The Atlantic

SEAS IN HISTORY
Series editor: Geoffrey Scammell

Forthcoming titles

THE MEDITERRANEAN

THE PACIFIC

THE BALTIC AND NORTH SEA

THE INDIAN OCEAN

The Atlantic

Paul Butel

Translated by Iain Hamilton Grant

London and New York

First published 1999
by Routledge
11 New Fetter Lane, London EC4P 4EE

Simultaneously published in the USA and Canada
by Routledge
29 West 35th Street, New York, NY 10001

Typeset in Perpetua and Bell Gothic by Routledge
Printed and bound in Great Britain by MPG Books Ltd, Bodmin

British Library Cataloguing in Publication Data
A catalogue record for this book is available from the British Library

Library of Congress Cataloguing in Publication Data
Butel, Paul.
[Histoire de l'Atlantique. English]
The Atlantic/Paul Butel; translated by Iain Hamilton Grant.
p. cm. – (Seas in history)
Includes bibliographical references and index.
ISBN 0–415–10690–7
1. Atlantic Ocean Region–Commerce–History. 2. International
trade–History. I. Title. II. Series.
HF4037.85.B8713 1999
382'.019182'1
98-38974
CIP

ISBN 0–415–10690–7

TO ROSELYNE

Contents

Contents

Illustrations

Map

Tables

Preface

Seas and oceans cover roughly two-thirds of the surface of the globe. Since time immemorial they have provided mankind with food. In our own age they have been found to contain a rich diversity of resources whose exploitation remains a matter of contestation. But the waters of the world are more than a prime instance of nature's munificence, or a handy dumping ground for the refuse of civilization. They can be formidable obstacles to societies lacking the will or the means to cross them. Equally they can be a powerful stimulant to technology and a challenge to the skills of those who, for any reason, seek to use them. They can unite the cultures and economies of widely dispersed and radically different peoples, allowing knowledge, ideas and beliefs to be freely transmitted. The ports that develop along their littorals often have more in common with one another than with the hinterlands of the states or communities in which they are sited.

Yet, since seas are in themselves so rich, and since for centuries they alone gave access to the wealth of many distant regions, land powers have put forward ambitious claims to exercise authority over them. In Europe, the justification or denial of such title has concerned thinkers and apologists since the days of Columbus and Vasco de Gama. Economic, political or strategic necessity, real or imagined, stimulate the growth of navies, fearsome expressions of the power of the modern state. Sea-borne commerce entailed the construction of ships which, however propelled, were long amongst the most expensive and technologically advanced products of contemporary economies. The shipping industries of the world support a labour force whose social organization and way of life differ radically from those of the rest of society.

But there is more to the history of the sea than the impressive chronicle of man's triumph over the elements, or battles fought, freights carried and ships launched. Everywhere, seas and oceans have had a significant cultural influence on civilizations adjoining them.

These and other themes are explored by Paul Butel in this study of the Atlantic. A scholar internationally acclaimed for his work in fields as diverse as

Caribbean buccaneering, the maritime economy of early-modern France and the history of opium, he now ranges wider still in time — encompassing some 2,000 years — and space. The outcome is an authoritative, fascinating and stimulating history of a formidable ocean which has played, and still plays, a decisive role in the affairs of humankind.

Geoffrey Scammell

Acknowledgements

The completion of this work would not have been possible without the invaluable help of friends and scholars, to whom I offer my warmest thanks: Marie-Hélène Berthault, Jean-Pierre Bost, Christian Buchet, François Crouzet, Alain Huetz de Lemps, Bernard Lavalle, Christian Lerat and Isabelle Lescent. Above all, however, I must acknowledge my wife, whose affection and help in overcoming times of discouragement deserves more recognition than any other, and to whom this book may stand as homage.

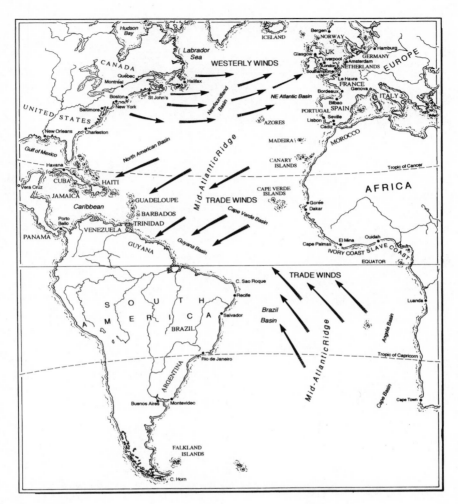

The Atlantic

Introduction

A legend states that whoever sees the sun go down over the Cabo de São Vincente, in Portugal, sees it a hundred times larger than it appears elsewhere; they would even hear the immense star steam and fizzle as it was extinguished by the waves. In the light of the sun, and of this legendary vision, the sea expands, its receding horizon always captivating men, attracting and repelling them at the same time. Hanno the Carthaginian, or Pytheas the Massilian – both merchants and courageous explorers – dared, although wary of monsters, to leap into this uncharted liquid expanse. Neptune and Mercury joined forces in the Atlantic to guide the sailors over the Sea of Perpetual Gloom, past the Pillars of Hercules and the limits of the known world.

On the other hand, the history of the Atlantic has gradually become inextricable from stories of a space made up of mysteries and wonders, not the least of which were the Fortunate Isles, where the Hesperides stood guard over the golden apples that Heracles managed to steal. The hostile, turbulent, violent swell and the immense, battering waves were so many obstacles, inspiring the greatest fears. '[I can] find no way whatever of getting out of this grey surf, see no way out of this grey sea',[1] the man who had the temerity to confront the ocean might exclaim.

In effect, seen from Europe, the Atlantic represented a formidable obstacle to all progress towards the West. In the temperate latitudes of the northern hemisphere, the dominant western winds were at the outset against setting sail from the old continent. One had to reach the higher latitudes of Norway to find more favourable currents and winds from the east that would allow westerly movement. They made possible the routes taken by the Irish monks and the Vikings, since further afield, in Greenland, lay the cold current of Labrador, leading ships to Newfoundland. While, between March and May, the easterly winds that had brought success in trade and fishing to fifteenth-century Bristol could still be found on English latitudes, they were stronger in the southern, subtropical latitudes. Thus, upon reaching Madeira and the Canary Islands parallels, sailing ships

1

could pick up the most favourable winds on a voyage towards the west: the trade winds that Columbus, and others before him, had used.

Very early on the ocean's layout allowed men to find regions where a rich maritime life could be led. The Atlantic area stretched out from north to south, standing apart from the much larger Indian and Pacific oceans. The two continental masses separated by the Atlantic, Africa and America, came closest at the northern tip of western Africa and Brazil, dividing it into two parts, opening onto the poles on either side of the equator. From Cape Palmas in Africa, to the north, to the Cabo de São Roque, in Brazil, in the south, is little more than 3,000 kilometres. Stretching through the Atlantic of the southern hemisphere, the largest marine space is unrelieved by land other than the presence, at its centre, of Ascension Island in the north, to St Helena and Tristan da Cunha in the south. Even though these islands offer the sailor some refuge, the roaring forties make for difficult conditions to the south of the latter. Towards the Antarctic continent, on the sixtieth parallel, the Atlantic assumes its greatest size, almost 6,500 kilometres.

In the northern hemisphere, the ocean seems distinctly less forbidding; one might even regard it as welcoming. It is, in effect, bejewelled with islands and coastal seas that link the continents, making its crossing easier.

To the north, the 3,800 kilometres that separate Ireland from Newfoundland are thus split up over several stopovers and while there are bogs and storms to be faced in the crossing, there is also good fishing to be exploited. Basques and Bretons, like the English and the Cornish, very soon learnt to practise cod fishing, leading them always further west. From the Faroe Islands to Greenland, the sailor can navigate between islands less than 600 kilometres apart.

In the tropical latitudes, in both the eastern and the western Atlantic, the navigator skirts the islands of various archipelagos that provide so many way-stations on the crossing. At less than 800 kilometres away, the island nearest Portugal is Madeira; the Canaries lie 1,200 kilometres distant, and the Azores at 1,300 kilometres, so that on both their outward and return journeys, Iberian explorers benefitted from islands rich in provisions, where crews were 'refreshed' and ships repaired. After Madeira and the Canaries, the steady breath of the trade winds carried ships towards the New World, while on the return, the great western winds took them back to the Azores. Once past Madeira, the speed of the voyage was surprising in relation to the relatively slow progress made until that point from Europe. In the eighteenth century, British naval vessels covered more than 191 kilometres a day between Madeira and the Lesser Antilles, making steady progress and navigating by the rear wind, whereas routine crossings from Plymouth to Madeira never surpassed 148 kilometres per day.[2] It took 18 days to cover the 2,300 kilometres from Plymouth to Madeira, and 27 days for the 5,000 kilometres separating Madeira from the Antilles.

On the other side of the Atlantic, the arc of the Antilles stretched out over 2,200 kilometres, from Trinidad to Florida. Its islands, on whose beaches Columbus and his crewmen first set foot in the New World, abut the much larger Mediterranean Atlantic, with the Caribbean extending to the north into the Gulf of Mexico and spreading over more than two million square kilometres.

Its coastal waters, together with its islands, offer the greatest riches in the Atlantic. In both east and west, they offer excellent fishing grounds and golden opportunities for transportation to connect them to other continents. These tributary waters of the ocean have facilitated relations between men and have thereby given the history of the Atlantic some of its most extraordinary characters. On the east side of the Atlantic, the English Channel and the North Sea, with their frequent fogs, the danger of the shallows and very often rough seas, have since antiquity had the heaviest traffic, despite the risks to sailing. In our time, more than 1,000 vessels a day are listed in Piccadilly Circus, and in the waters between the Dover coast and the Pas-de-Calais lies the major commercial and industrial axis in north-west Europe.

Along with the coastal seas of the European Atlantic, there is another determining element. The great rivers, like the Elbe, the Rhine, the Schelde or the Seine, flow into the North Sea and the English Channel, assuring their ports control over extremely rich hinterland which is also, therefore, Atlantic. More generally, the majority of the world's largest rivers flow into the Atlantic: the Mississippi, the Saint Lawrence, the Amazon, the Orinoco and the River Plate on the American side; and on the European and African sides, the rivers mentioned above along with the African rivers of the Niger and the Congo. The Atlantic can therefore provide an invaluable service to the adjoining continents. The Saint Lawrence Seaway and the Great Lakes of North America, for example, show this clearly: since it was opened to traffic in 1959, the modern lake route has become one of the major trade axes, with the Gulf of Mexico and the Mississippi, for the export of American cereals and the import of products serving the rich industries from Toronto to Chicago.

If the twentieth century has made possible the greatest activity the Atlantic has known, previous centuries laid the ocean open to the circulation of men and produce. Thus, from Columbus's discovery to the First World War, the Atlantic has lived to the rhythm of trade, generating fortune after fortune. First there were the Iberian galleons with the gold and silver of the New World; then the rich merchant fleets of Holland, Britain and France, whose activities, providing Europe with exotic and fashionable produce, also gave rise to later rivalries. From these naval confrontations, Britain emerged victorious. With conflict in the Atlantic culminating in an acknowledged British hegemony, nineteenth-century Europe crossed the ocean to provide an infant United States with the resources necessary to become a new power. In the following century overwhelming

American naval pre-eminence put an end to British hegemony, without, however, being able to prevent old Europe from reviving her activities in the Atlantic after the wars.

At the end of the twentieth century, the Atlantic is no longer the endless, shoreless ocean it once was, but does this mean that we have any clearer a view of it? Of course, in search of some vacation sunshine, city dwellers suddenly appear on beaches; more and more tourists taste the pleasure of cruises in the Tropics or the seas of northern Europe. Its legends gone, however, it has lost a great deal of the fascination it used to exercise over sailors and the colonizers of new worlds. Above all, its image is no longer the same: now the jet aircraft has killed the liner on long hauls, travellers' daydreams no longer focus on the great swell of the open sea. Few can recognize themselves in Melville's hero and share with him in the emotional state brought about by crossing the Atlantic for the first time:

> Why upon your first voyage as a passenger, did you yourself feel such a mystical vibration, when first told that you and your ship were now out of sight of land? Why did the ancient Persians hold the sea holy? Why did the Greeks give it a separate deity?[3]

The Atlantic can, however, be rediscovered in its most distant past. The long crossing through the centuries towards which its history beckons, makes us understand more vividly the dreams and the realties that inspired the development of a Western civilization that deserves the name 'Atlantic'.

Chapter 1

Atlantic legends and Atlantic reality before the Iberian discoveries

The legendary Atlantic

> There will come an age, in the far-off years, when Ocean shall unloose the bonds of things, when the whole, broad earth shall be revealed, when Tethys shall disclose new worlds and Thule will not be the limit of the land.[1]

The prediction made by Seneca's hero in the *Medea* would be realized with the explorations of the North Atlantic by the Irish monks and the Vikings, followed some years later by Columbus's arrival in the Caribbean. His prediction was written in the world of the ancients, for whom the idea of the Atlantic ocean was still swathed in legend. The very term 'Atlantic' reminds us of this, since it could have been derived from the name of the continent of Atlantis, sunk beneath the real ocean. Even the legend of Atlas and his brother Hesperus, spirit of the evening star, has helped to sustain the belief in a sunken Atlantis. Hesperus climbed onto his brother's shoulders in order to scan the horizon, but fell head-long into the sea, taking a piece of his brother's flesh with him; and Atlantis was born.

Atlas the giant, father of the Hesperides, had taken the side of the Titans in their struggle with the gods and was condemned by Zeus to bear the heavens on his shoulders. The ancients thought of him as residing to the west, in the lands of the Hesperides. To Homer, it was 'the malevolent Atlas, who knows the sea in all its depths and with his own shoulders supports the great columns that hold earth and sky apart' and whose daughter Calypso, the 'powerful nymph', kept the unfortunate Ulysses from his home.[2]

Again, we find the same images of a strange, foreign Atlantic in Virgil: at the edges of the ocean and the setting of the sun is the home of the Ethiopians. At the most distant part of the earth, mightiest Atlas turns on his shoulders the axis of

5

the sky, studded with its burning stars. On the Mediterranean side, these borders can be represented by the Pillars of Hercules marking the entrance to the straits of Gibraltar, Mount Calpe to the north, and the rock of Abylla to the south. Here we find what is claimed to be the conclusion of Heracles' labours, the point at which he set the limits of the known world. The legend of Heracles is added to that of Atlas, underlining the simultaneous attractions and repulsions of the unknown, beyond the *oekumen*, the civilized world. The Hesperides, nymphs of the western sky, were three sisters who maintained a vigil over the golden apples that the Earth (Ge) had given to Hera upon her marriage (to Zeus). Thanks to their help, Heracles was able to take the fantastic apples with him and thus to gain immortality. The ancients pictured the Hesperides' garden lying at the farthest reaches of the western world, beyond the Pillars of Hercules. A sculpture such as the one at the Olympian Temple shows Atlas helping Heracles: relieving Atlas from his daily labour, Heracles received the golden apples from Atlas in return. The Hesperides are none other than Atlas's own daughters, and are sometimes called the Atlantides. They may be taken for the Isles of the West, or the Fortunate Isles, becoming identified with the Cape Verde Islands, or the Canaries. Rising out of the heart of the ocean, these islands, the imaginary fruit of the reality of the tales of the first Phoenician adventurers in the Atlantic, are transformed in Plato's *Timaeus* into a powerful and wondrous empire, named Atlantis, which, by sinking, gave its name to the ocean: 'On the island of Atlantis, kings built a powerful and wondrous empire. This empire was master of the whole island, along with many others and parts of the Continent'. To reach it, one had to go by way of the real sea, containing a great many other islands, and the land that surrounded it, 'that may be called a continent'.[3]

The collapse of this continent creates the legend: 'The island of Atlantis disappeared into the depths of the sea. Hence to this day, exploring this ocean is an arduous, almost impossible task, due to the obstacle of the deep silt deposits that the swallowed island displaced'. Already presented by Plato, the image of the earthly paradise of Atlantis reappeared in a great many ancient authors. For Diodorus of Sicily, the island, found at high sea and situated in the west, has

> fertile, mountainous soil, with a flat area of great beauty; the island is irrigated by navigable rivers, from which one can see numerous gardens planted with all kinds of trees and orchards, latticed with springs of gentle water. The mountainous region is covered in dense forest, and even the air is so temperate that the fruit of the trees and other produce grow here in abundance throughout the greater part of the year.[4]

In the Middle Ages, a similar imagery came down from the Arab geographers, who believed in the truth of the legend, combining it with other traditions of the isles of the western seas, such as Thule, the isle glimpsed by Pytheas the Massalian amid the northern fogs; the Portuguese Antilia, or the Island of the Seven Cities; and the island of St Brendan and his Irish companions. Each had created their own legends. Antilia was the Island of the Seven Cities, founded in the Atlantic in the eighth century by Portuguese bishops fleeing the Arab invasion with their flocks. The isle was only to be rediscovered when the last infidel had been vanquished and, after the capture of Granada, Columbus could leave on his search in 1492. The Celtic legends were perhaps the most popular. Besides St Brendan's odyssey, his initiatory quest through the lonely Atlantic in search of a refuge favourable to prayer, and his celebrating Easter Day Mass on the back of a whale, there were numerous Breton legends. There was, for instance, the legend about the 100 monks setting sail over the Atlantic 'in order to contemplate the innumerable wonders of the ocean'. After three years of drifting, a statue in the form of the Virgin Mary appeared twice and pointed them in the right direction; a third apparition, this time of Moses, showed them an island with a golden mountain and a town also entirely of gold. This was the Heavenly Jerusalem, 'as resplendent as one of the most precious stones, like a crystal of jasper'.[5] After a meal of the food of angels, the monks left the island and returned after a few days to Brittany, where they found the world had since completely changed: while they had spent three years on their voyage, 300 had passed on the mainland.

'And the sea gave up the dead in it, Death and Hades gave up the dead in them' (Revelations 20, 13). Celtic myth has it that the Atlantic is the land of the dead, where the souls of the deceased rest before reaching the biblical paradise of Eden, lying in the east, in Mesopotamia. In this land of the dead that is the Atlantic, these lost, paradisiacal isles of contentment can equally represent the ascetic idea of purgatory, offering a step prior to the ascent to paradise proper.[6] There has always been, however, a certain ambiguity in this image, since the 'Fortunate Isles' may also constitute a hedonist paradise, where the sun generates gold and where existence is easy, painless and without labour, since nature provides everything. These isles offer marvels, *mirabilia*, that have fuelled dreams of the Atlantic.

There is also an ambiguity here, taking the form of a seductive vision that might vanish to reveal the threatening dangers which the sea brings down upon those who venture upon it. The theme of the siren, inherited from antiquity, reappears on the heads of columns on the Portuguese churches between the Douro and Minho rivers, where it constitutes a sort of exorcism against danger.

All these islands were drawn on maps from the fourteenth and fifteenth centuries. In 1306, Marino Sanuto's map counted no less than 350 Fortunate Isles, to the west of Ireland, that became the goal of voyages of discovery. In the eighteenth century, people still hypothesized about the existence of St Brendan's Island. The West's memory could not forget them. On English maps from 1853 one can still see a green isle, like a lost rock, marked at 44° 48' latitude north and 26° 10' longitude west.[7] After the Renaissance, however, an effort was made to rationalize myth. Of course, the legend of Atlantis was still accepted by Montaigne, Buffon and Voltaire, but they wished to uncover the reality. Atlantis was identified with America, Scandinavia and, especially, with the Canaries. The Etruscans, the ancestors of the Guanches, who inhabited the Canary Islands before the arrival of the Spanish, Basques, or the ancient Italians, were identified as its inhabitants.

This effort to get back to the reality of the Atlantic had begun earlier, even in antiquity. Thus the ocean's tides were themselves the object of Virgil's astonished attention:

> As the sea advances wave by wave, now rushing to the land, throwing foam over the rocks and soaking the edge of the sand in the bay; now turning and hurrying back, sucking down the stones and rolling them along in its undertow while the shallows retreat and the shore is left dry.[8]

Strabo even goes so far as to want to criticize a legend he considers ill-founded:

> It is ridiculous to believe that they [the Cimbri] left their lands through ill feeling towards ordinary waves, a regular phenomenon that recurs each day. Nor need we believe (since it is pure fiction) what is told concerning extraordinarily large waves. The ocean actually shows greater or lesser differentiation in this type of phenomenon, according, however, to definite rules and at predictable times.[9]

The same author unhesitatingly treats Pytheas, 'the man who gave an account of Thule', as an 'arrant liar'.[10]

Certainly, however, scepticism with regard even to the legend of Atlantis only appeared much later. It is only therefore at the beginning of the nineteenth century that German explorer and scientist Alexander von Humboldt considers that Atlantis does not belong to the domain of geographical fact but to that of pure imagination. For Humboldt, the fantastic image of the ideal state presented in Plato's *Critias* is a counterpart of the old Athenian state.

Suffused by an imagery quite as unrestrained as that of the Celts, the Arab geographers aim to base their story on realities experienced by their contemporaries. One Al-Idrisi recalls a story, in the twelfth century, just as legendary as that of St Brendan's voyage, or of the Breton monks from the abbey of Pointe de Saint-Mathieu: in his picture of the 'Adventurers of Lisbon', he recounts the voyage organized in the tenth century by eight Moslem sailors.[11] His heroes have just left familiar shores for, beyond the Pillars of Hercules, the Sea of Perpetual Gloom, the unknown ocean numbering no less than 30,000 fabulous islands at the edge of the world, with their man-eating monsters and covered in gold and silver. The fantastic aspect of the voyage is clear from the mention of 'adventurers' and in several passages noting the fear inspired by the ocean with its immense waves, its obscure depths and numerous reefs barely lit by the weak light. Without doubt, however, there remain genuine facts. The sailors probably landed at Madeira, called the Island of Sheep, and then in the Canaries, before ending up on the Moroccan coast after 37 days at sea. Safi was a port then at the height of its expansion on the Atlantic coast of the Maghrib. The Arab geographer's demonstration of the reality of a voyage has a precursory character, since it presages later European discoveries. It turned towards an unknown ocean, still of course feared, but often visited on its Iberian and African coasts. The geographers also managed to gather together the heritage of antiquity.

The realities of the ancients

Phoenician and Carthaginian voyages in the near Atlantic

It would be useful to distinguish the reconnaissance expeditions, such as those of Hanno of Carthage or Pytheas of Massilia, from the networks of maritime relations established by the ancient Thalassocracies. From the sixteenth to the fourth century BC, Phoenicia, with Tyre as its front-ranking port, dominated the eastern Mediterranean, its enormous expansion becoming apparent from the very beginning of the first millennium. Founded by the Phoenicians, Carthage solidly established its trade on the south of the western Mediterranean. In the same period, the Greeks greatly extended their networks at the Point of Euxin in the Aegean Sea; on either side of Sicily, Marseilles and the Etruscans were able to build up a rich commerce before the Mediterranean became the Romans' *Mare Nostrum*. Roman imperialism, however, only got underway slowly: in the fourth century, Carthage was able to sign a treaty with Rome to divide up trade in the western Mediterranean and, later, to make the Romans tremble before Carthage fell in 146 BC.

The ventures and voyages of Phoenician trade soon began to take shape in the ocean beyond the Pillars of Hercules. From the end of the second millennium before Christ, the most westerly Phoenician installation was Gades which Tyre had settled and governed, in all likelihood with a view to searching for the tin ore required for the production of bronze, in voyages across the Gulf of Gascony towards the Loire Basin, the Gulf of Morbihan, and as far as Cornwall in Britain. Strabo showed the role Portugal and Andalusia played as ports of call in the Phoenician period, exchanging Iberian salt against lead and tin from the

Cassiterides, Cornwall, or the Breton coast of France.[12] Diodorus of Sicily, however, set the extreme limit of the Phoenician diaspora further and deeper into the Atlantic, probably at Madeira, which was conquered much later by the Portuguese. A storm might have carried the Phoenicians to this enchanted isle with its rich soil, luxuriant vegetation and well-watered gardens. According to Pierre Rouillard, the Phoenician presence in Madeira should be understood in the context of Phoenician–Etruscan rivalry. The latter, informed of the discovery, wanted to settle there too. The event can be situated at the moment of great Etruscan dynamism in the seventh century BC, but it is really the Phoenicians to whom this voyage must be attributed.

In fact, on the strength of archaeological remains, only the settlement of Tyre at Gades, at the mouth of the Guadalete, gave the Phoenicians great renown, due to a temple at Melquart. The date traditionally assigned to this settlement, in the twelfth century BC, could correspond to the first voyage of the Tyrians towards the far west. Phoenician trade was already in full expansion, and the Bible attests to its magnitude in the western Mediterranean, even beyond the Pillars of Hercules: 'Tarshish trafficked with you because of your great wealth of every king; silver, iron, tin and lead they exchanged for your wares'.[13] 'The people's broker amongst the numberless isles', Tyre managed to find the principal relay for its trade with the west in Tartessus (the biblical Tarshish) on the Atlantic coast of Spain. The very name 'Tartessus' immediately evokes 'land of wonders', mines, ports, rivers, kingdom. It is to the west of Gades-Cadiz, on this Iberian Atlantic coast, that Huelva can provide the greatest testimony to the activities of the miners and metallurgists who helped make Tarshish the best port for Phoenician trade.

From the seventh century BC, Asia Minor dispatched the best of its mariners to cross the entire length of the Mediterranean in an unbroken voyage, to pass through the Straits of Gibraltar and to follow the African coast for more than 700 kilometres, until, facing Atlas (this time referring to the Moroccan range), they reached the island of Mogador. The Mediterranean sailors, navigating from the southern limit of their voyages to as far away as Cornwall, with Tartessus-Huelva being their principal trading axis, never ceased thereafter to visit the ocean's shores of Lybia (Africa) and of the Iberian peninsula.

It was almost two centuries later, under Punic control, that the Atlantic coast seems to have undergone its greatest expansion, combining voyages of discovery (the voyage of Hanno the Suffete) and commercial exploitation. The voyage Polybius undertook in the second century BC, on behalf of the Romans, in order to take an inventory of Carthaginian goods in the Atlantic, was very precise. In fact, Pliny the Elder reports:

Polybius says that Cerne is situate at the extremity of Mauritania, over against Mount Atlas, and at a distance of eight stadia from the land; while

Cornelius Nepos states that it lies very nearly in the same meridian as Carthage, at a distance from the mainland of ten miles, and that it is not more than two miles in circumference. It is said also that there is another island situate over against Mount Atlas, being itself known by the name of Atlantis.[14]

To André Jodin, the distances given by these authors, close to 1,500 metres, could allow the identification of Cerne with the island of Mogador, separated from the coast of the mainland by the same distance. The Phoenicians, and then the Carthaginians, exploited its purple, one of the most famous natural resources of the Moroccan Atlantic coasts. This exploitation would assume its fullest extent under the reign of Juba II, in the Augustan epoch, with the purple extracted from the shells of the island of Mogador proving a striking dye much appreciated by the Roman élite. Already, however, under Phoenician and Carthaginian colonization, Cerne-Mogador was the farthest limit of the trading routes.

In the fifth century BC, Hanno the Carthaginian completed his famous voyage in order to revive the ancient Phoenician settlements beyond the Pillars of Hercules that had lain dormant since the fall of Tyre. Since one of the most prosperous Phoenician trading posts, Lixus, south of the Straits of Gibraltar on the Moroccan coast, 100 kilometres from Tangier, had not disappeared like the other settlements, Hanno was therefore able to enlist help from this colony, and the Lixites provided him with pilots to face the most distant waters, and, in particular, to lead him to Cerne-Mogador, considered by Hanno as a reasonable limit to his colonies.[15]

Hanno's colonists were Libyphoenicians recruited on the Andalusian coast between Almeria and Gibraltar.[16] Almunecar, one of their cities, had existed for two centuries by Hanno's time. It was this city that was to have been the expedition's point of departure, rather than Carthage. Hanno's successful expedition took place when Carthage, between 475 and 450 BC, decided on an extremely vigorous effort of colonization. Hanno, however, intended to proceed with an exploration, probably at the same time, of the Atlantic archipelago of the Canaries, 700 kilometres off the Moroccan coast, and of the more southerly African coasts, as far as Senegal and even Guinea. The far-off Canaries lent themselves to being the site of the mythic sojourn of the souls of the elect on the Fortunate Isles, a name that had for a long time been given to this archipelago. Through his cruise, Hanno managed to renew the relations that the Punic sailors had with them.[17] By following the drift of the current for the exploitation of Mogador's purple, Punic ships had already been able to venture as far as the Canaries.

For Pliny the Elder, the narrative of Hanno's voyage was rich in ill-founded fables. The imaginations of the Punic sailors would have been stoked by the volcano on Cameroun Peak, the height and the eruptions of which would have seemed to be the chariot of the gods; the flaring volcano would have struck the Carthaginians dumb, however familiar the spectacle of the fires of Mount Etna in the Mediterranean. The 'women with hairy bodies' [that Hanno's interpreters called 'gorillas'] could simply have been pygmy-women rather than female monkeys. According to Jérôme Carcopino, we may however consider that Hanno undertook his expedition for good reason, in order to ensure Carthage's control of Sudan's gold.[18] Strengthened by the experience of the Lixites, Hanno had meanwhile extended the field of their voyage as far up as Sierra Leone, effectively Cameroun, well beyond the gold reserves of Rio de Ouro, the object of Lixus' commerce. Beyond Cerne-Mogador, however, Hanno left no more colonists, conducting his voyage as an exploration of the coast, turning to the east after having doubled Cape Palmas on a route unfamiliar to the sailors of Lixus. Hanno had served Carthage's mercenary politics as far as the Senegal Basin; further on, he conducted his voyage as a prospector in quest of gold.

Herodotus, reporting Hanno's voyage, underlined the importance of Carthaginian commerce in West Africa and explained its procedures:

> The Carthaginians also tell us that they trade with a race of men who live in a part of Libya beyond the Pillars of Hercules. On reaching this country, they unload their goods, arrange them tidily along the beach, and then, returning to their boats, raise a smoke. Seeing the smoke, the natives come down to the beach, place on the ground a certain quantity of gold in exchange for the goods, and go off again to the distance. The Carthaginians then come ashore and take a look at the gold; and if they think it represents a fair price for their wares, they collect it and go away; if, on the other hand, it seems too little, they go back and wait, and the natives come and add to the gold until they are satisfied. There is perfect honesty on both sides; the Carthaginians never touch the gold until it equals in value what they have offered for sale, and the natives never touch the goods until the gold has been taken away.[19]

For Jérôme Carcopino, it was undoubtedly Hanno's expedition that gave Lixus its lasting greatness in this trade with the black producers of gold. The powerful Carthaginian fleets procured the necessary logistic means for the link between Rio de Ouro and Cerne. The commercial exploitation, however, never got past the Senegal Basin, towards the west, in the Gulf of Guinea, and the expedition remained only an exploration. Later, in spring 147 BC, after Scipio Aemilianus had brought about the fall of Carthage and ruined, or more or less transformed, these trading routes: 'an era of normal commerce and shipowners supported by imperial politics was succeeded by one of illicit ventures and buccaneers'.[20]

The truth of Herodotus' words has been questioned, since in antiquity the conditions of navigating the African Atlantic coast would not appear to allow such a voyage.[21] Hanno's voyage would have been technically impossible. A sailor who came from the Mediterranean and arrived in black Africa could not get back again to the north. In effect, the winds on this part of the African coast prevent any northward ascent: blowing almost all year round, steady north-east to south-west winds could easily drive a sailing ship to the south; in the area lying between Cape Juby and Cape Blanc, by contrast, there are no winds that would enable the northward ascent. The monsoon winds that result from the inter-tropical front moving northwards blow from the south-west from July to October and enable one to return north, but only as far as Cape Blanc. Beyond this point, over the 850 kilometres between it and Cape Juby, no south wind can counteract the dominant north winds that block the passage. Nor, in this same sector, could oars compensate for the absence of a favourable wind: oar propulsion is slow, not to mention the difficulty of rowing against contrary wind, or the existence of the extremely strong north–south currents along the length of the coast. Providing for the oarsmen would also be extremely difficult, given that watering places are rare.

Finally, returning northbound into the wind would require the ship to stay close to the shore, tacking in order to hug the wind as closely as possible. Technological conditions in antiquity would prohibit this, however, since Punic ships bore a single central mast with a square or rectangular sail, used with the wind astern.

Raoul Lonis has challenged this argument. At the very least he refutes the technological impossibility of using a square or lateen sail, which was known from antiquity. Tacking against a head wind was familiar to Athens and Rome, and Carthage could not have remained ignorant of this technique. The steering gear of their ships, pivoting on its axle, was already highly developed. Lucretius shows a helmsman steering 'a mighty ship': 'however much way it has gathered, a single hand steers it – a single tiller twists it this way or that'. In his *Medea*, Seneca also testifies to ships' manoeuvring capabilities: 'Tiphys made bold...to write new laws for the winds' by skilful manoeuvring, and Virgil too writes of how Aeneas's companions are able to stand up to sudden and often violent variations in the winds:

> As one man they all set their sails, letting them out in time, first to port and then to starboard. As one man they swung around the high ends of the yard-arms and swung them around again as fair winds carried the fleet on its way.[22]

It would therefore be possible for a navigator who had ventured southwards beyond Cape Juby and Cape Blanc to travel the difficult route between the two capes again, in the opposite direction. Consequently, the northward ascent by Africa's Atlantic coast could take place. Hanno may not have been invented.

Since at least the seventh century, the Phoenicians had settled in Cerne-Mogador. Later, in their wake, the Carthaginians were to settle there. Navigators who headed south during the summer months, the *mare apertum*, from March to September, were able to make the northward return at the beginning of the winter months, taking advantage of the less violent winds. Having stopped at the ports of the Moroccan Atlantic, such as Lixus, the navigators would then leave for the Mediterranean in the following spring. Slowed down by an exhausting passage, Hanno would be able to stop at one of the colonies established on the outward journey in order to await the following spring before setting to sea once again.

Another hypothesis would be that he had begun his *volta*, as the Portuguese had subsequently done, by returning through the open sea, if necessary by the Azores; and, long before, hadn't the Phoenicians already discovered certain of the islands in this archipelago, as the presence of Phoenician money on the island of Corvo proves?[23]

Of course, this is a matter of only a few isolated voyages, so we must wait until the fifteenth century, the time of Henry the Navigator, a Portuguese prince, in order to see Guinea regularly visited by sea from Europe.

From Greaco-Roman to Arabic voyages in the Atlantic

By completing their voyages, both commercial and exploratory, the Carthaginians intended to ensure that no one contested their voyages beyond the Pillars of Hercules, or the wealth they generated. In this way, they managed to contribute to laying to rest the legends and the exaggerated difficulties sailors met with, once past Gibraltar. Returning from his great voyage to the Œstrymnides Islands, Ushant and its little islets, in search of Cornish tin, Himilco the Punican barely stopped talking about the perils he had faced: the shallows where he nearly ran aground, the hazard of seaweed, from which it had proved so difficult to get free, the fogs through which he had blindly progressed, the calms that had suddenly paralyzed him. According to the ancient authors, it really seems that the Punicans, demonstrating their hostility to every possible rival, had established a kind of blockade in the Straits of Gibraltar: Strabo, after Eratosthenes, explains that they would attack the ships that sailed close to the coast towards Sardinia and the Pillars of Hercules.[24] For Pindar, 'beyond Gadeira toward the gloom we must not pass...no further is it easy...to sail across the trackless sea beyond the Pillars of Hercules'. From such fearful views as the Greeks held of the Atlantic, we might think of them as having been ignorant of the ocean. The details of everyday life, however, render this opinion unsafe: some comedies evoke the success of

Gaditanian salt fish in Athens and, in *The Frogs*, Aristophanes alludes to 'Tartassian lampreys'.[25]

In fact, the Greeks' capacity for action was real enough, as the example of Pytheas the Massilian shows. Around 300 BC he had endless adventures. Departing from Massilia (Marseilles), Pytheas cleared the Straits of Gibraltar and headed north, rounded Brittany and reached the 'Island of Thule' (Iceland, or rather the western coast of Norway). In contrast to the numerous explorers of antiquity, who were motivated only by commercial or military concerns, Pytheas did important geographical work. He determined the latitude of Massilia, carefully observed the phenomenon of tides, recording differences in amplitude which he related to the phases of the moon. From his experiments with latitudes, he drew precise observations concerning the altitude of the Pole star. It is true, however, that Alexander had charged him with a mission to search for amber and tin; techniques for manufacturing bronze from an alloy of copper and tin were sought by the Phoenicians and the Carthaginians, as well as the Greeks. Pytheas's exploration enabled the British and North Sea coasts to be surveyed, perhaps as far as the latitude of Bergen. The frozen sea discovered near Thule, some 66° latitude north, was doubtless not an ice flow but an ice drift, a spectacle disconcerting to sailors accustomed to the sunlit south-western shores, rich in wine and salt. Such latitudes are doubtless too distant for the six days' sail north of Britain it is said to have taken the Massilian to reach Thule, which, therefore, could correspond only to Shetland.[26]

Massilian navigation, however, like that of the other Greek cities, very early took commerce, rather than exploration, as its sole object. In 630 BC, Colaios the Samian, driven by a providential wind, had cleared the Pillars of Hercules carrying Greek ceramics to Atlantic Morocco. The Greeks carried on the trade created by the Phoenicians and then the Carthaginians: salt and sea wares from Gades, tin from the Cassiterides, and purple from Mogador were exchanged for ceramics and fabrics. Doubtless more discreet than the Phoenician presence, the Greek influence is attested to by the presence of Attic and Ionian amphora in the Andalusian sites west of Gibraltar, side by side with Cypriot and Syrian vases. Preparing what, under Rome, would be the trade routes of Baetica and Lusitania, a triangle of towns – Huelva-Tartessos, Cadiz and Seville – benefitted from its land and sea links and proved to be highly active. Recent discoveries such as the two splendid helmets in Corinthian style, one found in the Huelva river and the other in the Guadalete, near Jerez de la Frontera, attest to the arrival of the Greeks and that they encountered no great hostility from the Phoenicians or even the Carthaginians.[27]

It was, however, under Rome that commercial activity in the Atlantic, beyond the Pillars of Hercules, towards Britain and the North Sea as much as towards western Morocco, became still more vigorous.

Going northwards, the Roman legions had to take on provisions in Britain and Germany.[28] The Mediterranean-Rhône route certainly took longer, at least in the direction of Britain, but it was safer than the Atlantic route, although the economies realized by taking the latter, gaining time and shortening the distance, were significant. More and more, this was the route to the camps on the upper Rhine that had favoured the Mediterranean passage. We cannot agree, therefore, that the ocean was the limit of the empire. Besides, without counting Caesar, other illustrious Romans undertook expeditions to Britain — for example, Agricola. Indeed, Dion Cassius shows that the Roman soldiers were so terrified at the thought of having to cross the Straits of the Pas de Calais, as Claudius had decided, for the conquest of Britain, that they rebelled and refused to march 'as if they had to fight beyond the inhabited earth'.[29] In his *Commentaries*, however, Caesar says nothing of the sort at the time of the expeditions of 54 and 55 BC. From the first century BC, relations between Britain and the Continent were very close. In the imperial era, the important needs of the army in Britain, the cargoes of provisions and fabrics, at least until the end of the second century AD, were satisfied by expeditions that were most often led from Baetica by way of the Atlantic. In this way, oil provided one of the principal components of the year's military provisions; the oil amphoras found on the French coast of Brittany and Normandy reveal the intensity of this trade.

At the dawn of the Roman Empire, under King Juba II's reign, the trading routes leading in the direction of the Moroccan south, towards Cerne-Mogador, became more intense. It is proper to speak of a permanent installation at Mogador, no longer a mere seasonal trading post as it was in the time of the Phoenicians and the Carthaginians. This activity was linked to the exploitation of purple, expanded to its fullest extent. Pliny the Elder cites the importance of the industry derived from this exploitation on the coast of Getullia on Atlantic Libya; he emphasizes its great renown but takes advantage of it to criticize Roman luxury: 'let us be prepared then to excuse this frantic passion for purple...it sheds lustre, and in the triumphal vestment it is to be seen mingled with gold'.[30] Juba II visited this Atlantic coast and perhaps got as far as the Canaries. He founded industrial settlements on the Purpurarlæ (the Purple Isles) on the site of Mogador to manufacture Getullian purple, highly esteemed in Rome. Salting bowls where the purple dye was prepared have been discovered on both Mogador and Lixus. The wealth of Juba's kingdom, evident from the expansion of a city such as Volubilis, tempted Caligula to rob Ptolemy, Juba's son, of his kingdom. Subsequently visited in an irregular way over the next two centuries, the island of Mogador became once more an active trading post in Severus's time, and Byzantium again fostered some trade there.

Between the voyages of the Phoenicians and the Carthaginians and those of the Romans beyond the Straits of Gibraltar, there was no continuity. After the time of

Byzantium and a phase of almost total maritime inactivity, lasting from the Visigothic invasion to the first period of Arabic settlements in the eighth century, Arab navigation in the Moroccan and Iberian Atlantic formed, from the beginning of the next century, a major step in the history of the Atlantic. Across the entire Andalusian and Maghribian coasts there followed a resurgence of maritime activity that ensured favourable conditions for the subsequent boom in Iberian discoveries. The daring of the Catalan, Genoan and Portuguese undertakings must be considered 'the extension of Maghribian commerce'. As Pierre Chaunu writes, 'the break in the eighth century was too unnatural, and the complementarity of the economies of the northern, southern and western Mediterranean was too overt for commercial links not to be maintained'.[31] From the ninth to the thirteenth century, Moslem sailing became a prelude to the decisive initiatives of the Iberians while, at the same time, maintaining the ancient traditions of maritime activity from the Iberian and African coasts beyond the Straits of Gibraltar.

We can, however, discern new factors in sea traffic in relation to the situation in antiquity. On the political level, the intense relations between Andalusia and the Maghrib implied the existence of an important fleet to control the passage through the Straits of Gibraltar. First with the Viking offensives and then with the appearance of the Portuguese fleet, it very quickly became apparent that patrolling the Atlantic was a permanent necessity. Commercial motives seemed just as strong, however: Andalusia seemed to have had an ever greater need for the cereals of the coastal plains of Morocco, whereas the Sevillians and the peoples of the Portuguese Algarve made more and more profit from their specialized produce, especially oil, as in the time of Roman Baetica. The commercial resurgence of the Atlantic coastline was confirmed after being interrupted by invasions.

The most striking example of the resurgence of the Atlantic coasts of Andalusia and the Maghrib in the beginning of the ninth century was the founding of Rabat by the Umayyadin. Their three capitals, Marrakesh, Rabat and Seville, were all located on the Atlantic side of their empire. Under this dynasty, Andalusia's demand for cereals from Moroccan Atlantic plains is much more important than gold or products hailing from the Sahara, at least as regards transporting them by sea routes.[32]

With the Andalusian Moslems, the commercial traditions of the Atlantic inherited from the Phoenicians, Carthaginians and Romans were resumed, and the trading routes were revived. Of course, we cannot ignore the limits of Moslem activity in the ocean, which are almost the same as those in antiquity. They are, first, geographical: towards the south, trading relations did not extend beyond the Wadi Draa, with the port of Nun Ramca as its final stage. Beyond this, the cargoes were transported overland. Marine currents and unfavourable winds prohibited regular sailing beyond Cape Juby. There were also seasonal limits to this activity.

Al Idrisi, the famous Arab geographer, remarked upon this regarding the ships calling in port at Safi, saying that, 'the vessels, after having discharged their cargoes, do not put to sail again until a favourable season, as soon as the weather is calm and the Sea of Perpetual Gloom is tranquil'. That is, during the rainy season, from April to September, when the easterly winds drive the ships northwards. Finally, we must note the psychological limits: the surrounding ocean is the *al-bahr-al-Mughim*, the Sea of Perpetual Gloom, rendered fearsome by the density of its cloud, the height of its waves, frequent tempests, violent winds and a multitude of monstrous animals. But for the presence of a few islands, one is conscious of the infinite character of the ocean, and sailors try not to get too far from its coasts.[33]

Amongst Arabic geographers there had been, however, some degree of knowledge of this Sea of Perpetual Gloom, beginning where navigation lost all familiarity, where fishermen could no longer reach. The sea contains the Atlantic islands, the Canaries marking the limit of the known ocean. There were other islands lying on the high seas, occasionally noted by expeditions driving adventurers or the shipwrecked far from shore, so that the Island of Sheep is assimilated, by some, to Madeira. The narrative of Ambassador Al-Ghazal, addressing the King of the Vikings, probably at Jutland, indicates a fear of the unknown sea, but also shows the possibility of crossing the customary limits of sailing.

In everyday Moslem navigation, certain staging posts clearly stand out. Until the tenth century, they had not passed the port of Salé, some 300 kilometres from the Straits of Gibraltar. Close to Salé, towards the south, a barbarian tribe called the Barghwâta lived at the edge of the Atlantic. Being independent of the Moslem provinces, they had determined its southern coastal boundaries for a long time, right up until the Almoravid conquest in the eleventh century, and so prevented normal relations. The Almoravids' action in the Sous allowed maritime trade between coastal ports on the Atlantic Sahara, the Iberian peninsula, and the entire Mediterranean.[34] In the summer months, ships reached Mogador and Agadir, descending as far south as the Wadi Sous and Nun. There were a huge number of anchorages and ships took no more than three to five days sailing the length of the coast. At Nun, we find ourselves nearly 1,300 kilometres from the Straits of Gibraltar and almost 2,000 from Lisbon. Al Idrisi notes that once past Salé, 'in ancient times, the last stopping point for ships', it took more than four days to reach Mogador and Nun. According to Al Idrisi, at Salé and Fedala (north of what is now Casablanca) ships loaded up with oil and all kinds of foodstuffs destined for the Andalusian coast. Andalusia and the Maghrib complemented each other: ships from the former went to Nun to fill up with agricultural produce and gold, where caravans arrived from Niger and Senegal.

The dynamic of the development of Moslem shipping was checked when the first *reconquista* reached the Atlantic coast in the middle of the thirteenth century, although Christian ships had already begun to arrive in Salé in 1260.[35] Taking over from the Moslems, the Genoese acquired the habit of sailing down the length of the Maghrib's Atlantic coast. While the Portuguese would only set foot upon Cape Bojador a century and a half later, Moslem pilots could serve as guides to the Italian merchants and sailors who displayed great ambitions towards the West before the Iberian dawn. In fact, the first Genoese attempts on Salé dated from the first half of the thirteenth century and from 1232 Ceuta was, in the main, open to Christians. The Genoese 'quest' for more and more southerly ports of call enabled them to take sugar cane from Sous and to transport it towards Flanders and Venice in the thirteenth century.

The lessons the Italians learnt from Moslem navigation of the Atlantic cannot be exaggerated. The ships were the same as those in the Mediterranean, but the sailing conditions with which they were acquainted were utterly different: the dangerous tides and swell of the Moroccan coast, sandbanks, different currents and winds. Some two centuries later the Portuguese success in their attempts to circumnavigate Africa was directly linked to the tradition of Atlantic coastal navigation that, since the tenth century, had taken root in Andalusian ports.

The Irish and the Vikings in the North Atlantic

Irish curachs and voyaging monks

With the Phoenician and Carthaginian voyages in the first and second millenniums BC, Mediterranean shipping expanded to the European Atlantic coast. This involved relatively large ships, equipped with sails, capable of transporting quite heavy cargoes.

In northern Europe, the first types of craft were rowboats, canoes suited to sailing on the calm waters of rivers, lakes and the fjords in Scandinavia. A wholly different type was capable of crossing the 'open seas', the North Sea, connecting the Continent to Great Britain, Ireland, or the islands located further north such as the Lofoten. Belonging to this group, the *curachs* of the west of Ireland, made from skins sewn together, appeared very early on, in the fifth century BC, in the time of Hanno and Himilco of Carthage. Relating the voyages of the *curachs* the writer Festus Avienus showed them to be capable of sea crossings. In his *Natural History*, Pliny the Elder sees the Bretons using them. At the end of the era of empire, fleets of *curachs* were even deployed in the Irish raids on Roman Britain. In the fifth century, St Patrick, taken from his native Britain at the age of 16 in the *curachs* of the Pictish and Scots pirates, reached Ireland by *curach* in 432, in order to further his evangelical mission past the west coast of England.

The *curach* was fast and suited to looting raids. At the same time, it was extremely well adapted to the rocky coasts of western Ireland, by Donegal, Connemara and Clare. It was the Irish *curach* that carried the Christian faith to the Hebrides and the Faeroes, the distant lands of the north. Large *curachs* had a mast and a square sail. They were frequently seen in the Irish Sea, the St George's Channel and along Ireland's and Scotland's Atlantic coasts. Oars were often used, but the sail was the principal means of propulsion. Due to their well-proportioned keel, *curachs* handled well at sea; the keel allowing the use of mast and sail.[36]

The source of the most beautiful legends of the wondrous Atlantic, the *Navigatio Sancti Brendani Abbatis* gives details of the construction of *curachs* in the second half of the ninth century: cover a pine wood craft with cowhide, use tar for the joins, mast and sail in the middle of the boat. The crew could comprise 17 men, laden with supplies, over 40 days. The popular and venerable St Brendan, however, was preceded and followed by many other hermits and monks sent from Ireland to the Continent, to France, Germany and even as far as Lombardy. St Brendan of Clonfert, the great Irish monastery, who died around 580, made at least one crossing from Ireland to Scotland and, further north, to the Hebrides. However, all the discoveries accredited to him are in reality the fruit of a collective maritime experience spanning several generations of Irish sailors. Criss-crossing the ocean with his 17 monks over six years, the seafaring bishop landed at the wondrous shores between Scotland and Shetland. Fantastic legends show him celebrating Easter Mass on the back of a whale he had mistaken for an island. The reality of these Irish discoveries, however, must not be forgotten.

In the second half of the sixth century, Irish missionaries had arrived at the Orkney Islands before discovering the Faeroes further afield, around 700. Most importantly, the Irish monks reached Iceland. When Pytheas the Massalian spoke of Thule, was it Iceland he intended to name, or rather one of the inhabited islands off the Norwegian coast, with climactic conditions similar to those described by the Greek geographer? On the basis of pieces of copper from the imperial era, during the reigns of Aurelianus, Probus and Diocletianus, being found on the south-eastern coast of the island, some have gone so far as to claim that Iceland had been visited by ships from the Roman Empire. Such a voyage at the end of the third century AD appears extremely improbable.[37] The vessels of Roman Britain were not equipped for the long Atlantic crossing up to Iceland.

On the other hand, with the *curach*, the Irish of the Early Middle Ages had access to a sailing boat that was extremely well adapted to Atlantic seafaring. Substantial experience had already enabled the Irish monks to reach the Faeroes by means of the *curach*. Similarly, later on, the Scandinavian *knarr* would enable the North Atlantic to be navigated.

The discovery of Iceland by the Irish marks the end of a progressive expansion in the Atlantic, preceded by the discoveries of Orkney, Shetland and the Faeroes. The earliest dated voyage on which Iceland was discovered is 795, but we may put the finding of the island of glaciers and volcanoes back to an earlier date. It would be followed a little later by the voyage to the Island of Sheep (the Faeroes). Ancient Celtic writings such as *The Life of Saint Columba* show that Iceland lies at the end of an unlimited ocean. A 'great silver pillar', perhaps representing an iceberg, is also mentioned, proving that a voyage to the west of Iceland had been undertaken, since icebergs are not found on the eastern side of the island.[38]

How can the discovery of Iceland by the Irish be explained? We could invoke the 'Arctic mirage':

> from time to time [particularly in summer, which in the early medieval era was the normal sailing season], when air rests on a colder surface and the observed image may be optically displaced, in a vertical direction, from its true location...which permits the occasional sighting of objects, such as islands and mountains, situated far beyond the normal distance to the horizon.

The rising sun creates the conditions most propitious for this phenomenon.[39] Another explanation might be that the Irish *curachs* had set out for Iceland following the route taken by migrating birds coming from the west of Scotland or the Faeroes. The route from the latter archipelago, with its strong easterly winds, would seem to be the most likely, pushing the craft towards the south-western coast of Iceland. According to Dicuil's chronicle, in 795 a group of Irish clerics left Ireland in January and arrived in Iceland on the first day of February, where they remained until the beginning of August. During the summer solstice, the monks remarked that the sun only went slowly down below the horizon, the remaining light being sufficient to allow a man to carry out some task such as 'looking for lice in one's shirt'. Dicuil confirms that, although it had been claimed that 'Thile' was covered in ice and cast into perpetual gloom in winter, this was utterly contradicted by the monks' experiences, as they were able to reach the island's coasts during the cold season without encountering any ice, and showed also that there was always an alternation between daylight and night except during the summer solstice. Since these indications coincide with the Viking sagas, Dicuil's 'Thile' is indeed Iceland.[40] For G. J. Marcus, the most interesting thing about Dicuil's narrative is that it does not present this voyage as at all extraordinary, or as representing a 'discovery'.

Doubtless preceded by other voyages, the expedition of 795 was followed by further departures, the narratives of which have been lost through the destruction of the libraries of the Irish monasteries during Viking raids. The link between Ireland and Iceland, however, was maintained, and Irish hermits still lived on the island of volcanoes when the first Scandinavians began to arrive in the ninth century. The Irish hermits, or *papar*, were then settled for the most part, although admittedly in small numbers, on the south-east of the island.

Some have speculated as to whether Iceland itself represented the limit of the Irish discoveries in the western ocean, and whether the Irish may have reached across the Atlantic to a 'transatlantic' island such as Greenland, or even to the lands lying still further to the west. Although no proof of this exists, we may still raise certain possibilities. Thus, on the voyage of 795, Dicuil's narrative speaks of a 'frozen sea' a day's sail north of Thile. The Irish craft went all around Iceland, venturing north until they encountered ice. Taking account of the phenomenon of the Arctic mirage, completing the circumnavigation of the island may have brought these sailors within sight of the distant mountains of Greenland. The elements of the legend of St Brendan suggest an awareness of the most western lands: his Pillar of Crystal may have been an iceberg, found only in the area of the Atlantic near Greenland; his great shoals of fish and dense fog suggest the approach to the reefs of Newfoundland; his swarthy dwarfs would be the Eskimos of Greenland; the fearsome monster with the tusks of a boar would be a North Atlantic walrus.

In the lands that certainly were frequented by the Irish the duration of their settlements was far from insignificant: a century on the Faeroes, between 700 and 800; and at least 80 years in Iceland. The means of these expeditions foreshadow those of the Scandinavians: the excellent performance of the *curach* at sea may have pointed the way towards the nautical excellence of the *knarr*; the Irish monks used the stars to navigate by, and a tradition in the Faeroes has it that they had made the voyage to Iceland early in the year to avoid the fogs and the bright nights of the later months (from May to the beginning of August) when, in high latitudes, the stars were invisible. In order to guide themselves over the vastness of the ocean, they depended on the sun and the stars. Like those of the Vikings, their craft were capable of doing hundreds of miles in the open sea without recourse to a magnetic or a gyroscopic compass, which would only be used in the North Atlantic some five hundred years later. They were the first genuine crossings of the northern part of the ocean, covering at least half the entire Atlantic crossing. Their expeditions may be considered as the 'test bed' for the Vikings' ocean voyages that followed soon afterwards.

The objectives of the Irish monks remain, however, very different from those of the Vikings. For St Brendan's companions, as for the other Celtic hermits, it was a question of finding saintliness in the solitude of the Atlantic. For the Scandinavians, navigation was ruled by the desire for pillage, for commerce, and for the colonization of new lands.

Viking navigation and colonization in the Atlantic

Ab ira Normannorum libera nos, Domine!

From the end of the eighth century, the terror the Scandinavians brought, not only to the coastal areas but far into a country's interior, by means of their rapid *drakkars*, spread westward.

The raiders were drawn to the ports and coasts of western Europe that were free of any serious defences: after two or three days at sea, they had direct access to booty, treasures, monasteries and churches, and slaves to take from terrorized populations. From 820 to 830, Holy Ireland was completely ravaged: the Book of Chronicles relates that 'not one saint, monastery, noble church or hermit's cave, not one island has escaped pillage'. Due to their important treasures, the monasteries remained the most coveted, and the monks began to hope that the great winter storms would bring them some respite. In the middle of the ninth century, the Frankish empire was shaken in its turn: in 845, 120 *drakkars* sailed up the Seine and pillaged Paris. Six years later, 350 Viking boats were on the Thames and terrorized London; Lisbon and the Tagus had already been pillaged; in 859, the Vikings were in Italy. The raids also reached distant Russia, where it was no longer the Danes or the Norwegians but the Swedes who pillaged Novgorod and Kiev in 865, pushing as far as Constantinople.

The first voyages of the Vikings, at least those known of in the west, had indeed been looting raids, but commerce and migrant colonization were very soon added.

Amongst the factors for the Vikings' raids and migrations, the demographic element must be ranked of the first importance. The net growth taking place in the population of Scandinavia, and in southern Norway in particular, forced groups of farmers to search for new soils. To this cause, political elements may possibly be added, such as Charlemagne's attack on the north of Germany, which represented a threat to a Scandinavian country like Denmark, just as the subjection of Frisia by the Carolingians contributed to an imbalance in the maritime and merchant forces of the north. The personal ambitions of certain Viking chieftains and the pull of adventure must also, of course, be considered an important factor.

The art of Viking seafaring

The most powerful contribution to the Viking offensives lay in the developments in shipbuilding and seafaring accomplished in the north. Two elements in particular must be highlighted in order to understand the developments in shipbuilding: first, an exceptional development in Norway's iron industry meant that tiller axles were made of iron, and a great many tools were also made of this metal.

Second, the Scandinavian forests represented an abundance of wood, remarkably well adapted to the needs of shipping, a wealth in practically unlimited supply.

Employed since the eighth century, the '*gokstad*' boat with its central mast and square sail, already displays the enormous dimensions of the *drakkar*: more than 24 metres long, more than five metres broad, and 2.13 metres deep at the central mast.[41] The material used was oak, the planks of which were assembled so as to overlap, covering over each other to form the planking. Stability was ensured by a deep keel and a high stem: to the rear, the ship was furnished with a poop deck. The most original characteristics of the craft were its extraordinary buoyancy and its pliability: given its construction, there was very little risk of a fracture. Propulsion was provided sometimes by oars and sometimes by sail; there were 16 oars on each side, each measuring some 5.5 metres, allowing steady manoeuvrability, with safety and precision enhanced by the presence of a lateral rudder turning on a vertical axis and acting as a second keel. Lowering the mast and yard arm when manoeuvrability required was the only time the use of oars was justified.

Merely having this ship, this excellent navigational tool, at their disposal, further improved at the end of the eighth century by the use of the *hafskip*, a merchant vessel shorter than the *drakkar* or *langskip* and better adapted to transporting merchandise, but still remarkable for its buoyant qualities, would not have been enough were it not for the simultaneous mastery of navigation. Some have attempted to explain the achievements of Viking seafaring and above all the daring of the sailors, the forerunners of other Atlantic discoverers, by accepting the existence of a sixth sense, perfectly noting the influence of the tides, the winds, the currents and the flightpaths of the birds. For Paul Adam, what must be put into practice is the observation of the geographical realities presented to the Viking navigators.[42] The distances in the North Atlantic, at the high latitudes between Norway, Iceland and Greenland, were far smaller than appeared on Mercator's projections. Mercator's maps increase the apparent distances on the northern latitudes. On the real map, the route from Bergen to Shetland and then to the Faeroes and Iceland is made up of staging posts barely longer – from 320 to 500 kilometres – than the Mediterranean staging posts between Minorca and Sardinia, Crete and Alexandria. Maintaining a constant latitude of 62° north by observing the sun and the stars, one would pass far to the south of Iceland without seeing its mountains and its glaciers. The clouds on the island, the shoals of fish and whales to the south of Iceland's continental plateau, were so many points of reference known to the Vikings. They then had to continue straight on until the mountains of Greenland appeared.

The qualities of the ships must, however, be emphasized. Extremely stable thanks to a solid keel, the *hafskip* bore a square sail and ran well in strong winds; a yard arm allowed the sail to be lowered and one took in reefs to limit the actions of the winds in bad weather. This enabled Iceland to be reached in close to three weeks out of Bergen. This ship has established the Vikings' nautical skills. It has never had the prestige, just as it never inspired the fear, that the *langskip* or *drakkar* did, a long warship whose stem was surmounted with a menacing dragon's head, shields hanging along the entire length of the ship's side, launching destructive raids on Europe's coasts. The *drakkar*, however, never crossed the western ocean; it is with the *hafskip* or *knarr* that the daring Scandinavian seafarers were able to launch into crossing the vast expanse of the ocean, over 1,000 nautical miles, between the Faeroes and a point on the east coast of Greenland, almost 60 miles from Cape Farewell. This crossing represents the height of Scandinavian maritime achievement, and we may say that the ships they used, rather than their destructive raids, represented for the Vikings what the temple did for the Greeks.[43]

The discovery of Greenland

To the Viking Eirik the Red, departing for Greenland represented an opportunity to escape the pursuits that justified his parricide, but also a chance to create a colony with his companions. Viking voyages had long been colonial undertakings through the migrations that, early on, accompanied the looting raids. The end of the eighth century witnessed raids launched by the Norwegians from Hordaland in Northumberland (the sacking of Lindisfarne) and in Ireland (the looting of the monastery at Lambay, near Dublin) in 793 and 795. Some years later, at the beginning of the ninth century, the peasant farmers of Agder and Rogaland, south-west of Bergen in southern Norway, were able to occupy the Orkney archipelago north of Scotland without any fighting. Shetland and the Faeroes were landed in the middle of the same century and in 874 the Vikings began colonizing Iceland.

The Swede Gardar Svávarsson, driven by adventure and the east winds, was the first to land on the north of an island that he called Gardarr, shortly before the Norwegian Flok Vilgerdarsson, who berthed in Breidhafjörd in western Iceland, where the crows he had released before spotting land had set down. Climbing a high mountain to glimpse the lay of the land, and seeing but ice drifts, he gave the island its definitive name, Iceland, the land of ice drifts. In the middle of the decade of 870, the age of the Viking colonization of Iceland began. A genuine expedition made up of families, the women and children following the warriors who left Norway with arms and livestock, perhaps fleeing the tyranny of Harald 'of the beautiful hair'.[44] The expedition berthed by the small islands to the south-west of the island. Its chief, Frijhof Arnason, did not forget to conduct a sacred rite prior to disembarking: within sight of the coasts, he began to throw posts engraved with his high office into the sea, conferring on the gods the task of deciding the site on which they should settle. The gods chose Reykjavik, the 'Bay of Steam', so called by virtue of its abundant hot water springs.

The colony reached its fullest proportions at the end of the ninth century. With emigration at a peak around 900, the best part of the 2,000 emigrants were already settled. A fleet of *hafskips* had already taken them there with their cargoes, which, along with livestock and provisions, also contained wood for constructing their houses. The majority of Scandinavians, who belonged for the most part to the coastal districts of south-western Norway, around Bergen, provided Iceland's population. With them, however, there were also Celts from Ireland and Scotland, Shetland and the Orkneys. Most appreciated were the Viking chiefs' concubine women, slaves who had been swept away after previous raids, or taken from ports of call during the voyage. The slaves were subsequently freed. Some women could also be at the head of the Viking expeditions: thus Aud the Wise, who came from the Hebrides, married the 'great king of the sea' whose son was a Viking king in Scotland; she boarded ship for Iceland with some 20 slaves and freedmen. Previous experiments in colonizing Ireland and Scotland conducted by the Vikings had proven invaluable for providing the workforce for more distant expeditions.

The discovery and colonization of Greenland at the end of the tenth century represented the farthest limit of Viking seafaring of which we know for certain.

One Icelandic tradition has it that, at the beginning of the tenth century, a sailor called Gunnbjörn Ulfsson, driven by bad weather, reached a group of islands towards the west, from which, facing to the west, he had seen an unknown shore. He made no attempt to reach it, however, but returned to Iceland. This tradition therefore attributes the first sight of Greenland to the Icelanders, but, once again, we could be speaking of the Arctic mirage.

While Gunnbjörn's children were still living by the Isalfjörd, in Iceland, a new colonist arrived from Norway with his family. Thomas Asvaldsson came from the Stanvanger region. After his departure, his son Eirik Raudi (Erik the Red) was accused of homicide. Having first set up in an inhospitable region of Iceland, since the good areas were already taken, Eirik reached Hemkadal, where good pasture was available for livestock, but he was banished from it after becoming involved in an argument with his neighbours. He found refuge on an island at the entrance to Hvansfjörd and was again chased away and banished for three years. It is possible that Eirik Raudi was aware of Gunnbjörn's narratives concerning the existence of an unknown western land, and that this incited him to attempt a first voyage, one that would have him reach the eastern coast of Greenland, with its high mountains and abrupt cliffs broken up by deep fjords encircled by glaciers. Past Cape Farewell, the south, where good pasture land could be found, became more welcoming. It was here that Eirik Raudi made his real voyage of colonization in 985 or 986. To attract his companions, he baptized this new land the Green Country: an expedition numbering no fewer than 14 ships and 400 people, with a similar number of livestock and tools, left Iceland to face some 800 kilometres of unbroken sea voyage.

Subsequent colonization was to make south-west Greenland in its entirety, from Eiriksfjörd to Vestribygd, a living country for raising sheep, some cattle, and still more fish. The fertile valley of Gardar in particular offered good pastures, in gentler climactic conditions than nowadays, and could feed from 10 to 20 head of cattle, and large flocks of sheep, per farm.[45]

The first genuine transatlantic voyage, made directly from Norway to Greenland, was carried out by Leif Eiriksson, the son of Eirik Raudi, in 999–1000. For G. J. Marcus, this expedition, rather than the discovery of America, which has for a long time been falsely attributed to him, represents Leif Eiriksson's principal merit. The route he followed was that of the Hernar parallel, a group of islands off the Norwegian coast, 48 kilometres from Bergen. He went far to the south to avoid the dangerous southern coast of Iceland. Crossing the ocean at its largest northern expanse (more than 1,800 kilometres) proved the excellence of the Vikings' ships and their seafaring mastery.

The Vikings and Vinland

Leif Eiriksson's renown, however, stems from the distinction of having led the Vikings as far as the coast of North America, to Vinland.

If Leif the Lucky and the other discoverers of the year 1000 undoubtedly never landed at Vinland, the land of the vine, on the New England latitudes, and still less south of the Hudson, there can be no doubting the reality of the discovery of the American coast, at least that of Newfoundland and Labrador. The *Groenlendinga Saga* tells of the first discovery of America, attributing it not to Leif Eiriksson, but to the Icelander Bjarni Herjölfsson, but leaving the greatest uncertainty hanging over the geographical position of the land discovered. In fact, leaving Iceland for Greenland, Bjarni and his companions sighted a land that was not mountainous like Greenland but composed of low hills covered in dense forest.[46] Faithful to his primary objective, to reach Greenland, Bjarni did not want to disembark. He would, however, have been the first discoverer of the unknown land located far beyond Greenland, which was already familiar to the Vikings, but would subsequently reach it on another occasion.

Hearing talk of his voyage, Leif, son of Eirik Raudi, purchased Bjarni's ship and hired a crew of 34 men. Then, leaving Brattahlid and the land of his father, he made for the south-west, following the route Bjarni had already taken. The first land he experienced was completely flat, rocky and desolate, and Leif called it Helluland, the land of flat stones. Setting back to sea, he reached another land that looked quite different: still low, the shore was composed of immense beaches of white sand, falling in a gentle slope to the sea, dominated by dense forest. Leif gave it the name Markland, the land of woods, because of this forested cover. This land displayed close similarities with the land that Bjarni sighted. After two days of renewed sailing, the third land they discovered was a completely different matter: the ship successfully navigated a river upstream, arriving at a lake where they disembarked. While exploring this appealing country, they found grapes and easily managed to fell some trees. There was no fog, and the river held abundant salmon. For Leif and his companions, this was Vinland, a paradisiacal land.

We realize that the Greenlanders had persevered, despite all the risks, ever further to the west. In subsequent voyages undertaken to Vinland, they met the natives and returned carrying cargoes of wood, skins and even grapes.

Markland and Vinland are not legendary islands, as was St Brendan's Isle. Adam of Bremen's accurate narrative, in his *Gesta Hamburgensis*, written around 1075, mentions information received from the king of Denmark, Svein Estridsson:

> Besides Iceland, there are many other islands in the great ocean, of which Greenland is not the smallest; it lies further away in the ocean.... Moreover, he [the king of Denmark] has said that an island has been found by many in this ocean, which has been called Vinland, because there vines grow wild and bear good grapes. Moreover...there is self-sown seed in abundance.[47]

The narratives of the sagas, however, are not at all supported by archaeological evidence, especially as regards Vinland. The Newport Tower on Rhode Island, like the Kensington Stone in Minnesota, have been shown to be forgeries manufactured in the nineteenth century, and the map of Vinland acquired by Yale University in 1966, is worth little more. The only genuine relic was found in L'Anse aux Meadows in Newfoundland, where the remains of eight Viking houses, with a forge and boat sheds can be discerned, proving the existence of a Scandinavian settlement going back to the last years of the tenth century or the beginning of the eleventh century.[48]

It is quite probable, especially at the end of the Middle Ages, that the Greenlanders occasionally ventured to Markland, but their appearance in Vinland is far less certain. Above all, there was no voyage of colonization similar to those undertaken from Norway or Iceland. While Iceland's shipping and manpower resources were sufficient for the colonization of Greenland, those from Greenland were not well suited to a colonization of Vinland.

Having Leif and his companions set sail from Newfoundland as far south as Cape Cod and beyond, doubtless stems from imagination rather than well-founded reality. Too many obstacles stand in the way of a discovery that ought to have ended in a real Scandinavian settlement. The Newfoundland waters are difficult, with frequent and dense fogs impeding navigation by observation of the sun and stars. Orientation techniques were tricky and took a great deal of time, of which the Vikings, no doubt, did not have much.[49] Expeditions to Vinland

followed soon after the colonization of Greenland, and only lasted for the generation of which Leif the Lucky was a part. The 'conquest' of Vinland that
Greenland's colonists dreamt of until they died out, required too many modifications to the Vikings' traditional route to the west. One had to leave a route with
constant latitudes of the 60th parallel and cross several latitudes in order to arrive
at Cape Cod. Little wonder there was only one badly organized exploration.

The discovery of the paradisiacal Vinland of the sagas conceals a reality that is
even more difficult to assess. This can only be done, however, if the Vikings'
nautical accomplishments are brought into sharper relief, although this may mask
the everyday reality of their life on the Atlantic, which focused on fishing and
trade. To the booty won from their piracy the Vikings had already added the benefits of commerce in Europe's seas, and they continued to do this in the North
Atlantic.

Fishing and trading were still tinged with both daring and a sense of nautical
realities. We should not be too quick to celebrate the exploits of these 'Kings of
the Sea' unreservedly, however, since the Vikings had had to take account of
numerous constraints imposed upon them by conditions in which it was always
difficult to navigate; and besides, they were not always successful.

Viking trade routes

The regularity of the relations established since the eleventh century remains
extraordinary, not only between Norway, the Faeroes and Iceland, but also
between Norway and Greenland, much further afield. To reach Greenland
certainly required much longer than the three weeks that Adam of Bremen
suggests it took for the crossing from Bergen to Iceland, or the eight days
required to get to the Faeroes. Not that the speeds at which the *knarr*, squatter
than the *drakkar* but highly manoeuvrable, could make the crossing were not sufficiently high. Of course, there was nothing comparable to the speeds reached by
the nineteenth-century clipper: nine knots cruising speed up to a maximum of 16
knots. The speed of the *knarr* can show an average of five to six knots, with a
maximum of eight and a half to 10 knots. Although the maximum speeds were
not insignificant, the long days of July enabled the distances travelled to be
further extended. Paul Adam estimates that a relatively unladen Viking boat could
stay afloat on the swell and if not exceed, then certainly reach its speed limit of 10
knots over a sufficiently long distance and with the aid of highly favourable winds.
One saga speaks of a return from Greenland to Norway at an average of more
than eight knots, that is, 192 miles a day, with a dominant west wind.[50] In high
seas and normal weather, a speed of five to six knots is more likely. A journey to
Greenland and back could, if necessary, be done in the summer months, but it
would be better to count on a winter journey.

Great difficulties remained in surveying coasts, particularly in Greenland, but also in Iceland where the south coast of the island was highly dangerous and only the west coast was easily accessible. In fact, shipwrecks were quite frequent in the offshore shallows, due to failures in the accurate estimation of the longitude. The sagas tell of many crews becoming confused and even highly distressed upon losing all sense of direction. They knew that the evil of *hafvilla* had taken hold of the sea when they were no longer able to orient themselves. The sagas tell that when reliable winds fail, the sails hang and ships can no longer be steered, and have to wait for a wind, a wait that lasts, however, for many long days.[51] One saga has a crew waiting in this condition for over a fortnight. 'That summer, they had to face a great deal of bad weather, a lot of fog, weak and irregular winds; they drifted far into the vast sea.' Calculating the route became impossible. This was the case with Bjarni Herjölfsson and his crew, who were the first to discover Vinland, when they encountered adverse north winds and, especially, the thickest of fog: 'they no longer knew where they were going'. This mention of the thickest of fogs indicates that they are entering the *hafvilla*. The fog does not lift for several days, and accurate calculations, the principal asset of Viking navigation, are lost. A *hafvilla* does not necessarily result in shipwreck, but it always seriously lengthens the journey and, above all, one can miss one's goal, thus reaching Greenland instead of Iceland.

In spite of these real difficulties, the trade routes were relatively regular. In Greenland, they were not interrupted until the end of the fourteenth century. Already in the course of the century, however, navigation had been made much harder by a cooling climate: the eastern coasts, whose fields of ice reached the sea, became more and more dangerous; moreover, there were icebergs, and cases of boats caught in the ice floes were even mentioned.

A good index of the regular relations between Greenland and Norway is provided by the list of bishops named at the see of Gardar in Greenland, usually consecrated in Trondheim Cathedral in Norway. It covers the best part of the twelfth, thirteenth and fourteenth centuries. The first report of a bishop is in 1126, the last in 1368.

For both Iceland and Norway, Trondheim was the first major trading port, then from the thirteenth century on, Bergen, became more important. Bergen was a cosmopolitan port into which came Icelandic, English (Norway and Iceland were closely linked in the fourteenth century with the ports on the east coast of England, especially Lynn), German, Danish and Swedish merchants. The merchants of the Hanseatic League seized control of the traffic at Bergen, which was their principal trading post in the Scandinavian north. They had also captured the Norwegian traffic in the Baltic and in the North Sea.

For Iceland's maritime trade routes, we have some data to go on. In the 1340s, there were fairly regular departures from Bergen: 11 ships in 1340, six destined only for the port of Stralfjörd in 1341, 11 in 1345, 12 in 1346, and 18 in 1347. The shipowners were the King of Norway, the Archbishop of Nidaros, the cathedral chapters, and the merchants of Trondheim and Bergen. A severe fall in traffic that became evident in 1350 can be attributed to the consequences of the Black Death in Norway.[52] Before the end of the century, traffic picked up again to some extent: in 1381, 10 ships were loaded at Bergen for Hvalfjörd; in 1389, 11 ships were sent to Iceland, seven in 1390, 11 in 1391, but only two in 1394. Norway's eclipse in the North Atlantic trading routes was decided when a sizeable number of English merchants began to appear in Iceland.

Greenland's trade is more difficult to appreciate for want of a reliable index of maritime movements. We can, however, use indications of western imports into Norway and Europe of seal and especially walrus skins, as well as the highly valued ivory from walrus tusks. Thus, in 1327, the papal legate received 250 ivory tusks from the diocese of Gardar as Crusade tithes and as Peter's Penny. At the Cologne trade fair, this same ivory was in as high demand as the skins. With walrus skins, they used to make an extremely substantial rigging with a reputation for durability. Another of the most appreciated imports from the west was the Greenland white falcon. It was introduced as a gift to the great or as ransom (hence in 1396, a son of the duke of Burgundy was bought back from the Saracens for 12 Greenland white falcons).[53]

Amongst the produce imported from Iceland, stock fish, i.e. dried fish, was most important, and was principally cod imported into Norway in great quantities and re-exported throughout Europe. Walrus and sealskins, along with their furs, also figure here. In the fourteenth century, these products were in hot competition with the Russian skins and especially furs imported by the Hanseatic League and the English merchants. The Icelandic falcons were as famous as the Greenland variety: in 1262, the sultan of Tunis received a present of Icelandic falcons.[54]

Commercial relations between Iceland and Europe were underwritten by human relations, with Icelandic merchants going to stay in Norway, children sent to Europe for their education, and bishops travelling from Skálaholt and Hólar in Iceland to Norway. Crossing the ocean had become almost routine. Reaching a peak shortly before the middle of the fourteenth century, the trading routes fell victim to Norway's decline at the end of the century. For G. J. Marcus, only 'the providential arrival of merchantmen from England saved the Icelanders from a fate similar to that of the Norse colonies on Greenland'.[55]

After the Icelanders, the Scandinavians were able to open the North Atlantic routes, but the Nordic region tended to slip away from them towards the end of the Middle Ages. For both the discovery of new lands and commercial practice, the initiative was to pass into the hands of the sailors and merchants of the Mediterranean and north-western Europe.

Chapter 2

A new Atlantic

From the fifteenth to the beginning of the sixteenth centuries

In the first Atlantic, the Phoenicians and the Carthaginians had exploited the abundant cereals on the Moroccan coasts, as well as rare products such as purple from Mogador and gold from Africa. Rome and the Arabs of Al Andalus had prolonged this prosperity. From the fifteenth century, a new Atlantic developed, extending its grip to the most distant regions of the sea and opening up a New World.

From the beginnings of the fourteenth century, the arrival of Italian, and particularly Genoese, sailors and money made possible the rediscovery of the archipelagos of the Mediterranean Atlantic: the Canaries, Madeira and the Azores. Knowledge of the Atlantic course was backed by the authority of a prince, Henry the Navigator, who was able to gather the best sailors together. After 1434, Cape Bojador, to the south of Morocco, ceased to be an insurmountable obstacle, and it became possible to navigate towards the Gulf of Guinea. The search for gold and slaves enriched the Portuguese to an even greater extent than exploiting sugar from Madeira, the Canaries, and finally from São Tomé. Choosing this southern course gave the Portuguese the advantage for several years, since it gave them access to the spice routes from India. Then came the time of Columbus and the discovery of America: the Catholic Kings of Spain reached west, where the ocean ceased to be the 'Sea of Perpetual Gloom' and no longer put up its dreaded barrier. Believing, even at the end of his life, that he had reached India, Columbus pushed back the limits of the Mediterranean world for good. Nevertheless, the image of an Atlantic ocean separating the New World from the Old only really appeared more than twenty years after Columbus's discovery, wiping away his fundamental error, when in 1513, Vasco Nuñez de Balboa reached the South Sea which, seven years later, Magellan called the Pacific.

A new Mediterranean Atlantic

Off Gibraltar: the maintenance and extension of the inshore navigation of the Atlantic

Along the European and North African coasts, the great inshore navigation of the Atlantic never stopped. Already important in antiquity, from the tenth to the thirteenth century it was driven by the enormous part played by the sailors of Al Andalus in the commercial exploitation of the riches in Andalusia and the Maghrib, where they had already encountered competition from the sailors and fishermen of Galicia and Portugal. At the beginning of the thirteenth century, and particularly in the fourteenth, new ambitious sailors and merchants intervened and took on this role. As Michel Mollat put it so well, 'gradually, beacons were lit from the Baltic to Gibraltar'.[1]

Two of the largest medieval navies, the Hanseatic and the Genoese, brought renewed activity to navigating the Atlantic. Between 1150 and 1250, under leadership from Lübeck, the German Baltic communities organized themselves into a commercial league, the Hanseatic, at the very moment that the countries of the littoral were offering their salted herring, wood and mined goods. The Hanseatic League was able to establish an extensive network in the hinterland, such as Brunswick in Saxony and Cologne in Westphalia. In the Mediterranean, the Genoese expanded their commercial networks to a far greater extent: 'So many Genoese were scattered through the world that everywhere they went, new Genoas took root.'[2]

Having at first been able to go by the Moslem trade route running north of the Mediterranean basin through the Black Sea, and following the loss of Constantinople and the Turkish market in the thirteenth and fourteenth centuries, the Genoese organized a turn towards the west in order to dominate trade routes such as the alum of Rome towards Flanders. At the same time, in conjunction with the Iberians, the Genoese turned towards the 'Mediterranean Atlantic' from the Azores to the Canaries.

Under the control of the German Hanseatic League, who had pushed northward into Viking Scandinavia as far as Bergen, the first opening up of the sound saw the Hanseatic ships leave the Baltic to enter into competition with the English in the North Sea, then, in spite of their difficulties, clearing the outcroppings of Brittany's coast and reaching Hispanic shores. In this decompartmentalization of western Europe, the Hanseatics were helped by the support of Breton and Basque sailors. The latter, far from *bricoleurs* making it up as they went along, showed themselves to be skilful practitioners of navigation.[3] The Hanseatic League began to desire access to profits from the south of Europe, encountered as they put into Bruges, and where they met Italian merchants. Each year after 1277, a fleet of

Genoese galleys left for the west, towards London and Bruges, where they met sailors from the Germanic regions, Slavs, and Scandinavians from the Hanseatic League. At the beginning of the fourteenth century, the Hanseatics had progressed as far as Lisbon, and in 1415, almost a century later, a German ship took part in the Portuguese capture of Ceuta.

French and Iberian salt went northwards, salt from the Atlantic that the Hanseatic ships carried to cover the growing needs of fishing in the North Sea towards 1300.[4] Every year, a salt convoy made the return from the Bay of Bourgneuf, south of the Loire. In addition, there were wines, alum and pastel. The wine routes from the Aquitaine became familiar to the English when, following the marriage of Aliénor d'Aquitaine to Henry Plantagenet in 1152, and the latter's accession to the English crown two years later, they took possession of a duchy that would remain British for three centuries. At the beginning of the fourteenth century, in the autumn after the vintage, wines from Guyenne and the Moyenne-Garonne were loaded at Bordeaux by fleets of between 100 and 200 sails heading in spring for Bristol, Southampton and London, from where part of their cargoes was forwarded to the Low Countries. In 1308–1309, up to 90 million litres were exported in this way. Almost half of these ships were English, although one out of five was Breton, and one out of 10 Bayonnese.[5] Like the Basques, however, the Bretons also went to load the Italian alum necessary for the textile industries of north-western Europe. For Jean Delumeau, the major share of transporting this product from Civitavecchia was undertaken by the Basques.[6] During the same period, the fleet destined for Flanders was laden with Castilian wool.

The re-opening of the Atlantic islands and the Genoese initiative

> More than anyone else, they had as much experience of the Atlantic as of Africa.[7]

For the Genoese, Morocco, as much as Andalusia, constituted an essential market where their merchants took wheat, oil, wax and fish. This renewed the Al Andalus trade routes, but on a far grander scale. From the thirteenth century onwards, the Genoese became visibly and increasingly invasive. Forced to reduce their activities in the Black Sea, they found massive compensation west of Gibraltar while the Venetians were fiercely defending their eastern Mediterranean positions. For the Genoese, the ports of the Maghrib were way-stations on their return journeys from London or Bruges. They imported Moroccan wheat into both the Christian and Moslem Iberian cities. However, besides the traditional trade in cereals, the southern routes led countries towards gold and slaves, with which the Genoese were soon familiar. At the end of the thirteenth century, the Genoese galleys were in London after having been at Bruges some 20 years earlier, and in 1291, the brothers Vivaldi of Genoa left their city to discover a new Atlantic route. In fact, they followed the course Hanno the Carthaginian had sailed on his voyage, along the African coasts up to the Gulf of Guinea, where they were lost, no doubt running aground in the shallows.

As Vitorino Magalhaes Godhiño has made clear, the motivation for the search for a southern Atlantic route, along the African coast was economic.[8] The hunger for gold, the lack of cereals in Iberia, the demand for sugar and the slaves to produce it, for gum ('the blood of the dragon'), and dyes for textiles; the demand for enlarged fishing areas due to Basque and Breton competition: all these reasons forced the Iberians and their Genoese partners to confront the obstacles of legend.

The 12,000 square kilometres of the Atlantic archipelagos (Madeira, the Canaries and the Azores), despite their limited size, were revealed as vital both for the nautical experiments that their discovery and their exploitation required, and for their capacity to satisfy economic demands. Moreover, at least the first two of them offered the paradisiacal landscapes from which they earned the name of the Fortunate Isles, inherited from antiquity and its imaginary. The mild climate and rich soil was as suited to the cultivation of cereals as to sugar cane, in Madeira to a greater extent than in the Canaries or the Azores, since the latter archipelago lay at the climactic limits for cultivating cane. The Canaries, with its Guanche population that had for so long proved difficult to control, also provided a workforce of slaves for the sugar plantations and to supplement that of Portugal.

The Genoese were the first to reach the Azores. Thanks to medieval cartography, we have some information available concerning their navigation in the waters around the most northerly Atlantic archipelago. Lying on the latitude of Lisbon, almost 1,400 kilometres separate the island of San Miguel, the most easterly of the archipelagos, from Lagos, the port from which the navigators departed. A Genoese map from 1339 shows two islands in the Azores. At this time, some Genoese, such as the Passagna, were already in the service of the King of Portugal. In 1351, a Genoese portolan places four islands in the Azores. Thereafter, there was an improvement in geographical surveys: we count seven islands in the Medici Atlas of 1370, eight on the Soler map of 1385. It was by dead reckoning that the Genoese sailed for and reached the archipelago, and once again, the certainties born of nautical experience are tinged with legend. In 1375, 10 islands figure in the Azores in the Catalan Atlas, designed by the Cresques of Barcelona, which suggests, however, that without doubt these islands are none other than the legendary Fortunate Isles cited by Isidore of Seville, following Pliny.[9]

In 1339, Angelino Dulcert drew the first map to provide an accurate outline of the Canary Islands. The Genoese had reached the archipelago of the Canaries in 1312, almost a quarter of a century earlier, and on the planisphere of 1339 the

Genoese Lanzaroto Malocello gave his name to one of the islands, which it still carries: the island of Lanzarote. In 1341, under the patronage of the king of Portugal, other Genoese set out to explore the Canaries. With only 115 kilometres separating it from Cape Juby, Fuerteventura was closest to the African coast, and the archipelago had probably been known to the Carthaginians and the Phoenicians who, from the colony at Lixus, had exploited Mogador's purple. However, the island possessing this wealth is situated at a latitude much further north than the Canaries. Hanno had undoubtedly found an important port of call in the Canaries during his voyage. The islands were some 1,150 kilometres from the Iberian coasts and lay at the limits of regular sailing from which the wind regime made the return possible.[10] This implied that it was very probably necessary to reach the open sea by west-north-west in order to find the most reliable winds and in order not to be caught by the coastal currents that pulled southwards. The Portuguese navigators already appreciated the value of the principle of the *volta* towards the Azores for their discoveries. It bound together the discovery of the Canaries with the other archipelagos, since Madeira lay on the route to the Azores, almost 600 kilometres from the Canaries.

Over the long years of the fourteenth century, legend and politics created a history of a far distant Canaries' archipelago. In 1344, an infante of Castile, tempted by the Crown of the Canaries, had himself titled the Prince of Fortune by the Pope, and declared himself master of the islands of Pluviaria (Lanzarote), Atlantica and Hesperida. In fact, Pope Clement VI confuses all the legendary islands – the Isle of Seven Cities, St Brendan's Isle, Satana, etc. – in the Bull where he conceded the Crown of the Canaries to Luis de la Cerda, the infante of Castile. These Castilian claims brought a reaction from the King of Portugal, who had already explored the Canaries and intended to reserve the right to conquer them for himself. During the long years that followed, before the fifteenth century, the archipelago was in dispute between the two Iberian kingdoms.

The time for exploiting the discovery had not yet come, even for the ambitious Genoese. Almost a century was to pass before they became interested in setting up a sugar economy, first in Madeira, then in the Canaries. Between times these islands were visited by the short-lived expeditions of the Norman Béthencourt.[11] Importantly, moreover, they remanded possession of the Canaries to the King of Castile, who had advanced the necessary funds. From 1420 to 1434, the Portuguese vainly attempted to regain the Canaries, but in 1431 the Venetian Pope Eugene IV recognized the rights of Castile over the archipelago.

The beginnings of the age of sugar in Madeira (1452–1498)

Like the Azores, Madeira was probably known to the Genoese, who reached the

Canaries from 1312, seeking the west winds, the 'westerlies', that allowed them to return to the Canaries and the African coast. Meanwhile, for want of ships capable of working to windward, the Portuguese, having used the maritime and financial services of the Genoese, maintained only sporadic relations with the Mediterranean Atlantic, constituted by the African coast to the east, and the archipelagos of the Canaries, Madeira and the Azores in the west, throughout the entire fourteenth century. It seems that the new economic conditions created in western Europe at the beginning of the fifteenth century had opened other horizons: after the fall in population of the fourteenth century and its repercussions on prices and wages, a net recovery was produced so that new economic ventures could be envisaged.[12]

In 1420, the Portuguese João Gonçales Zarco and Tristão Vaz Teixeira disembarked on the then deserted island of Madeira. A Venetian portolan of 1351 had signalled its existence, called Isla de Legname, Porto Santo and the Salvagens and Desertas Islands. For Prince Henry the Navigator's search, beginning in the 1430s, for a Portuguese settlement in the Canaries and for explorations of the African coast, the island offered a site for a port of call where fresh supplies were taken on. Its permanent occupation began in 1425,[13] but development remained quite slow until the 1450s, when the cultivation of sugar cane began. For the three crops, wheat, sugar cane and vines, that were to make the island's wealth, the introduction of Genoese capital was important.

At the beginning of the fifteenth century, the Genoese had introduced sugar cane into the Portuguese Algarve.[14] The Genoese then began to withdraw their capital from the East, where the Turks were increasingly threatening their trading posts in the Black Sea, to invest in the sugar plantations of Valencia, Malaga and the Algarve. Florentine and Venetian capital also favoured the sugar plantations that were going to establish a new area of production in the Mediterranean Atlantic.

We should not view the establishment of the sugar economy in the islands of the Mediterranean Atlantic as having happened overnight. In the middle of the fifteenth century, Madeira was still in the cereal phase of its economy. Wheat had been the first crop in the ground cleared by the colonists, both Portuguese and foreign – Italian, Spanish, Flemish and French, that Henry the Navigator, Master of the Island, had introduced. Wheat was both a crop that produced food and a crop to be exported to a metropolis deficient in grain. Amongst the resources that the Venetian Ca' da Mosto observes in Madeira in 1455, wheat assumes a high place, reaching its zenith, in fact, between 1450 and 1460.

For Ca' da Mosto, however, cane sugar is already one of the island's important resources, bringing more export value than the wood that gave the island its name. Cane production is 400 cantars, some 23 tonnes.[15] Of course, the visitor also notes the presence of wax, honey and 'the best kinds of wine', but none of these products can, in the immediate future, rival cane sugar. It was not until later, in the sixteenth century, when Brazilian sugar began production and became serious competition for Madeira, that wine became the island's principal resource.

In fact, in 1452, Henry the Navigator concluded the first contract relating to sugar production with Diogo de Teyer, who received the right to construct a water mill: 'this new engine has speeded up the rise of production'.[16]

Half a century later, in 1498, sugar exports from Madeira were approaching 1,700 tonnes (120,000 arroba). The island had become the great provider to Flanders (almost 563 tonnes to Antwerp), to Italy (183 tonnes to Genoa, 211 tonnes to Venice, 85 tonnes to Livorno for Tuscany, and 29 tonnes for Rome), to Portugal and England (99 tonnes to Lisbon and as much to London); in France, Rouen and La Rochelle imported 85 and 28 tonnes, Brittany, 14 tonnes, Provence (Aigues-Mortes), 85 tonnes. Even the Turkish empire was supplied from Madeira (211 tonnes to Constantinople and Chios).[17] For labour in the plantations and the 80 *engeñhos* (sugar mills), the Portuguese began to bring slaves from the Canaries and Africa, reaching almost 2,000 in number by the end of the fifteenth century.

Foreign participation in this economy cannot be disputed. When in 1461, the infante Dom Fernand, the adopted son and successor to Henry the Navigator in the administration of the island dominion in which Madeira is the jewel, responded to demands by the island's inhabitants to export its foodstuffs, he specifies that Jews and Genoese are not forbidden to purchase the goods mentioned – wine, sugar, wood, seed and flours – nor to rent land. The first consignment of sugar from Madeira arrived in Bruges in 1468, but was sold at a low price to compete with the old centres of production (Sicily, Messina). Dom Fernand favoured the setting up of a system of price controls for exports, resting on an agreement between the colonists and the traders, in which the Genoese played a considerable role. They showed themselves capable of securing the transition between the old Italian and Flemish imports of Mediterranean sugar and the new imports of sugar from Madeira.[18] Similarly, the Genoese were able to initiate the Portuguese into methods of selling that the latter had not mastered, since they possessed both the commercial connections and the capital. Coordinating the creation of what Jean Meyer calls a 'sales cartel', the infante clearly shows the international character of the market and the irreplaceable role of the Genoese or the Flemish in trade:

> I would have you know that a heavy fall in the price [of sugar] has taken place....We ought indeed to find a way to remedy this, since it seems to me that some have experienced serious troubles when the price was allowed to fall in this manner....I have sought advice from several persons who understand this type of thing well, and from this have

drawn the conclusion that this fall in prices would not have taken place if it had not concerned a very widespread foodstuff transported by sailors and other people to Flanders and other countries where it was sold off at a lower price than would have been reasonable. There is no other remedy than the following, which is to bring the whole sugar market, my own and yours, together into a single hand....I have had conversations with specialist traders from the city of Lisbon who look favourably upon my plan, which is made obvious by the fact that they will take both your and my sugars from me, produced in the island, and at reasonable and guaranteed prices.[19]

Amongst these specialized traders from Lisbon, the Genoese were of the first rank. Their mastery of this trade is illustrated by the example of Christopher Columbus, who in 1478 bought a cargo of sugar in Madeira for the account of Luigi Centurione, one of the big players in naval armaments and Genoese trade.[20] The Lomellini, other Genoese merchants, also counted amongst the major traders of Lisbon: in the middle of the fifteenth century, they exported Portuguese cork, exploited Madeira's sugar, and were also found in London.[21]

The example of the sugar economy in Madeira remains exceptional in the Atlantic world, since the Spanish were only introduced to cane sugar from the Canaries towards 1480, when it had already been familiar to them from the Levant. It is a crop whose destiny is strictly bound up with the ongoing development of international markets. This remained true for a long time, for over three centuries, in the economy of the Atlantic. Thus Madeira testifies to the utter originality of sugar plantation in the tropical Atlantic from the last third of the fifteenth century. Its economy was mastered by dynamic trading, the provision of slaves and control of outlets and prices.

This first Atlantic age of sugar, however, was realized while the Portuguese simultaneously undertook to survey the African coast in search of other objectives. They could certainly find slaves there to be used in the plantations, but this was secondary in relation both to the search for a new spice route and for gold. It would reveal the true dimensions of the Atlantic.

Exploring the African Atlantic

New Portuguese resources

We are well aware that, for a hundred years, the Kings of Portugal...[have] set sail in high seas.[22]

Beginning in the 1430s, the Portuguese lent a new vitality to the exploration of Africa's Atlantic coasts. They had the benefit of Genoese capital, already present in the Mediterranean Atlantic since the fourteenth century and, in particular, found one of the most efficient nautical devices in the caravel of Lagos.

Although fitted with an axial rudder fixed to the stern-post, the *kogge*, the Hanse ship with the enormous holds befitting a booming economy[23] that the Genoese adopted after the galley, was not well adapted for adverse winds, since it was rigged with square sails that were only suited to winds coming from astern. In another instance, carrying seed destined for Andalusia, North Africa, Catalonia and Italy, Nordic traders most often preferred to transship them into Portuguese vessels at Lisbon, in order to take on Portuguese salt, wines, cork and alum from the Orient and Italy.

The Bayonne *coque*, or skiff, may appear to be better suited to navigating the African coasts. Running high on the water, this round, rather short boat with a deck, was fitted with a square cabin on the poop and a forecastle on a triangular platform at the prow.[24] Fitted with a Bayonne tiller and an axial rudder on the stern-post, a large square sail, and a lateen sail on the mizzen, the *coque* was easier to navigate than the *kogge* when tacking close to the wind. After 1304, according to the chronicler Giovanni Villani, the *coque* had crossed the 'straits of Seville' and was used by the Genoese, the Venetians and the Catalans. Inheriting much from this type of boat, the Portuguese caravel of the early fifteenth century would be able to brave the high seas and was rigged for sailing close to the wind. It was the instrument of a new mastery of navigation in the Mediterranean Atlantic, between the Moroccan Atlantic coast, the archipelagos as far as the Azores, and the Iberian coasts. The successful exploration of the African Atlantic depended on this mastery. Apparently inaugurated fairly early on, when, by dead reckoning, the Genoese and Portuguese seafarers reached the Azores in the fourteenth century, the exploration of the African Atlantic was only regularly pursued in the following century. The *volta* drove the loop of the African route towards Lisbon as far out as the Azores, so as to avoid the trade wind and catch up with the westerlies, the west winds. The gradual introduction of the use of the compass may in this case have been an effective means to identify the route by latitude.

Finally, there were also powerful motives in the fifteenth century. Although the Christian ideal of the quest for an African or Asiatic ally (the legendary Prêtre Jean) against Islam might seem to be a powerful incitement to the seafarers, especially with the success of the Iberian crusade in the Maghrib, capturing Ceuta in north-western Morocco in 1415, the principal stimulant was the search for immediately exploitable resources, in particular gold and slaves. It was possible to double the gold passing through the Sahara by having direct access by sea to the gold of West Africa, while slaves could be used in the sugar plantations.

However, the prospect of creating a maritime route to the Orient, as the

Vivaldis had already envisaged at the end of the thirteenth century, became clearer as the geographical knowledge inherited from the Arabs was extricated from the constraints of legends that had been accepted since antiquity. Soon the Ptolemaic theory of the isolation of the oceans was contested in Italy. With the Arab geographers (Al-Beronni, eleventh century), it was admitted that the Atlantic and Indian Oceans were linked.[25] The dogma of a torrid and impassable zone, situated south of Ptolemy's *oekumen*, and the extreme feelings of fear it inspired, had disappeared, at least as regards the Indian Ocean, since the beginning of the fourteenth century. Abandoning the theory of the uninhabited, torrid zone was a breach in the medieval paradigm of cosmography, opening the future to discoveries on the African Atlantic. Thus, in 1484, before Diaz had completed the circumnavigation of Africa, Lorenzo Bonincontri, a professor of astrology at the University of Rome, bore witness to this transformation of knowledge:

> Ptolemy says that until then he had no knowledge of an inhabited place situated beyond the equator. Recently, however, Henri of Aragon [meaning, of course, Henry the Navigator], the King of Portugal, sent his ships to search these areas, and men have been found there; we now know that certain locales were abundantly populated, while some others were not.[26]

To minds that had for a long time been permeated by scholastic thought, the sailors' experiences set them apart. Still close to Ptolemy, one Genoese map of the world dating from 1457 showed an *oekumen* completely surrounded by the ocean; the Indian Ocean was no longer closed off like a lake, and Africa had become circumnavigable. Obviously, the influence of Ptolemaic thought remained enormous. It was profoundly stamped on Pierre D'Ailly's *Image du Monde* [*The Image of the World*], the favourite reading of Christopher Columbus, to the point of making him favour a flawed measurement of the meridian, one-quarter lower than Eratosthenes' exact measurement (assessed at 39,690 kilometres), so making the Atlantic appear relatively narrow: 'The water flows from one pole to the other into the ocean's basin and it extends from the tip of Spain all the way to where India begins over a width that is not terribly great.'[27]

By contrast, Eratosthenes' larger measurement of the size of the globe, retained by the Arab geographers and by the predominant Genoese and Catalans in Lisbon, created reason enough to prevent an ocean crossing and to force expeditions as far eastwards as Asia, which was preferably to be reached by the south. Lisbon's refusal, opposing Christopher Columbus's proposals for an expedition to the west, was inspired in part by Portugal's real intellectual and empirical advances in the first half of the fifteenth century.[28] In fact, experience could be put forward to refute Columbus's ideas: in his time, the maximum distance for a crossing on the high sea was still less than 800 nautical miles for a ship navigating by a known course, and according to the most favourable estimates, Columbus, on his chosen latitude, had between 6,000 and 6,700 nautical miles to cross.[29] To reach India, there was no choice but to circumnavigate Africa.

Exploration and exchange

Passing 'fearful Cape Bojador', situated on the West African coast on the latitude of the Canaries, marked the end of a period of fear and uncertainty. In 1455, Usodimare, a Genoese, even wrote that 'the waters come to an end here, as though in a pitcher'.[30] This was where ships ran out of the current bearing south along the Moroccan Atlantic coast, and met an opposing current. Furthermore, the return winds could only be sought further out to sea. In August 1434, in a very light craft almost 30 miles from the coast, Gil Eanes, working beyond the trade wind that had prevented his retracing the route taken by Hanno the Carthaginian, found the west winds in the midst of the Atlantic and initiated the Portuguese *volta*. This particular voyage opened the route to the south.

This was the result of the tireless efforts of the infante Dom Henrique. Henry the Navigator – the modern name by which he is usually known – seems an ill-suited description of this prince, who had undertaken only two short sea voyages.[31] A sailor from Lagos, the port from which the Portuguese left, Gil Eanes joined the ships' captains sent out by the infante to explore, with 'great patience', the African coastline. The year before the discovery of Cape Bojador, he had followed the same route as the others and was gripped by the same fear. Finally, he too went to the Canary Islands, from where he returned with a few captives. This performance reveals the somewhat negative role this archipelago had played for many years. Relatively easy to reach, it was attractive to navigators because they found slaves there, to be sold in Lisbon and, later, in Madeira. The Canaries could also be used as a base from which to exploit Saharan gold, a project increasingly nurtured by Henry the Navigator, who hoped at the same time to build himself a kingdom in the islands.

Gold and slave-trading firms had long been dominant, coming before the attempts at exploration that did not reach their full height until the second half of the fifteenth century, especially between 1470 and 1480. In 1441, a few years after Cape Bojador was passed, the Portuguese Nuno Tristão brought back the first Moorish slaves taken from the West African coast, won at the cost of fighting and raids. Becoming, after 1443, 'the pillar of all Portuguese discovery and colo-nization',[32] with every navigator requiring his authorization to venture onto the African coasts, Henry the Navigator intended to take advantage of what were lucrative explorations due to the markets for gold and slaves. In fact, in the same year, Antão Gonçales discovered gold on the Rio de Ouro: 'in addition to slaves...they also gave him gold dust, albeit in small quantities....In this region, there were merchants who traded with this gold.'[33] From the Rio de Ouro, the Portuguese first launched raids on the gold caravans returning to the Maghrib, and then turned to trade.

The search for slaves and gold on the African coast was in fact characterized by a process going from simple pillaging raids to commerce. In the 1440s, taking captives in order to provide for the first big sales on the Lagos and Lisbon markets, in 1444 and 1445 respectively, meant engaging in actual 'manhunts'. In 1445, the expeditions bringing back slaves were quite large scale: 26 caravels had left Lagos for the coast of Africa, with the fleet based in the Bay of Arguin, south of the Rio de Ouro. To protect their trading activities, the Portuguese had to construct a fort.

From 1445 to 1447, at the time of these great expeditions, the voyages began to grow commonplace. While passing Cape Bojador in 1434 was an almost mythical feat, the steady progression along the coast to Arguin and then to the mouth of the Sénégal river meant taking a route that was in large part known, thanks to the Portuguese 'seafaring revolution'.[34] A further step was taken in the 1450s, when Henry the Navigator, 'the first author to bring freight by the ocean from the Midi to the land of the Blacks',[35] began to employ professional sailors, in particular the Genoese, instead of recruiting exclusively from his own circle in Sagres and Lagos.[36] At the same time, slaves captured by violence, seized from poor fishing villages, were replaced by slaves bought and sold by Arab and Guinean merchants. The concept of trade replaced that of war.

In 1448, the probable limit of exploration lay at the level of Cape Verde, south of Senegal. Seven years later, the Genoese Usodimare sailed over the lower course of Gambia, and relations could be re-established with the empire of Mali. Casamance, the last staging post on the African coast known by Henry the Navigator before his death, was reached by this same Genoese, accompanied by the Venetian Ca' da Mosto, in 1456.

The search for gold on which the Portuguese had embarked produced opportunities for finding slaves. This search was undertaken in the sites of Bambouk on the upper reaches of the Sénégal, and Bouré in Upper Guinea, accessible from the trading posts in Gambia. Here, gold was exploited in conjunction with other rich resources: in West African commerce, Lower Gambia was a valuable source of sea salt, and from there there were commercial routes into the interior. Disembarking here, the Genoese and Portuguese sailors found a trade network already in place, extending across tropical Africa. The routes were used to transport products such as palm butter, cola nuts, fabrics, iron objects – and slaves – into the interior. The majority of the African societies practised the enslavement of prisoners of war. Slaves were transported towards the Maghrib, but were not the principal export, since gold and ivory were more important.[37]

Exploratory and trade expeditions sharply declined after the death of Henry the Navigator, but picked up again in 1469 on the initiative of a Lisbon merchant, Fernão Gomes, who received a grant of the rights for exploration. Beyond Cape Palmas, the course from India towards the east seemed to lie open along the coast of Guinea, and almost 5,000 kilometres of the coast were discovered by expeditions commanded by Fernão Gomes.[38] At the same time, the profitability of these enterprises was reinforced by other resources such as ivory, malachite and pepper from Guinea, and by access from the Gold Coast to the gold-bearing resources of Accra, in what is now Ghana. A profitable trade in slaves to sell to the tribes of Accra began to be established. Here, the Portuguese became much more involved than they did in Gambia in effective exchange networks: since the beginning of the fifteenth century in Begho (Ghana), Dyula traders had set up a commercial trading post into which all the produce of Western Africa flowed. The Portuguese competed with them and the Accrans, clients of both, used their gold to obtain a labour force.[39]

Doubtless in order to compete with the shady Castilian dealers on the coast of Guinea, the Crown of Lisbon broke Fernão Gomes's monopoly in 1475, and the circumnavigation of West Africa became the responsibility of the eldest of the princes of the royal house, infante Dom João. After his accession in 1481, he breathed new life equally into exploration and commerce. He adopted the principle of mare clausum, and the African Atlantic became a 'Portuguese' sea, and he meant to defend the fruitful trade in gold and slaves with whatever means necessary.[40] In 1482, John II, the 'Lord of Guinea', was to construct the fortress of São Jorge da Miña at the crossroads of the trade routes with the kingdom of Benin, where slaves were bartered against gold from Accra, near the mouth of the Volta. Some one thousand kilometres from there, discovered in 1472, the island of São Tomé witnessed a resurgence in the value of sugar cultivation that began in 1483, taking over from Madeira. At the same time, this equatorial island became a gathering point for the slave workforce from the coast, competing with the Cape Verde Islands, where slaves from Senegal and Gambia were held.

Increasing the profits of navigation with gold and slaves, John II gave the exploration of the south maximum scope. In 1483, Diogo Cão was on the Congo, and followed the coast until reaching latitude 22 degrees south in 1485. During the summer of 1487, his successor was Bartholomeu Dias, who left Lisbon with a mission to find a course through the ocean around Africa. With great daring, Dias departed from Cão's course towards the 27th or 28th latitudes south, and with the trade winds preventing him from going south-west, he went west in search of a favourable wind in order to reach the median latitude, the 40th degree, and to meet up with the westerlies, the west winds, that would allow him to touch solid ground almost 500 kilometres to the east of the Cape of Good Hope. The *volta* of the South Atlantic was inaugurated, opening up a course to the Indies.

The western ocean and the New World of the Iberians

Portugal owed everything to the sea. After a few African discoveries, it had given the Atlantic its largest extent in the austral hemisphere when, in 1487, Dias found the passage to the Indies to the south of Africa. It was nevertheless left to Castile to prove that, towards the west, beyond the archipelagos of the 'Mediterranean' Atlantic, the ocean was an exploitable space rather than a 'Sea of Perpetual Gloom' as had been feared since antiquity. Above all, in the eyes of those contemporaries (amongst whom Christopher Columbus was of the first rank) the western ocean ought to facilitate opening direct access to Asia and its riches, by a much shorter route than the long Portuguese route along the African coasts.

In fact, discoveries had rapidly expanded the dimensions of this ocean. The western ocean which Schoener's map of the world of 1520 had confused with the Caribbean Sea[41] had been supplemented since 1500, thanks to its discovery by the Portuguese Cabral, with an austral Atlantic, a *Mare Oceanus*, south of the equator (Cantino's Genoese map of 1502), bordering Brazil, a new world that Waldseemüller still called *Terra Incognita* in 1513. To the north, the western ocean was also expanded by the Portuguese Gaspar Corte Real's voyage in 1500 to Terceira, the central island in the Azores archipelago. Although after the Italian Cabot's voyage of 1497, in the service of the merchants of Bristol and King Henry VII of England, Corte Real discovered *Tierra Verde* (Newfoundland) and disembarked in the Maritimes. It is true that, in contrast with the discovery of Brazil, this discovery did not result in the establishment of Portuguese dominion of the New World. Nevertheless, Cantino's 1502 map shows it divided between Spain and Portugal and, in the eyes of his contemporaries, Portuguese pre-eminence was recognized since they had established a number of fishing grounds there and claimed exclusive rights to the fish on the Great Reef of Newfoundland.

Columbus and the Western Atlantic: the new Castilian world

Columbus confronts the Atlantic

Although it supported Cantabrian coastal activity, Castile did not achieve the rank of a great maritime power until the end of the fifteenth century, when Columbus's discovery opened new horizons for the Andalusian and Basque ports. Of course, Castile had directed its attention to the 'Mediterranean' Atlantic since the beginning of the fifteenth century, defending its rights over the Canaries against the claims of Henry the Navigator. However, with the Treaty of Alcobaça in 1479, it was compelled to recognize Portugal's monopoly on the African coast south of Cape Bojador, after having once challenged the Portuguese in the exploration of the Gulf of Guinea. In truth, Castile devoted everything to the efforts of the *reconquista*, and had to finance a costly war against the Moors of Granada.

Nevertheless, Castile was not so poorly off as regards its Atlantic ventures. In Seville, where the Italians had developed trading routes, Castile had access to the hub of their businesses. As in Lisbon, the Genoese dominated the place, but the Florentines were also there, notably in the person of Amerigo Vespucci, the director of the Medici subsidiary, who later become Columbus's friend and then usurped some of his glory.[42] It was Francisco Pinelli, a Genoese banker in Seville, who put up the largest proportion of the monies required for Columbus's first voyage. Moreover, this was a consortium supported by the Genoese capital that had been created by the treasury minister, Alonzo de Quintanilla, for Castile's first Atlantic venture, the conquest of the Canaries.[43] Finally, for a voyage of discovery to the west, Castile would not risk seeing its ambitions challenged by Portugal, which was looking to develop the exploration of Africa and, through Dias, opened the gateway to the Indies and was financed by Africa's coastal trading routes.

Meanwhile, Portugal's ambitions during the course of the 1480s, even as regards the exploration of the Western Atlantic, must not be completely dismissed. In 1486, John II of Portugal gave his consent to an expedition by Ferdinand Van Olmen of Flanders, whose Lusitanian name was Fernão da Ulmo, Captain of the Azores. Fernão undertook an expedition of discovery to the west of the archipelago and sank because he cast off at the end of the winter of 1487.[44] On the other hand, the fishermen of the Azores planned to discover other fishing grounds, richer than those in the waters of the archipelago and probably attempted launches into the North Atlantic in the decade of the 1480s. However, it was only in 1500–1502, with the Corte Real brothers, that the Portuguese discovery of the banks of Newfoundland took place.

Columbus: tradition, imagination and intuition

Christopher Columbus of Genoa managed to take advantage of the influence his compatriots had acquired in Castile, but it was nevertheless on the basis of his profound convictions that he applied his efforts to the pursuit of launching a mission of discovery in the western ocean. Columbus incontestably drew inspiration from the ancient myths of antiquity, revised in the light of his readings of the Bible: 'This island is Tarshish, it is Ophir and Cipango and we have called it "Espaniola" [Hispaniola].'[45]

In his 1502 letter to Pope Alexander VI, Columbus forcefully elaborated on this reference to the gold of Ophir he had seen at Hispaniola, the biblical gold that made the construction of the temple of Jerusalem possible. 'Islands spring up like mushrooms gestating in the imaginary of the Sea of Perpetual Gloom.'[46] Columbus was fed on an imagery created out of these mythical islands. Confirmed by precise testimony, bamboo and carved woods carried by the currents west of Porto Santo, north-east of Madeira, rumours of these islands proliferated in Lisbon and elsewhere in the 1480s.[47] Like others, Columbus confused these islands or new lands with an Earthly Paradise that was sought in the west during the Middle Ages:

> Sacred theologians and wise philosophers have indeed said that the Earthly Paradise is situated where the East ends, since it is a place of mild climates; now these lands that he [Columbus] has just discovered are at the end of the East.
>
> (Columbus's ship's log, 21 February 1493)[48]

Martin Behaim, whom Columbus knew, confused Antillia with the Island of the Seven Cities in his globe of 1492, placing it in the middle of the Atlantic.

We see, however, Columbus's real ambitions breaking out throughout his use of this island myth, based on his readings of Pierre D'Ailly's *Imago Mundi* or of the *Travels of Marco Polo*. It was necessary to him to find the Indies by a course to the west, across a relatively narrow stream, whose size he had reduced even further, to reach an Asia extending disproportionately into the east. According to Columbus's imaginings, the distance from the Canaries to Cipangu, the island off the Asian coasts, was only 2,080 miles, whereas in reality it was 12,000 miles.

Columbus's conviction that he had found Cipangu at Cuba corresponds well with the map of the Atlantic imagined by Martin Behaim in 1492, on which Cipangu is placed right in the middle of the Atlantic, well to the east of the Caribbean, with Cathay slightly to the north of Cuba. We can understand how Columbus could take the New World for a part of Asia (Marco Polo wrote that Cipangu lay 1,500 miles from the Chinese-Cathay coasts).

Contradictions were certainly no strangers to the mind of the discoverer: while remaining utterly convinced that he had landed on the imaginary islands of which he had been named governor before his departure, Columbus realized, at least on his third voyage in 1498 during which he daringly explored the north coast of South America from Trinidad to the mouth of the Orinoco, that he had landed on 'another world': 'I believe this is a matter of "another world", unknown until now.'[49]

It was while seeing the Orinoco Falls and being astonished at the volume of water borne by the river that Columbus expressed his awareness of the other world, but he still maintained that it was small and, above all, that these new lands were near Asia.

Columbus was a discoverer afflicted by his attachment to myth, although his numerous errors proved these myths were no match for Portugal's *cognoscenti*, yet he was also a sailor of inspired intuition.

All Columbus's talents were apparent in his study of the North Atlantic wind systems. In truth, he managed to acquire experience of these systems during a voyage undertaken in 1477 to Iceland,[50] where he had been able to hear talk of an island, in all likelihood known to the Icelandic fishermen, which was Newfoundland. At the end of the fifteenth century, attempts to cross the western ocean were made, before Columbus, in the zone of the west winds, the westerlies, blowing over the Azores. Sailing on a headwind, the navigator was on the other hand sure of being able to return to port, a consideration as important as the discovery. Sailors returning from the Canaries or Madeira by completing the *volta* in the 'Mediterranean' Atlantic were well aware of the advantages created by the Azores' wind system. At its most westerly point, the archipelago extended into the Atlantic by 31 degrees longitude west on the Lisbon latitude, and lay furthest to the north of all the Atlantic archipelagos, which was especially the case for Corvo and Flores, the two islands situated furthest into the Atlantic and the last to be discovered. At these latitudes, on the 38th and 39th parallels, one could hope to reach the new lands quickly. We could also imagine that, after his Icelandic voyage, Columbus was able to meet sailors from Bristol who were preparing to organize expeditions to discover the island of Brazil (Newfoundland) in 1480.

Nevertheless, the strength of the west winds put an obstacle in the way of every attempt led from the Azores: barely five years before Columbus's expedition, at the end of 1487, Fernão da Ulmo's expedition ended in failure.

Could it be that the certainty of Columbus's intuition regarding the choice of the return course, taking advantage of the westerlies, may have been acquired from an earlier discovery[51] alluded to by the text of the treaty of surrender of Santa Fe? Las Casas maintained that the 'legend' of the unknown pilot was 'common knowledge' in San Domingo around 1500, and that this represented the grounds for the assurance with which Columbus undertook the voyage and won the help of Martin Pinzon. The western course through the Central Atlantic met with no obstruction from the westerlies, so that a Portuguese or Spanish ship, returning from Guinea or the Canaries on its *volta* from the west, could be carried as far westward as one of the unknown islands. Columbus's idea was to leave from the Canaries, lying further south than the Azores where the strength of the winds put an obstacle in the way of every attempt. By the Canaries, he could use the trade winds in the hope of finding the west winds when he needed to return.

Columbus's expedition

At two o'clock in the morning on the night of the 11–12 October 1492, Rodrigo de Triana, then a lookout on the caravel *Pinta*, glimpsed straight ahead of him the white sanded beach of a small island, Guanahani, in the archipelago today called the Bahamas. Some hours later on the same day, Christopher Columbus, the Admiral at the head of three ships, the *Santa Maria*, the *Pinta* and the *Niña*, rowed towards the beach with a view to planting the flag of the kings of Castile and Aragon.

Although this date in the autumn of 1492 means much more after the event, for Columbus's contemporaries the course he discovered across the centre of the Atlantic, binding the 'Old World' to the 'New', which had until then been separated, proved only moderately important in the face of the cultural and political circumstances that Europe was then living through; and could, moreover, seem delusive to the sovereigns and financiers who had supported the venture. It went no further than an island world where no lush vegetation or natural resources could hide the inhabitants' relative poverty. The riches of Asia, as Marco Polo had described them, seemed barely present in Hispaniola or Isabella (Cuba). The most valuable Atlantic trading routes were still the sugar routes from Madeira, the Canaries, and São Tomé to Antwerp, which the Portuguese preferred to Bruges after 1488, and the gold and slaves from the African coast which, as Dias had just shown, opened onto another ocean and the Indies.

For a long time, people accepted this low assessment of the Genoese sailors' exploits. It might have seemed just one more step towards the extension of Europe's maritime frontiers, but there were few reactions in Europe beyond the Iberian and Italian peninsulas.[52] Shown in Basel, Nuremberg, Augsburg and Reutlingen in 1494, Sebastian Brant's *Ship of Fools* bore witness to Brant's recognition, as a celebrated humanist and lawyer, of the reality of the new horizons discovered:

> In Portugal they have found,
> As everywhere in Spain,
> Golden Isles and naked men,
> Whereof, only yesterday
> none could be explained.

This same Sebastian Brant had printed a second edition of Christopher Columbus's letter, which had appeared in Basel the previous year (1494) under the title *De Insulis noviter inventis* (*Of Newly Discovered Islands*).

One can compare this reaction with another, much more enthusiastic one, from Jerome Munzer, renowned in Nuremberg as a man of medicine and cosmographer, and a friend of Hartmann Schedel, the author of the famous *Chronicle of the World* of 1493. Travelling through France, Spain and Portugal in 1494–1495, Munzer shows great admiration for the court of the Catholic Kings:

> We have seen new men, unknown in our century, who, under your
> sovereignty, have been carried from the recently discovered islands of
> the Indies. Oh, what an incredible thing, unknown to many people....
> The dungeon of Christianity is in ruins![53]

Relatively exceptional for their time, these reactions cannot disguise the slowness
with which the fact of the discovery of the New World was noticed. As Bartolomé
Bennassar has emphasized, 'we must wait ten to twelve years between the event of
its founding and even the vaguest understanding of it'.[54] Knowledge of the real
continent was necessary so that the myth of the Asian island could slowly be abandoned. Columbus's navigation, like his successors', did not reveal any passage to
Asia at the latitudes in the region of the Caribbean, nor any straits enabling one to
continue westward by way of the sea. In 1513, Balboa crossed the Panama isthmus
and discovered the South Sea, and in so doing identified the most rapid route from
the Atlantic to the Pacific. We can at last gain a perception of the reality from the
point of view of Gonzalo Fernando de Oviedo, at the end of the 1520s:

> My opinion, shared by many others, is that it [the New World] is not a
> part of Asia, nor does it have any connection to the Asia of the ancient
> cosmographers. One could even go so far as to say that the Closed World
> of these Indies is another part of the world.[55]

Oviedo is writing after Magellan's voyage and his discovery of the passage south
of the continent, and after the failure of the Corte Real brothers to find a
northern passage.

We can therefore accept that, for the majority of his contemporaries,
Columbus's voyage was the discovery of a few new islands in the Atlantic. The
Chronicle of the World, published by Hartmann Schedel in Nuremberg in 1493,
enumerated Portugal's discoveries in the Atlantic and along the west coast of
Africa: the Azores, Madeira, the Cape Verde Islands and the Guinea Islands. The
previous year, Martin Behaim placed Cipangu in the middle of the Atlantic, taking
his share of Columbus's errors.

The arrival of Columbus and his companions on 12 October 1492, on a beach
at Guanahani, took place after some 34 days' sailing from the Canaries. The difficulties Columbus encountered in getting the expedition ready, and again in his
scrupulous preparations in the Canaries for adapting his ships for sailing in the
farthest reaches of the Atlantic, display the sailor's energy and talent as much as
the ability of the old merchant to find the necessary support.

Tied to the Portuguese world by his family and his past as a merchant,
Columbus naturally went to King John II with his project for finding the coast of
Asia by a westerly course through the Atlantic. The king, while intending to give

full scope to the search for a passage to Asia by the circumnavigation of Africa in the 1480s, did not turn the Genoese down from the outset. The circumnavigation had not yet met with success when, in 1485, the king asked his counsellors to study Columbus's proposals. These plans, massively underestimating the breadth of the Atlantic, were rejected by the Portuguese, who had more exact knowledge of its real size. Dismissed the first time, Columbus returned to Lisbon in 1488, but the capital had just learnt of Dias's opening of the route to the Indies by the Cape of Good Hope; it was no longer the time for John II to hear Columbus. The latter was unable to find support in England or France, who were still a long way from sailing in the Central Atlantic (in Bristol, the English were interested in the North Atlantic), so Columbus turned towards south-western Spain and its Atlantic seaboard. Spain had large interests in the Atlantic: fishing grounds, colonies in the Canaries, and experiments in navigation. But after Columbus had waited more than three uncertain years, and been rejected by the Catholic Kings at Salamanca, at the end of 1490, the year before Granada was besieged, Castile, proud after its defeat of the Moors, decided to take the Catholic faith across the world and to find out who would agree to undertake the expedition.

The Santa Fe Treaties of Surrender, of 17 and 30 April 1492, made Columbus into a representative of the Crown of Castile over lands to be discovered and secured his rights over his discovery. Such were the exorbitant privileges accorded to the admiral, with the right to collect 10 per cent from the cargoes brought back

> from all the isles of the Closed World, whatever goods these may be, whether pearls, precious stones, gold, silver, spices, or other things of whatever kind, name and description they may be, by purchase, exchange or discovery, acquired or obtained within the boundaries of the Admiralty.[56]

Columbus was recognized as the viceroy and governor of the New World.

In summer 1492, all activities in Seville and the other Andalusian ports, including Cadiz, were completely absorbed in preparing for the exodus of the Moors, recently conquered by Castile, from the Kingdom of Granada towards the Moroccan coasts. Christopher Columbus was therefore induced to turn to Palos, a port on the Spanish Algarve, where the Genoese could take advantage of the experience of two sailors, Martin Alonzo Pinzon and his brother Vincente Yenez. They practised trade, or rather piracy, at the expense of Portuguese and English ships on the Guinea coast or the Canaries. Martin Alonzo Pinzon helped Columbus find the necessary sailors: Andalusians from Palos, Moguer and Huelva, or from Seville, and a few Basques, as well as foreigners from Portugal or Italy. Pinzon could promise 'houses with tiles of Cipangu gold' and the most alluring riches to the 90 to 100 men he was recruiting for the expedition's three ships.[57] Two caravels, the *Niña* and the *Pinta* were found in Palos, and one vessel, the *Gallega*, rebaptized *Santa Maria*, of which Columbus was the admiral, at Puerto de Santa Maria near Cadiz. The rigging of this ship combined square sails on the two forward masts, and one triangular sail aft. The caravels changed their rigging to make them faster, the *Pinta* at Palos, and the *Niña* at the Canaries: they hoisted a square sail on the main mast (the forward mast) and kept the triangular sail to the rear. Wisely, Columbus loaded plentiful provisions – water for six months and foodstuffs for 15; nor did he forget to take some cheap and showy objects for possible exchange.

On 3 August 1492, Columbus and his sailors left Palos for the Canaries, where the ships arrived on 12 August. Here they completed the rigging and repaired the caravels on the island of Gomera. On 8 September, the north-west trade wind began to blow and the next day, the ships left the archipelago. Columbus had modified the caravels' rigging since he hoped, following the 28th parallel, for a following wind on the latitude of the islands. Setting a course full west showed that he chose the most direct route using the trade wind, while tacking, with the help of the compass, in order to maintain this westerly direction. With a constant wind right up to 20 September, they made a speed of over 180 kilometres a day, and on 25 September the captains estimated that they had covered a distance of 2,488 kilometres since Gomera. Columbus had stated the distance to the discovery to be 4,147 kilometres, so they could not believe they could have reached 'the islands at the entry to the Indies' so soon.[58] Despite numerous birds and abundant grass, giving favourable indications leading them to believe that land was near, and Columbus to remark that the water seemed 'curdled' since they had crossed the Sargasso Sea, worry gripped the crews. The order to 'return to Castile' began to go round. Ten days later, tempers became still more heated since they had done more than 4,420 kilometres since the Canaries and were therefore well beyond the distance Columbus had forecast, yet land was not yet in sight, and they had passed Cipangu without seeing any. On 9 October, the pilots of the *Pinta* and the *Niña* calculated that they had done more than 4,800 kilometres and as revolt brewed Columbus's men pressed him to give the order to return. The next day, however, birds, and, floating on the water, increasingly green trees and branches and carved wood were spotted. During the night of the 11 to 12 October, a seaman on the *Pinta* raised the long hoped-for cry, '*Tierra!*'

After some 36 days of sailing from Hispaniola to the Azores (10 January to 15 February 1493), Columbus returned to Palos on 15 March 1493, after storms had forced him into Lisbon. He took back to the Catholic sovereigns a discovery that might have appeared rather meagre in relation to the horizons which the course around the Cape of Good Hope had already opened up for Portugal. The islands of Santo Domingo and Cuba, that Columbus firmly believed to form part of the Asiatic world, the 'end of the East', and therefore to represent a gateway to the much sought-after Earthly Paradise, offered no gold, and still less any highly desirable spices. To Columbus's eyes, the proximity of this island world to Paradise explained the state of innocence in which the Tainos Indians of the island of Hispaniola lived.

Almost a year later, in the 1494 Treaty of Tordesillas, Castile and Seville established their domains in the New World. Pope Alexander VI had already confirmed Castile's sovereignty over the islands discovered 'towards the Indies' on condition that the Catholic Kings quickly sent missionaries there, by 4 May 1493. On the same date, the Bull *Inter Cetera* set the borderline between the Portuguese and Spanish empires at 100 leagues to the west and the south of the Azores and the Cape Verde Islands. At Tordesillas, the frontier was pushed back further west, 370 leagues from the Cape Verde Islands, leaving Portugal with the opportunity, in a few years, to conquer Brazil.

Columbus's three other voyages made it possible to observe the difficulties the Spanish had in confronting an Indian world from which they returned with only the riches of gold or spices they could conceal, which existed, moreover, only in the form of very limited quantities of gold. Of course, during these voyages Columbus's talents as a navigator were displayed in taking a more southerly route than the first time and making better use of the trade wind. The second and fourth voyages (1493–1496 and 1502) ended at the Windward Islands, Dominica and Martinique, while on the third, Columbus turned to reach the 10th parallel, the latitude closest to the equator, disembarking at Trinidad and then running along the north coasts of South America while reconnoitring the mouth of the Orinoco. Columbus was therefore able to explore the Caribbean world and, above all, to discover, without always being able to define its whole extent, a new Closed World.

Despite the new resources Castile put into exploration on the second voyage, on which Columbus had seven ships and 1,200 men at his disposal, there were great disappointments. Hasty raids and barter were rapidly depleting the world of the islands, and only imperfectly lived up to Spanish hopes. The real capture of the Spanish Caribbean took place during the 1510s, with successful expeditions to Cuba, Puerto Rico and Jamaica from 1509 to 1513, expeditions mounted with capital from the Hispaniola gold from which a few colonists had become rich. In the same way, from 1516 Cuba had to support the seizure of the Closed World that culminated in Hernan Cortes's conquest of Aztec Mexico. In turn, the riches of New Spain financed the colonization of Peru during the 1530s. Net investment of Castilian resources was therefore correspondingly reduced, only revealing their importance in the 15 years following the discovery. The profits from gold production on the islands enabled fruitful returns to Spain and a new wave of conquests. The New World in the Atlantic already nurtured its own expansion.

The Iberians in the South Atlantic

Cabral in Brazil

At the end of the fifteenth century, after Dias's successful circumnavigation of Africa and, moreover, Vasco da Gama's voyage to India by sailing around Africa, the Portuguese proved to be more and more attached to the exploitation of 'the spice lands', with Antwerp receiving the first cargo of Malabar pepper from 1502–1503. On the other hand, Portuguese interests in the Azores in the field of fishing grounds directed Lisbon to search for new areas to fish in a still unknown North Atlantic towards the Island of Seven Cities which Fernão da Ulmo had sought in 1487, with the voyages of the Corte Real brothers in 1502 coming to represent its culmination. However, navigating the Atlantic *volta* south of the equator – necessary for reaching the west winds in the southern hemisphere and arriving at the latitude of the Cape of Good Hope – was also going to lead the Portuguese to discover Brazil in 1500.

Three years earlier, Vasco da Gama, leaving Lisbon for India, tracking the course followed by Dias some 10 years previously, followed the most direct route in his four square-sailed ships, best suited to fully exploiting the liveliest following winds. He abandoned the traditional coastal route around Africa, and after having doubled Cape Bojador and the Cape Verde Islands, at the latitude of Sierra Leone, managed to take advantage of the westward running equatorial current to carry him directly west as far as the 20th meridian, 600 kilometres west of Ascension Island. Finding himself so far off course, south of the Tropic of Capricorn, he found the westerlies around the 30th parallel and on 8 November 1497 he arrived to the west of the Cape of Good Hope. Having had to spend three months at sea after putting in at the Cape Verde Islands, this was doubtless a testing voyage for the ships and men. But this long *volta*, due to the prevailing trade winds of the South Atlantic, was necessary and would thereafter be the course taken by Portuguese fleets to the Indies.

In 1500, Cabral tried a different approach. Leaving the Cape Verde Islands, he used the trade wind as crosswinds instead of the equatorial current and, only a month after putting out from the Cape Verde Islands, he came in sight of the Brazilian coasts on 22 April. Having left Lisbon on 8 March, Cabral took no more than six weeks on his voyage from Portugal to the Brazilian coasts. Leaving again for Brazil on 2 May, the navigator took a south-easterly course by the island of Tristan da Cunha on the 40th parallel, a more southerly route than the one Vasco da Gama had taken. Although supported by the Portuguese Crown, which managed to gather the necessary funds from Lisbon's Florentine merchants, and some 13 ships strong, with 1,200 men on board, sumptuously fitted out 'adorning the Tagus like a flowering garden in Spring',[59] Cabral's expedition did not result in the conquest of

Brazil. Cabral was happy to drop anchor off the coast of Vera Cruz, around 500 kilometres north of Rio de Janeiro, and he left again after 10 days in port. The chance discovery of a land in the Western Atlantic by the Portuguese might seem to be a fair compensation for the missed opportunity five years earlier, when John II dismissed Columbus, but it represented very little in the face of the commercial attractions of India that Vasco da Gama had just discovered.

If Cabral's lieutenant, Lemos, returned to Portugal at the end of summer 1500 with information on Brazil, the Portuguese Crown, while quickly establishing a monopoly over trading in brazil wood, a source of dye greatly valued in Lisbon and elsewhere, waited almost an entire generation, until 1530 (in the reign of John III) to launch an expedition by the de Sousa brothers, which led to the real colonization of the country.[60]

Did the Spanish precede or follow Cabral?

We can in no way believe that the Frenchman Paulmier de Gonneville's arrival in 1504 at the Rio São Francisco was the result of an intention to explore the Brazilian coasts. His arrival there was as entirely fortuitous as was Cabral's, since the Honfleur sailor was on a trading voyage to India. Caught in the storms of the roaring forties, near Tristan da Cunha, that had cost Cabral four ships, his ship *l'Espoir* was driven straight to Brazil. Paulmier de Gonneville, who had perhaps been preceded by other Frenchmen, nevertheless created a tradition of illicit pirate trade, to the detriment of the Portuguese.

On the other hand, the Spanish were greatly interested in an exploration for which Columbus had set the example by discovering the mouth of the Orinoco. Castilian claims to show their sailors had reached Brazil even before Cabral appear to have some grounds. Vincente Yenez Pinzon, one of Columbus's companions and one of the best navigators of Palos, in fact left that port on 18 November 1499. Having rounded the Cape Verde Islands, his four caravels navigated by wind on the beam, sailing along the southern fringe of the trade winds, and Pinzon took only 20 days between putting into port in the Cape Verde Islands and the Cabo de Consolación (Cape Saint Augustine), where he arrived on 26 January 1500.[61] He solemnly took possession of it in the name of Castile. Keeping what Columbus had taught in mind, Pinzon intended to seek the passage towards Asia by the south of the New World, but worked north-westwards and, for almost five months, followed the coasts up to the mouth of the Amazon, which he recognized. Facing the Rio Maranon, Pinzon wondered if he had found the Ganges;[62] the myth of seeking India and Asia in the west was still in the Castilians' minds. Since Spanish settlement would contravene the provisions of the Treaty of Tordesillas, this discovery did not result in any colonization. Pinzon left again for Hispaniola and Spain.

Perhaps Alonzo Velez de Mendoza went further south than Pinzon when, at Christmas 1500, he reached the mouth of the Rio São Francisco. Mendoza returned from the Brazilian coast with slaves and dye-woods, the brazil wood that Vasco da Gama had already brought back from India and which the Spanish had also discovered in the Antilles.

It is, however, the discoveries of the Florentine Amerigo Vespucci that have been the greatest source of debate. In 1499, even before Pinzon and Cabral, Vespucci, a Seville merchant, had gone with Alonso de Hojeda, one of Columbus's old companions, to reconnoitre the Amazon and then the Closed World as far as the Gulf of Maracaibo, returning with a rich cargo of pearls.[63] During another voyage in 1502 Vespucci reached the Bay of Guanabara. Arriving there on 1 January he named the place Rio de Janeiro. In 1506, in Florence, Amerigo de Vespucci published his *Letter on the Recently Discovered Islands*. Published in Latin the following year by Saint-Dié and edited by the German cosmographer Waldseemüller, the latter gave the new continent described in the text the name 'Amerigo', after Vespucci, who claimed the discovery.

The last mariner able to arrive at a complete knowledge of the South Atlantic and the American coasts is the Portuguese Magellan. In 1519, familiar with the spice route around the Cape of Good Hope, Magellan nevertheless intended to find a western passage to Asia and its riches. Rejected by Portugal, he took service with Castile, where Charles Quintus agreed to lend him his support. After having landed on Recife on 15 November 1519 and put into port in Rio, Magellan spent the summer reconnoitring the coasts as far as 45 degrees latitude south, reached at Puerto San Julian. Winter hindered the expedition and it was only on 28 November 1520, one year after having reached the American continent, that Magellan, after seven weeks' difficult navigation through the straits that bear his name at 53 degrees latitude south, emerged in the Pacific. For him, this circumnavigation would come to a tragic end on an island in the Philippines, where he died under the natives' arrows on 27 April 1521. His lieutenant Juan Sebastian del Cano did not reach San Lucar until 6 September 1522, returning with only 18 out of an expedition which had numbered 265 men.

In fact, Iberian interest in South America was only going to emerge very slowly after these voyages of exploration. In 1526, the Cabot brothers, in the service of Charles V, reconnoitred the Rio de la Plata and declared Castile's claims to Paraguay, but it was only after the colonization of Peru and the exploitation of the Potosi mines that Spanish interest emerged in a coast that was a new opening to colonies in the Andes.

The Europeans and the North Atlantic

Legends and trade in the North Atlantic

The search for a passage that would link Europe to Asia and its riches, and the desire to exploit the abundant fishing grounds in the deep waters of the North Atlantic was at the forefront of the minds of the sailors who reached these seas. As for Columbus and the majority of the other discoverers, however, the North Atlantic was inextricably bound up with legends and myths. The wonders revealed in narratives of the most ancient voyages, such as St Brendan's, coupled with narratives of the horrors faced by travellers venturing into the unknown, doubtless added, during the fifteenth century, to the growing attraction of real and mythical islands. The rediscovery of the Atlantic islands, Madeira and the Azores in particular, reinforced a belief in the existence of more distant islands in relation to the growing conviction amongst many that Asia stretched further to the east, with a string of islands amongst which Cipangu was only the largest. At the same time, they accepted the idea that the distance separating Europe from Asia was relatively narrow.

Fifteenth-century maps show how much these island myths had grown. Following the discovery of the western Azores, Corvo and Flores, in the middle of the fifteenth century, other islands were sought further north. Around 1470, Portuguese and Catalan maps had Brazil, the most frequently named of such islands, situated north-west of the Azores; they also showed how the Island of the Seven Cities was confused with Antillia: 'here is the Island of the Seven Cities, now populated by the Portuguese, where Spanish mariners say that silver is found on the sandy beaches'.[64] In 1490, cartographers had no fear of granting legendary islands a false reality.

Even the most vigorous economic activity is, however, suffused with myth. On the same map, Bristol's trade in Iceland is very precisely defined: 'As if it were money, the inhabitants exchange their dried fish for wheat, flour and other necessary items that the English brought them each year.' The attribution of fertility to island soils had already made Madeira and the Azores attractive. Further north, the search for fishing grounds was the more powerful stimulant to exploration. At the end of the Middle Ages, numerous French (Basque and Breton) and English fishermen ventured well beyond the limits of the continental plateau west of Ireland, where they gained experience of conditions on the ocean. Hence, during the first 25 years of the fifteenth century the English made several fishing expeditions to Iceland from the eastern ports of Lynn and Boston, and from Bristol in the west. Ships carried English cloth to the Icelanders, exchanging it for the fish the latter caught, and engaging in fishing themselves.

In the course of the century, the commercial route thus created was going to be extended even to Lisbon, Porto and the Algarve. Portuguese appeared in Bristol and in Ireland, at Galway and Limerick. A voyage such as the one David Quinn narrates reveals a great deal concerning the extent of the circuits completed in this way.[65] On 11 December 1479, the Bristol ship *Christopher*, laden with fruit, specifically figs from Faroe, left the Portuguese Algarve for Bristol. In this port, it took on a cargo for Iceland on 14 February 1480. In a few months, this ship had passed the 37th parallel at 65 degrees, on the latitudes of the 'Mediterranean' Atlantic to the most northern Atlantic, with no fear of navigating in the most northerly latitudes to reach Iceland. In the Algarve, the centre of Portuguese trade with West Africa, Captain Thomas Sutton was able to acquaint himself with Portuguese activities in Africa and to inform the Portuguese of Icelandic commerce. Iceland's dried fish were regularly imported into Lisbon by such ships, and Portuguese salt re-exported to Iceland via England.

English and Portuguese discoveries from 1480 to 1510

In the 1480s, the links between the Portuguese and the merchants and mariners of Bristol were extended into the Iceland traffic and voyages to the island of Brazil. The English were prompted to search for Brazil – or more properly, the island so called since the fourteenth century – in order to find new fishing grounds, due to the decline of the Icelandic fisheries and the consequent dwindling trade between Bristol and the island. The expansion of Portuguese commerce, on the contrary, with the increasing exploitation of sugar production in the Atlantic archipelagos and the trade routes with the African coast, called for the expansion of English cloth imports to Lisbon. For a long time, Bristol had vast amounts of dried and salt cod which could be exchanged with the Portuguese (or the Spanish). This was no longer the case. The Portuguese, too, were prompted to increase their fishing operations around the Azores, and their needs equally impelled them to search for islands and to open new fishing grounds.

The English were well acquainted with the Portuguese Atlantic islands. They sent some of their ships there. On the maps from Lisbon which were equally easy to find in England, all the islands appeared, whether unexploited or still to be discovered: Antilia, the Island of the Seven Cities, Brazil, Satanaze and the Green Isle.[66] They were able to join the Portuguese in the search.

'It is judged certain that the Cape of the said Land [that found by John Cabot in 1494 – Newfoundland] was *previously* found and discovered by the men of Bristol and was called the island of Brazil.'[67] Similarly, in a letter from the beginning of 1498 addressed to the 'Great Admiral' (Christopher Columbus), John Day, an English merchant, told of a successful voyage from Bristol by an unknown discoverer crossing the ocean looking for Brazil. The voyage of 1497 was successfully undertaken by John Cabot, who discovered around 600 kilometres of coast at Newfoundland and on the continent, but the letter clearly lends weight to a voyage having taken place 'previously'. This discovery was completed in 1481–1482, when three Bristol merchants and one Thomas Croft, a customs clerk who became the target of legal proceedings for indulging in trade, made the expedition to Brazil. Croft defended himself by maintaining that this was a matter of exploration rather than trade.

After 1481, Bristol's activities were shrouded in silence, since they had discovered new fishing grounds to replace Iceland's declining stocks, and were keeping them secret.

Simultaneously, in Portugal, expeditions were mounted from Terceira, the central island of the Azores, with the double objective of seeking a western course to Asia (they reached the Earthly Paradise and Cathay) and finding the fishing grounds the Azoreans wanted to use. According to Charles Verlinden, the expedition of the Lusitanized Flemish Van Olmen, organized by a royal diploma of 24 July 1486, to discover the Island of the Seven Cities, was preceded 'by a series of voyages, carried out for over a quarter of a century, into the deepest Atlantic, west of the Azores'.[68] In 1475, Fernão Teles in the Azores had received rights in relation to organizing such an expedition. This was bound up with the voyages that these same Azorean inhabitants were able to carry out in the direction of Iceland.

In consequence, the Portuguese and English discoverers were drawing on solid experience of navigating in North Atlantic waters when John Cabot completed his 1497 expedition, followed three years later by the Azorean Gaspar Real. Before his arrival in Bristol, around 1490, the Venetian John Cabot had tried without success to obtain financial backing from Castile and Portugal for a voyage of discovery to Asia by the west. He was able to make use of the Bristol mariners' knowledge of the Atlantic and, at the same time, to advance King Henry VII's maritime policies. On 3 March 1496, the king charged Cabot with a mission of discovery: to find the new lands to the west of England and Ireland towards the north, since in the south Iberian authority had to be respected. Cabot was granted the privilege of governing these lands in the name of the king and, as in similar royal concessions in Portugal, the discovery would cost the sovereign nothing, at least until it was established that there was something there to be exploited.

The first voyage of 1496 was a failure, but success came the following year when the *Matthew*, a small 60-tonne ship, left Bristol on 22 May, and sailed southwest to reach the latitude where the mariners thought they would find the islands. Sailing with an east-north-easterly wind, Newfoundland's shores loomed from the sea after 32 days. On 22 June, it was reached at a latitude 'west of the Bordeaux river'; the Gironde estuary is 45 degrees and 35 minutes north. Two days later, Cabot disembarked at Nova Scotia or Cape Breton Island, on a coast he took to be the Asia of the Great Khan (the mirage of Asia persisted). Indeed, for almost a century, Cabot was nearly a century out regarding the Mongols in China, whose rule had ended in 1368. He erected a cross and banners with the arms of the Pope and the King of England, recognizing English sovereignty and the Church's suzerainty. The mariners from Bristol who had accompanied him were satisfied since they had found abundant shoals of cod. Cabot made the return to London on 10 August, his voyage from America to England taking barely more than 15 days – a very fine achievement.[69]

On the third voyage in May 1498, Cabot had five ships at his disposal: four from Bristol, and one from London fitted out by the king and the City merchants. In fact, he had hoped for a fleet of 10 to 12, comparable to that Columbus had under his command on his second voyage. Certain merchant groups, however, remained sceptical regarding both the chances of reaching Asia and Columbus's claims, which Cabot had repeated, that the islands discovered were near to the 'spice lands'. There remained no news right up until the end of September, when one of the ships returned to Ireland with terrible damage from a storm in which Cabot's ship had disappeared. In 1512, Polydores Vergil reported what he thought had happened to John Cabot:

> We believe that he has found nothing of the new world, but that he went down to the bottom of the ocean with his ship, himself a victim of the ocean, since he has not been seen again since this voyage.

In 1501, three Portuguese from the Azores came to Bristol. One of them was João Fernandes, a farmer from Terceira, who, at the same time as Gaspar Real, Lord of Angra on this same Azorean island, had received a royal privilege for the discovery of the western isles on 28 October 1499. Fernandes did not appear to have been part of Corte Real's expedition of 1500. Was he disappointed, following the latter's success? He was a man of the people, while Corte Real was a gentleman. It was Fernandes who led the people of Bristol to a land called 'Labrador'. Returning in 1502, his expedition brought back three captives taken in Newfoundland, who dressed in sealskin and ate raw meat, and presented them to Henry VII. These were Indians, not Eskimos, and were the first Amerindians to set foot in England.

During this voyage there had indeed been cooperation between the merchants from Bristol and London and the Portuguese from the Azores, but the issue was that the latter were renegades, as in the case of Fernandes the farmer. Further voyages from Bristol took place in 1503, 1504 and 1505. The deception came to light since they realized that although the newly discovered land harboured rich fishing grounds, it was nevertheless hardly suitable for trade. The last great

English voyage of the early sixteenth century was made by Cabot's son Sebastian, who in 1508 left to seek a north-west passage, opening a new direction for exploration. Conscious that Asia had not been reached, the discoverers intended to circumnavigate the north coast of an America whose continental nature had now been established. Cabot seems to have entered the Hudson Strait, but ice forced him to turn back south, where he reconnoitred the coasts down to the 35th parallel in order to return to England with the westerlies. Upon his return, the death of Henry VII, a monarch favourable to exploration, led him to leave England for Spain.

On the Portuguese side, the Corte Real brothers were discoverers who, like Cabot, arrived at the North American coasts from the Azores. In 1500, Gaspar Corte Real left Terceira to sail northwards; he discovered a mountainous cape that Cantino's map, executed in Lisbon in 1502, had taken to be the position of Asia. It was, in fact, Cape Farewell that was in question, on the southern tip of Greenland by 60 degrees north. From there Corte Real reached the coast of Labrador further to the west. On his second voyage in 1501, he once again arrived in Greenland, sailed along Labrador, hit Newfoundland, which he called Terra Verde, and further south reached the Maritime Provinces and Maine, where he enquired about finding masts for his ships. There was some contact with the Indian communities, ending with the enslavement of about 50 Amerindians. One of the ships brought them back to Portugal, where this human cargo 'suited to all tasks' caused a sensation,[70] whereas Gaspar Corte Real himself was lost along with one of his ships. Of the three Corte Real brothers, only Vasco Annes was to survive the discovery: Miguel, who left in 1502 to search for Gaspar, was also lost after having reconnoitred Labrador and Newfoundland. Vasco Annes brought the Portuguese fisheries of Newfoundland to their peak.

The dream of discovering unknown islands in the North Atlantic did not therefore produce results comparable to those the Iberians obtained in the Central or South Atlantic. Nevertheless, we cannot ignore the impetus it gave to the English maritime interests in the Atlantic that were to triumph under the reign of Elizabeth I. Soon the North Atlantic would witness the efforts of Verrazano and Cartier to make discoveries in the service of the King of France. Through the stimulus that its navigation gave to the maritime enterprises of north-western Europe, and to ambitions that soon became dangerous for the Iberians, the North Atlantic already seemed to constitute a theatre of confrontation from the fifteenth to the beginning of the sixteenth century. However, because of the range of the lands they already dominated on the coasts of the Central and South Atlantic, for many decades the Iberians would reap the benefits of having discovered the New Atlantic.

Chapter 3

The Atlantic and the Iberians
Sixteenth to seventeenth centuries

The hopes and realities of Columbus's America

Columbus and his companions were inspired, in 1492, by hopes of reaching Cipangu and Cathay, and the riches Marco Polo had so enthusiastically described to the Europeans. An utterly naive wonder gripped the discoverers upon their first contact with a paradisiacal land and the surprising generosity of its inhabitants. However, this could not obscure the primary objective, which was the quest for the riches to be gained, the great quantities of gold that remained the real motivation for the voyage. On his return from America, writing to the Intendant Luis de Santangel who had financed the expedition, Christopher Columbus noted that in the interior of 'the wonder that is Hispaniola', a number of mines for gold and other metals were to be found.

These first illusions were to be followed by a greater knowledge of the reality of the Caribbean; of islands with limited resources, sometimes inhabited by the peaceful Arawaks, sometimes by Caribbean warriors, but none far removed from the Stone Age. They were certainly superior to the most primitive hunter-gatherer tribes in the Orinoco basin who, when encountered by Columbus on his third voyage, were capable of cultivating manioc and engaging in sea fisheries (the Caribbean canoes were capable of achieving great distances in the Caribbean Sea). Nevertheless, the Indians disappointed the conquerors: caught out by the food, the Spanish had little enthusiasm for the cassava of marioc, a cake of indisputable nutritional value, but requiring delicate preparation to rid it of the plant's harmful elements. They preferred to import wheat from the Azores or Spain, and to pay for it in gold. Above all, the resources of gold on Cibao proved to be extremely limited.

More importantly, this was the gateway to the sophisticated empires of Mexico and Peru, where copper metallurgy for the ornamentation of temples had already been mastered. Moreover, their agricultural communities obtained regular harvests of maize from the Mexican plateaus, and maize and potatoes from the steep Peruvian valleys, creating in the Spaniards' minds an image of the Indies 'paved entirely in gold and silver'. The treasures of the high Amerindian plateaus with their sedentary populations invited conquest and population. The European economies' need for precious metals created favourable conditions.

The spiritual aspirations to match the crusading spirit still pervading Seville were to be added to the attractions of material wealth. The Amerindians appeared better disposed to evangelization than the Moslems of Africa. Church and Crown justified the enterprise of conquest already glimpsed in Columbus's reports.

Doubtless fooled by the first tales of the natives of Guanahani and the other islands in the Bahamas, regarding the abundant gold actually to be found on the north coast of Hispaniola and then on Cibao, the mountainous part of the island, Columbus retained his illusions about the islands. '*Oro sin cuento*': the gold was incalculable, together with spices – and slaves. On departure from Guanahani, on 14 October 1492, Columbus suggested that the Indians brought on board could be kept captive on the island, 'where one could make them do what one wanted[...]they are good for whatever one commands them to do, so that they can be made to work, to sow and to do whatever else is necessary'.[1] From the beginning, the expeditions of *rescate* or plunder that rapidly multiplied in both the world of the islands and Tierra Firme (the Spanish Main), combined commerce and barter, and then resulted in acts of conquest. When in 1519 Cortes disembarked in Mexico, several characteristics of the Castilian *reconquista* were already reproduced on the other side of the Atlantic: pillage, raiding, enslavement and exploitation under the sign of the Cross; but it lacked another element of the *reconquista*: populating and colonization.

The catastrophic decline in the native population, the gold reserves and the linen to be obtained further west, left this island society the victim of the spirit of adventure that sought island after island throughout Tierra Firme, the mainland that formed part of this insular space. These marauders were more concerned with pillage than with territorial gain.[2] 'There is no good conquest without peopling, and if the country is not conquered, its inhabitants will not be converted. A conqueror's maxim must be "to populate"' (Hernan Cortes).[3]

In fact, the initial means of conquest were in conflict with such an objective. Financially, it was sustained by resources from the areas that had already been exploited. In this way, Iles, then New Spain, financed the subsequent conquests of Peru, and then Chile. The *compañias*, associations of merchants and financiers who shared the capital and the risks in a limited project, in which Genoese and Germans played a large and central part, demanded the swift return of the funds invested. For the conquest of fringe frontiers with poorer returns, such as northern Mexico and southern Chile, state aid became indispensable.

Silver, the principal resource of the high Mexican and Andean plains, was 'the motor' *par excellence* of the colonial economy since its discovery.[4] It strengthened the Atlantic trading routes, and, from the middle of the sixteenth century on, represented slightly more than half the value of exports from the Indies. When ore processing had been greatly improved through the use of Peruvian mercury from Huancavelica (300 kilometres from Lima) in the ore amalgam, replacing the more expensive Spanish mercury from Almaden, there was a spectacular upsurge in imports to Seville. From 11.9 million pesos in 1571–1575, they rose to 29.3 million in 1581–1585.[5]

La *Carrera de Indias*: trade and ports

The boom in the production and importation of silver from the Americas into Seville provoked an equally significant rise in Atlantic navigation, due to the need to transport these treasures. In 1506–1510, 225 outward and return journeys were counted on Spanish Atlantic routes; a century later in 1606–1610, their number had more than quadrupled, and rose to 965.[6] This evidence remains flawed, however, since it conceals an even sharper increase in transport capacity: Pierre Chaunu evaluates the total merchant tonnage of treasures on this same route at 20,000 tonnes in 1511–1515, rising to 275 thousand tonnes in 1606–1610, nearly fourteenfold. Yet this shift was already clearly marked during the first half of the sixteenth century, so that from 1506 to 1550, when the traffic rose from 35 to 215 ships, their capacity increased from 3,300 tonnes to 32,000 tonnes. Tonnage in 1550, only a few years after deposits began to be mined in Zacatecas in Mexico, and Potosi in Peru, far exceeded the mean annual tonnage, estimated at 25,546 tonnes over the whole period from 1504 to 1560. It is true that since 1610 there was an overall reduction in return journeys to America. This tonnage also proves to be far higher than the levels accepted by Garcia Baquero for the eighteenth century, from 1717 to 1778, who put the mean annual tonnage at 12,346 tonnes.[7]

On the outward journey to the Indies, it was necessary to put in at an early port of call, as Columbus had previously done at the Canaries, where vessels took on water and provisions. On average, the ships took about 12 to 15 days to cover the 900 nautical miles separating Seville from the Canaries, crossing the Mediterranean Atlantic. The currents carried them to the Canaries on leaving the Moroccan coast, while in summer, the north-westerly trade winds veered largely to the north up to the Azores. In June, the trade wind blows most frequently, from 90 to 95 per cent, whereas in winter, depressions swell over the Atlantic, and in January the frequency of the trade wind is barely higher than 50 per cent.[8] So we can understand what Pierre Chaunu calls the 'winter silence' in Atlantic sailings from January to March, when the trade wind is less pronounced, relative to the intense activity of the summer.

The supporting role of the Canaries' port

The convoy system very soon made it possible to guarantee a safe navigation. During the 1530s, a distribution of sailing periods was established that was as rigid as the turn-around of the convoys from New Spain and Tierra Firme. Ships from New Spain left Seville in June with a view to reaching the Canaries at the beginning of July; those from the Tierra Firme and the Panama isthmus left in May and therefore passed the Canaries at the beginning of June. This succession allowed provisions to be distributed in the form of abundant and high quality fresh foods, and marketed better than in Spain, since the Canarian population was quite small and there was an enormous excess of seeds, fruits and wines. The Canaries thus became the 'nutritive' port, indispensable for a safe crossing of the *Golfo* from the Atlantic right up to the Antilles, which was relatively rapid for around 30 days on average when the trade winds blew, although any delay could become dangerous, with the consequent risk of having insufficient water and provisions.

In order of importance, the ports in the Canaries in 1550 were Lanzarote (33 per cent), Gomera (31 per cent), Gran Canaria (12 per cent) and Tenerife (5 per cent). In late autumn and in winter, the archipelago was copiously drenched by maritime tropical atmospheric depressions. The south winds brought heavy rain, particularly over Gomera and Gran Canaria, the most westerly of the islands. North-west of the archipelago, Lanzarote, the most easterly of the islands, is less well served, and even seems to be a little arid.[9] The paucity of the rainfall in Lanzarote was compensated for by agricultural techniques that kept the soil moist. The best conditions were still found on the western part of the archipelago.

The sugar plantations, especially developed in Tenerife, could have proved a threat to re-supplying the convoys, but competition with Brazil during the latter half of the century, and, of course, with Madeira and São Tomé before that, had reduced it in scale. Moreover, for want of sufficient rainfall, it could not be extended to Lanzarote and the other, eastern islands. It was wheat and wine, the two basic provisioning products on the *Carrera*, that created wealth in the port of the Canaries. Apart from providing for crews, the archipelago also sent shipments to the colonies in the Antilles and Tierra Firme. In the following century, however, becoming greater in the eighteenth, an imbalance caused by the invasion of the vine in cereal or vegetable growing country began to show up. There was even a cereal deficit when, in the second half of the eighteenth century, persistent drought caused several farm workers to emigrate from Lanzarote and Fuentaventura to Gran Canaria and Tenerife.

Although they had lost a great proportion of their lush forests through the rise of agriculture, the islands, especially in the west, offered ships wood to load, and the same wood was used for repairs undertaken in the shipbuilding yards. Crews were refreshed by consuming fresh supplies, and the sick were looked after in hospitals: in Tenerife, the port of Laguna alone had three hospitals at the beginning of the sixteenth century.

The crossing and the ports of the Carrera

Crossing the Atlantic posed no major problem to such well prepared ships and men. To the north of Trinidad and Tobago, the northern trade wind blows for 300 days of the year, enabling a relatively fast passage from the Canaries to the American islands. Once past the arc of the Antilles, ships had to cross the Caribbean between the Tropic of Cancer and the equatorial zone (around 10 degrees latitude north). A huge space had to be covered there, almost 1.9 million square kilometres, and if we add the Gulf of Mexico, the area is more than doubled to 4.6 million square kilometres. The crossing could be difficult, due to the existence during the summer (the equatorial winter) of *invierno*, or wintering, and the rainy season which, from July to September, produced dangerous cyclones. Such incidences were well known in the Antilles, Yucatan and far into the Gulf of Mexico, although the southern shores of the Caribbean Sea, from Guiana to Colombia, were relatively free of them.

The north equatorial current runs from Guiana northwards to the islands level with Martinique, where combined with the effects and the influence of the trade wind, it changes its direction to the west, and thereafter to the south-west, and, known as the Caribbean current, it reaches Jamaica and the south coast of Cuba. The trade wind dictated the convoys' route. These favourable tendencies can, it is true, disappear from July to October, when the trade wind sometimes gives way to the south or west wind, at which time sailors experience the most threatening turbulence due to the current of warm, equatorial waters that can even flow back into the Atlantic.

Taking advantage of a set of favourable conditions, however, the convoys regularly followed courses imposed by the winds and currents. The course for New Spain passed the port of the Lesser Antilles, most often at the level of Dominica, between Martinique and Guadeloupe, in order to make for the north of the arc of the Antilles, passing Santo Domingo and the south coast of Cuba, reaching Vera Cruz at the base of the Gulf of Campeche. The course from Trinidad to Tierra Firme and the Panama isthmus went along the southern coast of the Caribbean Sea and, after putting into port at Cartagena, arrived at Nombre de Dios, the port of the isthmus. For the former, the most favourable winds were in July, blowing from the south-east to the north-west, whereas in winter, in January, the wind turned to north-east to south-west and drove the ships onto the inhospitable coasts of the Gulf of Campeche.

The most important thing was the date of arrival, whether at Nombre de Dios or Vera Cruz. Apart from the relatively brief time taken crossing the Golfo between the Canaries and the Antilles, seldom more than about 30 days, we need also to add the time spent navigating through the more difficult regions of the Mediterranean of the Americas. In fact, this is a vast area in which the changing winds from July to October can slow ships down. In the case of an excessively prolonged journey, ships sometimes had to face cyclones which, originating from the east in the Atlantic, most often drove northwards, ascending to the arc of the Antilles and perhaps going as far as Yucatan. To reach Vera Cruz, sailing conditions were therefore more restricting than those that existed on the coast of Tierra Firme and the isthmus.

Arriving in Nombre de Dios posed its own problems, however, not least medical ones, since most convoys settled here in the first fortnight of July, and the rainy season then prevailing over the isthmus was the most unhealthy.[10] On average, the convoys took some 75 days (including halts) to reach Nombre de Dios, a journey time comparable to the voyage between Seville and Vera Cruz.

Nombre de Dios and Peruvian commerce

After the 1540s, convoys handled Peru's trade in Nombre de Dios. During the *Feria*, the port witnessed the shipping of silver from Potosi, imported via the Pacific *Carrera* to Panama and then carried by mule portage over the isthmus to Nombre de Dios on the Atlantic. The poor shores of Nombre de Dios did not guarantee good conditions for putting into port and, in 1598, a more reliable 'fore-port' at Porto Bello in Panama replaced it. However, its traffic was by far the most important on the *Carrera* from the middle of the sixteenth century, and over the period from 1541 to 1650 its value represents from 55 to 60 per cent of the exchanges between Spanish America and the Old World.[11]

Life at the port of Nombre de Dios remained precarious since it was dependent on the arrival of the fleet of Tierra Firme from Seville, and the fleet from Peru to Panama that was the system's nerve centre, controlling the traffic that enlivened the Atlantic coast some 100 kilometres distant over a portage route that cost a great many human lives. The largest port of the Atlantic *Carrera* and the second Pacific port in the New World were directly linked, forming a unique complex. Up until the end of the seventeenth century, there was no link to the Pacific by way of the South Atlantic, so this complex monopolized the Panama isthmus. In Nombre de Dios, it was only normal that two fleets, one from the Pacific and another from the Atlantic, arrived at almost the same time, and according to Pierre Chaunu, this happened once every two years.[12]

Yet Nombre de Dios was only a very poor harbour, exposed to the high seas with no real shelter, and without stable trading posts for the traffic. Each time the stay was prolonged during the period of the *invierno*, the mariners were exposed to terrible attacks of the *calentura*, the devastating yellow fever that sapped the strength of the *Carrera*. If the weather was too bad, if an enemy became afraid, they withdrew to Cartagena, the arsenal and the military port on the road over the isthmus, on the near coast of Colombia. At Nombre de Dios there were no more than 150 to 200 inhabited houses when the fleet arrived on the high seas, and all were abandoned when it left, empty, that is, for an average of almost 10 months of the year. Meanwhile, the *limenos* agents of Panama were also active here, where distinguished guests of the fleet were lodged during the *Feria* when the convoys rested. Sanitary conditions were worse than poor: as in the other ports of the *Carrera*, there was no drinking water so there were no fresh supplies there. Death took a heavy toll, with a rate of some 6 to 7.5 per cent, almost 300 men out of a total of the 4–5,000 of the convoys' crews died every year in the swamps of Nombre de Dios.[13]

The port was also exposed to enemy raids (Drake's attack in the years 1570–1580). At the end of the sixteenth century, the risk of English or French attack was lessened by increasing the transportation of goods by coastal navigation to Cartagena, which acquired an exceptional position in exchange between 1596 and 1600, compensating for the fragility of the isthmus with a remarkable capacity for defending these riches over the 450 kilometres from Nombre de Dios to Porto Bello alone.

Access to the ports on the isthmus shows a clear seasonal rhythm. On average, the influx of provisions and precious metals coming from Panama, Peru and Colombia preceded the fastest arrivals from Spain by a month. Provisions were accumulated to meet the needs of crews and merchants, produce to be loaded with the briefest possible delay. At the end of the *invierno*, from the beginning of September to the beginning of November, the largest slack period began, and then, from the end of November to January, a revival of maritime activities took place, followed by a new slack period in the spring, preceding the enormous activity of the summer months (the equatorial winter), during the *invierno*.

Via Panama, the isthmus attracted the Peruvian silver that constituted the core of the trade with Spain, but Lima exported just as many provisions to the isthmus, necessary to the human settlements of the merchant *Feria* from Nombre de Dios to Porto Bello. The quickest and safest land transit from Panama to Nombre de Dios required convoys of mules lead by the *arrieros*; almost 850 mules were thus used to carry objects of value while heavy goods took the Rio Sagre from the Atlantic as far as Cruces. The mule convoys were at risk from many dangers, with an abundance of reptiles and wild animals in the forests, and with the slave workforce employed in the convoys always tempted to make pacts with the *cimarrones*, fugitives who had escaped their masters and dared to attack the rich convoys, and who were the best servants of the buccaneers from the sixteenth to the eighteenth centuries.

Early on, in 1533, to protect themselves against attack from the buccaneers,

Spain installed a fearsome arsenal at Cartagena, on the near coast of Colombia. Upon departing the isthmus, the convoys made an obligatory call here for repairs and taking on supplies before crossing the Caribbean Sea towards Santo Domingo, and, from the mid-century, towards Havana where the treasure ships gathered before setting off again for Seville. The seizure of Peru by Pizarro had required the reinforcement of military power on the isthmus of Tierra Firme. The port of Cartagena was well protected against the bad weather but, above all, against the corsairs who began to appear in the Caribbean in the 1530s. It was also the opening to the new realm of New Granada, Bogota and Antioquia, whose traffic, however, was not equivalent to that carried over the isthmus to Peru. The best of this traffic was the gold from Buritica, but its shipping remained rather irregular, and in the Seville Atlantic all the consignments from Cartagena represented just 25 to 30 per cent of the importance of those from Peru.[14]

Cartagena protected the coasts of the isthmus by maintaining a powerful squadron of fast galleys. This expensive defence was, on the whole, successful, despite attempts by the English, such as Drake's in February 1586, and later by the Dutch when, in the seventeenth century, they settled in Caracas, half way along the coast of Tierra Firme, between Trinidad and Cartagena. From here they were able to launch raids and above all to undertake considerable amounts of smuggling, and, to the detriment of Seville's monopoly, to supply the Spanish with slaves and valuable goods.

Vera Cruz: the opening to the New Spain

At Havana, convoys from the isthmus met up with fleets coming from Vera Cruz in Mexico. After Cortes' conquest, traffic from New Spain was concentrated in this port. After having passed the arc of the Antilles parallel to the Windward Islands, a convoy from Vera Cruz, taking advantage of the impetus from the Caribbean current and a lively trade wind, gained easy access to the coasts south of Santo Domingo, an island lying in the trade wind's path, but which, since the middle of the sixteenth century, was the major route in the *Carrera* that led to Cuba and the Gulf of Campeche. Santo Domingo had then lost any importance in the treasure trade, its gold deposits had been exhausted since the 1510s, and there had been a decline in its shipping of sugar and skins. After 1550, Havana completely took over Santo Domingo's role as the centre of the Americas.[15]

Navigation in the Gulf of Campeche, south of the Gulf of Mexico where ships entered after having passed the Yucatan Channel between Cuba and the mainland, did not benefit from the most favourable conditions. The greatest danger was not so much the cyclones, which were concentrated between July and September, as the far more frequent violent winds from the north that drove sailing ships onto the Mexican coast. The number of losses at sea off Vera Cruz was far higher than it was off the isthmus, despite a lower volume of traffic. On the other hand, however, the extreme perils of the sea gave more protection to the coast of the Gulf of Campeche than to the isthmus, exposed to enemy raids.

In addition, climactic conditions were worse. The low-lying, marshy coast, ravaged by fevers, consisted of some 600 kilometres of desert, and the site of Vera Cruz lay at the place where the low-lying plains dwindled away and the plateau drew near. The position of the port was not without its own risks, however. Ships had to cross the ridge of the Antigua river, at the mouth of which, where the port was found, the estuary was silted up and the vessels risked running aground. Moreover, ships often remained at anchor off the island of San Juan de Ulua, which was fortified by the Spanish, and small shuttle craft were used to unload them. There was a lack of drinkable water, which had to be drawn from a neighbouring, brackish lagoon. In 1600, a new port was established further south with better water supplies and, being closer to San Juan, protected by its defences.

As in Nombre de Dios, the precarious means for operating loadings and unloadings are striking: the port had no more than 600 negroes and when a fleet arrived the number of shuttles proved insufficient. From April to June 1585, during a period of great prosperity, 18 ships left Vera Cruz; from July to September, 37 entered it, to which the Portuguese trade in negroes from Angola must be added. Twenty years later, in 1605, during a 'brief flash of prosperity' after the peace with France and England, there were 15 ships in port from January to March, 38 arrived between July and September, and 34 left from October to December.[16] Such fleets represented from 2–4,000 men, more than the port's permanent population. Upon their arrival, a fleet of *arrieros* came down from the Plateau of Anahuac, with a view to maintaining the port's operations and the transportation of the cargoes across Mexico. The population of the town then tripled. From Seville, Vera Cruz received wine, oil, and wheat when colonization began; Spanish mercury from Almaden came here too, necessary for processing silver ore from Zacatecas, as well as iron, and valuable goods such as cloth, books and jewels.

The port sent treasures back, of course, and also cochineal, over which Vera Cruz held something of a monopoly, and which was of far greater value than the skins that were also loaded. Along with these shipments destined for Seville, cargoes for Havana, the most important port on the return journey, were also sent with provisions for refreshing the convoys. The *arrieros* mule trains brought them down from the plateaus by means of *caminos* from Castilla. They were brought together in a staging post in Puebla, midway between Vera Cruz and Mexico, in the heart of a rich agricultural region.

Havana, crossroads of the Caribbean

Before returning to Seville, the last port in the *Carrera* was Havana. The two fleets arrived during the summer, spending the winter in the Indies. In January, the fleet from the isthmus prepared to depart, the ships heading north-west to reach Havana; in February, the vessels from New Spain left Vera Cruz, climbing against the trade wind to arrive at Havana towards March, and were met by several galleons that had left, further south, from Honduras. Arrivals in Havana could, however, arrive later: thus, in 1585, the largest of the convoys only arrived between April and June, 18 ships from Vera Cruz, six from Honduras and five from Nombre de Dios that had put into port in Cartagena.

The concentration of fleets at Havana lent this port its great importance, largely eclipsing Santo Domingo. Havana was an important and substantial port. Between the island that protected it and the coast, there was space for from 500 to 1,000 ships; the harbour was well defended by a chain of fortifications that were reinforced at the end of the 1590s. Havana then became the 'key' to the Caribbean, in the same way as was Cartagena on the isthmus route, or San Juan on Puerto Rico, at the point where the convoys from Seville arrived. Leaving Havana with the fleet from New Spain in January 1599, Champlain admired it as one of the most beautiful ports, with an entrance so narrow that an iron chain was sufficient to bar passage. Havana was 'the warehouse where all the riches of America were held, and the Spanish have taken great pains to fortify her'.[17] Some years later, in 1625, the English Dominican Thomas Gage asserted that the Spanish had put Havana on a par with the citadels of Antwerp, Milan and Pamplona: the 'twelve disciples', twelve guns 'of extraordinary proportions', made the artillery of Moro, Havana's fortress, fearsome.[18] The growth of Havana's military post provided the convoys with almost total security, at least on the American Atlantic seafront, with the exception of Dutchman Piet Heyn's success against a convoy from Vera Cruz in 1628, near Havana, on the Cuban coast of the Bay of Matanzas.

Havana had superior shipbuilding and repair yards. Long waits in tropical seas seriously damaged the ships: their worm-eaten hulls came apart. Urgent repairs were carried out, but the 'creole' ships found in the *Carrera* could also be built in these yards, which, at the end of the sixteenth century, were second in the Spanish Atlantic only to those of northern Spain. Pierre Chaunu highlights the case of the *Nuestra Señora del Pilar*, a heavy galleon of 640 *toneladas*, that in 1610 left the Cuban shipyards and was broken up in Vera Cruz 13 years later. This ship had one of the fastest turn-arounds, making one outward and one return journey in a year on its first voyages.[19] By the middle of the seventeenth century, Havana's shipyards had become the equal of those of the Basque Country and the Cantabrian coast; from 1640 to 1650, the shipyards of northern Spain and Cuba each represented 40 per cent of the *Carrera*'s entire material resources.

After an indispensable rest in the port of Havana, the fleets left Cuba for Seville from the end of July to September, taking the Bahamas Channel to reach the Bermuda archipelago some 1,650 kilometres from Havana. Here the ships took advantage of the powerful flow of the Gulf Stream (from one metre to a metre and a half per second), but if their departure was delayed they could also suffer greatly from the hurricanes blowing from the Antilles to Florida from the end of August to October. Thus in 1622, the *Nuestra Señora de la Concepción*, a mediocre Andalusian vessel of 116 *toneladas*, lost all hands and cargo in the Bermuda area, 'killed by a hurricane at the end of August'.[20] The ship had made just one single voyage from Seville to Vera Cruz, and was lost during its return. On a scale of losses, Bermuda would rank as high as Havana or Vera Cruz, both ports with difficult approaches, and well above the isthmus, where several losses in the Bahamas Channel itself must also be counted.

Once past Bermuda, north of the 30th parallel, the ships found the westerlies, which blew more or less regularly, and also took advantage of the North Atlantic drift of the Gulf Stream to reach the Azores archipelago, the last halt before Seville. It could take between 60 and 65 days from Havana to the Azores. After long days at sea, the Azores archipelago allowed ships to be restored and men to be refreshed. Here, masts and hulls were often repaired, and exhausted men could at last find abundant food and water. In fact, the Azores were a well run and productive cereal growing area, since, due to its more northern latitude, the sugar economy was never very successful. The use of this port is all the more remarkable because the archipelago remained Portuguese, apart from the short period of the union of the Crowns of Madrid and Lisbon, between 1580 and 1640. Although no one wished it, collaboration between the Iberians was still necessary for the exploitation of the Atlantic.

Ships could discharge the goods that weighed them down and hampered their defences while completing the last stage of the crossing of the ocean sea. In fact, engagements with pirates from the west or from the Barbary Coast were not infrequent at sea off the Cabo de São Vincente. The amount of treasure, whether plentiful or whether the loads had grown smaller, could be assessed in the Azores, and a fast ship, sent on from the archipelago in advance of the convoy, carried the news on which Seville's markets thrived. As the role of the Azores declined during the first half of the seventeenth century, and less and less treasure was sheltered there, Havana was becoming the principal refuge before the Atlantic crossing.

Seville, a cosmopolitan port

After slender Mediterranean galleys had tacked the often difficult passage from the Azores to the Iberian coast (it required some 20 days, and there was always the risk of storms hitting and inflicting losses; even Columbus nearly fell victim to them during his first voyage), heavier galleons finally passed through the

Guadalquivir Channel. They had to journey upriver for almost 90 kilometres, since Seville lay at the topmost point of an ascent from the sea. Its port thus offered the great advantage of security and easy access to a rich hinterland. Seville experienced all the prosperity of a metropolis 'at the confluence of two worlds' in the life of the *Carrera de Indias*.

The spectacular growth of its population demonstrates this increase in wealth: in 1530, Seville contained more than 50,000 inhabitants, exceeding 100,000 at the beginning of the 1560s, and reaching 130,000 inhabitants around 1590.[21] It was both national and foreign immigration that made this growth possible. Drawn by the volume of trade in Seville, many merchants came from all over the peninsula: from Burgos, with their long experience and their powerful commercial networks, they came to trade textiles destined for Flanders and Italy, while there were many Basques involved in banking and the iron trade at Biscay, necessary to the mining activities of the New World. The Flemish, the Portuguese and the Genoese, followed by other Italians, the French and the English, gave the place a cosmopolitan character. The Genoese financed the export of seeds and cloth to America, the export of Andalusian goods to northern Europe, the negro slave trade and, above all, the bank. After 1566, they obtained export licences for American silver and dedicated themselves thereafter to banking activities. The Flemish, who had also been settled for a long time in Seville, bought wines, skins and sails, while those from Antwerp, who enjoyed the advantage of relations with northern Europe, provided America with goods that Spain could not give, and took an equal interest in American dye-products, such as cochineal and indigo, as in skins. At the end of the century, there were as many as 200 Flemish houses established in Seville.[22] The Portuguese tended to monopolize the slave trade that their compatriots had controlled on the African coast since the fifteenth century.

La *Carrera de Indias* and the Atlantic economy

Seville's monopoly

For Spain, the route to the Americas played an essential role. The *Carrera* brought the monarchies of Charles V and Philip II the means to be politically dominant in Europe, since it enabled the mobilization of the wealth discovered in Mexico and Peru, so that there was a continual increase in trade during the sixteenth century. Following the creation of the *Casa de Contratación* in 1504, Seville became the staging post for the *Carrera*, distributing gold and then silver to places in Europe such as Genoa, Venice and, above all, Antwerp.

After Columbus's first departures in 1492 and 1493, Seville asserted her rights to a monopoly over the Spanish Atlantic, in particular with the royal schedule of

14 February 1503, which recognized the *Carrera*'s first successes and established its prerogatives. Seville had the indisputable advantage of its geographical position. In relation to a voyage begun in Seville or Cadiz, the voyage between Europe and America lasted about 15 per cent longer if the departure took place from Galicia, rising to nearly 20 per cent from the Basque Country. Costs similarly rose by 20 to 25 per cent.

The *Casa de Contratación* provided Seville with indispensable administrative and naval means to control shipping and to create a corps of ships' captains. Even if the Council of the Indies that controlled the administration and politics of the colonies was established in Madrid, Seville had a *Consulado* of merchants, a commercial tribunal playing a pre-eminent role in defending the monopoly.

The assertion of this monopoly was nevertheless made on shaky grounds. Journey times of 40 days to reach the Lesser Antilles, around 60 days to Cuba and almost 75 days to Vera Cruz and Nombre de Dios, although they were long, creating a time–distance relation specific to the era of the galleon, must not obscure the length of the real commercial circuit. When it benefitted from an exceptional confluence of circumstances, the circuit could be completed in 18 months, but bad weather or war could mean it took up to five years.[23] The turn-around time for the convoys was, of course, shorter, but still took from 14 to 15 months in the best cases. Times of laying idle – loading and unloading, waiting for winds – amounted to between eight and a half to 10 months against only five and a half months' actual sailing. During long periods of war, idle times were far greater; costs increased and ships suffered when woodworm rotted their immobilized hulls in the warm seas, so that they had to be repaired in Cartagena or Havana.

The successes were nevertheless quite remarkable, since despite raids by the English, Dutch and French, the *Carrera* kept up the constancy of its activities. The capture of treasures by the Dutch in 1628 and the English in 1656 were still exceptions. A slowdown in consignments, delivered much later than they were expected, took place in the middle of the seventeenth century (1646–1656), but this was far more the result of a rise in smuggling than direct attack.[24] There had never been a shortage of precious metals in Seville's Atlantic, and these were increasingly important to the world's economy. The great west–east flow that brought silver from America to Europe was never interrupted, and Spanish piastres struck from New World silver were an essential instrument for international payments whether in Europe or Asia, in India and China, who sold much more to Europe than they bought from it, and who were therefore controlled by these precious metals.

Seville's success is therefore inseparable from the prosperity of the other leading Atlantic regions, amongst which Antwerp must be counted in the sixteenth century. The success of the great region of Scheldt is confirmed by its role as the major world market:

Antwerp weds the north to the south; they come here equally from Danzig and Leipzig as from Venice, Lisbon and London; *whether foreign or native, all these merchants do business, a trade both incredible and marvellous, as much in the exchanging as in the depositing of merchandise.*[25]

Here products from the colonies came together with English cloth and German metals. The influx of precious metals from America was re-routed to Antwerp when the Iberian monarchy had need of the services and capital of the great businesses established in Antwerp. The region's economy was stimulated by its tight bonds with the traffic from the Indies.

At the end of the sixteenth century, when the market at Antwerp was broken up due to the Low Countries' revolt against Philip II, other staging posts appeared and the silver convoys were turned away from the Mediterranean, Italy and the Alps, and Amsterdam was elevated to the first rank. Seville, however, maintained its vitality: the region's Atlantic traffic reached record levels between 1606 and 1610. It was only in the course of the seventeenth century that two new Atlantics – the Dutch and the British – asserted themselves, playing a growing role in the European economy and, in some degree, to the detriment of Seville's Atlantic. They nevertheless remained strictly dependent on the latter and hopes of the treasures to be captured or even dominated remained an essential element of the naval politics of the north-western Europeans.

Returning riches

The influence of American precious metals in the Atlantic economy grew progressively. In the Atlantic islands of Hispaniola, Puerto Rico, Cuba, Tierra Firme and Golden Castile, during the first quarter of the sixteenth century, gold was the most important constituent of Seville's imports. After 1530, these imports exceeded the African gold imported by the Portuguese. Almost 100 tonnes of gold reached Seville as late as 1560, although after 1550 the share of gold was greatly reduced, accounting for little more than 13 to 15 per cent of Seville's imports. With the discovery of Potosi in Peru, in 1545, Spain's imports of silver doubled: from 1541 to 1550, more than 177 tonnes of silver arrived in Seville. When the amalgam with mercury and the forced labour of the *mita* system in the mercury mines of Huancavelica or the silver mines of Potosi had been introduced, Peru became the first producer. At its maximum, Seville imported 2,700 tonnes from 1591 to 1600, worth more than 100 million *pesos*.[26] Thereafter, imports fell: from 1601 to 1660, almost 550 million *pesos* of gold and silver, that is, some nine million per year, were imported; from 1660 to 1700, the monopoly imported 580 million *pesos*, 14.5 million per year, showing a significant rise in inflow, which was more fully confirmed in the eighteenth century when, from 1730 until the end of the century, the imports of precious metals from Spanish America tripled. From 1730 to 1745, annual imports were 12 million, the increase becoming more apparent in the second half of the eighteenth century when, in 1790–1795, almost 150 million were imported, thanks to a leap forward in Mexico's silver production.[27]

To establish the real value of the imports of American metals, it is necessary to take account of the prevalent fraud at the monopoly's expense. At the beginning of the sixteenth century, when the Castilian Crown created the *Casa de Contratación* in Seville, it was essentially to control the *Carrera*'s trade. In 1717, the monopoly system passed from Seville to Cadiz, and on the eve of the liberalization of trade by the Bourbons in 1765, only Seville and Cadiz could do business with the New World, while in the Americas the only cargo ports were Vera Cruz and Porto Bello.

In theory, the value of the silver loaded in these ports was carefully recorded by the *maestrios de plata* so as to inform the administration. In Seville, foreign merchants and consuls received this precise information on the value of the silver a convoy was carrying by way of the *navio de aviso*, sent from the Azores before the convoy departed the archipelago, and almost a month later the Amsterdam newspapers also published the total amount of the cargo. These records of transportation were the focus of fraud, but fraud was also practised in the records of production. The Crown saw the *quinto*, a tax of a fifth of the metals' value, effectively reduced to a tenth during the middle of the sixteenth century in Mexico and later, in 1735, in Peru. In fact, the *Mercurio Peruano* of 1789 estimated that fraud enabled two-thirds of production to avoid taxation. This observation, made in Lima, gave an account of fraud as it had developed in Potosi over almost a century. Since there was also fraud in the records of the production of the mercury in Huancavelica (which was required for the amalgam), a parallel market was able to sell nearly 130,000 tonnes of silver per year in Peru. One final element preventing the imports into Seville being seen as an exact reflection of production was the exportation of silver by way of the Pacific from Acapulco in Mexico in the direction of Manilla, and the use of precious metals in the sumptuous decorations of religious and civic buildings in the Spanish colonies.

Whether introduced by the monopoly or by fraud, precious metals did not simply remain in Spain. These riches were circulated like a currency 'common' to all nations. Spanish purchases of wheat, metals, gunpowder and canons within Europe; the activities of the German and Italian bankers in Spain; foreign craftsmen working there, and the rich colonists from Mexico or Lima buying textiles and jewels, all meant that the precious metal circulated throughout Europe. We could apply to other countries the image given by François Crouzet of France as the 'financial leech' of Spain: over three centuries, due to the surplus of their commercial balance, the European countries drew in the white metal from Spain.[28]

The demand of the courts and armies, provoked by the growing population during the sixteenth and seventeenth centuries, in the face of supplies reduced by war and the drift of monies towards Asia, provoked an increase in all the long-term prices during the sixteenth century. Beginning in Seville, it spread throughout all Europe. In fact, the increasing mass of metal brought about by the influx of American precious metals, had profound repercussions for the movement of prices and business. In 1566, the Lord of Malestroit wondered at 'the strange increase in the price of everything that we see day by day, and how much everyone, however great or small, feels it in his purse'.[29] It was then possible to believe in the role played exclusively by the New World as the driving force, as events sped faster and faster in Europe and inflation multiplied.[30] It was as much the pull exerted by the development of trade around new commercial poles from the end of the sixteenth to the eighteenth centuries, in Amsterdam, London and the French Atlantic ports, however, as the pressure of American production of precious metals that created the conjunction of prosperity in the Atlantic. Above all, it induced their merchants to want to make as much profit as possible from the Iberian riches. Capturing the galleons with their fabulous treasures and possessing the colonies for themselves, the source of so many dreams, was what drew the attention of the powers in the Low Countries and in London, and inflamed the popular imagination. In order to do this, it was necessary to challenge Seville's monopoly and to bring war and pillage to the Caribbean.

The Iberian Atlantic is opened to foreigners

The first violations of the monopoly

While it was challenged by certain sovereigns, such as King François I of France, Spain's monopoly had all but escaped direct attack until the 1530s. Before this, the only foreign presence in Spanish America were the French mariners and merchants who, having left Brazil's coasts, where they were looking for 'brasil wood' for use as a cloth dye, ventured into the Caribbean during the war between France and Spain. Raiding expeditions against Portugal in Brazil began to take place very early on, since if this kingdom had doggedly defended its spice monopoly in the East India trade it would have been too weak to preserve its possessions in America from foreigners. The French in particular ran an illicit trade there, since the carrying trade wind had made the sail to Brazil easy; the 'pirate' ships that frequented the Guinea coast in the 1500s in order to operate a slave trade there, very soon appeared on the coast of Brazil. Thus, sailing out of Honfleur on *l'Espoir*, Paulmier de Goneville of Normandy reached the Brazilian coast 'by the good fortunes of the sea', in January 1504. In his diary of the journey, Goneville makes it clear that 'despite some experience in this, albeit years ago, from Dieppe and Saint Malo, along with other Normans and Bretons, they are going in quest of red dye wood, cotton, monkeys and parrots'.[31]

Ten years later, the new governor of Panama was given authorization to attack and punish the Frenchmen he had met in the Indies, and in 1522 Santo Domingo was attacked by the French. In 1528, the Margarita Islands off the coast of Tierra Firme, rich in pearls, were the target of raids from La Rochelle. The French corsairs showed themselves to be increasingly daring: in Puerto Rico, the town of San Juan was sacked in the same year, while Puerto Plata and Yaguana, towns on Hispaniola, were similarly attacked in 1539 and 1543; on Cuba, Baracoa and even Havana suffered the same fate in 1539 and 1546.

These ships left from Dieppe and Honfleur in Normandy, La Rochelle in Saintonge, and Bayonne and Saint Jean de Luz in the Basque Country, making it possible to speak of a continuous French presence in the Caribbean Sea during the second quarter of the sixteenth century. Their activities were not limited to raiding and pillaging, since they also engaged in trade: in Guinea, they loaded up with 'black gold', or negroes, thus violating Lisbon's monopoly and offering slaves to the colonists on the coasts of Tierra Firme. However, their actions took place during a state of war between France and Spain which, between 1494 and 1559, was almost constant; at the same time, however, their actions were individual enterprises, plundering Spanish settlements or seizing their coasters if they were unable to attack the treasure galleons.

The English did not yet come to relieve the French because Henry VIII's England wanted to maintain its alliance with Spain against France. In the Low Countries, dominated by Spain, there were important English commercial interests, and, until the Reformation, cross-Channel opinion attacked the greed of the French pirate-entrepreneurs far more than the Spanish. In Seville, there were numerous English merchants who desired to profit from the *Carrera*'s wealth. There was, therefore, no reason to undertake raiding campaigns in the Americas. Merchants from Plymouth, Southampton and Bristol in the West Country traded in products from the Iberian colonies and were associated with the merchants of Spain. Thus, from Bristol, English interests were carried over the islands of the Mediterranean Atlantic: the Canaries, Madeira and the Azores. After the treaty of Medina del Campo between England and Spain in 1489, English merchants could trade in Spain and the Atlantic islands like the Canaries, where English agents had settled to purchase sugar, in particular, but also wine.

However, during the years 1530 to 1540, religious tensions increased. Henry VIII broke away from Rome in 1532 and opinion in England began to turn against papist Spain. Legitimate English commerce in Seville was going to be under threat; English pirates seized Flemish ships in the Channel and some predatory merchants even became overtly hostile to the Spanish, launching several pillaging expeditions against them: Robert Reneger, who seized a silver ship returning from the Indies was considered a precursor of Drake or Hawkins.[32] They were hardly representative of the pioneer community's view as regards privateering, however; the vast majority of West Country merchants took no part in these enterprises and, furthermore, merchants from London completely abstained from them, because in the middle of the sixteenth century they still had strong links with Antwerp, which was the major centre of Iberian produce, controlling the trade in the Mediterranean and northern Europe, and where the venture merchants of London exported English fabrics.

Slave-trading expeditions and English illicit commerce

It was through Africa and the slave trade that the merchants of Plymouth, Southampton and Bristol, like the French a few years earlier, became interested in the Iberian Atlantic. Around 1540, the Portuguese found themselves constrained to withdraw from Morocco, where, since the fifteenth century, they laid claim to a commercial monopoly. Lisbon's withdrawal gave the English the opportunity to find new markets in which to sell their textiles and to buy sugar. In 1551, a London shipowner sent his ships to Safi and Agadir. A few years later, trade on the Barbary Coast and Guinea was supported by merchants from the Muscovy Company who had interests in several slave-trading expeditions at the end of the 1550s. As well as slaves, the English imported gold, ivory and malaguetta from Guinea. The voyages were marked by violence. In 1553, Thomas Wyndham, on one of the very first voyages, received help from Portuguese renegades, who guided the English to the coast of El Mina. Fevers drastically reduced crew numbers, and Wyndham himself perished. Of the three ships in his expedition, only two came back to Plymouth, with only 40 out of the 140 men engaged upon departure.

This was the area of Africa that was to create the initial renown of one of the greatest of the English predators of the sixteenth century, John Hawkins. His father, William Hawkins, was amongst the number of the West Country merchants present in the Spanish ports and the Canaries.

> Master John Hawkins, having made several voyages to the Canary Islands, and there, thanks to his cordial manner, having earned the peoples' favour, studiously learnt from them about conditions on the Antilles, about which his father had already given him some little instruction. Being, amongst other things, fully convinced that the negroes would make a very fine commodity in Hispaniola, and that he could easily acquire them on the Guinea coast, he resolved to attempt an expedition and formed an association with his friends from London.[33]

Celebrating the heroes of his *Principal Navigations of the English Nation* at the end of the sixteenth century, Hakluyt was able to show the reasons for Hawkins' success. At the time of his first slave-trading expedition in 1562, Hawkins had been able to win support for his cause from the City merchants and several grandees of Elizabeth's court.

Negroes had been introduced into the Spanish colonies from the beginning of the sixteenth century (the first cargoes of 'black gold' were unloaded in Hispaniola in 1503) and the island was the principal market of a trade that was practically monopolized by the Portuguese. The first three decades of Spanish occupation had in fact seen Hispaniola's population dramatically decline. There were some 800,000 Arawaks at the time of Christopher Columbus's discovery of the island, but by 1510 they were no more than 60,000, and they had almost disappeared by 1520. When, after almost 50 years, Hawkins decided to make his voyage, the needs of the sugar cane plantations required this black workforce, and in 1562 close to 20,000 blacks were divided among Hispaniola's 30 plantations. The majority of the slaves lived in the capital, Santo Domingo, but there was also a demand for them on the other islands, such as the coast of Tierra Firme, from Cumana to Cartagena, on the Panama isthmus and in Peru and Mexico.

Evading the Portuguese monopoly in Africa, the ships came for the most part from the Canaries, where the Spanish traded freely with the Portuguese, Italians, Flemish, English and French. The Spanish monopoly was also evaded, since it required that slaves bought under licence or *asiento* on behalf of the *Carrera*, left from Seville. Many Portuguese traders illicitly supplied Spanish America from São Tomé, taking advantage of the pressure of rising prices.

At the time of this first expedition, John Hawkins did not intend to act as a pirate, due to the prevailing peace between England and Spain. Nevertheless, his three low-tonnage ships of 120, 100 and 40 tonnes respectively, were well armed. In the Canaries he found valuable support from the merchants already linked with his father. Pedro de Ponte provided him with a pilot and advised his associates in the Antilles of his coming. At Sierra Leone, Hawkins procured 300 negroes. It seems that his cargo did not include high-quality textiles, such as linen and the Rouen cottons prized in the colonies, that were fraudulently sold by the Norman or Breton ships present in the Caribbean.[34] The slaves were sold without difficulty on the north coast of Hispaniola, and Hawkins took on skins, then the major product of the island, ginger, sugar and pearls. Some of his ventures even enabled him to charter two additional ships, which he sent to an English merchant in Seville. Although this cargo would have brought a healthy profit back to Plymouth, the operation was to suffer a setback when the ships he chartered were confiscated. The authorities of the *Casa de Contratación* did not accept what was an act of *rescate*, trade by force, violating the monopoly, while the colony's administrators were seen to be well disposed.

Conditions on John Hawkins' second voyage in 1564–1565, were different. Anglo–Spanish relations were beginning to deteriorate: in the Channel, corsairs committed acts of piracy against Spanish ships while English vessels were seized in Spanish ports and the Inquisition employed violence against several of their mariners. For some time trade between the two countries was suspended, and finally the two nations entered a phase of religious antagonism which was to increase. In addition, while the voyage of 1562 did not constitute an attack of pillaging comparable to those the French had undertaken in the Antilles, the violence of 'trade at pike-point' marked Hawkins' new voyage. Poorly supplied by their metropolis, the Spanish colonists, at least those on the islands and on Tierra Firme, demonstrated an unflagging desire to buy slaves, as well as other produce.

Hawkins certainly did not behave like the French pirate François Le Clerc, who, in 1555, burned La Yaguana on Hispaniola, and even dared to attack Havana. Le Clerc operated during a state of war between Henri II and Spain, and French raiding and pillaging multiplied on the coast of the Spanish Main during the 1540s. The war notwithstanding, a great deal of force had been used. The expedition had the advantage of much greater fire-power than its predecessor, and had the backing of the Queen, several senior members of her Court, and the merchants of London. The *Jesus*, from Lübeck, was armed by the Crown, had a capacity of 700 tonnes and was accompanied by three other, smaller ships. In the Canaries, the Spanish connection still guaranteed the necessary commercial and naval support: Pedro de Ponte got Hawkins a pilot and procured him provisions. In Sierra Leone, 400 negroes were loaded and the expedition reached the Caribbean at Dominica. Hawkins steered his ships towards the coast of Tierra Firme, the Spanish Main, where commercial prospects were greater than those on Hispaniola and where, in particular, the rich banks of pearls on Margarita, near Trinidad, were particularly attractive.

However, the authorities' welcome was far less favourable than it was two years earlier on Hispaniola. Margarita's governor informed the audience in Santo Domingo of the arrival of these 'Lutherans', and the cities of the Spanish Main received the order to refuse all trade. Thus in Burburata, north-west of the current site of Caracas, in a port engaged in the tobacco trade, Venezuela's principal resource before cocoa became the great product of the end of the sixteenth century, a trade that was simultaneously reassuring and worrying took place 'at pike-point'. Hawkins felt he had to disregard the authorities' resistance, and even demanded a licence to trade, insisting he had come to sell his slaves and to buy produce from the colonies, while at the same time making his determination known: 'If this petition were not accepted, I will find my own solutions.'[35]

In order to make himself more acceptable to the town, Hawkins had used the *arribada maliciosa*, claiming he had been forced to enter Burburata due to the damage sustained by his ships: 'I have been impelled by contrary winds to these coasts, and as soon as I find a suitable port, I can repair them.' Hawkins won his case and even managed to brush aside a supplementary tax demanded by the Spanish, of thirty ducats per slave sold. It is true that he was giving a demonstration of his strength by having deployed 100 armed men throughout the town. He succeeded in selling the slaves, albeit at a lower price than the Portuguese traders. Adopting this same 'pike-point' commerce, the English, 'keeping the peace and doing no harm to anyone', put into port at the Rio de la Hacha, the port of pearls, and here too sold their slaves. From these sales on the coast of the Spanish Main, Hawkins' sleeping partners were going to realize a return of more than 60 per cent on their outlay.

There were calls to repeat such voyages: in 1566, Hawkins entrusted a ship to John Lowell who directed his slave-trading expedition to Margarita, where he came across the ship of the famous French slave-trader, Jean Bontemps. Violence had broken out at the port of Burburata, where Lowell did not shirk from taking Spanish hostages in order to obtain his licence to trade. Despite this, Lowell had to be content to sell few negroes, which was all the worse for Rio de La Hacha, where he had to disembark 92 negroes, all old and sick, without managing to secure payment. According to Andrews, this voyage was a failure.

The voyage of 1567, on which Hawkins' fame was based, was going to be quite different. This expedition was far more important than previous ones, and he assembled six ships with a total capacity of 1,333 tonnes. The *Jesus* and the *Mignon* were royal warships. Supported by the Court and some City merchants, John Hawkins gave the impression that his expedition was defending the pride of Albion when, before departure, he wanted to humiliate the Spanish warships docked in Plymouth by demanding that they salute the English flag.

The first part of the voyage was completed without incident, because after putting into port in the Canaries, as usual, and capturing 500 slaves between Cape Verde and Sierra Leone during a three-month stay, with three extra ships having been added to his fleet, Hawkins was able to reach ports on Tierra Firme that he had already visited. He rested for a month at Burburata, where, in spite of the official ban on all their commercial activities, the English sold their slaves at night. 'Being pleased to see us, the inhabitants voluntarily began to trade', Hawkins remarked in his ship's journal. Similar scenes of smuggling took place in Santa Maria and Rio de la Hacha, where, however, violence, setting fire to a quarter of the town, pillaging and hostage taking, marked this out as a matter of 'pike-point trading'. Hawkins abandoned the idea of going near Cartagena, because the *Carrera*'s arsenal was too well defended, but the town's *cabildo* was complaining about the seizure of several richly laden ships by pirates. Pearls, tobacco and even silver ducats were crammed into ships' holds when they left Tierra Firme to reach the Florida Straits and to return to Europe by way of the Azores, following the course of the great west winds. In order to do this it was necessary to cross the entire breadth of the Caribbean Sea, over 1,600 kilometres, without putting in to port in some 25 days at sea. When they tried to double the western point of Cuba at Cape San Antonio, the vessels endured violent storms, since by now it was the season of the *invierno*, with its fearsome hurricanes. With their hulls and rigging seriously damaged, the ships had to be repaired and Hawkins decided to make for shelter on San Juan de Ulua, the fore-port at Vera Cruz, which was the nearest anchorage. He entered it on 15 September 1568, which was quite a feat, since it lay at the heart of the treasure route.

The good fortune that had thus far protected Hawkins and his men was, however, to abandon them at San Juan. Hawkins had only been able to gain entry to this port due to a mistake by its inhabitants, who had taken the English sails as belonging to the galleons expected at Vera Cruz. So on the morning of 16 September, the *flota* was in sight and Hawkins was no longer dealing with the colonists eager for contraband, nor with corruptible authorities, but with the Viceroy of New Spain, who arrived with the fleet, and Captain General Don Francisco de Lusan, metropolitan rather than creole Spaniards whose careers, if not their lives, depended on respecting the monopoly. Philip II's mariners, in a fight where they had the advantage of numbers, easily defeated the English, only three of whose ships reached England again.

The expedition of 1567–1568, despite the sale of some pearls and silver, was a financial disaster, but acquired some value as a *cause célèbre* illustrating the Spaniards' treachery. Hawkins had vainly attempted to negotiate with the Viceroy, and there was no state of war between England and Spain. The insult warranted revenge, and the subsequent exploits of Elizabeth's Sea Dogs were thus legitimized.

Meanwhile, in the very short term, this was the end of the English slave-trading and commercially illicit expeditions to the Americas. In Africa (compared with the powerful Portuguese traders) the purchase of slaves lacked the necessary foundations, and in the Caribbean the English had none of the high quality textiles to dispose of, such as Rouen cotton, or extremely fine linens, that the French sold to the colonists for skins or tobacco. At the same time, the years 1568–1572 represented a political turning-point: the long years of peace were over, and they were entering a violent phase that was to last until the beginning of the seventeenth century. Open war did not break out between England and Spain until 1585, but privateering expeditions multiplied, with no less than 30 in eight years from 1570 to 1577.

Important political and religious factors compelled this conflict between the two kingdoms. In May 1568, Mary Stuart's escape to England threatened to unleash a counter-revolution in that country, supported by Spain and France. In the Low Countries, the Duke of Alba triumphed over rebels, and in France, the third civil war was England's chance to back La Rochelle with arms and silver.

English sailors joined up with French Huguenot pirates to attack the Catholic fleets of Spain, France, Flanders and Portugal. On the south coast of England, the ships carrying silver destined for the Duke of Alba's troops saw their cargo confiscated. This was a cold war pitting the English against the Spanish in Europe as much as in America, where Panama became the theatre of their conflicts.

English raids on Panama

Francis Drake, one of Lowell's mariners, had commanded the *Judith* on the third voyage in 1567. His impassioned Protestant faith drove him to avenge the defeat of San Juan de Ulua on his three voyages of 1570, 1571 and 1572 to the Panama isthmus, where he was aiming for the heart of the treasure route. In the course of the first two sparsely equipped voyages (two ships in 1570, only one in 1571), Drake managed to attack the Sagre estuary near Nombre de Dios, and carried off a booty comprising silver and precious textiles. Above all, however, he acquired a thorough knowledge of the conditions under which the treasures were transported, when the whole isthmus was bustling with men bearing silver from Peru, stockpiling it in Panama towards the Atlantic before the *flota* arrived. He thus knew of the presence on the portage route of the *cimarrones*, fugitive negro slaves who were always hostile to the Spaniards. In 1572, Drake, perhaps on the advice of the French pirate Guillaume Le Testu of Le Havre, who was protected by Coligny and had taken part in Villegaignon's expedition to Rio de Janeiro and joined the English, realized the Panamanian authorities' worst nightmare: an alliance between white pirates and black bandits.

Financed by Hawkins and the merchants of London, the expedition of 1572–1573 had a force of 73 men on two ships, the *Pascha*, 70 tonnes, and the *Swan*, 25 tonnes. They left Plymouth at the end of May 1572. However, the raid against Nombre de Dios began with a defeat, with the pirates relying on seizing treasure, but the *flota* had already departed. They turned away, and Drake had to be content with cruising the length of the coast of the Spanish Main for almost six months, with his crews exhausted by fevers. In January 1573, he had only around 30 men at his disposal, although success finally came thanks to making contact with the *cimarrones*. At the beginning of the year, in fact, the blacks had informed the English of the arrival of the *flota* from Peru in Panama. Guided by them, Drake's men set about surprising the mule convoys carrying treasure to the Atlantic coast. At Venta de Cruces, midway on the road over the isthmus, the bars of silver had already been taken; however, the pirates were unable to surprise the Spanish, to whom the blacks had remained faithful and had alerted, so the booty was meagre. In March, with the aid of the Huguenot Guillaume Le Testu, the raid was successful: 20 Frenchmen, 15 Englishmen and around 40 negroes surprised the convoy arriving from Venta de Cruces, two leagues from Nombre de Dios.

The pirates have befriended and are in league with the *cimarrones* of the hinterland, who are more than three thousand in number and who aid and guide them. They have stolen more than one hundred and fifty thousand pesos of gold and silver.

The *cabildo* of Nombre de Dios bitterly deplored Drake's boldness. The Spanish reaction, however, was brusque: soldiers arrived from Nombre de Dios and chased the pirates back to their ships.

Drake was back in Plymouth by August 1573, with treasure on board, but at the cost of heavy losses: two of his brothers and half his men had perished, the victims of Spanish bullets and yellow fever. Nevertheless, the *Carrera*'s weakness had been highlighted, and alliance with the *cimarrones* promised the success of subsequent raids. All of Drake's other projects, in 1577, 1585 and 1595, were marked by this desire, relying on the support of the rebel negroes in order to bring about the downfall of Panama, the gateway to Peru.

It is true, however, that for three years after this raid the English contented themselves with raids in the Caribbean, along the coast of Tierra Firme, the Spanish Main. But in 1576, Oxenham, one of Drake's old companions, took up the project of attacking Panama and its treasures, with the negroes' support. With rare daring, Oxenham, abandoning a frontal attack on the portage road, with the Spanish strengthening its protection, developed a new plan to arrive on the Pacific coast and attack ships coming from Peru on their way to Panama. At the heart of Cordillera, he discovered the villages of the *cimarrones* in the dense jungle that covered the slopes on both the Atlantic and Pacific sides, and set about constructing a light craft 'commanding twelve oars on either side', a fishing vessel that enabled the English to disembark at the entrance to the Gulf of Panama on the Archipelago de Las Perlas. On 15 August 1577 Panama's notables, stricken with panic, described this raid:

> Fifty Englishmen, fearing neither God nor Your Majesty, crossed the Gulf of Acla to the Gulf of San Miguel.[...]They went to the Las Perlas Islands where they took and stole a great quantity of pearls and jewels of gold and silver, giving seventy head of slaves employed in pearl fishing and trading, including women and children, to ten *cimarrones*. More keenly felt was the lack of veneration that they showed for the saints and the worship of God: they smashed images and the crucifix, upturned the altar, used the albs and the chasubles as cooking aprons and committed many other offenses.[36]

The Spanish, however, rapidly recovered, destroying the vessel that was to take the pirates back to England on the Atlantic coast and, most importantly, clearing the jungle of its gangs of *cimarrones*. Their capital, Vallano, was taken and at the end of 1577 the Spanish captured Oxenham, who was executed in Panama. In fact, he had acted alone and was not backed by the Queen, who could not countenance open warfare with Spain over Panama. As Andrews has emphasized, Elizabeth was a realist, not an imperialist.[37]

The *Carrera*'s defences were strengthened: two galleons were sent to Cartagena in order to cruise along the coast of Tierra Firme as far as Trinidad, and their efficient operations enabled six or seven French ships to be taken during 1578. They never again experienced a renewal of the direct attacks on the road over the isthmus. The attack Drake attempted in 1585–1586 showed equally disappointing results in Santo Domingo and in Cartagena. Elizabeth, finally having decided on war against Spain, hoped that seizing Cartagena, which was the gateway to the Caribbean, would paralyze the convoys. Francis Drake's expedition, financed by the Queen, with an armada of 17 ships with 2,000 men aboard, left Plymouth on 12 September 1585. Progress, however, proved difficult: 200 men died of scurvy during the three weeks that the voyage took from the Canaries to Dominica. At Hispaniola, the raid yielded only a minimal hoard. More spectacular was the raid launched against Cartagena in February 1586, but the town, informed of the English arrival, had time to evacuate a large part of its riches, so that pillaging did not bring in what Drake had expected. Having set fire to the cathedral, the Augustinian and Dominican monasteries and several houses belonging to the notables, Drake managed to obtain a ransom of 107,000 ducats. The result was still modest, because despite extravagant efforts, the treasure route was not eliminated, and some 10 months later, on 5 November 1586, Don Juan de Guzman entered Seville with the galleons from New Spain, bringing with him one of the largest treasures of the end of the century.

The reaction from the Spanish side was not to wait. Madrid sent additional galleons to defend the Atlantic fleets; well-armed frigates were used to send silver, as in 1588, when two galleons sped to Santo Domingo, Cartagena and Havana respectively, and Antonelli, an engineer, fortified Havana, Cartagena, and San Juan de Puerto Rico, the gateways to the Caribbean. Although the treasure was indeed well protected, the defences were not sufficient to preserve commercial activity in the Caribbean. They had not set up a local fleet suited to rid the Caribbean of the pirates that infested it. Of course, the entire Caribbean area east of Cartagena and Havana had no great strategic value, was not commercially very attractive, and was difficult to defend. There was a massive slump in Hispaniola's sugar plantations, and pearl production on Margarita had lost its value. Jamaica, Hispaniola, Puerto Rico and Venezuela were too far from the Mexican and Peruvian empires that were especially favoured for their precious metals. The Lesser Antilles, without Spanish occupation and peopled only by Caribbeans, were abandoned.

Operations as powerful as Drake's in 1585, or Hawkins' raid in 1595, remained exceptional, and ran up heavy losses. Far more frequent were the raids by one or two ships that were not suited to seizing hoards of treasure or garrisoning a town, but which had the important cumulative effect of contributing to unsettling the trade routes. The 74 expeditions numbering 183 ships, which took place from 1585 to 1603 from the English coast, dealt a severe blow to commercial relations between the colonies and even threatened the areas around Havana and Cartagena, where galleons suffering from a lack of silver and from impoverished crews very rarely took to the sea.

The Armada and the battle of the Atlantic

In 1585, Elizabeth and her ministers agreed on open war with Spain. Although the treasure route was not cut off in the Americas, they nevertheless believed for several years that they could deal a mortal blow to Seville's America by occupying the Azores archipelago, the port that was indispensable to returning galleons. On the other hand, the English had also hoped to block the Spanish war machine in the Low Countries by threatening first of all its marine supply routes. The Queen's objectives were not, however, entirely shared by her ministers, whose Protestant gentry mentality sought glory rather than profit at sea. Ralph Davis has shown how the English mentality changed: in 1540, France was where a gentleman sought honour, but in 1580, this was to be found on the Atlantic. Whereas Raleigh wanted to shatter the Spanish Empire, Elizabeth intended to take account of English interests in Europe: in the face of a Catholic France where the League was still a threat, it was better to help the Protestants to limit French ambitions. Moreover, the cost of all-out war could prove disastrous to a still weak England.

Nevertheless, by sending Drake to the Caribbean in 1585 to support the Dutch rebels, Elizabeth only managed to encourage Philip II to eliminate England. Plans for an expedition by an 'invincible' armada were therefore drawn up during 1586 while Elizabeth was still trying to negotiate. The King of Spain intended to sweep the sea clean: the Spanish Way, leading to Flanders via the Gulf of Gascony and the North Sea, was less expensive than overland routes, but since the 1560s communications in the Atlantic, from the north to the south, were dominated by the English in alliance with the Dutch and French Huguenot sailors.

This objective had to be reconciled with the other pole of Spanish politics, which was to reinforce the *Carrera* by providing the Azores archipelago, its essential way-station, with every security. In the summer of 1557 it was this defence of the treasure route that was successful in the end, a fleet having been sent at full speed to the Azores. After the annexation of Portugal in 1580, Spain's naval forces were strengthened by Portuguese sea-going vessels. In total, at Lisbon before the

Armada's departure Philip II could count on some 300 ships with a capacity greater than 57,000 tonnes. The cost, 10 million ducats, was impressive, six years' worth of the revenues of the English Crown, but this force entailed some considerable logistical weaknesses: insufficient supplies, weak artillery (this was the major handicap in their confrontation with the English), a lack of naval repair yards, and the poor state of health of crews too long immobilized before departure.

The English could provide a comparable opposing force of 140 vessels; the centrepiece of their fleet consisted of the Queen's 34 ships and, furthermore, they had excellent ship repair yards like Chatham at their disposal, while in Plymouth they had a large base at the entrance to the Channel.

Leaving La Coruña on 12 July 1588, Medina Sidonia's 130 ships, with 7,000 sailors and 17,000 soldiers on board, were to meet Parma's troops coming from Flanders with landing craft. Passing the banks of the Pas de Calais proved extremely difficult and at Gravelines insufficient artillery brought about the defeat of the Spanish fleet. It was prevented from returning to base via the Channel, which was blocked by the enemy, and, due to contrary winds, it had to go back towards the North Atlantic and return via Ireland, where a storm scattered many of its ships.

The scale of this defeat must not, however, be exaggerated. In fact, the English had the greatest difficulty exploiting it. In 1589, Drake proposed an expedition against Lisbon and Seville, then on to the Azores. By strangling Seville, City merchants hoped to gain new profits from the Portuguese Empire in the Indies and Brazil. At the same time, the Queen intended to destroy Santander and San Sebastian, where the remnants of the Armada had taken refuge, and only afterwards to start operations against Lisbon and the Azores. The results were pitiable: at La Coruña, as in Lisbon, the English were beaten back and were unable to reach the Azores. As yet, the Elizabethan state lacked the resources necessary to create a dominant sea power, and had to rely too much on private trade for capital and for a navy.

In 1590 and 1591, the Azores was the object of further English attempts, but with no decisive result. The galleons and carracks from the Indies continued to pass. Most importantly, under the leadership of Don Alonso de Bazan, the Spanish fleet was rebuilt: around 20 galleons managed to defeat the English at the Azores. Spain could once again appear to be a threat. Of course, in 1595, when Drake and Hawkins suffered disaster at Puerto Rico on the isthmus route, Essex succeeded in sinking the galleons in Cadiz, but he did not attack Lisbon, and neither did he destroy the fleet from the Indies. Despite further Spanish humiliations in October 1596, when her galleons were scattered by a storm off the coast of Cape Finisterre, the English expeditions against her ports on the Cantabrian coast or in the Azores ended in defeat.

For the English, the only realistic option was privateering operations on a reduced scale, which cumulatively, however, proved extremely costly to the enemy and ruined her trade in the Atlantic and the Caribbean. The 1590s saw the wave of English maritime offensives reach its peak. It was extremely popular, with the Protestant victory over the papist Armada celebrated in images and pamphlets, and Hakluyt sent out a message of maritime imperialism when he published his *Principal Navigations of the English Nation in the year following the Armada's defeat*.

The new Dutch arrivals from the end of the sixteenth century

Dutch privateering and illicit trading operations in the Caribbean were an essential element in the weakening of the Iberian Atlantic. Its first phase is bound up with the period of revolt preceding the truce signed in 1609 between Spain and the United Provinces, and the second followed the formation of the Dutch West Indies Company, created after 1621 for open warfare against the Iberians in the Atlantic. It saw Dutch businesses manage to settle a colony in Portuguese Brazil and the creation of an entrepôt for illicit trade in Curaçao and St Eustatius in the Caribbean, and one in Elmina in Africa for the slave trade.

In the first period, when a way was cleared for winning global commercial supremacy, the Dutch benefitted greatly from the position they still occupied until as late as 1580 in Seville's Atlantic. They provided the *Carrera* with some of its ships, while their merchants were active in the peninsula's ports, distributing American products across northern Europe and the Mediterranean, and finding commodities that the colonists valued. In 1585, when Antwerp, re-taken by the Spanish, saw its ships blockaded by Dutch control of the Scheldt estuary, Philip II decided to place an embargo on Dutch ships and goods in Spain and Portugal in order to crush the rebels' resistance. The Iberian peninsula's trade with the Baltic, which until this time had been taken on by the Dutch more than by the Hanseatics (in 1584, 93 Dutch ships had left the peninsula for the Baltic, compared with 51 Hanseatic ships), collapsed in a spectacular fashion.[38] There were only 22 such Dutch voyages in 1586, 12 in 1587, four in 1588 and three in 1589, and part of the trade passed into the hands of the Hansa towns where numerous merchants had come from Antwerp and were engaged in seeking a profitable refuge for new businesses.

Philip II, however, battling against great difficulties in provisioning the peninsula at the beginning of the 1590s because of extremely bad harvests, could not count on sufficient naval provisions and cereals through the Hanseatic network, and decided to lift his embargo in 1590. The Dutch completed 101 voyages from the peninsula to the Baltic in that year, and 169 in 1591. It was then that Holland and Zeeland became the great European entrepôt for products from the Iberian Americas as from East India, since the blockade of the Flemish coasts maintained by the rebels prevented Antwerp from continuing to play its role as the centre of Iberian colonial trade.

In 1598, King Philip III decided on a new embargo on Dutch ships and goods in the peninsula, which had a devastating effect.[39] Direct Dutch voyages from the peninsula to the Baltic fell from 107 in 1598 to only 12 in 1599, and 26 in 1600, while from Amsterdam to the peninsula they went from 201 in 1598 to 15 in 1599. By reducing the products arriving in the Low Countries from Iberia and Iberian America to a tightly controlled trickle, Madrid thought it could dismember the Dutch commercial networks in Europe. However, closing the Iberian peninsula to their ships forced the United Provinces to seek direct routes for accessing colonial wealth.

Émigré traders from Antwerp, such as Balthasar de Moucheron, Jacques de Velaer, and the brothers van der Meulen, were the first to create a slave-trading network in Guinea.[40] They were then joined by other Dutchmen such as the brothers Bicker. The first phase of their trade was devoted to trafficking in gold, ivory, rubber, and also sugar, from São Tomé, since the embargo prevented them from taking these products to Lisbon. Although there were more and more Dutch (from 1599 to 1608, no less than 200 Dutch ships made for the African coast), they only gradually took an interest in the slave trade. Their Caribbean trade did not emerge until relatively late, in 1593–1595. In 1596, Moucheron, the great merchant of Middelburg, sent two vessels to the coast of Venezuela; other ships were sent to Hispaniola, where their captains forged links with the Portuguese New Christians, who were descended from the Jews and had migrated to Spanish America and engaged in illicit trading.

The 1598 embargo was to have decisive effects for enhancing Dutch traffic in the Caribbean. The Dutch had to go on obtaining necessary products such as salt for the fish by finding new markets, since they could not get access to the Iberian peninsula. Thus in 1596, ships from Hoorn sailed to the Cape Verde Islands for salt, but three years later a new port opened when the Dutch fleet appeared on the Tierra Firme coast between Cumana and the Margarita Islands, at Punta de Araya. From the summer of 1599 to the end of 1605, 768 ships set sail for Araya for salt; one out of every 10 was loaded with expensive goods bought by the colonists at Maracaibo, Rio de la Hacha and Caracas, while the rest came as ballast.

The heightened value of products sold as contraband compensated for the relatively low number of ships carrying them: the finest cloths among the rich draperies they carried were sold to the colonists of New Andalusia from the Guaira Mountains in Trinidad in exchange for tobacco from the rich plantations of Nueva Ecija, near Cumana, or pearls from Margarita. According to the Spaniard Suarez de Amaya, in 1603, each inhabitant of Nueva Ecija was a *rescatador*, freely trading with the foreigners.[41] This trade, however, was still marked by violence, and on occasion the fishing boats used for smuggling did not hesitate to engage in attacking coasters from Cartagena or even the Greater Antilles.

The Dutch were also present in Hispaniola, Cuba and Puerto Rico, and each year from the beginning of the seventeenth century they employed some 20 ships there to sell linen cloth, draperies, paper and wines in exchange for the skins that were still produced in these islands. The contraband circuits were similar to those the French and English had used: anchoring their ships in inlets far from the Spanish garrisons of Havana, Santo Domingo and San Juan de Puerto Rico, they thus procured silver, pearls and some tobacco.

Spain's reaction, however, reorganizing its naval forces during the 1600s, was forceful: in September 1605, Seville sent 18 galleons to Venezuela, attacking the Dutch fleet at Punta de Araya, seizing several ships, burning others and proceeding summarily to execute a considerable number of mariners who, along with the famous Daniel de Moucheron, *el grand corsairo flamenco*, were hung from gibbets erected on the spot. The cultivation of tobacco was prohibited in the Cumana region and the colonies of Nueva Ecija were forced into exile. In Hispaniola, the north-west part of the island was also cleared of any Spanish presence, and its colonists were scattered. This was a scorched earth policy, which was ultimately very damaging to the Spanish economy in the Antilles.

While some in the United Provinces wished to transform the hitherto relatively peaceful expeditions into decisive aggression against the Iberian colonies through the establishment of a West Indies Company, the 1609 truce between Spain and the United Provinces put an end to these activities for the time. The far-off Caribbean salt circuit became useless, Iberia's ports were reopened and many merchants resumed their business connections with the Iberian Americas through Seville and Lisbon. It was in 1621, with the breaking of the truce and an embargo once again placed upon Dutch trading in the peninsula, that the Dutch were led to take up once more the invasion of the Iberian Americas, this time by creating the WIC, the West Indies Company. Contraband, which until this point had been the principal form in which they had intervened in the Caribbean, was replaced with expeditions for capturing treasures and settling colonies or large entrepôts for their businesses.

In Matanzas in Cuba in 1628, where Piet Heyn attacked the galleons off Vera Cruz, taking more than 15 million florins in booty, as much as in Brazil, where after initial defeats the company managed to lay its hands on the Portuguese cane sugar plantations in Recife and Pernambuco, the Dutch asserted their pre-eminence in the Americas. Indeed, during the first half of the seventeenth century, a new Atlantic was created, belonging to the merchants of Middelburg and Amsterdam. It was driven by a commercial revolution, and in the second half of the century, with the breakthrough of English trade under the Stuart Restoration, it was to result in turning the Atlantic into one of the essential bases of the wealth of north-western Europe's maritime powers.

Chapter 4

The Atlantic and the growth of the naval powers
The seventeenth century

In the seventeenth century, the Atlantic ocean was no longer the exclusive preserve of the Iberian monopoly. Rather, in the New World as in Africa, the north-western Europeans would demonstrate new ambitions to dominate trade and to set up their own areas of colonization. The Atlantic of precious metals, the age of the Hispanic *Carrera*, which prospered so well in the sixteenth century, would be succeeded by an Atlantic of plantations, first tobacco, then cane sugar, the latter of which would bring into being the institution of a system of slavery and slave-trading on a far greater scale to those of the Iberian Americas. Another Atlantic took form in the seventeenth century with the colonization and peopling of North America, from French Canada to the English colonies on the mainland. The Atlantic of the plantations inspired the first movement of northern European immigration to the New World. Based on cultural systems similar to those in Europe, it originated directly from the exploitation of the sea's riches in Newfoundland and throughout the entire North Atlantic, as far as Greenland and Spitsbergen.

The commercial and colonial empires of England and France would emerge during this Atlantic age and veer towards the development of a bitter rivalry between the two countries, before the Treaty of Utrecht established English predominance in 1713. From this date onwards, *Britannia ruled the waves*, and for almost two centuries the English reigned over the sea. None of this would have been possible, however, or the evolution of this new age would at least have been slower, had there not been a dazzling Dutch expansion during its first phase, in the first half of the seventeenth century and even beyond. It was really this that contributed most to giving a powerful boost to Atlantic trade, to favouring the establishment of the plantation system, and to creating indispensable commercial networks in Europe.

The precocity and scale of Dutch ambitions

In the position of parasites, or indeed predators who wanted to challenge the Iberian empires of the sixteenth century against a Spain strengthened by the annexation of Portugal in 1580, the north-western Europeans were content until the beginning of the seventeenth century to launch raids and piratical attacks. At first they did this in the Atlantic Mediterranean and the African coasts, and later in the Caribbean. They could not boast, however, despite the ambitions of a few, such as Raleigh or Gilbert in Elizabethan England, or Coligny in Valois' France, to have founded colonies capable of disputing Spain's imperial monopoly in the New World. Despite the lightning strikes of Hawkins or Drake, their actions were shown to be too weak to shake the *Carrera* whose strength was confirmed by its arsenals in the Caribbean, at Cartagena, Havana and San Juan de Puerto Rico, while at the same time, and with some vigour, continuing to undertake the transportation of silver to Seville where, at the end of the sixteenth and the beginning of the seventeenth centuries, record imports of precious metals were attained.

The 'upstart' merchants of Middelburg and Amsterdam were able to take advantage of the experience acquired by some amongst them in Antwerp or Lisbon, first to make a name for themselves in the illicit trade in the Spanish Main (the Venezuelan and Colombian coasts) and then to claim to found colonies. A merciless war with the Madrid Crown had made them believe in the success of their projects – in Pernambuco in north-west Brazil, on the one hand, and on the other, in the Caribbean and African entrepôts at Curaçao, Saint Eustatius, Elmina and Luanda.

The Dutch could draw on part of the wealth of Northern Europe, focused on the Atlantic trade, which experienced no crises, at least until the middle of the seventeenth century. The Mediterranean and Hispanic-colonial worlds of the Sevillian Atlantic, by contrast, simultaneously experienced a demographic downturn and economic decline. Meanwhile, thanks to the spectacular take-off in the production of precious metals, Sevillian traffic had stimulated economic activity but remained an exception, having more to do with the vagaries of Peruvian and Mexican mining than to real developments in the European economy. By contrast, Dutch navigation took its first profits from the mastery that the merchants of Amsterdam and the other ports of the Low Countries gained early on over the transportation of heavy goods from the Baltic and the Atlantic: seeds and wood, resin, potash and hemp. This trade sustained all the others, always requiring more ships and mariners, and exceptionally cheap terms for freight enabled the Dutch to gain supremacy in the Baltic, to the detriment of other merchants. In exchange for these Nordic products, they provided salt from the Atlantic coasts and France, from Portugal and Spain, and wines from France. Finally, after the middle of the fifteenth century, sales of herring, the staple product of the Dutch North Sea fisheries, also contributed to the wealth of the numerous ports of Holland, Zeeland and Flanders.

From the 1560s these trades employed, in Holland alone, almost 1,800 ships with 30,000 mariners,[1] who came not only from Amsterdam and Middelburg, but also from numerous ports in Fresia, Holland and Zeeland. But the developments that would lead to the establishment of the Dutch European entrepôt proper to the great commercial firms, emerged slowly. Up until Spain's seizure of Antwerp in 1585, Holland and Zeeland lacked two essential elements to sustain their commerce: on the one hand, the presence of large firms whose networks and capital might have been able to support trade; and on the other, the industries, especially in textiles, whose production would have stimulated carriage. On the eve of its fall, Antwerp had these assets and had begun the majority of its activities. After 1585, its merchants' departures for the northern Low Countries and the establishment there of powerful industries thanks to the migration of textile workers to Leiden and Haarlem, created the proper conditions for the growth of the Dutch international entrepôt. Thereafter things moved on very rapidly from the exchange of heavy goods between northern and southern Europe by means of the Dutch fleet, to a trade in light high-value goods, which played a decisive role in the Dutch 'breakthrough' in the first half of the seventeenth century.[2]

As Jonathan Israel strongly emphasizes, this shift was doubtless partially disguised at the end of the sixteenth century by the operation of two factors: first, there had been very important deficits in cereals in Mediterranean Europe during the 1590s, which contributed to strengthening the trade in seed from the Baltic southwards; also, the political bearing of the Spanish embargoes that closed the Iberian ports to the Dutch resulted in putting the brakes on the launch of the trade in valuable products that had begun in the Levant, and in the countries under Spanish influence, by the merchants of the United Provinces. By the last decade of the century, however, new Dutch merchants became interested in the exchange of rare and expensive goods – furs and caviar from Russia, spices, pepper and silks from the Levant. The predominance of the United Provinces developed slowly in the Mediterranean trade: in Aleppo, one of the great markets of the Levant, Dutch sales and remittances of silver in 1604 would still fall far short of their Venetian, French and even English rivals.[3] The war with Spain then constituted a further handicap and, as soon as the truce was signed, the United Provinces increased their trade in the Levant: in Aleppo in 1613, Dutch sales represented double those of the English (500,000 ducats against 250,000 ducats).

The United Provinces crossed a new threshold to accede to the domination of global commerce when the English and the French threw themselves into colonial ventures in the New World, in the Caribbean and in Virginia as well as in

New England and Canada. London and Paris had to leave a large share of the commercial exploitation of these colonies to the Dutch in order to provide for the daily requirements of their settlements and to bring them back into the global market. The two nations had to do this because they were far too completely absorbed with their political and religious disturbances until the middle of the seventeenth century. However, they also suffered directly from Dutch mastery of a far superior maritime and commercial technology, which took every advantage of the enormous loading capacities of their numerous, low-laden ships, and drew on rich networks of substantial capital.

The Dutch were to take their place in the North Atlantic fisheries, even in the large cod fishing areas from Iceland to Newfoundland where they could not contemplate mounting a challenge to the English, the Spanish and French Basques, or the Bretons; it was indeed their quasi-monopoly in herring fishing off the Scottish North Sea coast that released them to send cod fleets to Newfoundland. Very early in the seventeenth century the Dutch pinned their ambitions on whaling in order to obtain the oil, a commodity indispensable to everyday life, by means of which Europe lit its lamps and worked its textiles. By the middle of the century in Spitsbergen, the Dutch Compagnie du Nord and the privateers occupied an essential place and, after the 1620s, had greatly reduced their rivals' takings in the English Muscovy Company.

The Atlantic boom, in which the Dutch played the leading role, was in contrast to the downturn in the Mediterranean economies. The fortunes of the merchants of Amsterdam and the other towns in the United Provinces (Amsterdam did not represent the total wealth of the country by a long chalk) supported it beyond the mid-century. Meanwhile, whether due to the contraction of their trade in northern Europe towards 1650–1660, on which, until then, their growth had depended, or whether because of the new maritime and colonial ambitions of their English and French rivals, the Dutch had to share the spoils of the Atlantic that, until then, they had dominated. The measures taken by England and France to protect their shipping and their trade (the English Navigation Acts of 1651 and 1660, Jean-Baptiste Colbert's tariff-list and ordinances of 1664, 1667 and 1674) had a long-term effect. Added to this were the consequences of the naval conflicts, in particular those of the first Anglo–Dutch war of 1652–1654, where English seizures of enemy vessels amounted to a minimum of 1,000 ships and enabled the merchant fleet, which until then had been condemned to remain at a relatively low rank, to be rapidly enlarged.

Having experienced an uncontested zenith in their economic activity, based largely in the Atlantic, the United Provinces saw their growth slow down between 1650 and 1672, in the course of international disturbances aggravated by the war between Louis XIV's France and the Dutch Republic in 1672. Their Hansard and English rivals (the former using neutrality from the outset of the conflict, the latter doing likewise from 1674 rushed to take advantage of their difficulties. The time of the United Provinces' economic hegemony was at an end.

If the Dutch Atlantic had never experienced a 'reversal of the secular tendency' (Braudel), but maintained its prosperity beyond the 1650s, then neither were the British and the French to undergo a turn-around in economic circumstances in the Atlantic. There were transferrals of power and, at the end of the seventeenth century, the maritime Atlantic, if not colonial, had come to be dominated by England, which had brought its 'apprenticeship' to an end when it became aware of a commercial revolution based on two principal elements, namely, a spectacular growth in exports to Europe, and the increasing movement of capital, often of foreign (Dutch) origin, necessary to the development of commerce.

Dutch participation in the Iberian Atlantic, 1609–1621

Barely two years before the signing of the Twelve Years' Truce between Spain and the United Provinces, a project to create a Dutch West Indies Company was put forward. Supporting this so as to make it an organ of warfare in the New World, the merchants of Middelburg, Amsterdam and Rotterdam also intended to develop the Guinea trade and the trade with Iberian America. Zeeland forts appeared during the same period on the Guyana coast and at the mouth of the Amazon. The states of Holland and Zeeland received petitions demanding that they undertake to send a convoy of troops and arms to these settlements. The Middelburg Zeelanders were the most zealous in wanting to pursue war, having made great use of privateering and illicit trade activities on the coasts of Brazil and the Spanish Main since the 1590s. Their spokesman was William Usselinx, who, when he published his pamphlet *A Demonstration of the Necessity, Utility and Profit for the Low Countries of Preserving Freedom of Trade with the West Indies*, challenged the Iberian monopoly, vaunted the merits of a company as an organ of overseas expansion, far more capable of ensuring the Republic's economic growth than the United Provinces' European trade alone, which was judged to be too vulnerable to enemy attack (the Spanish corsairs of Dunkirk were fearsome).

These projects were abandoned with the truce, however. In effect, the States General agreed to cease their attacks against Spain's fortresses, sea traffic and trade. The directors of the various Guinea companies in Amsterdam, Rotterdam, Delft, Utrecht and Middelburg protested that their trade in gold, rubber and ivory would be ruined. With the cessation of hostilities, Dutch sea traffic, which had suffered heavily from Philip II's embargo of 1598, took off again in the direction of the Iberian ports and the traffic between the peninsula and the Baltic, which was returned to Dutch hands after it had been run for many years by the Hansards. From 1608 to 1620, out of 156 ships each year linking the Iberian peninsula to the Baltic, 118 Dutch and 34 Hansard ships were counted, loaded with olive oil, almonds, grapes and above all salt from the Atlantic coasts of Spain and Portugal.[4] In this sea traffic, direct voyages from Setubal in Portugal to Danzig or Riga multiplied, and the Dutch shipowners were able to control the vast majority of the shipments of salt indispensable to the north European fisheries by reducing freights of a commodity that, at the beginning of the seventeenth century, was already at a fairly low level. They did likewise with the transportation of Nordic naval supplies such as wood, metals, hemp and tar, as they did with grain. Around 1630, already well into the Republic's golden age, Dutch minds proudly kept up the memory of the beginnings of this prosperity: 'During the Truce, we, through our skill and good management, swept all nations from the seas, took over nearly all the trade of other lands and served the whole of Europe with our ships.'[5]

The enthusiasm generated by this boom impelled Grotius to demand, in his *Mare Liberum* of 1614, the freedom of the Atlantic without, for all that, demanding the same for the Indian Ocean, where this freedom worked against the Dutch. The Dutch had just recently gained control of two-thirds of the trade at Sund, at the entrance to the Baltic: out of more than 6,000 ships passing Sund in 1608, more than 4,500 belonged to them,[6] at the expense of their Hansard, English and Danish rivals. To ensure the security of the traffic, once the truce with Madrid had been obtained, the Republic imposed without hesitation a *Pax Nederlandica* over the waters of the North Sea and the Baltic, allying themselves in 1613–1614 with Lübeck and Sweden against Denmark and forcing the latter to reduce its customs tariffs in Sund.

This incontestable boom enabled Holland to develop its exchanges in valuable Mediterranean and Oriental products, so that various textiles, pepper and spices began to arrive in the Amsterdam markets in ships of the Dutch Indies Company, while Seville also provided it with Castilian quality products. Fernand Braudel has endeavoured to show how the bond of money, strengthened by the truce between Spain and the Republic, served Holland's interests. For him, the secret of the 'termites' of Amsterdam lay in the patient extraction of piastres from Spain that were exchanged in Italy or the Levant for silks and other fine textiles. As buyers also of cochineal and indigo, indispensable for the dyeing of European textiles, the Dutch created the wealth of Spanish America. In particular, the importation into Seville of Nicaraguan or Guatemalan indigo, the principal resource of Spanish Central America, little valued by Seville which was waiting for Mexican or Peruvian silver, increased thanks to a European demand stimulated by Dutch commerce.[7] Furthermore, there was smuggling on a vast scale, and these imports were greater than that of Mexican cochineal.

These successes, however, had their downside. In the waters of the Caribbean, the salt fleets from Hoorn no longer loaded up in the Punta de Araya and the fine tobacco trade from Ecija in Venezuela had disappeared, Madrid forcing itself to respect their monopoly. The entrepôt at Lisbon for Brazil had taken on its full role, and Amsterdam's merchants, importing brazil wood, were the delivery men for the *asientistas*: farmers in Lisbon, and the monopoly's salesmen. While it is true that an important illicit trade was maintained and that the Dutch managed to transport perhaps a half to two-thirds of Brazilian sugar to Amsterdam,[8] there was also a certain paralysis in Dutch business's direct exploitation of the New World's resources. This was to lead to some merchants getting the project back on its feet for an aggressive Dutch West Indies Company, a company capable of making count Holland's right to navigate freely from America to Europe.

The Dutch West Indies Company and the great Atlantic projects

Although Holland was to bring renewed vigour to its war in the Atlantic with the founding of the West Indies Company, Seville's monopoly had realized record imports of silver on the eve of the signing of the truce and kept exchange at this pitch until the break of 1621 saw the 'reversal of the overriding direction of traffic'.[9] The tonnages of galleons in 1608 reached 70,000 tonnes, reducing to 40,000 and then 30,000 tonnes by the end of the 1630s and 1640s. Spain's transatlantic commerce with the New World went into a long-term decline. It has, however, been shown that the fall in silver production was not as drastic as has been put forward, and that a growth in smuggling was about to compensate for the reduced levels of silver arriving in Seville from the *Carrera*. It has also been established that the navigation of the Spanish Atlantic was maintained with some degree of regularity.[10]

At the same time, the continental European economy saw consignments of Nordic grain to the west fall in an impressive way: from more than 110,000 lasts in 1618, they fell to less than 40,000 in 1624 and bottomed out at only 12,000 in 1630. This reflected the direct effects of the bad harvests in northern Europe, and, over many years, of the Thirty Years' War, which disturbed exchange. In the longer term, after imports began to pick up again at the end of the 1640s, thanks to bad harvests in the west, the trade in grain from the north entered into a long period of decline after 1650, by virtue of a lowering in demand in the west where agriculture was becoming more productive. However, the long period of expansion throughout the sixteenth century was prolonged in northern Europe until the middle of the seventeenth century, and the trade in textile fibres, linen and hemp was to compensate for the decline in cereals.

For the United Provinces, it was not so much the fluctuations in European commerce that hampered exchanges but rather the war with Spain, which began again in 1621. The relative insecurity created for Dutch navigation – more by the Dunkirk corsairs than by the Spanish fleet – caused an increase in the traffic of their Hansard and English rivals. The effects of the embargoes vigorously imposed by Philip IV of Spain cannot be overlooked, since their consequences were spectacular: from 400 to 500 Dutch ships visiting the Iberian ports each year during the truce, there were now no more than 20 to 25 a year,[11] and the Hansards largely took over from the Dutch. From 1621 to 1641, fewer than 13 Dutch ships left the Iberian peninsula for the Baltic each year, while the Hansards were able to place some 29 vessels a year on this sea route, more than double that of their rivals. The creation in 1624 of the Almirantazzo in Madrid marked an important threshold in the increase of insecurity: it prefigured the confiscation of neutral ships and cargoes, while the principle of the flag under which the merchants sailed was no longer respected by the numerous corsairs from Dunkirk and Flanders: from 1627 to 1635, 413 Dutch merchant ships and fishing vessels were sunk, 1,606 captured by the Flanders squadrons and the corsairs.[12] The situation would only improve after Tromp's victory at Downs in 1639, with only 495 ships taken between 1641 and 1646.

The importance of the Dutch fleet made effective protection difficult: in 1636, in Holland alone, 1,750 ships and 600 fishing vessels were counted.[13] The French conquest of Dunkirk before the peace of 1647 finally brought appreciable improvements. In the Baltic, meanwhile, the Dutch immediately performed some spectacular actions, such as the naval demonstration of 1645, which saw a squadron of 47 warships and 4,300 men escorting the merchant ships.

In the face of these difficulties, overseas expansion made a striking contrast both in the New World and in Asia. The Dutch entertained great hopes and thought it possible that the Spanish and Portuguese Indies might be broken up. In the event, however, at least in the Americas, the expansion proved difficult, perhaps because of the late foundation of the West Indies Company, which was only created when the truce ended in 1621, more than 15 years after the initial project. Moreover, due to the resistance of Fresian ports such as Hoorn, which dominated the salt trade in the Caribbean and had no wish for a monopoly, it was only ready to act in 1623.

To attract shareholders, the company directors presented the general malaise of which Dutch trade was the victim in Europe's seas. The trade in Baltic grain had just collapsed there, and Madrid's embargoes reduced its shipments. They contrasted this with all the benefits of a colonial trade based on closely defended trading posts and plantations, which would give stability to commerce by expanding Dutch markets.

This propaganda was only partially successful, and the share subscription for the company was rather slow in taking off. The largest investors were a few merchants who had played a major role in the first expansion in the Caribbean, in Brazil and Guinea: Bartholotti put in up to 100,000 florins, while Balthasar Coymans risked 20,000 – both men belonged to a group of merchants who were immigrants in Antwerp and who gave new vigour to Dutch trade. The Regents' oligarchy emerged as the most favoured, without however being able to claim to monopolize investment, or even manage it. In particular, Amsterdam's share was not very high in relation to the town's importance, making a total of 1,700,000 florins from a share issue greater than 6,600,000. It was in certain towns in the interior, far from the sea, where religious and political zealotry fuelled heightened efforts in the war against Spain (the company had also to be an instrument of aggression against the Iberians), that the most active participation could be found. Leiden and Utrecht contributed 270,000 and 215,000 florins, Groningen 400,000.

The projected action against Portuguese Brazil is explicable in terms of interests already held by Dutch merchants in the trade with Lisbon before the embargoes: from 1609 to 1621, the majority of Brazilian sugar was transported in their ships. Moreover, before the truce, they had practised pirate raids against Pernambuco, in the heart of the richest cane sugar plantations, attacking Recife in 1587 and 1595 with the Englishman Lancaster; in 1604, seven Dutch ships forced their way into the port of Bahia, took a ship laden with cargo and burned another. Brazil's wealth also attracted the French, due to their trade in brazil wood and sugar, but in 1615 the Frenchman La Bavardière surrendered at San Luis de Maranhon, marking the ultimate failure of French attempts.

In 1623, after having seized 70 Portuguese merchant ships in Brazil, the company attempted to take Bahia by force, swiftly dispatching 23 large ships and a few smaller vessels to that port in May 1624. The capture of the town yielded a booty of 3,900 crates of sugar and brazil wood, but after the departure of the Dutch fleet at the end of July, a Spanish mission hastily assembled by Olivarès in Cadiz and Lisbon enabled Spain to recapture Bahia in April 1625. In the same year, the Dutch suffered bitter defeats in Puerto Rico in the Greater Antilles and in Elmina in Guinea. The company did not manage to establish itself in Brazil until 1630, undergoing a further defeat off Bahia in 1627, where Piet Heyn had to content himself with a raid yielding 2,700 crates of sugar.

These defeats could not disguise already remarkable successes. First in Africa, where they were developing their trade, importing 12 million florins of gold between 1623 and 1636, not to mention the trade in rubber and ivory. Above all, there was Piet Heyn's famous attack of 1628, in which he seized the vast majority of a New Spanish silver convoy in the Bay of Matanzas, close to Havana: 15 million florins of silver were taken by his men. Added to this was the loss of an entire year's worth of indigo exports from Guatemala and cochineal from Mexico, the most important cargoes, other than precious metals, carried by the galleons. A wave of madness gripped Amsterdam after this haul of treasure, impelling the further development of the Brazilian adventure, albeit with insufficient funds. Amongst the successes must also be placed the numerous captures, some 547 ships between 1623 and 1636; the value of their sugar cargoes alone reached almost 8 million florins.

It was even more important to accept the necessary heavy investments: in wages alone, paying the sailors and the troops, the company spent 18 million florins in the 13 years between 1621 and 1636, an equivalent undertaking to that of funding the United Provinces' army against Spain for more than a year and a half.[14] During these same years, some 220 ships had been bought, as well as guns and munitions.

Nevertheless, in 1630, all hopes were pinned on Brazil. An impressive armada was sent there, comprising 3,780 sailors on board 35 ships, accompanied by 3,500 soldiers; the firepower with which these vessels were equipped was raised to 1,170 canon. The Dutch war machine put an end to the resistance at Recife and reinforcements of 42 ships and 4,000 soldiers hurried there four years later, giving the colony a wide reach. Upon the arrival of the new governor, Jean Maurice de Nassau, in 1637, the future of Dutch Brazil looked highly promising thanks to the restarting of sugar production, making Pernambuco, close to Recife, one of the largest of the world's producers. Its conquest allowed Amsterdam to dominate the European market for a period of a few years: the combined imports of private merchants and the company in actual fact went from 5,687 crates in 1638 to 14,542 crates in 1641, then, it is true, to fall again, although only gradually, since there were still 10,739 and 10,772 crates in 1642 and 1643, then 8,598 and 7,279 crates in 1644 and 1645.[15]

After 1646, the real decline set in. It can be explained both by the effects of the Portuguese renewing resistance in Brazil and by the spectacular growth in production in Brazil that still remained in Portuguese hands, around Bahia and Rio de Janeiro. Competition for Portuguese sugar on the European markets became fierce: in 1641, Lisbon had received 20,000 crates; in 1645, its imports climbed, according to Frédéric Mauro, to some 40,000 crates.[16]

The restoration of the Portuguese economy's superiority in the end ruined the company's shareholders; on the other hand, it favoured the interests of certain Dutch merchants. The proclamation of Portugal's independence in 1640 effectively allowed the Dutch ships freedom to resume their navigation to Lisbon, which thus escaped the Spanish embargoes. Out of 98 foreign ships entering the Tagus in 1643, there were 54 Dutch against 16 Hansards and 22 English; in 1647, out of 107 ships, there were 49 Dutch, 19 Hansards and 34 English. Rivals to the Dutch over the Atlantic routes began to show up in Lisbon, as, indeed, they did in Brazil. Genoans, and Germans from Lübeck and Hamburg, were going to the Azores to take on emigrants for Bahia or Rio de Janeiro. The Dutch merchant, however, was still the most powerful.

International networks and a sugar industry still far and away the foremost in Europe, sustained the activities of the Dutch. Along with naval construction, sugar refining absorbed most capital in the middle of the century, since the merchants of the United Provinces exported to the whole of Europe: to France and England, as well as Poland, Sweden, Denmark, Bohemia, Austria, Moravia and Germany. In Amsterdam, immigrant Jews from Lisbon played a major role in this industry and in the sugar trade.

Already well established in the slave trade before their conquest of Brazil, although more by seizing Portuguese traders' cargoes off the Brazilian coasts than by trading in Africa, the Dutch developed this trade at the same time as the sugar economy. The Pernambuco *engenhos* had to be supplied with a labour force and the needs of Spanish America had to be met by illicit trade. The year following Jean Maurice de Nassau's arrival in Recife, the Portuguese trading post of Elmina reverted to the Dutch and the latter also settled in Angola in Luanda, and on the island of São Tomé where ships replenished or 'refreshed' the cargoes taken on in Elmina and in the other trading posts in the Gulf of Guinea. From 1636 to 1645, almost 24,000 slaves, more than 2,500 a year, were sent to Brazil from Angola alone. They were transported by company ships, which maintained their monopoly over the slave trade while the sugar trade was open to private traders. Slaves destined for Curaçao became more and more numerous, and after capturing the island in 1634, the Dutch had an excellent port close to the coasts of the Spanish Main in Venezuela and Colombia, where the traders hoped to find new outlets.

Meanwhile, when the Portuguese *moradores*, the plantation owners of Recife, heavily indebted to the company, began to stop buying slaves and went into open revolt after 1646, the Elmina merchants, like those in Curaçao, experienced immense difficulty in trying to sell stocks that were too large. Curaçao, too far from the indigo plantations in Guatemala, Nicaragua and Vera Cruz, had been able to absorb the slaves to cover the demand for manpower in the Mexican mines, but did not live up to the hopes of the slave merchants. These difficulties were to force the Dutch to seek a market in the Antillean plantations to which to send their captives, and to develop a new sugar economy. In fact, the downturn experienced by Dutch Brazil was accelerating and in January 1654 Recife surrendered. For the company, its finances exhausted in the colonial effort, the disaster had begun much earlier. The peace with Spain of 1647 had moreover removed its *raison d'être*, and the war against Iberian America was over.

A new Atlantic age: the Antillean plantations

The Dutch had been able to draw on the enormous resources of the Iberian Atlantic empires, rerouting a share of the produce to Amsterdam's advantage, and to the detriment of Lisbon and Seville, while nevertheless remaining unable to grow beyond an intermediary rank and become a true colonial power. The defeats in Brazil and the difficulties in being able to find in Curaçao the necessary Spanish American markets, caused them to redirect their traffic to the Caribbean. They never owned any plantations, since, although they may have been excellent for slave entrepôts and the exchange of goods, the rocks of Curaçao and Saint Eustatius did not provide soil suitable for plantations. They did, however, offer irreplaceable services to the new plantation colonies of the north-western Europeans: the English in Barbados and the Leeward Islands; the French in Martinique and Guadeloupe. The Marrano Jews (the New Christians) who, in Lisbon and Antwerp, had already played a major role in the redistribution of colonial produce throughout northern Europe, had settled in Amsterdam where their experience in commerce and sugar refining became extremely precious.[17] They had also set themselves up in Dutch Brazil and after the surrender of Recife some took refuge in Europe, in Holland and England, while others left Brazil to reach the Caribbean, where they were to establish powerful networks, be it in Curaçao or on the islands of Barbados, the Leewards, then in Martinique and Guadeloupe in the 1650s. There, they introduced sugar cultivation and refining. The Marrano Jews and the Dutch were the essential agents in the establishment of a Caribbean Atlantic developed around the sugar plantation.

As Spain and Portugal had done in Central and South America, England and France founded and populated colonies in North America which proved able to develop forms of subsistence agriculture that meant they had no need to resort to importing vital everyday provisions. They were able, at least in the English mainland colonies, to develop their own commercial networks, even if, in the southern colonies, tobacco from Chesapeake turned into an export crop strictly dependent on the European markets. This characteristic of the settlements remained, and their inhabitants increased, both by demographic growth and immigration.

In the Antillean plantations, the Europeans could not survive for long on their own resources. Economies were created in which invested capital, often coming from abroad, played a predominant role around strictly specialized production, with a view to responding to market demands. The state retained a presence in the Iberian Atlantic economy in order to control production and transportation. Also maintaining a presence within this economy were the Dutch, the Genoans, the Florentines and the Germans, who invested their capital but only developed a large-scale plantation agriculture in the nearby colonial areas where transport costs for slaves and goods were not too high. Similarly, Nicaragua and Guatemala in Spanish Central America, despite favourable conditions for the plantation of cocoa and indigo, saw no plantations develop with a dynamism comparable to their counterparts in the Antilles. In the Iberian Atlantic, only the Mediterranean

Atlantic, at Madeira and the Canaries, and Brazil witnessed large-scale sugar plantations.

It is therefore necessary to distinguish between the 'near' Atlantic – the archipelagos of the Eastern or Mediterranean Atlantic – and, as in Brazil and the Antilles, a 'distant' Western Atlantic where only the mining economies attracted capital, the high value of the treasure compensating for the higher transportation costs. More than in Madeira or Brazil, however, there developed right from the start in the sugar plantations in the Antilles a 'savage capitalism',[18] where the search for maximizing profits driven by constant adaptation to the demands of the international markets was in operation right from the start of the sugar plantations. Of course, Cromwell and Colbert, as defenders of the colonial treaty, attempted to reserve the produce of the Antillean colony for the needs of their home countries alone, and to turn their colonial possessions into protected markets, keeping foreigners out of colonial trading in accordance with the laws of exclusive rights. However, there were several wars consequent upon international violations of this law, and the geography of the islands left them open to illicit trade: their jagged coasts provided a great deal of cover for smuggling, and foreign colonies were close by. The development of a plantation culture for the European markets, such as tobacco or cane sugar plantations, strictly limited the production of provisions, leaving the Caribbean area wholly dependent for the supply of foodstuffs on either the home countries or, more profitably, on the North American colonies. Very early on, the 'New Englanders' maintained tightly connected networks for supplying foodstuffs, flour, fish and wood, and buying sugar or molasses, a by-product of the refining process, for manufacturing rum.

The English presence in the Atlantic

Subject to Dutch commercial hegemony over many years, even in the English Antilles, the sugar plantation was going to become progressively freer from it much earlier in English than in French possessions. There had in fact been a progressive erosion of the Dutch advantage due, on the one hand, to the application of strict measures to protect the home countries' trade, and on the other, to the consequences of the naval wars that pitted England and France against the United Provinces.

British Atlantic navigation

The mercantilist doctrine that presided over the English and French measures were applied by the strongest states, in Cromwell's England during the Restoration following the end of the civil war, and in Louis XIV's France after the Fronde. The English Navigation Acts of 1651 and 1660, like the French ordinances of 1664 and

1673, had as their object the elimination of the Dutch from trade in the two countries' American colonies. These measures were taken despite the hostility of the plantation owners, who wanted only to transport their products at the best price, something the Dutch, until this point, had managed very well. It was, however, on the English side that the plan to be free of the Dutch intermediaries succeeded most quickly. There was a simple reason for this, which was the remarkable increase in the size of the English merchant fleet, which had come about through England's three wars against Holland, in which the English had made a large number of captures. This was especially the case at the time of the first war in 1652–1654, in which they were able to make a minimum of 1000 captures thanks to the actions of the navy and the corsairs. The tonnage then seized from the Dutch, according to Ralph Davis, may have amounted to the equivalent of the entire English merchant fleet.[19] Above all else, these ships were of very high quality and were suited to all kinds of traffic, so that they could be steered by smaller crews and loaded up with heavy cargoes. Their acquisition enabled British commerce to enjoy a new competitiveness amongst European trade in northern as well as in Mediterranean Europe, which ensured the best outlets for transatlantic commerce by re-exporting the produce of the Caribbean plantations.

The English merchant fleet, still only 115,000 tonnes in 1629, climbed at the end of the Restoration to some 340,000 tonnes,[20] and the tonnages the fleet required to serve the overseas possessions, which stood at 126,000 tonnes in 1663, grew to more than 190,000 tonnes in 1686. In 1664, London had seen 45 ships leave for the American Islands; in 1686, their number quadrupled and it was of course the Antillean plantations that stimulated the majority of this traffic, since, between the same dates, sailings from London destined for the English mainland colonies had barely doubled.[21] English ships were happy to come to Newfoundland, where the activities of their cod-fishing fleet reached its peak before the civil war, to take the cod from the New England fishing boats. Iceland, which had attracted a quarter of the English ships in 1615, was in overall decline, and in Spitsbergen, dominated by Dutch whaling, English fisheries had been in complete decline since the 1660s.

The success and the limits of English trade in the Caribbean

The spectacular growth of its fleet after the Stuart Restoration, pursued in the aftermath of the Glorious Revolution, enabled England to experience a remarkable boom in exports of American produce, both from the plantations in the English Caribbean (Barbados, the Leeward Isles, Jamaica) and from those in Spanish America, where merchants practised smuggling. In this, England had the basis of a commercial revolution constituted by the opening up of new markets with the aid of close-knit commercial networks.

The activity of the commercial firms established in London, where they made their fortunes in the latter half of the seventeenth century, became the most important weapon in the success of this commercial revolution. The protectionist environment created by the Navigation Acts doubtless facilitated economic growth, but they nevertheless recognized already existing trade that they had not created and, following their own interests, these merchants did not hesitate to break free of them.

In effect, these firms controlled both the importing of colonial products into England and their redistribution throughout Europe. Following the beginnings of the Reformation, they scored a partial success in replacing the Dutch networks with their own trade. A share of their power was confirmed in the Antillean world. In order to set up a large-scale cane sugar agriculture, in Barbados at first and then in the Leeward Islands and Jamaica, they in fact had need of capital that came originally from the Dutch. Of course, in the beginning, during the pioneering phase, cane cultivation was still combined with other crops. Fertile soil was required and these crops would make the land rich. Thus in Barbados there was an expansion in small-scale operations simultaneously devoted to tobacco, indigo and cotton as well as cane sugar. Small-scale mills meant that processing the sugar took rather a long time. In his journey to Barbados in 1658, the Frenchman Charles de Rochefort was struck by the small dimensions of these mills, that had been adapted to suit fields of similarly modest scale:

> Many of the inhabitants are not yet able to have a sufficiently large boiler and to procure for themselves the great machines in which the canes are ground, but have little cylindrical mills set in motion by two or three men or drawn by a single horse....With one or two boilers, they purify the juice obtained and make a good sugar.[22]

However, the scale of the properties and the mills grew rapidly. In 1647, when Richard Ligon visited the plantation of one Colonel Hilliard in Barbados, he recognized the model of the great Brazilian *engenho*: the field was more than 200 hectares and was cultivated by 100 black slaves. The cane was grown over a little more than 100 hectares, tobacco, cotton and ginger were spread over a dozen hectares, with places for foodstuffs – manioc, maize, potatoes – occupying about 30 hectares while the remainder was reserved for pasture for the animals required to work the mill and the harvesting carts, or for the wood to provide fuel for the boilers. The price of land climbed quickly: in 1642, Hilliard had paid £400 sterling for his 200 hectares, while five years later, Samuel Modyford had his purse emptied of almost 20 times as much – £7,000 sterling – for barely half.

Paying for land and buying slaves cost a great deal, and the first profits to be made were eagerly awaited. Of course, the colonists formed associations to procure capital, but more often than not they turned to the services of Europe's merchants. The most prominent among those who provided this indispensable credit were from Amsterdam, at least until the 1660s. They had no problem about waiting for a year and a half, indeed, even longer, to have the funds they had advanced return to their possession and, most of the time, demanded no interest. In fact, the cost of borrowing money was quite significant, since the plantation owner had to adjust the advances while finding his bills for European goods and slaves become more expensive. In his mid-century *Description of Barbados*, John Scott presents the Dutch as

> the great assistants to the Plantations since they give large credits to the inhabitants and during the misfortune of the civil war in England, they administered all the trade in the western colonies, provided the islands with negroes, coopers, boilers and many other things.[23]

The Navigation Acts passed in 1651 and 1660 legalized the political will and the desire of certain groups of merchants to remove from the Antilles the Dutch merchants, who had been too successful. Passed under Cromwell, the 1651 Act protected the interests of the home country, albeit not completely. In effect, it determined that no colonial product would be imported into England or Ireland, or into any other colony, unless by way of English ships, and that European goods would only be sent to the colonies on board these same ships or in craft belonging to the country producing the goods. However, since the colonies' trade was not restricted solely to England, they were able to send their products to the European continent while also providing themselves with goods produced in these countries.

The Act of 1660, at the start of Charles II's reign, was far more restrictive. It required the importation of certain 'denominated' colonial products, such as sugar, tobacco, cotton, indigo, ginger and dye-woods into England before they could be re-exported to foreign markets, which could no longer directly receive these goods. Foreign goods were not excluded from the colonies, but could only enter them by way of England where protectionist laws would be levied in order to preserve English interests. The same laws affected colonial products coming from other European countries imported into England.

In application, however, this regime showed its limits in its first years. On the one hand, it provoked the anger of the plantation owners who, until then, had been closely bound up with Dutch commerce. In 1664, plantation owners in the Leeward Islands of Antigua, Montserrat and Saint Christopher demanded that free trade be re-established 'due to the unbearable difficulties' bearing down on their exchanges.[24] The islands of Saint Eustatius and Saba, lying no more than a few miles from the Leewards, displayed ample provision, by the Dutch, of slaves and European goods that the colonists avidly sought, so that illicit relations were maintained between these Dutch entrepôts and the English (and French) plantations. In 1671, the great majority of the produce from Nevis and Antigua was transported to Saint Eustatius on Dutch ships, from where they left for Amsterdam, where the sugar was christened 'Saint Eustatius sugar'. In this way, the plantation owners were economical with the laws that London had imposed on the entry of their goods into England and found the goods they wanted. The necessary foreign connections, particularly with the Sephardic Jews from Brazil, were numerous amongst the English possessions.

The governors of these islands were not unaware of the many pressures of which they were the object and often, won over by corruption, applied these acts less than rigorously. Even in Barbados, in 1666, despite being some 300 miles distant from the Dutch entrepôts, Governor Willoughby dared to write: 'the life of all the colonies depends on the freedom to trade'.[25] He said this despite the fact that England had been absorbed in its second war against Holland for more than two years, with the exclusion of the Dutch from colonial trade at stake. After the peace of 1667, the governor of Antigua allowed the Dutch and the French onto his island. As on Nevis, Saint Christopher and Montserrat, Antigua's coasts were extremely jagged, replete with many sheltered inlets, offering a smuggler's paradise so that the foreigners could supply the plantation owners and ensure their outlets with impunity.

In 1673, London replied to the many violations of the Navigation Acts, hitting its own colonists on the mainland who had already shown themselves to be the most zealous smugglers. From now on the laws would be applied to all 'denominated' products transported from one colony to another. They were aimed at the 'New English' merchants of Boston, Salem, New York and Philadelphia, who transported sugar and other colonial products directly to Europe while ignoring English stopovers. In a petition of 1676, London's merchants showed the importance of such trade:

> All kinds of goods produced in Europe are directly imported into New England and transported from there throughout every one of the King's colonies in America, to be sold far less expensively than it would cost to ship them to England. In exchange, they take colonial goods shipped to Europe without coming to England. This brings great harm to our country's navigation, depresses the King's receipts, causes trade to decline and impoverishes many of His Majesty's subjects.[26]

English traders and Europe

On the other hand, even when the acts were seen to be applied, it became apparent that they had unexpected effects, at least during the earliest years. In his *New Discourse of Trade* of 1669, the London merchant Sir Josiah Child proudly emphasizes that his country had eliminated raw Portuguese sugar from the European market and reduced the price of refined sugar in Lisbon. According to him, the Brazilian fleets that used to bring from 100,000 to 120,000 crates of sugar into Lisbon now brought no more than 30,000, augmenting the profits of the Barbados plantation owners.[27] The sugar from this colony being imported into London had in effect gone from 7,061 tonnes in 1655 to an annual average of more than 10,000 tonnes in 1699–1701, while from Jamaica and the Leeward Islands, the sugar imported in minute quantities in mid-century had risen to an annual average of more than 12,000 tonnes by the same date. From 1682–1683, the English islands put almost 19,000 tonnes on the market, much more than the French colonies which yielded less than 10,000 tonnes (although their consign-ments had doubled in less than ten years) and, above all, more than Dutch Surinam, whose sugar exports did not exceed 2,524 tonnes.[28] Still at 29,000 tonnes in 1650, Brazilian exports collapsed and amounted to no more than 17,000 tonnes at the end of the century.

This 'exuberant' wealth creation, however, already present in Barbados by the middle of the century, then in Jamaica from the 1670s, gave way on the eve of the Glorious Revolution of 1688 to an important recession, since the massive quanti-ties of English sugar entering the European market provoked a very pronounced price collapse. Moreover, overburdened with customs charges and bearing the costs of re-exportation, the London firms were not in a particularly favourable position to trade large quantities abroad at lower and lower prices.

However, this situation, destabilizing, 'savage' competition, gave the strongest the chance to raise a challenge to the market which resulted in the establishment of new commercial structures in America's plantations, which we have to say subjected the plantation owners to the domination of trade.

A good example of these traders managing to dominate the markets is provided by the case of Charles Marescoe during the years 1660–1670. Originally from Lille in the Spanish Netherlands, Marescoe, from the age of 22, associated himself with a London merchant originally from Hamburg, in order to engage in the trade between Scandinavia, the Iberian countries and the Mediterranean, and to maintain close relations with the Hanseatic base.[29] Belonging to London's Huguenot colony, Marescoe was able to form family alliances that would give him the support of the largest traders: his brother-in-law, Peter Joye, was a director of the Royal African Company and a supplier to the Admiralty. He developed his networks by making Hamburg out to be a privileged place, since there, London's merchants would find the entrepôt necessary to the growth of their re-exportations to Europe, capable of competing effectively, owing to the wars, with Amsterdam and other Dutch ports and cities.

The great port of the Elbe had access to a vast hinterland through which colonial, Mediterranean and Asiatic goods could be redistributed. Relations with Hamburg contributed a great deal to improving England's place within the world market in the 1660s. From Marescoe, Hamburg received grapes from Xanthi and Malaga, and especially the sugar from the Antilles where production in the Leeward Islands and Barbados had already outstripped Portuguese Brazil. In 1668, Marescoe distributed one-third of his shipments of sugar through Hamburg, although he worked less with Amsterdam.[30] Without colonial posses-sions, neutral throughout all the century's naval maritime wars, Hamburg became a market where merchants from several maritime powers competed mercilessly. Its population amounted to only one-tenth of London's, and a quarter of Amsterdam's, but its trade gathered together merchants from the four quarters of the earth and an enormous body of Dutch, Flemish, Portuguese and English knowledge and experience. Particularly expert in international payments, they made the city play a major role in the negotiation of letters of exchange.

However, the market underwent phases in which there were gluts of sugar, cotton and indigo from Barbados and the other Antillean islands, as well as from Brazil, Cyprus and Guatemala. Prices fell and in addition to the regular arrivals from British and Dutch ports there were ships carrying illicit merchandise that did not respect the Navigation Acts and entered Hamburg having come directly from the Levant or the Antilles, their cargoes altering the market's dealings. Thus, English ships came *adroittura* from Barbados and Jamaica paying no attention to going through the British entrepôt. Moreover, Hamburg was also being provided, equally directly, with sugar through Lisbon, cotton from Smyrna and Cyprus and indigo from Guatemala through Amsterdam.

The important profits realized in London by merchants like Charles Marescoe through their re-exportations did not therefore come about without having to go through such competition. Meanwhile, after 1674, the British made their country's neutrality work to their advantage during the maritime war pitching France against the United Provinces, and London's triumph was confirmed rela-tively soon. In 1667–1668, Amsterdam imported less than 3,262 tonnes of sugar; in the same period, London was bringing in just under 9,000 tonnes.[31] Getting as quickly as possible out of a war that 'caused poor trade, almost all merchants being without sales', the re-exporting merchants in London who had effectively seen their consignments fall in 1673, took back the initiative on the Hamburg market. They did this while the city was experiencing the effects of a long depres-sion and while the supply of colonial commodities in London had become overabundant. A few, however, knew how to adapt to these difficulties, taking

110

orders and buying while speculating, it is true, on present and future political events, such as an imminent war between England and France in 1675, or, a year earlier, the brilliant naval campaign of the Frenchman François D'Estaing against the Dutch islands.

London's success

The often risky, always patient work of trading explains the fact that success returned to London through the re-exportation of colonial commodities right up until the end of the century and, at the same time, through their importation. Arrivals of ships of Caribbean origin made London into England's largest port for the Antilles on the eve of the Glorious Revolution: in 1686, 225 ships arrived from the English islands with Bristol, the second largest Antillean port, receiving 42 in 1687.[32] The ships departing for the Antilles, with 161 craft leaving London in 1686 and 56 leaving Bristol in 1687, puts London in the same position in relation to Bristol.[33] This volume of traffic came well above that of North America, despite the importance of tobacco imports from Chesapeake: London received 110 craft from Virginia, Maryland, Newfoundland and New England in 1686; Bristol, 31.

This activity rested on re-exports amounting to more than half the sugar imported, which was sent on to Hamburg, Holland and France until the 1680s. It would then be reduced due to a growth in internal consumption and French imports from Martinique and Guadeloupe.

The same merchants who were active on Europe's markets set up trade on commission, an original system, in the Antilles. In Hamburg as elsewhere, more often than not the lowest price for sugar would prevail; this led the commercial firms to turn to this kind of trade. Avoiding sending cargoes of European produce and carrying colonial commodities at their own expense, they received products like sugar as a deposit from the plantation owners and merchants of the Antilles, undertook to find markets themselves, negotiated treaties with their correspondents and found them the necessary credit to purchase supply goods such as mill wheels, boilers, slaves and provisions. A system of contracts permanently binding these brokers to the plantation owners gave the latter assured crop sales and access to purchasing English and European goods. In this commercial environment, which was much to their advantage, London's merchants managed to create a *de facto* monopoly. To operate it, they required enormous financial reserves to cover the necessary advances, such as only London possessed. Already provided with privileged access to commerce between the West Indies and east India, to the slave trade with the Royal African Company and the Levant, through their links with the Antillean plantations, London found the means to slow down the development of outports such as Bristol for some years to come, until the end of the century. Merchants in the port of Bristol, like those later on in Liverpool and Glasgow, were in effect almost completely excluded from this trade on commission, and traded on their own account in the most difficult conditions by employing agents in the colonies who would purchase goods there in exchange for European merchandise consigned to them.

London, the nub of the credit and exchange networks that made this commercial revolution possible, was freed from Amsterdam's tutelage and at the end of the century became the most important European colonial entrepôt. Some amongst its merchants had not hesitated to invest in the Antillean plantations, as in the case of the famous Sir Josiah Child who, in 1672, as the sugar economy reached its pinnacle in Jamaica, entered into an association with a Port Royal merchant to settle a plantation of enormous dimensions – more than 550 hectares – on condition that he provide slaves, technical equipment and provisions.[34] Jamaica had by this date just put a period of buccaneering behind it, and for many years the island was far better known for the exploits of the corsairs than for its plantations, with Thomas Modyford, its first governor, preferring raw buccaneering raids to refined investments in cane sugar. Excellently situated facing the Gulf of Mexico and Central America, the island could inflict serious damage upon the Spanish colonies. The triumph of the sugar plantation here marked a new success for London's trade. In spite of the difficulties encountered in the wars at the end of the century, and despite sometimes making use of buccaneer capital (Morgan invested the booty from his raids on Panama and Porto Bello in it), the plantation reached a peak that betrayed the new dimensions of British power in the Caribbean.[35]

At the same time as the English Antilles were becoming America's primary producer of sugar at the end of the century (24,000 tonnes in 1700 against 18,000 in 1683), London also saw growth in its imports of dyeing products, essentially indigo and cochineal, which surpassed an average of £3,000 sterling per year in value from 1663–1669 to 1699–1701 (at the latter date, England's imports amounted to £85,000 sterling). This peak was reached thanks to the imports from Spanish America being made on English ships since, at the same time, English purchases in Seville and Lisbon of these same products were stagnating and Dutch imports were growing only slowly. This growth answered the needs of the English textile industry and a decline in the shipments of indigo from India. In exchange, and by way of links with illicit trade, the English introduced slaves from Jamaica required by the Spanish plantations. In this, however, they were in competition with their Dutch traders in Curaçao and, after 1701, when the Spanish trade was given to France, the bitter rivalry between the maritime powers became still stronger. Louis XIV's kingdom gave notice of its ever greater ambitions both in the trade with Iberian America and in the colonization of the Caribbean.

The French challenge: from Newfoundland to the Antilles

François I, King of France, was one of the first sovereigns to contest the Iberians' monopoly, and by founding the new port of Havre de Grace in 1517 he appeared to be mounting a challenge to Charles Quintus' Spain and Henry VIII's England. After all, a few years later he even sent the Florentine Verrazzano to the coasts of North America, supported by capital from the Normans and the Lyonnais. His will to contest the Spaniards' claims to sole rule of the newly discovered western lands compelled him to grant his support to an official expedition to North America in 1534. Jacques Cartier from Saint-Malo received the order to set sail for 'the New Lands' in order to locate 'certain islands and countries where they say great quantities of gold are to be found'. However, the harshness of the Canadian climate and the devastating effects of scurvy that killed many of Cartier's men as they wintered on the site where Quebec now stands, did little to encourage a repeat of such expeditions. It was further south, towards the tropical lands, that a few French Protestants lead by Jean Ribaut founded the short-lived settlement of Charlesfort in Florida, in 1562, which, three years later, was savagely laid to waste by the Spaniard Menendez de Aviles. We must wait for more than half a century to see the French contemplate settling once more, and more permanently, further south still in the Caribbean area, while at the same time having returned to follow the path of the Saint Lawrence estuary under Samuel Champlain in 1608.

The civil and religious wars in France during the second half of the sixteenth century did not favour colonial expansion. Even the privateering expeditions, of which, since the beginning of the century, there had been a great many, from Dieppe, Honfleur, Saint-Malo and La Rochelle towards Portuguese Brazil or Peru, and to the islands and coastline of the Spanish Main in the Caribbean, had begun to slow down. In fact, they were dependent on the capacity of the Huguenot ports of western France, which had been more weakened than strengthened by the religious wars.

The French ports in the North Atlantic

Meanwhile, trade in the North Atlantic and the fishing off Newfoundland still drew many more ships from France's Atlantic ports, from Rouen to Bayonne. Every summer, an increasing number of ships crossed the Atlantic to fish the Great Reef off the Saint Lawrence estuary and around Newfoundland, working as quickly as possible in order to return with fresh fish, salted on board, to the ports of France's Atlantic coast.

We can assume that the Bretons and the Basques were participating early on in the construction of an 'empirical' fishing route across the North Atlantic towards the cod stocks of Labrador and Newfoundland, the former since the second half of the fifteenth century, well before it was officially settled by Cabot and the Corte Real brothers. However, by the beginning of the sixteenth century, shipping became more important around Newfoundland. A large number of small ports on the Brittany seaboard, especially on the north coast from Saint Pol de Léon to Saint-Malo, were riven by a feverish race to equip themselves for large-scale fishing. By the middle of the century, their number was reduced and such enterprises became the exclusive preserve of three principal ports, at Binic, Saint-Malo and Nantes, the latter port having the advantage of an already bustling trade with the Iberian countries and the nearby availability of salt from the Guérande marshes, exported by Le Croisic. In 1517, a Newfoundlander equipped in this latter port had just transacted the first sales from the port of Gironde in Bordeaux,[36] while the latter appeared not to have been equipped for large-scale fishing before 1530. The primacy of Breton shipping would only be found again further south, in Bayonne, with the Basque expeditions.

Beginning officially, according to the available sources, at the end of the 1510s, this was a new kind of navigation. If, in Saint-Jean de Luz or Ciboure, they specialized in cod-fishing (and whaling) equipment, the variety of traffic led the merchants to alternate large-scale fishing expeditions with long navigations around the European coasts towards the Spanish ports in Galicia, or even in Portugal, as well as to Normandy's ports. Thus, cargoes of resin and cork left Bayonne to be exchanged for iron from Biscay, wool from Castile and in Lisbon, cotton, brazil wood and ginger.[37]

It seems that the same concentration of resources that took place in Brittany, to the benefit of Nantes and Saint-Malo, also came about in south-west France, benefitting Bayonne, Bordeaux and La Rochelle. Some 20 cod-fishing ships were rigged out in Bayonne in the middle of the century; Bordeaux went so far as to send some 60 ships to Newfoundland in 1560, while La Rochelle had sent 49 during the previous year. Four years later, Rouen was able to equip 94 cod-fishing ships.[38] In 1565, on the eve of the start of the religious wars, these three ports had been able to fit out 156 ships for large-scale fishing, solely for their own use, more than the English navigator Pankhurst had estimated in 1578. Pankhurst, making enquiries for some London merchants who were thinking of setting up a Newfoundland company, assessed the number of French ships present in Newfoundland during the 1560s at some 150 out of a total of 350 European ships. He then put activity in Newfoundland at 100 Spanish ships, around 50 Portuguese (after the fifteenth century, the fitting-out yards in the Azores became extremely important), and some 50 English ships. However, it seems his estimate was too low for the latter, as indeed it was for the French.

Cod fishing took on a largely international character, so that even in 1600 the

Spanish and the Portuguese disputed the cod off the Newfoundland reefs with the English and the French. Meanwhile, the Portuguese left the English to supply Madeira and Bahia, the Atlantic islands, and Brazil, areas which, with their slaves, created the highest demand for cod, which was for them a relatively cheap, high-quality foodstuff. In the seventeenth century, the Spanish market was already largely open to English ships, few of which took advantage of fishing themselves, but instead bought cod from the fishermen of New England and Maine. In this way, these *sack ships* supplied Cartagena, Alicante, Tarragona and Barcelona, taking wines, olive oil, fruit and money in return. From the beginning of the seventeenth century, the French, competing with the English for this market, found it, like their English rivals, to be the basis of a fruitful 'triangular' trade in the North Atlantic between their ports of registry, Newfoundland and the Iberian ports. The importance of the French cod fleet, which around 1580 had reached from 300 to 400 ships, cannot be explicated without the opulence of the outlet that was to be opened up to a still greater extent in the second half of the seventeenth century, thus establishing the great fortune of Saint-Malo.

A conclusive advantage to the French was the availability, south of Brittany, of the largest fitting yards in Nantes and Bordeaux, along with salt deposits that enabled them to supply the cod ships. There was also a very high domestic demand, stimulated by the Catholic observance required by the Counter Reformation in the time of Louis XIII and Louis XIV, which restricted the use of meat. Green cod, freshly salted on board ship, was thus sold in Nantes to be sent to Paris via Orléans, Auvergne and Lyon. English and French fishing methods were to prove quite distinct in this respect.

The English dried all the fish they caught and used less salt in order to sell their catches on the markets of Mediterranean Europe. This led the powers, under the Restoration of 1660, not to place cod on the list of so-called 'denominated' products that were obliged to be returned to the English entrepôt before being re-exported. Fish was sent directly from Newfoundland to the ports of Spain and Italy, while sugar, indigo and tobacco had to go back to the English stopover before being resold. For the English in Newfoundland, drying had to be done on land, the still fresh fish being laid out over 'stands' set up over the beaches. Their fishermen therefore fished in the coastal zone and in the Great Reef south of Newfoundland. The French, who sold a great deal of 'green' cod, rushed back to their ports. They fished a larger area, west and north of Newfoundland, as well as on the Cape Breton coasts and in the Gulf of Saint Lawrence. It was only later, in the seventeenth century, that they imitated the English in order to fulfil Mediterranean demand, so that they too set about drying their fish. Distancing themselves therefore from the Newfoundland site proper, they were led, even before Cartier's arrival, to penetrate deeply into the Gulf of Saint Lawrence and to make contact with the Indians there to practise a trade in furs.

The fashion for beaver-fur hats, greatly appreciated by the French élite during the reigns of Henri III and Henri IV, demanded this fur trade. Equipping out a Basque ship from Ciboure in Bordeaux for cod fishing and whale hunting 'in the great bay of Newfoundland', the participating Girondon merchants included the fur trade in their expedition: while the fish were drying (the ship was not sent here to fish for green cod) and the whale oil was being melted down, the captain would go 'to traffic and trade with the savages on the coast of the Great Bay'. In his *Great Book of Islands and Piloting* of 1586, André Thevet even predicted the fur trade:

> Every year, great numbers [of whales] and principally on the Sagueney river [a tributary of the Saint Lawrence], the greatest trade in which merchants may engage beyond that in the whale itself, is its fat, which they melt down; they also trade with these barbarians for their various fine and beautiful skins, which they then exchange to foreigners for other merchandise.[39]

The fur trade is thus closely tied to cod fishing and whale hunting, and it was practised by each of the many Basque whaling vessels leaving Bordeaux: almost 15 from 1584 to 1600. The activities of the fur-trading monopolies that were established at the beginning of Louis XIII's reign, and from which the Basques were excluded, did not prevent them from continuing to kill whales there, even coming as close as Tadoussac. In his report of 1637, Father Paul Lejeune saw them trying to 'take the innumerable porpoises and white whales that pass before Quebec'.

As it was for the English West Country ports, the fishing trade constituted an exceptional education in Atlantic navigation. In 1584, the first Royal Marine Ordinance, already drawing to an end almost a century of French traffic in the ocean, was making provision for casting off for far-flung destinations such as Newfoundland by requiring that ships sail in groups 'without abandoning each other except in cases of overriding necessity', with a view to avoiding simultaneously the dangers of the sea and the naval risks arising from competition between the various European fleets. The Ordinance also did this for ships bound for the coasts of Guinea and the West Indies. At this point, in effect, the French Atlantic ports, even Bordeaux, despite being more geared towards trading over the long European coastal navigation, were equipping privateering ships for Africa and America.

Piracy and trade at pike-point

It is beyond question that Rouen, Dieppe, Honfleur, and later La Rochelle, the

Charente and the Huguenot Normans, were the first to engage in expeditions to Guinea, Brazil and the 'Peruvian' islands (the Antilles). Bretons and Normans frequented the Brazilian coasts in search of brazil wood; from 1521 to 1550, there is practically not a single year in which ships were not seen leaving either Dieppe, Honfleur, Rouen, or finally, Saint-Malo. Beginning during the 1520s, privateering campaigns to the Caribbean were redoubled after 1530 in order to capture caravels, and to sack and burn towns, and raids followed from Cuba to Puerto Rico in the northern Caribbean and on the coast of the Spanish Main to the south.

Doubtless more rare but just as daring, merchants from a Bordeaux port still little interested in the New World, turned their enterprises around to invest in expeditions to Guinea, Brazil and the Antilles. In 1544–1545, the *Baptiste*, a ship from Saint Jean de Luz, went to Bordeaux for finances and to get rigged out in order to set off for the Guinea coasts and their 'maneguette', a pepper-like substance. The shipowners were merchants from Bordeaux, and another of the town's merchants had advanced their capital; in 1579, a La Rochelle ship was sent for the slave trade; in the subsequent two years, another two ships, again leaving from Bordeaux, set off to trade between Guinea and the islands.[40] Trade and piracy were still indivisibly bound together, as was the case with a ship sent to Fécamp from La Rochelle in 1572 to 'trade with the inhabitants of the cannibals' islands [the Lesser Antilles] in sheets, canvases, knives, daggers and hardwares' before conducting buccaneering raids around Puerto Rico.[41]

The first French Antilles under Richelieu

These sixteenth-century expeditions had not brought about a programme of colonization, since piracy and trade at pike-point constituted the sole objectives of the merchants who dared to invest in these expeditions. In the seventeenth century, it was left to Richelieu and Colbert to bring an entirely new scope to the Antillean projects. In December 1626, Richelieu, the Grand Master, Chief and Superintendent General of Trade and Navigation, was to present, by way of Marillac, the Minister of Justice, a maritime bill bearing not only on naval shipping, but also on commercial navigation, overseas trading and the colonies. He intended to overthrow the basis of a commercial doctrine to which even Colbert adhered: sell as much as possible to foreigners and buy as little as possible from them. The foreign successes fascinated him just as they impressed Colbert: 'Genoa, which had only rocks to share' was, to Richelieu, Italy's richest town; Holland, 'which produced nothing but butter and cheese, provided every nation in Europe with the majority of what they required'. France could only gain by exporting their various products along with those that the distant lands could provide them with.[42]

The Michau Code of 1629 and the Great Marine Ordinance of 1631 presented the principle of a navy capable of keeping the sea free and protecting merchant shipping and large-scale fishing. Really a Navigation Act, the monopoly was theoretically recognized as belonging to the French fleet: foreigners could not, in the kingdom's ports, load 'any foodstuff, merchandise, nor any goods whatever, with the sole exception of salt'; although, it has to be said, with the following addendum: 'unless they come to be in these ports in ships belonging to the King's subjects'.

The principles of the exclusion were announced in the Isles of the Americas, but the reality was going to prove to be different: tobacco, the main crop of the first plantations, was sold on the Amsterdam market far more than on the French; Curaçao and St Eustatius, the Dutch entrepôts in the Antilles, stocked the colonies since the ships sent by the Saint Christopher Company, and then by that of the Isles of the Americas, became extremely rare. Richelieu's mercantilist views effectively led him to colonial projects in the Antilles, in the immediate vicinity of those that formed the basis of the Dutch [West Indies] Company created in 1621. It was a question of attacking the Spanish in the New World: the Isles were 'the suburban avenues of the Indies, the entrance to Peru', from which one could bring ruin to Spain's possessions. Could it be that the meeting he had with a pirate captain, three months prior to the Assembly of Nobles before whom Marillac had presented his bill, forced him to champion an expedition, in 1627, to the Island of St Christopher, for purposes of piracy and colonization?

At the beginning of the 1620s, Belain D'Esnambuc, a ruined gentleman, left to be a pirate as one would leave for the Crusades. His meeting with Richelieu in October 1626 laid the foundations of the Saint Christopher Company, in which financiers from the Cardinal's entourage took up positions. Aggression towards the Spanish colonies was on the associates' agenda, but the principal objective was commercial: to profit from the sale of tobacco, a product that was still relatively rare, but for which a fashion had developed since the reign of Henri IV.

> After a short while, we expedited a quantity of petun or tobacco from these foreign countries without paying any entry duties....[O]ur subjects, because of slow sales, took it [tobacco] all day, causing losses and a change in their health.

The monarch himself had high hopes of making some profit from the fashion and decided to charge 30 sols per pound weight on foreign tobaccos but to exempt produce arriving from Saint Christopher from the duty.

The company designated Le Havre the port for the arrivals and departures of its ships, and Belain D'Esnambuc had future colonists embark; 530 men on the *Catholic*, the *Cardinal*, and the *Victory*. On 24 February 1627, the fleet was made ready and on 8 May was in sight of the coast of Saint Christopher after a crossing of more than 60 days, made longer by the conventional stopover in the Canaries. The commission given to D'Esnambuc clearly laid down his course:

> They will report what they will have captured and recovered from the pirates and others of ill repute, including those who hold up French merchants, and then go on to navigate the south coast beyond the Tropic of Cancer and the first meridian of the Essores off the west coast.[43]

To do this was to be in violation of the Iberian monopoly, yet they too intended to take advantage of tobacco cultivation, the crop to which the colonies established by the Englishman Warner on this same island had already been devoted for almost a year.

Meanwhile, difficulties were rapidly piling up, and in the autumn of 1627, D'Esnambuc's comrade, Urbain du Roissey, had to turn to France in search of provisions. The aid sent proved insufficient, and the colony, despite Richelieu's mercantilist views, was unable to survive without support from Dutch merchants. Thus, the 'Flemish' fleet, consisting of 12 Dutch ships in two squadrons, returned from loading salt from the shores of the neighbouring island of St Martin with dried meats, flour and cheeses for the islanders, taking on the first tobacco yields. The English, with whom D'Esnambuc had an understanding regarding the partition of Saint Christopher, were better provisioned, since the vessels returning from Virginia stopped over at the island.

In 1629, when the 17 galleons of Don Fabrique de Toledo chased the colonists from Saint Christopher, it was the Dutch from Saint Martin who came to the aid of the fugitives wandering through the Leeward Islands. The resettlement that followed – for the Spanish reaction was short lived – took place in even more difficult circumstances. Once again, provisions were lacking and, more seriously, the tobacco in London declined in the face of an ever-larger volume of imports from Virginia and Barbados, where access to the market became impossible. The colonies' products were not of a sufficiently high quality, while the preparation of 'Verinas petun', from Virginia, needed great care, and the very strong 'Amazon petun', imported from Trinidad, had to be matured from one to two years, necessitating an investment that the inhabitants, under pressure to make sales, could not make. Antillean tobacco was criticized by many; John Winthrop, the eldest son of the founder of the colony of Massachusetts found the tobacco from Barbados that he was sending his brother, who had settled in the colony, 'very badly prepared, full of leaves, foul-smelling, and of poor colour'. London's City merchants also turned their backs on taking Antillean tobacco in favour of that from Virginia, which was more highly regarded. Only the Dutch continued to buy the Antillean varieties.

These difficult conditions did not, however, stop Richelieu persevering in his programme of colonial settlements in the Antilles. In 1635, he decided to wage open war against Spain, and one of his objectives was to dispute the Iberians' claim to the islands, the 'second Peru'. In fact, the heavy demands of the war in Europe prevented the monarch from effectively sustaining his effort in the Antilles, despite the help of powerful financiers such as d'Effiat and Fouquet. While Rouen dominated France's international trade during the 1630s, it was the merchants of Dieppe who, supported by capital from Paris and Rouen, granted Liénart de l'Olive the means to assemble ships and men for an expedition to Martinique. Dieppe had already been extremely active in the sixteenth century when, at the beginning of the previous decade, it took on the vast majority of overseas businesses, while in Quebec its merchants enjoyed a virtual monopoly in the New France trade.[44] In 1627, however, Richelieu established the Canadian Trade Company, called the Company of a Hundred Associates, and revoked the rights of the Dieppe merchants by forbidding them to trade in New France. Dieppe was therefore obliged to withdraw to the Antilles.

On 25 June 1635, to the singing of the hymn *Vexilla Regis*, Liénart de l'Olive planted a cross and a *fleur-de-lys* flag on Martinique's west coast, between the sites of Saint Pierre and Fort de France. However, judging the island too mountainous and too stripped of resources, he and his men boarded again and set sail for Guadeloupe. Later, from St Kitts, D'Esnambuc would make a start in his colonization of Martinique. Of course, by 1635, D'Esnambuc had received some 16 ships from Le Havre and Honfleur, and was able to establish the staging post necessary to the colonization of Martinique and Guadeloupe. On Dieppe's sides, apart from Le Havre, the port of Guadeloupe, the port of Saint Christopher, Martinique, and others were beginning to equip themselves for the Antilles.[45]

In 1629, one of Sables d'Olonne's ships had been chartered by some merchants from Nantes for a return journey from Saint Christopher 'to the Loire river', and Nantes retained exclusive links with Saint Christopher right up until 1645, its merchants joining forces with the Dieppese in order to send ships there. Martinique began to receive ships from Nantes after the middle of the century. Despite frequent complaints lodged against their presence, foreign merchants who had settled in Nantes, amongst whom the Portuguese and the Dutch were the most active, stimulated trade, and the merchant élite grasped the importance of the Antillean zone. In exchange for tobacco, merchants from la Fosse central to Nantes' businesses, were employed to provide the colonists with meats, canvas, and above all a workforce of white servants who preceded the black slaves in working the plantations. In a fragmentary notarial document, doubtless at one remove from reality, Guy Saupin thus noted around 16 indenture contracts between 1643 and 1647, witnessed by these merchants' go-between. To their great profit, the ships combined the great European coastal sea route with the long passage through the tropical Atlantic. Thus a large cargo ship of some 250 tonnes, the *Grand Armand*, could be docked in Martinique towards the end of 1646 and return the following year to leave for England and Ireland, carrying salt from Guérande and tobacco from the Antilles. Thus, around 1640, a rather cautious turn to the Antilles began to take shape in Nantes, perhaps in reaction to the domination of the 'brazen Dutch merchants'. This turn would be confirmed under Colbert.[46]

Even with the encouragements to resettle arising from the appearance of new crops such as cotton, and especially indigo, which atoned for the increasingly obvious weakness of tobacco production during a fall in prices,[47] Martinique and Guadeloupe had no more than 8,000 white inhabitants around 1664, whereas, since 1640, Barbados' white population had reached 10,000, proportionately the same as in Massachusetts and Virginia. Meanwhile, despite the establishment of regulations for limiting its cultivation, tobacco production had continued, with Dutch vessels still coming to collect it, whereas the trade in French ports remained more modest: in the 10 years between 1654 and 1664, Dieppe and La Rochelle launched no more than 65 expeditions and 49 ships to Martinique.[48] At the beginning of Louis XVI's selfish reign, public opinion was stirred by the scandal represented by the overpowering position taken by the merchants of Amsterdam in the Antillean trade. The planters, however, remained tightly bound to these merchants' services, so it was only slowly that the 'Frenchification' of the Islands of the Americas set in, due more perhaps to habits of trading and cultivation than to any real lack of means.

French ports turn to the Antilles

In 1664, when Colbert launched a maritime inquiry prior to re-establishing his battle fleet, the situation was not as bad as he wanted to make people think when he blamed Mazarin for having neglected the sea. The French merchant fleet was at this time almost the equal of the English commercial navy that bore the handicap of seizures during the last Anglo–Spanish war, and had not yet been transformed by the vigorous trade of the Restoration. The French possessed a tonnage of nearly 150,000 tonnes, a large proportion of which were smaller ships, although Colbert's inquiry took account only of heavy freighters of more than 100 tonnes, creating the appearance of an immense deficit.[49] While these lesser tonnages were perfectly suited to the Atlantic crossing, the majority of the voyages from Le Havre, Dieppe, Rouen and Nantes, even until the middle of the century, were accomplished by ships of a capacity of less than 100 tonnes, or, indeed, even less than 50. In 1664, there were no more than 208 heavy freighters in Saint-Malo, Nantes, Le Havre, La Rochelle, Bayonne, Bordeaux, Dunkirk and Marseilles, and even counting ships from other ports, such as Dieppe, we would find no more than 329 ships.

In fact, the Norman, Breton and Charente shipowners preferred to take on indentured servants – the price of their passage being more profitable for their captains – than merchandise, since they were hoarded in under conditions that were hardly different from those that slaves or the emigrants of the nineteenth century were subsequently to experience. In addition, the West Indies Company, founded in 1664 by Colbert, showed itself to be incapable of gaining control over the traffics remaining in Dutch hands. More given to changing his ideas than has been assumed, in June 1669 Colbert decided to withdraw from the company the privilege of granting passports for the Antilles, and in 1671, on the eve of war with Holland, even passed fiscal measures exempting exports to the islands from any taxation and lowering duties upon their return, decisions that would bring about the closing of the colonies' ports to foreigners. Moreover, the minister encouraged the fleet's growth by granting subsidies for naval construction and grants for the purchase of foreign ships.

Despite the war, throughout the decade of the 1670s, and especially in the early years of the 1680s, the ports took a turn to the Antilles. In 1686, the ports cited in the 1664 inquiry rigged out some 591 ships. The example of a single port, however ill-disposed it was to switch its attentions towards the Antilles at the beginning of Louis XIV's reign, is significant here: by 1671, Bordeaux had still rigged out just 13 ships for overseas; almost 15 years later, however, a total of 49 ships had been equipped.

A revolution in the sugar trade that took place on the islands was instrumental in bringing about this progress, although the age of tobacco and other crops such as cotton, ginger and indigo did not come to an end altogether. The shift to cane sugar cultivation in Martinique and Guadeloupe happened later and more gradually than in Barbados, where it had been accomplished since the middle of the century. Thus, on Martinique in 1671, almost one-fifth of cultivated land was still given over to tobacco, against which, meanwhile, the majority – almost 67 per cent – was given over to cane sugar.[50] As opposed to Barbados, Martinique's crops were not therefore based on the cultivation of sugar alone, but developed by conjoining the cultivation of cane sugar with that of provisions and tobacco. However, the costs remained very different than they were under the tobacco 'estates' suitable for small planters. Even for a plantation of modest scale with around 20 slaves, the purchase of slaves, mills for grinding the cane and ovens to cook the *vesou*, as well as the wait for a crop that took more than eighteen months of cultivation, all combined to increase the amount of investment.

On Martinique there were 111 sugar plantations and 6,382 slaves in 1671, while in 1685, there were 172, with 10,343 slaves. By this date, the productivity of the French islands had almost doubled, increasing from some 5,000 tonnes to little less than 10,000, still, of course, far from the productivity of the English islands. The indispensable element necessary to achieving this was the possibility of finding a relatively cheap workforce to bear the extreme hardness of the labour: the black slave, present since the end of the fifteenth century in the plantations in Andalusia and the Portuguese Algarve, then in Brazil's Atlantic archipelagos, was the instrument of the revolution in sugar cultivation, whereas the employment of white servants corresponded to the age of tobacco. The indentured servant was very expensive; his contract in the French colonies was for only three years, and even before this time was up it was necessary to replace those who died from epidemics or due to exhausting labour. Remaining high before 1650, the price of slaves then collapsed when the Dutch traders, having lost their Brazilian market, were able to offload their slaves. Despite Colbert's projects for developing French trade, the majority of these slaves were still provided by Dutch traders.

In Guadeloupe in 1670, de Baas, the governor, underlined for Colbert the requirement under which the planters found themselves, of having both slaves and capital at their disposal in order to gain wealth from sugar:

> Clearing and cultivating the earth can only be done according to the strength and ability of the inhabitants. That is to say that the strong are those who have many negroes, horses or cattle to plant and harvest the cane and to turn their mills without respite; and those who do not have these things can grow little more than a little tobacco or indigo.[51]

Ten years later, on Martinique, another governor, Blénac, made an initial assessment: all lands, 'those clean and commodious', were taken for growing sugar. As for what was left, too far away on the slopes of the *mornes* or hillocks that were too difficult to cultivate, 'the expense of carrying sugar to the sea being so great, no one would wish to undertake it'.[52] Land and slaves became concentrated in the hands of the richest and, in particular, those who were most involved in the import trade. One constant factor, however, interfered in both French and English plantations: the dominant power of trade in the great Atlantic ports. This power had become apparent since the age of tobacco, rather to the advantage of the Dutch, and it would become even clearer during the age of sugar. Jacques Petit-Jean Roget thus noted that in Martinique, over the years 1650–1670, powerful Dieppe merchants were taking control of the 'estates sold by a certain number of good old boys who did little more than create beautiful plantations which they then sold, completely planted with provisions and tobacco, at a rather low price, to newcomers'.[53]

The Santo Domingo effect

A new stage was to be reached with the colonization of the western part of the island of Santo Domingo. French penetration into this Greater Antillean island, where the Spanish had founded their presence first on mining for precious metals and then on rearing livestock, both for the skin trade and for working the plantations (cane sugar had certainly been cultivated in the sixteenth century), was similar to the English in Jamaica. In reality, profits from piracy preceded profits from the plantations. Like Jamaica, the island was as well situated for raids on Havana and Vera Cruz as it was, in the southern Caribbean, towards the Spanish Main. On the Île de la Tortue on the north coast, a mixed population of several individuals from various parts of Europe had launched attacks against Spanish ships and cities since the 1630s. The preponderant element on the island was English, but the French, mostly originating from Saint Christopher, but almost all Protestants, and therefore exiled from that colony, set themselves against the English, who were forced to retreat to the Isla de Providencia, facing the Honduran coast. For a few years, Le Vasseur, the chief of these freebooters, established a pirate Huguenot republic on la Tortue, with many of his comrades practising buccaneers, hunting livestock and living in a state of savagery. Raids were launched on some very sparsely populated Spanish plantations on the interior of Santo Domingo.

Upon Colbert's death, the naval strength represented by the Santo Domingo freebooters was far from negligible, with some 17 ships with crews of almost 2,000 men, whose principal base remained la Tortue. Bertrand d'Ogeron, whom Colbert had named governor of the French part of Santo Domingo in 1664, would settle some of these freebooters by substituting tobacco cultivation for the practise of buccaneering. He continued, however, to rely on the pirate raids they led against the Spanish and the Dutch, at least until the day following the Nimègue peace treaty, for expeditions such as Cumana's against the Spanish Main in 1678 or against Vera Cruz in 1683.

On Santo Domingo, tobacco found fresh soil and inhabitants of frugal means who were only too happy to take part in its cultivation. In 1674, the foundation of the royal tobacco monopoly marked a turning-point with disastrous consequences. Responding to consumers' tastes, the Antilles effectively went to buy tobacco from Virginia and Maryland, the English colonies on the mainland, as well as in Brazil. Large amounts of this tobacco were placed on the market during the war of the Augsburg League, so that many of these English purchases were sold. The outlets for Santo Domingo tobacco closed and the colonists might once again have been tempted into piracy. But tobacco had in fact allowed the first expansion of the colony, where there were 1,500 whites in 1665, and 10 years later, 5,000. Numerous small-scale planters came from the Windward Isles, Martinique and Guadeloupe, where the beginnings of the sugar economy were raising the price of land and concentrating property.

Santo Domingo's entry into the age of large-scale sugar plantations was to mark a new period of growth. The island's 26,000 sq. km, more than double that of Jamaica, the largest English island in the Antilles, offered fertile soils. Officially ceded by Spain in 1697 at Ryswick, the 'Coste' of Santo Domingo produced practically no sugar and was even in crisis following the collapse of tobacco exports during the war of the Augsburg League. Some 15 years later, in 1714, in spite of the war, production reached almost 7,000 tonnes, and more than 10,000 tonnes in 1720. The slaves necessary to its cultivation had risen from 3,400 in 1686 to 47,000 in 1720, and Santo Domingo became the English Antilles' most dangerous rival.

The decision to abolish the refining industry on Martinique and Guadeloupe, taken at the end of the seventeenth century (1695), stimulated the installation of refineries in the home countries which still required raw sugar. More and more frequently, however, they were handling sugars that had already been improved by a claying process, since the planters had an interest in sending muscovado that lost less moisture than raw sugars by seepage through the barrel during the crossing, and took up a much reduced volume in the holds. Kitting them out with the necessary boilers and earthenware moulds was certainly expensive, and was a factor that favoured the concentration of property and capital aid from the trading ports.

Corresponding to the growth in Santo Domingo was a mutation brought about during the last years of the seventeenth century by the network of French ports in relation to the Antilles. Whereas the shipyards of Dieppe, Le Havre, Honfleur and La Rochelle had undergone an initial expansion during the age of tobacco, Nantes and, to a lesser extent, Bordeaux, Saint-Malo and Marseilles grew rich after the final breakthrough in the sugar economy. In accordance with Colbert's wishes, an élite of adventurous traders with huge capital at their disposal that they were ready to risk in both the Atlantic sugar trade and the slave trade that went with it, dominated exchange. The demand for European markets grew: towards 1673, before the sugar revolution in Santo Domingo or even in Jamaica, the entire American sugar business in Brazil and the Antilles produced almost 50,000 tonnes; in 1700, it reached 80,000 tonnes. This growth in production answered to the falling prices necessary for enlarging its market: on Amsterdam's market, Brazilian white sugar fell by two-thirds from 1655–1690.[54]

To follow on from this fall, the planters had to lower their production costs, which they did by generalizing the employment of a servile, black workforce. In 1713, the French isles had 75,000 slaves, while the English islands, with 133,000 captives labouring on them, had almost twice that number at their disposal. On the English side, there was a larger number of imports from Africa: 263,000 had been introduced by their traders, against 156,000 by the French. Throughout the entire century, however, the principal importer had been Brazil, with 560,000 captives, with imports from the Spanish empire running in second place with

292,000.[55] The Iberian imports, however, were more staggered through time than were those of the English and the French who had brought in their imports principally between 1670 and 1700. These were not in answer to the growth in large-scale sugar plantations, which required a higher yield of their slaves than in the Iberian colonies, a yield entailing far higher losses. The triumph of large-scale plantations on the Windward Isles, the Leewards and the Greater Antilles, brought about in barely the space of a generation, demanded heightened imports at an increased human cost.

Accomplished by the French islands despite the wars at the end of Louis XIV's reign, this expansion would not have come about, at least with this speed, despite Colbert's mercantilist efforts and the progress of the colonial fleet, without foreign cooperation. Over long years, the Dutch lent their help, until this role was increasingly taken over by the colonial English merchants on the mainland who, in the eighteenth century, were to assume a very large role in the activities of the French Antilles, but who had begun to do this in the seventeenth century.

The New English and the Antilles

Since the beginnings of the Antillean plantations, the English colonial ports of the North American mainland formed relations with the Caribbean islands. The routes that had to be taken across the Atlantic uniquely favoured such relations. A comparison of the trajectories being taken from the ports of Boston and Bordeaux in order to get to the arc of the Antilles clearly demonstrates this: less than 2,600 kilometres separate the former from Santo Domingo, while there are more than 7,000 kilometres to cover from Bordeaux, by the fastest trade wind, before reaching the Windward Isles, Martinique and Guadeloupe, in the eastern Caribbean; crossing the Caribbean Sea to return to Santo Domingo requires a journey of an additional 1,000 kilometres. If, on the outward journey, the North American ships were not aided by favourable conditions, upon their return the Gulf Stream currents from the Bahamas Channel would be favourable to their northward ascent.

From the end of the 1630s, New England became a market for the by-product of sugar refining in Barbados – molasses, which enabled the manufacture of rum. Subsequently, the stream carrying this 'magical' beverage did not stop before reaching Newfoundland, where the fishermen took courage from it to perform their rough tasks. Later, rum would be carried by slave ships from New England, New York and Philadelphia towards far-distant Guinea, and served in particular to enable exchanges in fur-trading with the Indians, a great many of whom were 'duped' thanks to the *guildives* or 'kill-devil': the drink that killed the devil.

Despite the interdictions of Colbert's Exclusive, renewed by an accord between Louis XIV and the English Stuart king, James II, prohibiting any trade between the colonies, the English mainland colonies provided the French Antilles with indispensable supplies for the maintenance of factories, with slaves, cod from the large-scale fisheries, flour from Pennsylvania or the colony of New York, and wood for cooperage or construction, in exchange for molasses. Until the beginning of the eighteenth century, the French colonies bought North American products from the English Antilles, which acted as an intermediary, and paid in colonial or European products and in kind. Due to the taxes on molasses imported from the English islands and the official prohibition on importing molasses from the French Antilles, an intense smuggling operation animated this traffic. The establishment of sugar claying on Martinique and Guadeloupe at the end of the seventeenth century, and then on Santo Domingo, was nevertheless to provide the planters with molasses to sell or to distill into rum. As the colonists could not export molasses back home, the Royal Declaration of 24 February 1713 having forbidden the manufacture of every water of life in France other than wine, there was no other market available to the French than that of the still poorly developed African one, and we can easily understand the immense pull that the North American market exerted. In the colonial Atlantic, under the rules of mercantilism, the north–south exchanges between the English North American and the French Caribbean colonies became increasingly favoured by the naval conflicts that restricted exchanges between France and her colonies. The eighteenth century thus caused the northern European naval powers to lose control, at least in part, of an Atlantic economy originally created for their benefit alone.

The French challenge, launched first at Holland by Colbert, jealous of her wealth, then at England, strengthened by a naval might acquired to the detriment of the United Provinces, had in part been met.

Of course, one of the essential instruments of Colbert's commercial politics, monopoly companies, clearly became an obstacle. There was the fall of the Levant Company in 1670, the fiasco of the Compagnie du Nord from 1669 onwards, and the abolition of the West Indies Company in 1674. It was the merchants' initiatives, doubtless stimulated by some of Colbert's measures, that drove expansion and that constituted the true challenge. The initiatives taken in the Antilles marked a new orientation and had already achieved notable results during the decade of the 1670s: on 16 August 1678, in Rouen, the London firm to which Benjamin Beuzelin drew attention in a letter to Charles Marescoe

> because still there comes to us a great number of sugars from the French estates of America and, in a few days, we have sold it at L. 22 t. as a good, although rather low, average; thus nothing can be done with Barbados sugars at 22 s.d. 6d.

Sugar from the French islands competed very well on the French market with sugar from the English islands.

France and the Spanish Indies

The same initiatives sustained the French trade with Spanish America, where it competed strongly with that of the other Europeans, this time on an open market rather than one protected by the Exclusive, as in the Antilles. The profits to be drawn from the arrival of the fleets from the West Indies were the object of the most daring speculation, and ports such as Saint-Malo sped their best frigates to Cadiz to take delivery of American piastres in exchange for luxury products, especially the finest textiles that were so prized in the American colonies. Some 26 French ships had thus been sent at the beginning of the year 1670, and the traders' excitement reached its height when they learnt of the entry of the *flota* into Cadiz: on 21 February 1670, Robert Oursel, a Rouen merchant, exclaimed

> we have news from Madrid, by a letter of the fifth of this month, of the arrival of the fleet from the Indies, numbering 17 ships, in San Lucar, God be praised! This is good news that makes the merchants of this town rejoice heartily.[56]

Very actively engaged in the Spanish American traffic since the sixteenth century, Rouen's traders could only congratulate themselves on the happy and long-awaited event, but remained conscious of the fierce rivalry that threatened French projects. Oursel knew of the arrival 'of the effects of the Spanish fleet within your [London's] districts, and in Holland', but reassured himself that 'an equally large number is expected in this country, which will enable our affairs to be kept in balance'.

In fact, in 1686, a year of record imports of American piastres, exceeding its 1595 peak (35 million piastres), France had reached Cadiz first, making sales of almost 17 million livres, Saint-Malo's share counting for almost half of this total. This success allowed the French to gain almost 40 per cent of Europe's shipments to Spanish America via Cadiz, more than double the expeditions from Genoa, the second largest exporter (7.3 million), and almost three times those from England, the third largest exporter (6.2 million). This testifies to the successes of French industry, which found its best foreign market in the Iberian Atlantic.

Even with products that appeared to be the privilege of the United Provinces, or indeed Hamburg, such as whale oil during the 1670s (the Dutch whaling fleet then numbered almost 160 ships, while Hamburg's fleet was around 70), the French market took on provisions in its own ports, which it had not done in the middle of the century: in June 1679, the Rouen firm of Amsincq signalled to Jean

David, Marescoe's successor in London, that 'Paris wants no oils from Holland due to their stink, while the Basque oils made or burnt at sea have barely any smell', and the merchant was supplied in the previous autumn with Basque oils.[57]

Despite the obvious failure of the monopoly companies, were we to deprive Colbert of the merit of having profitably directed trading activities we would be jumping the gun. The merchants were conscious of the advantages that the monarch's decisions had given them:

> If [you] observe that the value of what are strictly your own merchandise is falling at home and that thereby, something had to be done when sending them by way of France, they can be served by the privilege of the entrepôt that the King has granted traders, which is to say, the free access and departure of goods that are supposed to be sent beyond the Realm without paying any duties. We will always have good Ships loaded in harbours for Cadiz, Alicante and Marseilles.[58]

The London merchant was invited by Oursel to Rouen to take advantage of the provisions of the edict of March 1669, which, in order to stimulate French traffic in the Levant, had granted Marseilles an exemption from customs. Beyond this group of companies, French traders intended to use the privileges favourable to them. They were to do so, with still greater success, in the eighteenth century, in order to share with the traders of London and the other English ports the profits of an Atlantic commerce in full bloom.

Chapter 5

The golden age of the colonial Atlantic
The eighteenth century

England and France: the two great rivals

The conditions of their mutual challenge

From Utrecht to Waterloo, rival French and English ambitions reigned over the Atlantic. In the middle of the sixteenth century, the Atlantic still had just one single master, Iberia, whose authority was challenged, of course, very early on by pirates and illicit traders from Holland, England and France. The seventeenth century saw the ocean shared between the competing appetites of the north-western Europeans, still officially bound by the Iberian monopoly throughout the greater part of the century. It was only later, in 1670, that Madrid's monopoly was finally shattered by an Anglo–Spanish treaty recognizing England's occupation of Jamaica, and, in 1697, by the Treaty of Ryswick, in which the Spanish accepted the return of the western side of Santo Domingo to France.

In the eighteenth century, the wealth of the plantations in the Antilles and the Chesapeake in English North America gave a powerful boost to transatlantic trade. In many ways, European ports from Cadiz to Hamburg took this wealth to be a secret sign of a new expansion, but the crossroads of the great entrepôt trade, exporting free of all taxation, were still the most highly regarded in both Great Britain and France. The basis of the former's expansion certainly turned out to be more complete and more stable. It did not rest, of course, on Antillean products alone, but also on the trade of the English North American colonies from which tobacco from Virginia and Maryland, rice from the Carolinas, and wood and seafood from New England's waters were exported.

Given the rising value of both the colonial possessions of the two countries and the rich mines of a Spanish empire increasingly infiltrated by foreigners, the confrontation between English and French Atlantic politics was to become the justification for a merciless struggle that was, albeit only later, to shatter Great Britain's superiority over France. The 'blue water' strategy to control an Atlantic dynamic was doubtless far better received in Great Britain, focused as it was on the sea, than in France, which remained in large part continental, and it profited immensely from the relative withdrawal into which Holland was forced after the exhausting wars of the end of the seventeenth and beginning of the eighteenth centuries. The logic behind the economist Adam Smith's thinking and the vigorous oratory of Pitt, idolized by the people after the great British victories in the Seven Years' War, came to the same conclusions: the dearest wish of every man in the state had to be to see his country reign alone over the Atlantic by dominating commerce and navigation – *Britannia rules the waves*.

The entrepôt system and Britain's advantages

The market for exotic goods such as sugar, coffee, tobacco, tea and indigo opened up in a mercantilist age during which the countries of Europe were closed to English and French manufactured goods by their protectionist politics but, thereby deprived of important transatlantic commerce, remained open to the re-exportation of American and Asiatic products that were taxed either lightly or not at all. In the two countries an entrepôt system was set up, characterized by important customs advantages granted to re-exportation merchants, while high tariffs protected national markets from foreign competition. At the same time, transatlantic commerce itself was freed from the constraints of monopolies and favoured companies. While the traffic from Asia was still supported by a system of commercial companies endowed with powers of sovereignty, the traffic of the European Atlantic, like that of the American Atlantic, was freed from any corporate privileges.

Meanwhile, in the political and economic duel that set it against France for the domination of the Atlantic, Great Britain enjoyed one essential advantage: that of being at the head of a common quasi-market that gave unequalled value to its exchanges.[1] Following Scotland's entry into the United Kingdom in 1707, the Gaelic countries, Scotland and Ireland, the English colonies in North America and the Antilles joined together to trade within a large market, which, however, remained incomplete to the extent that certain products, such as cereals from the mainland colonies, and a few agricultural products from Ireland, were prohibited in England. In the British exporter's favour, however, there was indeed a free exchange zone, creating a protected market able to receive products that were 'Made in England'.

In this zone, demographic expansion created another factor favourable to the creation of a very powerful consumer market. It was realized here, of course, at a very much faster speed than it was in England itself. From 1670 to 1770 the population increased by more than 70 per cent, growing from 96,000 to 480,000 inhabitants in the English Antilles, and from 112,000 to 2,148,000 inhabitants in the Thirteen Colonies, whereas Ireland, passing from 2 million to 3.6 million inhabitants, experienced a speedier demographic increase than all other European countries. In England and Scotland, the population increased more slowly, passing from 5.3 to 6.9 million and from 1 million to 1.3 million, respectively.

Although there was also a significant increase in France's population, with figures rising from 22 million in 1700 to 24.5 million in 1750 and 29 million in 1800, it was again in the far Atlantic, in the Antilles, that the increase was the swiftest. In 1713, the French part of Santo Domingo numbered fewer than 10,000 inhabitants; by the middle of the century, its population had already reached 172,000 inhabitants, more than 17 times the level obtained at that date in Utrecht, and, with 513,000 inhabitants in 1789, it had tripled in relation to 1753. Between these two dates, the annual rate of increase was 25 per thousand, a rate unknown at this time in the rest of the world.[2] In Martinique and Guadeloupe the increase was also significant: from 45,000 and 22,000 inhabitants in 1720, the populations of these two colonies rose to 102,000 and 117,000 in 1789, doubling in the former, and more than quadrupling in the latter. This Antillean increase remained artificial, however, due to the enormous contribution of the trade in black slaves from Africa, especially in Santo Domingo, where the number of these slaves in 1789 was more than 465,000.

This progress contributed greatly to the enormous vitality of the French Atlantic market, in the production of colonial goods as well as the consumption of European produce, since it was necessary to feed and clothe the slaves. Meanwhile, France did not possess a consumer market in the Americas comparable to that open to Great Britain through its mainland colonies because, although the Antilles had grown in a spectacular manner, French Canada was far from reaching a rank comparable even to that of Santo Domingo in the middle of the century, since its population did not manage to reach one-third that of the inhabitants of the Antillean colony. Some 20 years later, English Canada, with its 110,000 inhabitants, was still far behind its mainland colonies on the demographic level. It was in Europe, especially northern and central Europe, that French trade was able to find a market capable of absorbing the increasing volume of exotic products. The population growth in Germanic Europe, easily perceptible in certain regions such as Prussia or Saxony, and which accelerated after 1815, was already sizeable by the second half of the eighteenth century.

The growth in the consumption of exotic goods

Eighteenth-century Europe had seen a rise until then unequalled in the consumption of exotic products. Consumption of tobacco – for smoking, snuff or chewing – had more than doubled; its import into Europe had risen from 50 to 125 million lbs; the increase in other products was still more remarkable: the consumption of tea had risen from 1 million to 40 million lbs; of chocolate, from 2 million to 13 million lbs; and of coffee, the growth of which was easily the most spectacular, from 2 million to 120 million lbs.[3]

Sugar and new drinks

The European fashion for sweetening exotic drinks by means of sugar gave the Atlantic sugar trade an unprecedented dynamism and explains the increasingly demanding taste for the product that had contributed most to giving the great Antillean slave-worked plantations an exceptional place in the Atlantic economy. Less than a century after the sugar plantations took off in Jamaica, and hardly more than half a century after their advent in French Santo Domingo, by the 1770s sugar was an indispensable prop for aristocratic, bourgeois, and even plebeian, drinks: chocolate, coffee and tea. Chocolate was taken particularly in the south of Europe, in Spain and Italy; coffee in Holland, France and Germanic Europe, and tea was above all the drink of the British. These drinks were no longer passing fashions, but necessary elements of everyday life, from morning breakfast to the family or afternoon social get-togethers. It was, however, in Great Britain that sugar consumption rose most rapidly, reaching the highest levels in Europe by the end of the century: in 1800, its consumption had risen to almost 10 kilos per head per year, so that its sales at market exceeded 93,000 tonnes.

Through the practice of sugaring drinks in Great Britain, stemming, for the most part, from adding sugar to wine, a long-term familiarity with sugar had existed at least since the sixteenth century. In 1617, an English writer named Morgson drew emphatic attention to a certain élitism in the uses of sugared drinks: 'only vulgar men take large amounts of beer and ale; gentlemen take to wines that they mix with sugar, far more, indeed, than in any other kingdom'.[4] However, a more and more pronounced taste was emerging and the sweet tooth of the average Englishman, more than that of any other European people, demanded that bitter drinks like coffee, tea or chocolate be sweetened with sugar. However, it remains difficult to date the origins of this practice with any precision. In 1657, at the beginnings of the Cromwellian period, Thomas Garway was still recommending that tea be sweetened with 'virgin honey' rather than sugar.[5] In the Swedish court during the 1680s, the doctor Johan Fechlin gave the same advice but this time using sugar, at least for *Bohea* tea (black tea). In 1715, the French recipes of the *Cuisinier Royal et Bourgeois, nouvelles instructions pour les confitures*, took account, in preparing tea, of sweetening it with sugar, 'each adding sugar to taste'.[6] From the middle of the seventeenth century, chocolate was also being sweetened with sugar, as, before long, was coffee. Other sugared drinks were also being prepared, such as lemonade, anisette, cordial and sherbet, which were introduced into France from Italy during the time of Catharine de Medici.[7]

In England, the fashion for tea, which was soon inextricable from sugar, became a passion due to a revolution in the dietary regime, in particular in the institution of taking breakfast: from a meal based on porridge, a gruel of oats taken with ale or beer, people shifted to a hot, sugared drink accompanied by bread, milk, and then cold meats and eggs.[8] Added to this was the taking of tea in the afternoon, in the family or social circle. This explains the spectacular growth in tea imports from east India, which in 1720–1726 amounted to 320 tonnes a year, climbing at the end of the century to almost 10,000 tonnes in 1792–1798.[9]

This change in manners also reached the Continent, with the use of sugar there introduced into French and German breakfasts. In his *Physiologie du Goût* (*Physiology of Taste*), Brillat-Savarin recommended coffee with milk and sugar at the beginning of the nineteenth century, but this practice had begun a century earlier in Paris under the Regency, while in Germany breakfast remained closer to the English than the French style. The fashion for these exotic drinks was all the more celebrated since they were supposed to harbour exceptional medical virtues, especially tea, which, according to Madame de Sévigny, 'visibly revived' the landgrave of Hesse Cassel in 1684; and tea even cured 22 diseases, according to a treatise which appeared one year earlier, by Jean Gérin, a Lyon bookseller.[10]

In England, meanwhile, enthusiasm for tea sparked an increase in consumption of the drink together with that of sugar. At the end of the century, Malthus could declare that 'the peasant who is compelled to work for several extra hours in order to obtain tea and tobacco, will prefer his rest when compared to purchasing a new piece of clothing'.[11] The ever more pronounced taste of the consumer made him accept new sacrifices in order to satisfy his need for exotic products. This explains how Great Britain and Ireland were able to absorb almost all the British imports of sugar on the eve of the war with America, up to almost 94 per cent, while the balance went abroad or to the Thirteen Colonies. Great Britain would only regain her position as a major exporter with the Blockade and the cessation of French imports during the Revolution: she exported 64,939 out of 158,224 tonnes of imports, that is, 41 per cent[12] of the sugar introduced into her ports, despite the increase in its consumption. To contemporary eyes, the reasons for this were a buoyant tea market which increased its distribution throughout all social classes. This tendency began early on: in 1724, a London merchant saw 'an extensive use of tea and coffee that had sharply increased, especially given the good price of tea, which will further augment its consumption'.[13] Thus, a few years earlier, in London, they thought it was necessary to take 12 to 16 lbs of sugar for a single pound of tea. By the middle of the century, in 1744, the use of sugar, independent of tea, was noticed in Scotland, where it was mixed with water to make lemonade, brandy or rum.

From this it is clear why a number of sugar refineries sprang up on British soil, intended to satisfy the increasing needs of the national market. While a similar multiplication of refineries in France was essentially associated with the satisfaction of foreign needs through re-exporting their produce, the British establishments, particularly concentrated around London, where there were 80, or in the western ports such as Bristol, where there were 20, sold within their own borders. In 1751 a refinery was created in Edinburgh, where the firm declared in its opening declaration that 'the consumption of sugar in the city of Edinburgh and its environs has been greatly augmented'[14] and traders added that a trade had developed between Leith, the nearest port to the Scottish capital, and the English sugar colonies in America, so that the trade in and manufacture of sugar could be extremely profitable. During this same period, Ireland equipped itself with refineries, possessing around 40 in 1766, while in 1780, Dublin alone maintained 22.[15]

On both sides of the Channel, these changes in everyday habits were able to bring about a new appreciation of drinks, not only within the familial setting, but also in the broader context: tea, coffee and chocolate were enjoyed more and more in the increasingly fashionable establishments of the French cafés and British coffee houses. In the reign of Good Queen Anne, London's coffee houses numbered up to 500, and every respectable Londoner had his favourite coffee house where his friends and clients knew they could find him at certain times. One of the most famous establishments in London during the time of the Glorious Revolution belonged to Edward Lloyd, and was soon to become a meeting-place for all who had business in Atlantic navigation: ships' masters, shipowners, traders and insurance agents. The last became Lloyd's best clients, and the association destined to become the largest insurance company in the world was born in their midst.

The expansion of European overseas trade through these products, and the sociable environments in which they were consumed, formed a major part of the cultures of both Great Britain and the Continent. In a coffee house one could be served things other than tea or coffee, and less innocent drinks could be found there, such as whisky or rum, or the so-called spa waters from Bristol or Bath. It was also possible to treat oneself to delicacies like sugar candy, oranges, or cakes made with already sugared grapes. Most importantly, however, coffee houses were respectable places, clearly held in higher regard than inns or taverns. Outside the familial or social consumption of tea, in which the woman, the mistress of the house, took the principal role, the coffee house was reserved for a male clientele, as the cafés of the Near East had been, where men came both for business and to enjoy the rest they sought, so that later on these places were naturally enough to take on the respectable character of the club.

The passion for tobacco

At the end of the eighteenth century, both in Great Britain and on the Continent, tea and coffee, taken with sugar, provided many, including the poorest on the other side of the Channel, with a cheap source of calories, easing the physical sensation of hunger, while at the same time sustaining an air of healthy relaxation. However, it was tobacco, as the first exotic product, which, through mass distribution, made the most profound impact on European taste. This had been happening in England since the Stuart Restoration, in the form of smoking tobacco, which, according to Goodman, was used by a quarter of the adult population at the rate of one pipe per day.[16] In France, mass consumption only arose later, towards the middle of the eighteenth century.

Europe's Atlantic expansion had facilitated tobacco's introduction into Europe, where it furnishes one of the best examples of the success of the plantations on American soil, first in the Caribbean world, and then, with much greater scope, in production and commercialization on the English North American mainland colonies.

Largely consumed during the pre-Columbian age by Amerindian societies, from the forests of Canada to the south of Argentina, it was only later, towards the end of the sixteenth century, that the cultivation of tobacco was started by Europeans in the New World, when its use as a medicinal property in the Old World's societies began to be noticed. Spanish colonists first traded it from its Indian producers in Venezuela before they turned, following the end of the sixteenth century, to making it into a product highly esteemed by European, and especially Dutch, merchants, much to the detriment of the Iberian monopoly. However, it was in 1620s Virginia that Europe found what it took to satisfy an ever increasing hunger for tobacco, through developing the Chesapeake plantations to a far greater extent than was happening at the same time in the Antilles, first in Barbados and then on Saint Christopher. At the beginning of the eighteenth century, Virginia supplied the majority of Europe's markets, with Europe drawing on it for 80 per cent of its consumption, the remainder being furnished by Brazil.[17]

As with tea, coffee and chocolate, the consumption of tobacco acquired its own faithfully observed rituals within certain cultural or social sets. The consumption of the product had been Europeanized in the form of pipes and cigars, chewing tobacco and snuff. At first, Europeans imitated and then transformed the Indian rites, in most countries initially integrating them into the culture of the tavern, where they could accompany the consumption of alcoholic drinks. The Indians' religious uses of tobacco in rites and shamanism as well as its social use as an offering to guests had thus been completely altered, banishing its religious aspect and leaving only the social.

The atmosphere could be as intimate as a seventeenth-century image by the Flemish painter David Teniers, which shows an elegantly attired woman in an inn about to light a pipe that her companion has just refilled. Arnoult's eighteenth-century work, *The Charming Smoking-Den*, is equally calm. In it, Arnoult shows three elegant women sitting round a table, with two of them smoking from long pipes while the third prepares the tobacco.[18] The more popular modes of consumption, however, may have been quite different, as practised by mariners from Dutch or Hansard whaling-crews, or the numerous Newcastle colliers in London since the seventeenth century, in the taverns and the real smoking-dens, which were an integral part of the large merchant ports. Here, although rarely, smoking a pipe may have been a way of resisting the temptations that ports held for mariners, drawn to binges that made them forget the hardships of their life before casting off for overseas. Of course, in port towns from Bordeaux to London, Amsterdam and Hamburg, the shipowners' and traders' houses in the decent districts may have housed charming, serene smoking-parlours, far from the taverns that were the preserve of the crews who had come to spend their pay in a frenzy.

It was without a doubt in the salons of the wealthy bourgeois merchants, and in those of the aristocrats of the towns of north-western Europe, that what was going to be the greatest fashion of the eighteenth century began to develop – the consumption of snuff. At the beginning of the seventeenth century, the Spanish and the Portuguese had begun to take snuff-tobacco. In France, this mode of consumption expanded considerably during the eighteenth century, and in 1789 some 80 per cent of the production of manufactured tobacco from the 'Farm's' establishments was composed of snuff-tobacco (12 million out of the 15 million lbs produced). The same mode of consumption had reached Holland and Great Britain, where a decline in pipe smoking was observed. The progress of the vogue for snuff-tobacco may explain the relative stagnation of individual consumption, since the volume required for snuff was less than that required for a pipe.[19] At the end of the eighteenth century, each inhabitant of Great Britain consumed 1.5 lbs per year; in France, 1 lb. The use of tobacco had expanded but it was not as intense as it is at the end of the twentieth century, when individual consumption has reached 3 lbs per year in France, 4.5 lbs in the United Kingdom, and 7.5 lbs in the United States.

Poverty and the burden of tobacco taxation may also account for the relative slowness of progress in its consumption. It is, however, worth taking into account the presence of the smuggling that was widespread in every country, especially in France and England. Although the cultural isolation of the rural population should not be forgotten, the fashion for snuff-tobacco was above all an urban one. This tobacco was the easiest for women to take, and snuff could also be used in work-places where smoking was dangerous or unacceptable. A subtle rite surrounded snuff-tobacco: often, the consumer prepared the tobacco, so a snuff-box with a grinder were indispensable elements. Snuff-boxes were genuine works of art, made from ivory, fine porcelain, or even gold; they were 'all the rage' amongst both aristocratic and bourgeois clientele. In his *Tableau de Paris*, Sébastien Mercier shows how the seasons dictated the occasions on which it was used: 'such are the boxes for every season: the winter box is heavy, the summer one, light....One excuses someone for not having a library or a natural history collection when he has three hundred boxes for snuff.'[20] Marie-Antoinette managed to carry off some 52 gold snuff-boxes from amongst her wedding-presents. There were many different qualities of snuff-tobacco. In England, up to 200 varieties were available at the end of the century. Tobacco could be sweetened with sugar, orange blossom, jasmine or bergamot, although the mass market ignored the most perfumed tobaccos.

The triumph of the fashion for tobacco explains the growth in western Europe's consumption, which in 1710 had been close to 70 million lbs, but which by 1800 was accounting for up to 120 million lbs. Increases, however, were still uneven between urban and rural environments, and, to be properly measured, must also be considered in relation to Europe's demographic boom, in which the population rose from 162 million to 200 million in the half-century between 1750 and 1800. The fashion, and, in the case of snuff-tobacco, more often than not the *passion* for the drug, enabled the Atlantic trade, in particular in England and Scotland, to find one of its best markets with this exotic product.

Expanding markets

British successes

Sustained by the demands of a market that was answering to a new taste for exotic products, trading activity in the Atlantic relied on the existence of flexible chains of credit, which ensured the financing that was indispensable to commerce. In this field, British superiority seemed clear since the eighteenth century, as much in importing colonial merchandise as in selling it on the domestic market or re-exporting it. Nevertheless, French traders also took advantage of this same system of credit.

On this point, London had the great advantage of the presence of its bankers, brokers and 'capitalists' who could make the necessary capital available to trade. Just as, on the other hand, the West India merchants did not go on to make any investments in industry – François Crouzet has ascertained that direct investments of 'colonial' capital in nascent big industry were relatively infrequent[21] – vast sums of capital were ready to hand at the hub of commerce. The banks in particular, who naturally found investing their reserves in government securities an extremely attractive prospect, were particularly fond of financing commerce by drawing drafts, and drawing on fixed sums, making temporary advances, as much for purchasing colonial goods as for exporting articles back home. In fact, credit played a huge role: Daniel Defoe, cited by Jacob M. Price, has clearly shown the role played during the 1720s by London's 'wholesale men', who granted credit to provincial merchants and even to traders from the ports in such a way that domestic and foreign commerce were in large part conducted on the basis of the capital of those who were playing the role of brokers and wholesalers.[22] For overseas expeditions, there was often credit spread out over 12 to 18 months, whereas those reserved for domestic trade ran for no longer than six to eight months.

An example of successful trade: the Chesapeake tobacco trade

The Chesapeake tobacco trade, and the development of the colonial plantations it brought with it, can reasonably be ranked amongst the greatest successes of British trade in the Atlantic. Sustained by European modes of consumption, the re-exportation of tobacco also benefitted from the monopolistic regimes established in France, Spain, Portugal, the Habsburg Empire and the numerous smaller German and Italian states. The fiscal yield of these monopolies rose from 6.4 to 7.3 per cent of the revenues of the realm in France from 1763 to 1789, and up to 25 per cent in Spain during the same period.

Of course, the Chesapeake plantation did not have a monopoly on production: the Bahia region of Brazil had an important yield destined not only for the Portuguese markets, but also for Europe and even Africa, where tobacco was exchanged for slaves. Expeditions carrying Brazilian tobacco to Africa began towards the end of the sixteenth century, and at the end of the seventeenth, the discovery of gold in Brazil having increased the need for slaves, trade expanded again, with Brazilian tobacco being taken by all the Portuguese, Dutch, French and British slave-traders.

Spain had a state monopoly that could count on the colonial produce of Venezuela, and later Cuba. Known under the name of Verina tobacco, Venezuelan tobacco was extremely sought after in Europe where it cost twice as much as Virginian tobacco. The Dutch smuggled tobacco from Curaçao, and in the seventeenth century Amsterdam received more than Cadiz and Seville. Smuggling continued into the eighteenth century, with the exception of a period at the end of the 1730s when the new Company of Caracas, a regional monopoly, augmented what they sent to Spain, but the Anglo–Spanish war of 1739 interrupted this trade.[23] In the eighteenth century, Spain decided to increase its voyages to Cuba, which was closer to Europe and above all a stopover for the *flota* coming from Vera Cruz in Mexico. Before its cigars were so famous, Cuban tobacco was prized for its carefully selected leaves, which made it highly suitable for snuff, which was so fashionable in Enlightenment Europe. Tobacco, Cuba's major export, was also smuggled to the French, English and Dutch Antilles to be re-exported to Europe, where its largest markets were Hamburg and Amsterdam. However, the monopoly strengthened its hold throughout the eighteenth century, so that Spain managed to receive more than two million lbs per year from 1740–1761.[24] Since, however, demand required some 3.5 million lbs per year, tobacco also had to be imported from Venezuela and Brazil via Lisbon, and even from the Chesapeake. Great Britain sent 1.2 million lbs of tobacco to Spain in 1729–1730, and more than a million lbs again in 1762–1768. Even the Seven Years' War, during which Spain allied itself with France, did not interrupt British sales in Madrid.

In contrast to Spain and France, the British government entered the tobacco trade under the framework of a monopoly. It preferred to sacrifice the highest possible receipts for the state in order to develop the colonies. The French, by contrast, abandoned colonial production at Santo Domingo as it did at home in order to base their manufacture of both snuff-tobacco and smoking-tobacco on tobacco imports essentially from the Chesapeake, the Farmer Generals charged with the management of the monopoly constituting one of the most important pressure groups that took an interest in it.[25] In Great Britain, importers paid higher customs duties – up to 200 per cent of the price of the product at the end of the eighteenth century – but in exchange, they were encouraged to re-export, since the traders who practised it received a reduction in the total amount of the duties settled at customs, with the exception of a halfpenny per lb. During the 1720s, Scottish and London merchants entered into a bitter competition, and Walpole agreed to abandon the demand for this halfpenny. On the European markets, this system made British prices far more competitive than those of the Germans, the Dutch and the other Continentals when prices were low (from 2 to 2.5d per lb). This explains the tripling of the British tobacco trade from the beginning of the 1720s to the beginning of the 1770s. On this latter date, re-exports accounted for 85 per cent of imports.

The largest purchases were made by the French monopoly after the end of the seventeenth century. During the war in the 1690s, French corsairs seized many ships loaded with Virginia tobacco, the taste of which was preferred to French and Antillean tobacco by smokers and snuff-takers, which they sold on cheaply to the monopoly. Following the peace of 1697, the tobacco firm bought more than a million lbs per year from England, regularly increasing its purchases throughout the eighteenth century. On the eve of the American war, they climbed to more than 23 million lbs per year, and even during the Seven Years' War, the licences granted enabled them to receive almost 12 million lbs per year. The rise in French purchases was an essential factor in the boom in British imports from the Chesapeake, Virginia and Maryland. In Glasgow, Scotland benefitted more than

London from the market's expansion: the rate of increase of its imports was more than 4.5 per cent per year after 1740, whereas the average growth rate in British purchases was no more than 2.4 per cent. After 1762, Scotland reserved 40 per cent of the market for importing, London less than 40 per cent. After the middle of the century, the French preferred to get supplies from Glasgow. By 1775, Chesapeake's business formed one of the major poles of activity in the Atlantic, employing more than 330 ships and 4,000 mariners.[26]

Who harvested the fruits of this boom, the plantation owner or the trader? Actually, the latter appears to have benefitted more. In the system of consigning his tobacco, the plantation owner forwarded his produce to a firm in London, selling and making advances for the following harvest. Large plantation owners joined forces to produce large consignments and thus assured themselves of credit from the traders in London and controlled the production of their less important neighbours. However, after 1745 a new type of selling appeared, based on direct purchases by local factors, and, due to the new competition this created with the previous system, prices soared. The firms that dominated the traffic from local factors in Virginia and Maryland were Scottish – mainly from Glasgow – offering higher prices and using their ships to better effect, loading them quicker than the consignment plantation owners. The voyage from the Chesapeake to Glasgow, a port further into the Atlantic than London, was faster. Numerous small-scale plantation owners were interested in this new mode of exchange. The London Tobacco Merchants – Buchanan, Russell and Molleson – retained the confidence of the larger plantation owners, to whom they granted huge credits. By 1773, after a sudden reversal in the tendency of the market, the larger traders of London sustained losses. This crisis clearly revealed the speculative character of the business, in a trade based on credit. Tobacco's high prices in the aftermath of the Seven Years' War had heightened the purchasing power of the plantation owners, to whom London-based commission agents sold European merchandise, while agreeing to advances secured by tobacco or by bills of exchange, and giving their debtors up to a year's credit. By 1770, the market was beginning to be saturated after plentiful harvests, and prices fell violently; since tobacco had been sent on the basis of higher prices to cover the plantation owners' debts, authorized overdrafts were far too large and could no longer be balanced, while the cargoes sent to Virginia from London were selling badly. Huge collapses hit London's firms at the end of 1772 and 1773. Clearly less engaged in these credit chains, Glasgow came out of the business far better off.

Through the tobacco trade, the Chesapeake, a 'captive market', contributed more than any other market in North America to increasing the importance of colonial trade for Great Britain. Although the plantation owners' networks of debt could, as in the crisis of 1773, turn out to be full of risks to commerce back home, the increase in their purchases in exchange for their colonial sales accorded an even greater importance to North America than to all the other markets Great Britain had available to its exports. North America's share thus climbed from 5.7 per cent of English exports at the beginning of the century to 25.3 per cent in 1772–1773, and after the American War of Independence, Great Britain was soon able, in the decades following the conflict, to recover the North American markets, placing 25 to 30 per cent of its exports there by the end of the century.[27]

Great Britain's Caribbean markets

In the English trade associated with the Antilles, the same speculative character that we met with in the Chesapeake trade can be found. This does not, however, detract from the enormous success of the North American markets. Of course, in order of value, of the colonial products imported by Great Britain, sugar comes first for the most part: in 1771–1775 its value reached £2.4 million sterling, whereas tobacco rose to no more than £1 million, and coffee and indigo each accounted for £3–500,000 sterling. The sugar trade, on the same dates, required 459 ships and more than 5,500 mariners, and the total imported of West Indian origin rose to more than £3 million sterling, whereas from the mainland colonies, they remained lower, at £2 million sterling.

The situation in the English Antilles was, however, very uneven, since on some islands the soil was exhausted and could no longer support sugar production, as was the case in Barbados where sales fell to an annual average of 5,715 tonnes in 1771–1775, whereas the Leeward Islands (Montserrat, St Kitts, Nevis, Antigua) delivered 25,654 tonnes over the same period, and Jamaica, more than 44,000 tonnes. This commercial situation was to the advantage of the regime of protected markets, and English imports from the Antilles tripled from the beginning of the century. The pearl of the Antilles was Jamaica, which came late to the sugar economy and in which, in 100 years from 1670–1770, the number of plantations had multiplied by seven, amounting in 1768 to almost 648 with their 100,000 slaves, producing more than 60,000 tonnes of raw sugar, each slave producing some 0.6 tonnes per year. The island exported almost 86 per cent of the total yield, while the island's 12,000 whites consumed 1,219 tonnes, that is, more than 100 kgs per person, far more than the English did in the same period.[28]

Commerce was still at the mercy of highly irregular climactic conditions, where droughts and hurricanes could destroy harvests and damage installations, while the cane fell prey to disease. Expeditions began in mid-March, at the end of the season of the 'rollers', which began in January. Ships attempted to be first to arrive in order to fetch the best prices in London, Bristol or Liverpool, and one or two days' delay could cause their cargoes to suffer heavy losses because sales were very slow due to plentiful arrivals. The first sugar came into Bristol at the end of May, and maritime activity peaked from 1 April to the end of July. At the end of these months, the risk of hurricanes brought a halt to the expeditions since the insurance rates became too high.

In fact, Jamaica's sugar was not the most highly regarded: London's traders criticized its low quality, far inferior to sugars from Barbados or the Leeward Isles. The rum the island produced, on the other hand, was very highly prized. The largest amount of molasses, a by-product from refining raw sugar, went to Jamaica for distilling this much sought-after rum, of which the island produced more than 168,000 hectolitres. Local consumption, as with sugar, was relatively high, with the colony taking 28 per cent of the rum produced, that is, more than 47,000 hectolitres. Each white man drank up to 117 litres per year, although each black adult male, driven by 'gargantuan' appetites, drank as much as 4.5 litres a week.[29] In London, it was held that Antilleans had bodies like those of Egyptian mummies due to their abuse of rum. The free blacks and the mulattos each consumed 90 litres a year; slaves, 13.5 litres. Great Britain and Ireland were first among the rum markets, taking three-quarters of it. We might also note that the English mainland colonies were only rarely supplied from Jamaica, taking the majority of the 86,000 hectolitres imported from the Antilles from the Leewards and Barbados. The North American consumer was satisfied with a rum of very much lower quality than Jamaica's, provided by imports and, increasingly, by mainland production using molasses imported from the foreign Antilles, especially the French islands.

Sugar production dominated the West Indian economy far more than it did that of the French Antilles. By 1770, sugar and its by-products – molasses and rum – comprised more than 89 per cent of Jamaica's exports, coffee playing a minimal role, only produced in notable quantities in the islands France ceded in 1763, Dominica and Grenada, the value of which had been growing since the middle of the century.

Due to prices being higher in England than in continental Europe, the sugar plantation owners experienced a golden age in the aftermath of the Seven Years' War, having managed to eliminate from the British market the serious competition represented during the war by occupied Guadeloupe and Martinique, which were not annexed under pressure from the colonial lobby. Thanks to the changes introduced in the Navigation Acts, Ireland and Scotland received their sugar directly, Ireland also received its sugar from Bristol and Liverpool, while simultaneously expanding their voyages to the Antilles: worth £35,000 sterling in 1682–1683, their value rose to £287,000 sterling in 1773–1774. Delivering salt-meats, butter and linen to the islands, the Irish market found the secret of enormous prosperity in this Antillean trade.

In the West Indies, trading relations between Jamaica, Tierra Firme and Mexico increased the importance of the colony, which received piastres from them, and in exchange exported manufactured goods from the home country into these markets.

As in the Chesapeake, trading relations more often than not made the plantation owners dependent upon trade in their home countries for sustaining Antillean commerce. Thanks to the system of buying on commission, London's powerful firms controlled the majority of Antillean commerce. Consignees for sugar and other colonial goods were responsible for selling them and buying products from Europe. Larger advances were granted to the plantation owners whose harvests varied depending on the weather and the value of their slaves, since wars could block imports of captive Africans. These inequalities in the sugar expeditions put plantation owners into dire straits when they were unable to cover the credit that had been granted them.

Permanent financial assistance sometimes resulted in direct associations between merchants and plantation owners. Credit against the harvests ran for a minimum of nine months in Jamaica at the end of the seventeenth century, and for buying slaves could be extended for as long as two years. Increases in the prices of European goods sold to the colonies paid for the advances, from which, more often than not, the interest was not deducted, so that there were always two prices – cash and credit – the latter naturally being the higher. The system pivoted around commissioners from London, Bristol or Liverpool, who bought provisions and equipment and sold Antillean merchandise. In London, for example, the great trader Lascelles had been extremely active in Barbados since the seventeenth century, and adopted a relatively liberal attitude towards the plantation owners, investing relentlessly in property. In Bristol, however, Pinney wanted more guarantees and was less willing to grant credit.

London controlled the market, at least as regards Bristol. Liverpool was capable of developing a practice of dropping the sale price of sugar on the domestic market and thus proved relatively independent of London's rates. By contrast, Bristol anxiously awaited the opening of the London market in order to fix prices.[30] In times of large imports, the collapse of prices in London badly affected the market in Bristol, where the refiners waited for the port's traders to lower their prices accordingly and hoped to buy large lots at more attractive prices in London. Kenneth Morgan notes how the fleet's arrival in Bristol from the Antilles controlled market conditions: too large a number of ships resulted in a saturated market, leading to lower rates; by contrast, the arrival of ships relatively lightly laden with sugar in a market with low supply entailed good prices. Information on the volume and quality of the harvests, principally in Jamaica, also constituted an essential factor regarding the market's behaviour.

War created an altogether different situation: in 1780–1781, during the American War of Independence, speculators had put their money into government securities rather than Antillean businesses. Sugar from foreign islands like

Saint Thomas and Tortola was offered at attractive prices, and brought about the collapse of sales from the English Antilles. Upon news of the peace, negotiated at the end of 1782, sales to Bristol were stopped and commerce suffered heavy losses. The only available options were to sell the sugar quickly or to keep large stocks and wait for the rate to pick up. The plantation owners pressed for the former, since more often than not they wished to sell quickly in order to recover their funds. On balance, it was a duel, pitting traders, importing factors and consignees against refiners and factors.

While taking account of the upsets endured under these circumstances, the picture of trade in the ports of the home country nevertheless remains one of the prosperity the merchants created on the basis of profits they realized from both the commissioning of colonial merchandise and the sale of European products exported to America. On the other hand, there is no need to accept the gloomy view advocated by some, despite the plantation owners' many remonstrations. In their study of the Worthy Park plantation in Jamaica, Michael Craton and James Walvin observed that average revenues during 1776–1796 (12 years of war and nine of peace) were equal to, if not higher than, those of the period preceding the American War of Independence, and were certainly double those of the years prior to 1750, making the average rate of return from 15 to 20 per cent of capital investment.[31]

'Captive markets' and the British export boom in the American markets

Commerce was deliberately concentrated on the Atlantic markets that enjoyed imperial protection because of the considerable extent to which the protectionist politics of several European states reduced the capacity of their markets to absorb manufactured products. English mercantilist legislation, like that of the French, strongly supported exporting such goods to colonial markets. When the English Commercial and Navigation Acts were passed in the middle of the seventeenth century, colonial trade represented no more than 10 per cent of English overseas trade. As Jacob M. Price writes, 'the legislators' most extravagant dreams turned out to be modest in comparison with the exuberant growth of the following century'.[32] In fact, in Ireland, the North American and Antillean colonies, and on the coasts of West Africa, English exports were increased by more than seven times from 1669–1701 to 1772–1774, representing less than one-fifth of the total exports in the first period, and almost three-fifths in the second.

On unprotected markets, the exporter's task was distinctly more difficult. Sales of English goods in southern Europe only increased by 50 per cent, while sales in northern and north-western Europe were even tending to decline. In the 'naval stores', the markets from which England bought strategic goods such as iron for anchors and capstans, rigging nets, masts, and hemp for cables and rope, exports covered only 20 per cent of imports in 1772–1774. To make good the deficit, they had to count on re-exporting colonial goods, and on English credit transfers coming from other areas of commerce. Colonial protection could turn out to be partly harmful to the grand politics of exporting. After 1705, parliament voted in a law subsidizing imports from the naval stores in the North American colonies. By 1740, London tried to subsidize the production of British linen in Scotland and Ireland, in order to replace imports of this textile from central Europe, and to export the necessary linen for clothing slaves in the American plantations. Central Europe retaliated by thoroughly reducing its purchases of English cloth.

In the face of the difficulties posed in Europe by the imposition of mercantilist policies, Great Britain turned increasingly back to the transatlantic markets, where the attractions of the Iberian colonial markets added to those of the British colonies. Their development had been one of the issues at stake in the Spanish War of Succession between France and England. In Utrecht, the annual ship, or *asiento*, that Madrid granted to London allowed British exporters to realize their hopes of selling manufactured goods and captured Africans to the Spanish colonies. Charles III's Spain, however, replied with the same protectionist politics, and later, at the time of the Spanish colonies' independence in the Americas in the 1800s, traders' minds could encompass new dreams. George Canning went on to boast that 'the New World called into existence would re-establish a balance in the Old'.[33]

British America, however, was to prove the better client throughout the entire eighteenth century. Almost 90 per cent of the goods imported by the colonies in 1770 from back home were manufactured or semi-manufactured.[34] For British firms, keeping this colonial clientele was a permanent concern. It required heavy financial sacrifices on the part of parliament, which subsidized exports of sugar from English refineries to the North American market in order to enable its price to remain competitive and even to win over new clients. Almost half of England's exports of copper goods, as well as irons and ceramics, cotton, linen and silk textiles, were sent to colonial markets: Benjamin Franklin knew what he was doing when he threatened London with closing these markets. The colonies could have produced the goods they imported themselves, but goods manufactured in England remained of a higher quality, so that taste and fashion dictated purchasing from Great Britain.

The remarkable terms offered to the English colonies in North America for settling their purchases from Britain also need to be underlined. British commercial firms granted long-term credit; transportation was at rock bottom prices due to a reduction in the cost of freight; above all, however, the colonists possessed enormous purchasing power because of their commercial links, both legal and illegal, with other countries.

A good example of these links is provided by American imports of molasses originating from foreign Antilles, in particular, the French islands:[35] in 1770, Santo Domingo produced some 404,684 hectolitres of molasses, of which more than 65 per cent was exported. France took 49,500 hectolitres, a relatively small amount; Germany, Italy and Holland made gin with this same molasses; but English North America was the best client, importing more than 196,000 hectolitres, either to be consumed in that form or to manufacture rum. In fact, molasses was substituted for sugar on colonial tables, and sold far better. In New England, sought-after confections were made with molasses, which were served in the traditional manner on feasts such as Thanksgiving Day. The Germans of Pennsylvania enjoyed apple pie, which was also cooked with Antillean molasses; at Christmas, many children were treated to gingerbreads, for which molasses was also used.[36] In 1728, a middle-class family of nine used up to 32 litres of molasses each year for cooking.

Imports had been increasing, however, for making rum. Since 1713, France's markets had forbidden the manufacture of any spirit apart from wine-spirits, taking only a paltry amount from the islands which was destined for export to Africa for the slave trade. To supply Boston's 36 distilleries, Newport's 16, New York's 17 and those in Philadelphia, the Americas also imported molasses from Guadeloupe and Martinique; on the island of Martinique alone, some 126 American ships loaded 25,875 hectolitres, that is, almost 2 tonnes of molasses per ship. These same ships also put in to Dutch Guyana, where molasses was extremely low-priced and where, in summer, there was no risk of hurricanes. In Sainte-Croix, in the Danish Antilles, ships from the mainland colonies were also to be found taking on French molasses that had been smuggled in. Overall, the French colonies were by far the major supplier, providing more than 87 per cent of America's imported molasses. The rum manufactured in English North America was of poor quality, barely comparable to Jamaican rum; lacking the colour and aroma of its Antillean counterpart, its price remained far lower. In 1770, New England covered two-thirds of its needs with North American rum. This enabled the extremely high consumption of rum to be sustained. According to John McCusker, in a single year the colonies drank almost as much rum as America does today, with 100 times the population. The mainland colonies consumed a total in excess of 340,000 hectolitres,[37] that is, 14 litres per year per inhabitant, whereas at the same date – 1770 – England and the Gaelic countries consumed no more than two and a quarter litres. The drink provided the requisite energy for New England's sailors and fishermen, the trappers of Pennsylvania and New York, as well as the lumberjacks from these same colonies.

While there was a certain amount of transatlantic export – 12,330 hectolitres sent to Newfoundland, 14,220 hectolitres loaded up for the African trade – the African market was relatively minor in scale. In 1770, less than a third of the rum exported by the mainland colonies was sent there.[38] In fact, these colonies were only playing a minor role in the slave trade: between Utrecht and the Seven Years' War, only Massachusetts and Rhode Island sent a few ships. The Seven Years' War saw an unprecedented expansion in the mainland colonies' maritime traffic, particularly with a new engagement in the slave trade, selling slaves to the occupied French and Spanish islands (19,000 slaves to Guadeloupe from 1759 to 1763; 11,000 to Cuba from August 1762 to January 1763). Subsequently, however, this traffic fell again, and in 1770 only 29 ships left the mainland colonies for the African coast, each loaded with 440 hectolitres of rum, while the number of slaves imported was only 4,400, barely 4.2 per cent of the total imported by the European slave trade, and 7.4 per cent of those taken by the British (104,761 slaves were then transported by the Europeans, 59,459 of which were for the British).[39]

Purchases of Antillean products were largely paid for by the North Americans' sales. Of course, in 1768–1772, Great Britain and Ireland remained the primary clients – out of £2.8 million sterling of exports, £1.6 million was headed for the United Kingdom, 57 per cent of total exports. However, the English and foreign Antilles represented the next most important client, taking £0.7 million's worth, more than 27 per cent of total exports, while for £0.4 million, southern Europe bought 14 per cent. There still remained a trade imbalance, of course, maintained by the mass of goods bought back home, but in 1766, Benjamin Franklin clearly identified a solution to this:

> The balance is paid by transporting our products to the Antilles and selling them in the French, Spanish, Danish and Dutch islands, and by transporting them to Spain, Portugal and Italy in Europe; in all these places, we either receive money, bills of exchange, or products that can then be delivered to Great Britain along with all the profits of the activities of our merchants and mariners deriving from these circuitous voyages; thus the cargoes won by their ships are at last brought to Great Britain, thus restoring the balance and paying for the English manufactured goods employed in the province or sold, by our merchants, to foreigners.[40]

On the eve of the American War of Independence, facing a trade imbalance averaging, in 1768–1772, £1.4 million sterling, the North American outfitting yards brought in almost £0.6 million, other 'invisible' revenues yielding £0.2 million, that is 58 per cent of the deficit paid for by merchants' profits. Added to this, revenues from government expenditure on the colonies of £0.4 million sterling brought in important cash.

The 1733 Molasses Act, placing prohibitive duties on the importing of foreign molasses while at the same time authorizing sales of wood, livestock and provisions, was not applied, and the supply of provisions and wood to the Antilles was a source of increasing revenues, regardless of British mercantilist measures. In 1768–1772, American flour sold in southern Europe and the Antilles alone rose to a total of 44,307 tonnes, 20,653 tonnes of which were sent to the Antillean plantations. New York and Pennsylvania were the most successful in these sales, sending 15,014 tonnes to the Antilles. On the other hand, in the export of salt fish to the Antilles and southern Europe, at a rate of 9,826 and 5,854 tonnes respectively, Massachusetts took first place, sending 13,363 tonnes.

In effect, the Antillean expansion created a growing demand for products from the North American mainland, raising their prices and increasing the revenues of the Thirteen Colonies. For most American products, prices rose more quickly in the middle of the century than they did for the products of English industry: with a given quantity of wheat, a farmer could buy many more cloth or metallurgical products. After 1760, this tendency was reversed, but the prices of seed and flour continued to rise when England decided to buy grain and the Portuguese market grew extensively.

Moreover, commercial operations between the homeland and its colonies very often included arrangements for bartering product against product: tobacco for linen sheets, raw iron for hardware. British suppliers had to buy tobacco and iron to enable them to amass the outstanding capital and to accelerate the circulation of their funds. In fact, credit remained the fundamental basis of all Great Britain's colonial relations: she invested up to £9 million sterling in credit chains in North America, the Antilles and Africa on the eve of the American War of Independence. Indeed, it was the flexible way in which Great Britain financed its Atlantic trade that meant it could count on meeting the challenge posed to it by the boom in France's Atlantic markets.

The fragility of the astonishing French success

France's situation in the Atlantic at the beginning of the eighteenth century

At the end of Louis XIV's reign, England's progress created a clear distance between the two countries. As contemporaries observed:

> France will become dependent on the English, just as Spain is dependent upon her foreign neighbours for providing what cannot be found within her Realm, in which case our industry and our navigation will die out and England will become strong by the growth of her subjects, her business and her wealth.

In 1714, this memorandum, sent to the Marquis de Torcy, Secretary of State for Foreign Affairs, expressed a fear that would persist in the minds of the majority throughout the eighteenth century.[41] However, not only did France close a part of this distance, she even proved herself capable of outstripping her rival in the Atlantic colonial trade.

London had won important concessions at the Treaty of Utrecht, signed the previous year. Spain, humiliated, had granted the English an *asiento* for negroes – the provision of Spanish America with African slaves passed into British slave-traders' hands; she also allowed a vessel – known as an 'annual ship' – of 300 tonnes loaded with English merchandise to be sent each year to the American Indies. However, Spain's climb-down could also be seen to be France's. It was indeed true that threats that had already been made in the negotiations leading up to the peace had been carried out by 1711, when a French Royal Commission for Foreign Affairs asked that English demands for 'two concessions in the South Seas' be rejected:

> We must be persuaded that, as deserted as it [the island of Juan Fernandez off the Chilean coast] may be today, if it passes into England's possession, then in a very few years, there would soon be a large number of inhabi-tants, ports would be established, and it would quickly become the largest entrepôt in the world for European and Asian manufactured goods, from which the English would supply the kingdoms of Peru and Mexico...[in exchange for the] 60 million in gold and silver leaving their mines every year, that would be the aim and the result of their industry; what efforts would this nation, so skilled in commerce and powerful in ships, spare in order to lay hold of this immense revenue from America![42]

However, these fears were to prove largely unfounded. For one thing, the use of the annual ship did not bring in as much as might have been hoped. According to J. H. Parry, there had only been eight annual voyages from 1714 to 1738 for the trade fairs in Porto Bello and Vera Cruz.[43] It was rather the sale of English prod-ucts during illicit trading voyages, often in the face of a Spanish fleet that was still highly active, that enabled Great Britain to tap into the flow of Mexican piastres; but disappointing trade was to drive London into war against Spain in 1739. However, the British had extended their control of the Brazilian maritime economy by exploiting the means that the 1703 Treaty of Alliance with Portugal had given them: they shared in the Brazilian gold boom, selling their cloth and other products on the Portuguese market and creating a surplus of exports there that could only be balanced by the supply of gold from Brazil. In the Spanish Empire, on the other hand, it was France that, over more than half a century, managed to extend its trade either through the intermediary of its colonies or through direct relations.

In 1715, however, the English advance seemed unstoppable. England had profited from the advantage it had seized over the Dutch in three successive wars in the second half of the seventeenth century, from 1652 to 1674. She managed to quell Dutch pre-eminence in the sugar and tobacco trades, as well as the traffic in fur and slaves. Most importantly, the crises of the seventeenth century had not struck England as they had France: in the 'dark seventeenth century', the French economy suffered at the very least from stagnation, if not decline, and Colbert's commendable efforts to struggle against this tendency seemed destined to fail. This largely suffices to explain the widening gap between the two countries. Frequent economic and demographic crises in France brought about a lowering of revenues and consumption. By contrast, the English economy, which certainly experienced difficult periods during the civil war and some years of war against Louis XIV, was not afflicted with violent crises, and there was a real increase in the average income of each inhabitant. English colonial expansion was precocious and during the 1660s the re-exportation of exotic products constituted the principal factor in the growth of overseas trade, whereas France's colonies and her colonial trade remained negligible for a long time. In 1715, the English merchant fleet was more important, and the accumulation of commercial capital proportionally higher, as was trade.

Nevertheless, this general tendency should not conceal the reality of a growth in certain sectors of the French economy, the signs of which were apparent at the end of Louis XIV's reign. Despite the jolts created by the war, overseas trade experienced a certain expansion, traffic with the far Atlantic – the Spanish colonies and the Antilles – grew, accompanied by constant trading in Europe, where the northern countries were reached through the intermediary of Holland and could receive up to one-third of total exports. The policy of devaluing the royal currency, due to monetary revaluations at the end of Louis XIV's reign in 1713, created favourable conditions for exports. When the Anglo–French commercial treaty, which had been the subject of much deliberation, was negotiated, the British Atlantic merchants expressed their fears:

> The war has devalued French exchange rates, the *livre tournois* has fallen from 18 to 12 pence, which gives the advantage to French merchants....[T]heir manufactures have begun to sell well for us, and if we impose only moderate duties on their imports, we will be overrun with French products.[44]

The signs of renewal came from the Atlantic, where France had taken hold of the markets in the Antilles and in Spanish America. French since the Treaty of Ryswick, Santo Domingo experienced the start of the sugar economy which was to make it so very wealthy in the course of the century. Favoured by a certain effacement of the sugar economy on Britain's Antillean islands, and the falling back of Brazilian production, the Greater Antilles were struck, after 1701, by a fever for sugar mills: 'fifty-two rolling sugar mills [for processing cane sugar], with another thirty ready to roll in three months, and ninety that have already begun'. For de Gallifet, the governor, writing to Minister Pontchartrain, the colony was entering the age of the great slave plantations.[45]

French growth in the eighteenth century

As François Crouzet has clearly outlined, the data is well known: French overseas trade went from an average of 215 million *livres tournois* in 1716–1720, to more than 1,060 million in 1784–1788, increasing its value fivefold. Taking price rises into account, we must arrive at a threefold increase at least. English overseas trade rose from £13 million sterling in 1716–1720 (on average) to £31 million in 1784–1788, expanding more slowly than its French counterpart.[46]

This dynamic growth was due in large measure to the Atlantic. In Spain and, via Cadiz, in Spanish America, the French maintained the position they had acquired during the reign of Louis XIV, and France remained the most important provider of manufactured goods on these markets. The greatest advantage of this expansion was the 'Americanization' of trade: colonial traffic increased tenfold from 1716–1720 to 1784–1788, while exchanges with non-European countries represented 38 per cent of all trade at this latter date.

In Santo Domingo, the expansion in the cultivation of sugar cane, like coffee, 'as sudden as lightning',[47] on these new soils, yielding a product at rock-bottom price, very competitive on Europe's markets when compared to goods from the English islands with their exhausted soils and higher production costs, constituted the basis of this boom in colonial traffic. Thereafter, France was able to establish its dominance in the markets of northern Europe, where trading in its Atlantic ports multiplied the re-exporting of colonial goods eightfold. This boom was even more significant than British re-exports, which, although they were still sizeable in 1700, when they represented half of the total volume of exports, fell sharply after the 1720s, at least as concerns sugar.

France's golden age in the Atlantic had its best years before the Seven Years' War, traffic expanding hugely from 1735 to 1755, while the value of overseas trade doubled in barely 20 years. A slump became apparent during the Seven Years' War with catastrophic effects, since the British Navy chased French ships from the sea, and recourse to neutrals' ships could not compensate for the effects of enemy cruisers. Average annual trade then was barely half that of previous years. During the American War of Independence, trade was still falling sharply, from 725 million *livres tournois* in 1777 to 450 million in 1779. It is true, however, that the war had been preceded by a clear renewal and that a new boom in the years preceding the French Revolution appeared in the balance sheets for the years 1787–1788.

In fact, independently of the influence of wars, structural weaknesses in trade revealed themselves. First, its growth became increasingly dependent on the Antilles alone: in the 1780s, Santo Domingo alone was responsible for three-quarters of the exchanges with the colonies, and provided the largest amount for re-exporting. When compared with Great Britain, another weakness appeared: the proportion of industrial products in French re-exports remained relatively modest, never exceeding two-fifths, whereas in England it accounted for two-thirds of exports. First among these were coffee, sugar and wine, then came fabrics and silks. Another weakness in the French Atlantic was that its colonies had not seen the creation of social structures comparable to those back home, particularly as regards the emergence of the middle classes and their higher purchasing power. England's Thirteen Colonies did possess a middle class with a standard of living close to that of Europe's middle classes. In the French Antilles, a white minority, partly composed of absentee plantation owners, could not aspire to play such a role. Finally, and this was by far the most serious defect on the French side, the British mastery of the seas could never seriously be challenged – sea power remained the privilege of Great Britain.

The success of Santo Domingo, the 'pearl of the Antilles'

If therefore there were serious reasons to doubt the future of a commercial empire that remained fragile, French success made a no less strong an impression on the contemporary world, and its most distinctive symbol was Santo Domingo's unashamed wealth.

Colonial towns always drew admiring astonishment from voyagers in the time of the Enlightenment: the 'Paris of the Antilles', the Cap Français (now Cap Haïtien), on the island's north coast, best represented the success of the plantations and the traders. After 1743, the Jesuit Margrat showed that the Cap, 'which, in the beginning, was nothing but a random collection of a few fishermen's huts and stores for loading, is now considerable'. Forty years later, at the peak of the traffic, Moreau de Saint Méry clearly outlined the town's activities:

> It is a very interesting sight to see in these two streets [Moreau had just shown the Rue du Gouvernment 'completely filled with traders' and has now added Rue Sainte Croix] the long row of shops where vessels from every port parade merchandise manufactured in these ports…and also lay out what has been taken from foreign ports. In front of each shop is a table of around three feet in length, containing a detailed inventory of

the cargo being sold there, the names of the captain and of his ship. One might think that in a few moments, one could run through all France when one hears first a Gascon accent, followed by accents from Normandy, Provençe and Dunkirk.[48]

By then, the Cap's population had tripled since the middle of the century, reaching almost 20,000 inhabitants. Not all, of course, profited equally from the town's boom, and Moreau de Saint Méry notes that one out of every six whites had no property, and contented themselves with 'speculating about uncertain events'. The Cap's wealth, however, coming from a port that held on to the majority of the traffic, was striking. In 1788, 465 ships were sent from ports in France to Santo Domingo; the Cap welcomed almost two-thirds of them, some 320 ships. With traffic on this scale, its port accounted for more than 40 per cent of the transatlantic movement destined for the French Antilles: 783 ships left France for the Caribbean during that year. Almost 15 years earlier, in 1773, 296 out of the 570 that left France for the American islands were welcomed in Santo Domingo. At this time, French navigation in the Caribbean held pride of place in the Atlantic: the English Antilles received 459 ships and the Chesapeake colonies 330. Out of a total activity of 1359 ships crossing the ocean to take tobacco, sugar, coffee, indigo and cotton, Antillean traffic from France represented almost 42 per cent of the total.

The intensity of the activity in the Cap's port is reflected in the feverish loading and unloading imposed on the ships' captains arriving from France. Shortening the time taken during the stopover by gaining the best wind conditions was a priority. For this reason, they hurried to rent the best placed shops and did not hesitate to pay the most expensive rents. In 1784, from 1,000 to 1,200 livres a month were thus paid out by captains anxious to have the best shops at their disposal.[49]

An enormous diversity of cargoes was discharged: provisions, especially flour, wine and meats, still comprised a high proportion of the products introduced, while 'dry goods' often of high value, were also part of these cargoes. To this, material supplies should also be added, such as wheels and drums for the sugar mills, and copper boilers for cooking *vesou* from the juice of the sugar cane, and even construction materials such as slate from the Loire, stone from Gironde like the paving stones from Barsac used in the construction of the pavements in the streets of the Cap. Ships from Bordeaux discharged almost 20,000 tonnes of flour alone at the end of the 1780s, despite the severe competition the Americans from Philadelphia or New York provided. According to statements from Moreau de Saint Méry, some 20 bakers from the Cap needed almost 70 barrels, that is, almost six tonnes of flour each day, so as to offer to the inhabitants white bread similar to the bread back home.

The captains, however, scrupulously noted the prices and the quantities of 'dry goods' in their sales records. Doubtless fashion and the desire to appear in the latest clothes, rather than the habitat, inspired behaviour on the islands. Buying fine shirts, lingerie, silk stockings or lace waistcoats satisfied the Creoles' vanity. At the same time, back in France, these sales stimulated occasionally vigorous growth in the manufacturing of luxury goods in Cholet, Valenciennes, Ganges, Lyon and Saint-Etienne. In 1788, the value of exports to the Antilles was 77 million, of which textile products exceeded 34 million livres, decidedly higher, that is, than provisions (29 million livres). In Bordeaux, hosiery alone, especially the most renowned article, the Cholet handkerchief, was of sufficient value to make about 1.5 million in exports. For the mariners and their ships these products formed the basis for 'private' operations for their own benefit. These were *pacotilles* that were not included in the cargoes sent on behalf of shipowners or other traders. Purchased, in most cases, on credit, these goods provided an opportunity to engage for the first time in the islands' trade to merchants who, lacking the means, could not take a share in the cargoes.

The prices of these goods remained very high, the value of *pacotille* often reaching from 10–12,000 livres, or even higher. With such sums, one could procure the most expensive colonial goods such as indigo or, better still, Spanish piastres. It seems that, in the Antilles area, a double circulation of these moneys was taking place in the eighteenth century. On the one hand, piastres were most often off-loaded in Cadiz, where ships from Marseilles, Bayonne and Bordeaux met after having crossed the Atlantic to put funds into the islands' markets, which more often than not suffered from cash shortages. Ships' captains with 'silver in their hands' bought colonial goods at the lowest prices. However, piastres also came to Santo Domingo and Martinique from Tierra Firme or Mexico, and were illicitly exchanged for *pacotilles*.

Some Portuguese-Jewish firms that had set up in Bordeaux, the Cap Français or Port-au-Prince seem to have made such exchanges their speciality, conducting them not only in the colony but also throughout Spain's possessions. Salomon Raba, a founder of one of the largest Portuguese firms in Bordeaux, made profits emerge from this trade: 'the Spanish buy things of the highest quality from us, such as silk, lace, velvet, silver and golden threads, and silk stockings'.[50] Established in Bordeaux in 1765 before founding a subsidiary in the Cap with 80,000 livres of capital, less than 20 years later the firm controlled assets that had risen to more than 4.3 million. In the 1780s, there were almost 150 Jewish firms in Bordeaux, with links to communities in Amsterdam, London and Curaçao, that consolidated into networks.

The wealth of the plantation owners and the traders of Santo Domingo enabled them to display clothing and lay tables of a luxury that surprised visitors, and by selling products from the plantations, their wealth grew further. The plantation owners of Santo Domingo dominated the North Atlantic sugar market from the 1740s. At the beginning of that decade, they controlled more than 40 per cent of the market, practically as much as they did 30 years later,[51] whereas British sales accounted for no more than 28 per cent of the market, which was mostly conducted in Great Britain, Ireland and the North American colonies. According to Drescher, if we compare the production of Santo Domingo alone with that of the entire British Antilles, around 1745, we can see that the Greater Antillean island exported half of the total. It was, in fact, between 1720 and 1740 that Santo Domingo got the better of Jamaica in the production and export of cane sugar, since the proportion of British sugar re-exported fell by at least 10 per cent in 1734–1738, while French sugars gained at least three-quarters of this trade.

The Seven Years' War gave the British the chance to reverse this situation. Leaving to one side the importance of Guadeloupe, which the English occupied but did not retain after the peace, the islands France ceded to Great Britain – Grenada, Dominica and St Vincent – sharply increased the capacity of the English Antilles: in 1787, the 18,630 tonnes of sugar they produced represented almost 18 per cent of their gross product; the English could begin re-exporting significant volumes during the 1780s to northern Europe, where they were competing with the French. In comparison, Tobago and Santa Lucia, the islands France acquired after the American War of Independence, producing close to 3,200 tonnes, made only a tiny contribution to the growth of production on the French islands, which, however, was still higher than that of the English Antilles, since, along with the giant Santo Domingo, which made more than 86,000 tonnes, it rose to more than 125,000 tonnes.

In the wars of the second half of the century, Great Britain actually had the advantage thanks to the success of her navy; French superiority in the sugar economy was proportionally no longer as large at the end of the *ancien régime* as in the middle of the century. At this time, positions were tending to become established and even at the level of exports, Jamaica made up some of its lag behind Santo Domingo.

On the eve of the French Revolution, coffee rather than sugar was the most dynamic element in the wealth of the greatest island in the French Antilles. Its dazzling boom took place after the Seven Years' War, on the new soils, along the slopes of the small mountains to the north and south of the island. Despite the expansion of sugar cane plantations, this crop never took up all the land. Around 1770, coffee exports accounted for a quarter of the total value of exports from the French Antilles, whereas they made up only 11 per cent of the value of exports from the English islands. On Santo Domingo, far from the plains and the irrigation necessary for cultivating sugar cane or indigo, coffee trees were planted in their thousands in the larger hillside properties. The sugar colonists who had suffered huge losses during the war, due to the sudden collapse in prices, sold off their fields for new land. Buttressed by large, capital-rich businesses, the coffee front also benefitted from small-and medium-sized owners, within whose organizations people of colour often held important office. This explains the position occupied by Santo Domingo in the French coffee trade at the end of the *ancien régime*: out of 39,000 tonnes received in France from the Antilles in 1788, 34,000 came from Santo Domingo.[52]

Cotton, the last crop to contribute to Santo Domingo's growth, expanded due to high European demand. Its production benefitted from the breach made in the English mercantilist system when, in 1766, free ports were opened in the Caribbean islands of Dominica and Jamaica. Cotton from Santo Domingo and the other French islands found its best market in England, where, unlike sugar, it was not yet hampered by higher duties. Santo Domingo owes more to the cotton boom than it does to sugar or even coffee, as regards the spectacular increase in its slave workforce in the years following the American War of Independence. Then the colony doubled its imports of Africans, whether sent by French slave-traders or by the English from Jamaica, where traders used the free ports: each year in the 1780s, some 30,000 slaves were unloaded on Santo Domingo. Exports of cotton from Santo Domingo rose by almost a third from 1783 to 1789, while sugar exports grew by only one per cent. The value of the cotton exported was higher then than that of indigo (16.7 million *livres tournois* against 10.4 million). The example of a port like Bordeaux shows the importance of English demand as regards these exports: in 1785, seven ships had left, loaded with cotton, for England; in 1789, 19 were sent to the British market, 15 of which went to Liverpool.

France was, however, far from being the only country on the European continent to re-export cotton to Great Britain, since its share of British imports was close to one-fifth. In 1789, out of the 32 million pounds of cotton imported by Great Britain, more than 10 million came from European ports: Brazilian cotton from Portugal, Demeraran from Holland, and Santo Domingan from France.

To contemporaries during the 1780s, however, Santo Domingo's renown was based more on its sugar and its coffee than on its cotton: in 1788–1789, the Great Antillean island exported more than 72 million lbs of coffee, six times more than 20 years earlier. In Europe, a consumer boom took place in which the price of coffee from Morocco and the Near East, having been prohibitive for a long time, fell noticeably after the middle of the century. At the end of the *ancien régime*, even in Great Britain, it was recognized that the French colonies had beaten the British on the European and North American coffee markets, whereas in the sugar markets, the West Indies' plantation owners had made up a proportion of the lag that took hold in the middle of the eighteenth century.

The 'fabulous' success of Santo Domingo's plantation owners seemed to dominate the Atlantic economy. However, it was far from exclusive, and threat-ened to come to an end. The weaknesses of a colonial Hercules, in whose wealth Moreau de Saint Méry could see 'one of the greatest successes obtained by the European powers overseas', were to reveal how far it was from a greatly over-romanticized vision of things.

Threats to the French Atlantic

The view of the islands as a paradise with luxuriant vegetation and an enchanting climate had for a long time kept Christopher Columbus under its spell. Some three centuries later, Santo Domingo had seduced just as many visitors. However, this was far removed from the experience of the savage Antillean in the plantation colony with no experience of the changes introduced by the Europeans, and whose work was permanently on the increase.

Girod de Chantrans of Switzerland, doubtless more lucid than others, had difficulty adjusting to the turbulence of the great port that was the Cap Français: 'the world's wealth is so vast, that the streets are always full of people coming and going despite the burning heat of the sun'. While he may have longed for the calm of the countryside, he had gone there to find

> a certain dark thrill produced by the chaos and noise of the sugar mills alongside the carts trundling along with their crops, in addition to which one can occasionally and indistinctly hear blows being dealt to animals and negroes. From ovens and boiler rooms, plumes of smoke can be seen extending high into the distance and falling to the earth, or rising in the form of dark clouds.

Other travellers declare themselves struck by the cheerful spectacle of the country-side and the fertile soils, and cannot avoid giving in to a kind of colonial romanticism. Perhaps the reality lies somewhere between these two views.

THE REALITY OF THE ANTILLES

However optimistic or pessimistic the view, the reality of the natural environment was unavoidable: a climate of great contrasts, where the gentle spring or autumn that Columbus observed is far from permanent. Amongst the natural catastrophes that in a few hours could destroy the plantations, the typhoons and hurricanes of the winter months from August to October hold pride of place. Described as 'the Plagues of Egypt', they were often preceded by long months during which 'great droughts' held sway, afflicting both plants and men: river levels fell and the cane could bake. These effects were accentuated by the savage deforestation that had ensued due to the recent planting of coffee bushes: the forest mantle was destroyed, the earth no longer held, and beneficent rains became more rare: 'The rains are much less abundant than they used to be. The mountain settlements are quite injurious to the plains; the more of the country they clear, the less it rains.'[53] Of course, in the last years of the *ancien régime*, a huge effort was made to offset the consequences of the five to six months of drought experienced on certain parts of the island, and irrigation networks were set up using water from the rivers that flowed down the low mountains; but this was not enough. All too often, the hoped-for rains came down with too much violence. These were the 'swallowers': canes were flattened, huts and roofs from dwellings and sugar houses were carried away by rivers that had burst their banks.

Hurricanes affected all the islands. On 10 and 12 October 1780 a single hurricane devastated first Barbados and then Martinique. On the first island, more than 2,000 slaves and some 700 whites perished, and several houses in Bridgetown were destroyed; in Saint-Pierre, on Martinique, the sea swept houses away and trees were uprooted. Four years previously, Bordeaux's shipowners refused to discharge their cargoes at Guadeloupe, which had just been hit by a hurricane, for fear of finding the plantation owners unable to pay for their goods,[54] since they had lost practically all their crops. From 1780 to 1785, Jamaica experienced no fewer than six hurricanes. Of all the Antilles, however, due to its enormous riches, Santo Domingo's economy was worst hit by the dramatic repetition of such catastrophes.

The devastating effects of natural catastrophes can be worsened by a lack of human foresight. Girod de Chantrans was able to identify clearly the dangers to which an ill-considered exploitation of the land exposed Santo Domingo during the 1780s:

> In the district of Marmelade, which has not been cultivated for twenty-five years, the mountains are still wooded or planted with coffee bushes up to their summits, and are everywhere covered over with a significant bed of earth. The same is not the case on the earliest mountains to be cultivated, whose hilltops and peaks have become infertile and been abandoned, exhausted, entirely denuded and spiked with rocks in the form of needles.[55]

In the French Antilles, and most particularly on Santo Domingo, a fragile, natural environment was in part threatened by sometimes foolhardy developments in the economy of the Atlantic plantation. Can we for all that accuse the plantation owners of remaining insensitive to the problem and, by looking for only the most immediate profit, endangering the colony's future?

Again, Girod de Chantrans was quite clear on this point. An unchanging routine governed agriculture, passed on from one to another, applied without any modifications whatever to all soil types. This is, in effect, the case brought against the plantation owners:

> always preoccupied with the idea of returning to France and guided by an old, flawed example, seeking only to draw hastily from their land all that it can produce at the lowest possible cultivation costs, without troubling themselves with the following generation.[56]

This observer from home was led to pass judgement all the more severely on the agriculture and management of the plantations, obviously at one remove from reality, since there existed a strong inclination in both England and France to condemn a plantation for relying on slave labour, which was abhorrent to humanitarian views. Adam Smith was one of the first to highlight the superiority of wage labour over slavery, and the theory of the decline of the colonial plantations was accepted by the École Liberale, under increasing pressure, at the end of the century.

PROFITS AND PLANTATIONS

On the part of the British, this decline had given rise to the abolition of the slave trade, and then of slavery. The plantation classes in the West Indies had begun to become aware of this in the aftermath of the Seven Years' War, and the country's economic interests demanded the abandonment of the slave trade and slavery itself. The upsurge of industrial capitalism led to a weakening of the plantation owners' cause. Although the theory is also applied to the French islands and therefore to Santo Domingo, the 'dereliction' of the English Antilles became clear after facts that were often invalidly generalized, such as the exhaustion of the soil, or the rise in absentee plantation owners, were believed to be flaws. In particular, the latter had placed their fields under the control of managers who were rather unscrupulous, both as regards treating the soil properly and the use of a slave labour force.

These generalizations may appear invalid, and they are contradicted by the precise observations that studies of the plantations present. In Jamaica, Michael Craton and James Walvin, in the Worthy Park plantation from 1776 to 1796, generated an average revenue that was equal, if not superior, to that of the revenues obtained before the middle of the century; average profits here were 15 to 20 per cent of the capital.[57] On the Fleuriau plantation on Santo Domingo, Jacques de Cauna was himself also asked about the profitability of the plantation, and he estimated that, other than the difficult times of the Seven Years' War and the 1770 earthquake, the results were more than decent, and had noticeably improved after the American War of Independence. Gross income was tripled, and net profits were taken to more than 15 per cent.[58] This put the plantation, near to Port-au-Prince, into the upper ranks which, according to Girod de Chantrans, were able to bring in more than 15 per cent net profit. Of course, lower revenues are given for many other plantations, but, as de Cauna wisely notes, the theoretical revenue estimated in goods does not take account of the possibility of subsidiary profits from illicit trade, profits drawn from smuggling. There was a dynamic attitude on the part of the managers who, between the American War of Independence and the French Revolution, were pressing for the plantation to be modernized by increasing purchases of slaves, establishing new kinds of agriculture and refitting buildings.

A similarly precise analysis confirmed the famous Hilliard d'Auberteuil's assertions and soothed the plantation owners' anger: well-managed sugar refineries yielded 15 per cent net per year, thus reimbursing capital at the very least within seven years. The plantation owners could only protest against such views implying a certain increase in wealth that did not correspond to the losses that they had advanced to justify the delay in scheduling their debts to trade and the home country. Absent proprietors and managers complained unanimously and, as Pierre Pluchon correctly points out,

> little by little, the absentee owners followed their inclinations, with the self-interested collusion of the colonists who remained on the islands: the average annual income of a colonial estate raised just about 6 to 7 per cent, or indeed 5 per cent.[59]

In fact, the profits came from the 'colonial secret' and, in 'discreet' exchanges of letters, this was itself often raised.

Nevertheless, the real problem lay with French Atlantic trade, which found itself facing unavoidable changes that led to alterations in the structure of the entrepôt economy on which its wealth had been based for more than a century. These structures involved respecting the protected market constituted by the legislation of the colonial Exclusive monopolies. It gave privileged French ports the *exclusive* right to trade with the colonies, in order to procure necessary European products for them and to let their products flow into the markets at home and abroad. In these latter markets, traders had developed a fruitful export trade by taking advantage of the entrepôt's customs regime, so that re-exported goods were free of duty. Since the middle of the century, war had led to the decline of such regimes: the astonishing superiority of the British navy in the Atlantic considerably weakened maritime relations between the French ports and her colonies, which had to resort to the services of neutrals and forced the colonists to focus on a trade far closer to home, with the Thirteen Colonies of the

English Atlantic, in violation of both British and French legislation. In the aftermath of the Seven Years' War, modifications that took account of the *de facto* state of things were introduced in the Exclusivists' legislation in order to soften its harshness and to authorize certain links with foreigners; this had happened anyway after the American War of Independence. Certainly, the situation created in the aftermath of this conflict was new to the extent that the old colonies that had become independent in the United States were officially prevented from trading with the West Indies (in the 1783 Navigation Act) and were therefore forced to turn towards other Antillean markets.

The intrusive presence of the 'New English of America' on the land and in the waters of Santo Domingo and the other French islands was undoubtedly in the interests of the plantation owners, but it was a real threat that was capable of ruining the traditional structures of the colonial economy for good. 'The extent to which foreigners have been allowed to trade has proportionally diminished our own, as consequently, it has our navigation.' This bitter reflection from a Marseilles trader in January 1785, barely a few months after the establishment of a slimmed-down Exclusive monopoly in August 1784, favourable to North American interests, had also occurred to many other traders.[60]

The ageing plantation economy had not therefore 'run out of steam' prefiguring the decline of the sugar islands in the face of the new forces landing on other exotic shores such as India. Louis Dermigny's views do not square with the realities observed on Santo Domingo.[61] Rather, it is the structural transformations in the colonial market, considered from the point of view of traders from home as a decline, that must be examined. Without going so far as to follow in blind faith the *pro domo* complaints of the traders, who affirmed that the island trade was ruinous to them, 'that it was kept up only to keep their ships employed', deficits were indeed noted in commercial accounts: sales of European products in the colonies did not produce enough of a profit to cover the losses recorded in exporting colonial goods. Blame fell on the speculation that developed at the end of the American War of Independence; too many ships were sent, entailing lesser cargoes, an excessive rise in colonial products and the 'depreciation' of merchandise from the home country. Denouncing the 'thanklessness' of business in America, the Bordeaux Chamber of Commerce painted an extremely pessimistic picture: 'There are barely ten shipowners in Bordeaux who have made a profit in their trade since the peace, the remainder have made greater or lesser losses.'[62]

THE PLANTATION OWNERS IN DEBT

Of all the evils thus exposed, the most serious seemed to be the slowness or even the catastrophic delays in the plantation owners paying for slaves and products from the home country, which bled the coffers of commercial firms dry. Nantes encountered the same difficulties as Bordeaux: on the eve of the Revolution, eight large shipowners from Nantes had credits in the Antilles exceeding eight million livres (160 million francs in 1995). At the end of 1792, the firm of Paul Nairac in Bordeaux, one of the largest slaving-ship owners in the port, had more than 2 million livres unpaid from three voyages carried out by his ships in 1790–1791.[63] There was strong tendency to increase the overdrafts extended to the plantation owners: during the time of the Seven Years' War, Santo Domingo's debts to the slave-trading shipowners from Nantes was 10 million, and certainly far exceeded this total in 1789.

Meanwhile, sales of slaves by shipowners from the French Atlantic ports were to constitute one of the most important sources of profit, since the costs of a slave workforce had risen considerably in the second half of the century due to the increased demand attendant upon clearing the land for coffee and cotton on Santo Domingo. Thus the price of an adult slave was on average higher than 2,000 livres (40,000 francs in 1995). However, the system of payments in the slave trade – and it was the same in the 'honest' trade between the Antilles and the home country – led to the plantation owners accumulating debts. In reality, in contrast to the British firms that employed the services of permanent correspondents or 'postmen', French firms more often than not preferred to entrust their sales in Santo Domingo and the other islands to their ships' captains. With difficulty, they managed to find important and independent correspondents. When they did make use of local links, it was generally through the intermediary of their branches, managed by younger associates who were often relations of the firms back home, who financed these branch managers as limited partners. Ships' captains still had an essential role in selling the cargoes of African slaves: in the majority of cases, the large slave-traders, carrying between 250 and 400 slaves, had two captains. Once the slaves were disembarked and the return cargoes were loaded, the ship left under the command of the second captain while the first remained on the island for at least a year in order to collect the funds arising from the sale of slaves. This was a profitable activity for him, since he took five–six per cent as a commission on these recoveries. At the same time, he looked after loading the colonial goods that were the products of these funds on ships chartered for that purpose.

The means for paying for slaves and goods from the home country involved bonds. A certain proportion of these, though rarely the majority share, was paid in cash, in piastres or bills drawn on their local traders, or in colonial goods. The larger share was however settled in promissory notes from the plantation owners or their representatives, the traders from the ports of Santo Domingo, who paid in colonial produce over 12, 18 or 24 months. By contrast, Liverpool's traders had generally, since 1750, received the yield from their sales 'on shore', before casting off from the port of the West Indies, either in merchandise or in negotiable bills of exchange.[64] Increasingly used to settle the purchase of slaves, British

163

slave traders preferred bills of exchange to returns in goods. They were drawn by the 'factors' or the traders more than by the plantation owners, and were easily accepted back home. This was hardly the case for bills of exchange drawn by the plantation owners on the French islands, and the explanation for the prevalent distrust towards the latters' signatures is provided by measures taken in legislation providing creditors with recourse against their colonial debtors. In the plantations in the West Indies, especially after the law on colonial debts of 1732, slaves, live-stock and equipment could quickly be seized to settle a loan. In the French Antilles, Colbert's Black Code also allowed for the possibility of seizure, but it was very rarely used and all that was ever seized were crops.

THE AMERICAN INVASION

Heavily indebted to French commerce, the plantation owners warmly welcomed the Americans who, although they often paid in cash, sold at much lower prices and took molasses, the by-product of cane sugar. A proportion of the produce of the Antilles was therefore redirected to the interests of the North American trade. Two merchant networks were in competition, and increasingly numerous foreign firms were getting the best deals on flour, cod and slaves, and securing an outlet for sugar, coffee and other colonial goods in contravention of the provisions of the Exclusive monopoly. The Seven Years' War saw their activities begin and at the end of the conflict, plantation owners and the North American traders pursued closer ties: in 1768 exports from Martinique and Santo Domingo to the Thirteen Colonies via free ports opened the previous year reached 5.7 million livres; by 1769, 2.2 million livres; from Guadeloupe they reached 1.2 million in 1766. Almost half of the Caribbean's imports from the English Thirteen Colonies in North America were carried through in the French islands at the end of the 1760s.[65] The American War of Independence provided an opportunity to redouble this trade, and made the Antillean market aware that North America was irreplaceable: 'Without the Americans, we would be unable to exist in the colonies for any length of time. They are absolutely necessary to us for fine foods and wood.' On Santo Domingo, in October 1776, Governor d'Ennery and the plantation owners were worrying about a possible break in this traffic. They were swiftly reassured since the treaty of friendship and trade between France and the United States, signed in 1778, authorized all ships from neutral or friendly nations to enter the islands and, in return, to carry colonial goods of whatever nature they might be.[66]

Recognizing the situation this created, the decree of 30 August 1784, taken by the King's Council, established a moderated Exclusive monopoly: three ports were open to American ships on Santo Domingo – the Cap, Port-au-Prince and the Cayes; on Martinique and Guadeloupe, Saint Pierre and Pointe à Pitre were similarly opened; even on Santa Lucia, the port of Le Carénage was open, as was Scarborough on Tobago. Of course, the introduction of American flour was still forbidden, the low price of which – in 1776, an American barrel cost half the price of a French one, £50 sterling as opposed to £100 – was at a premium on the market, and smuggling flourished. The same thing applied on the return journeys, for which only molasses and syrups were allowed, although ships from New England, New York, Philadelphia and Baltimore took on large amounts of sugar and coffee. The owners of coffee plantations who had earmarked their crops for trade with the home country to balance their debts, preferred to load ships for the Americans who agreed to settle in cash with the foreigners for the flour, timber and cod they required.

> When I went to Cayes, I found evidence of illicit trade throughout the entire journey....In the homes of the inhabitants who welcomed me, I found barrels of American flour. They made no attempt to disguise the fact that this was the basis of their subsistence and sold a quart at a better price than from Bordeaux. Sr. D., the Cayes toll collector, had just entered a group of 102 negroes onto just one [American] boat, and in spite of the threat of public notoriety, he could not be convinced.... Some of the [naval] station's officers ended up sharing the sentiments of the inhabitants with whom they passed their time. They were reluctant to cross swords with the smugglers, and declared that they could not prevent a trade that brought life and prosperity to the southern party, without which, they could not survive.

Barbé de Marbois, the Intendant on Santo Domingo, reported to Castries, the Naval Minister, the extent of the fraud on the southern coast of the Great Antillean island, neglected by the slave traders and other French ships.[67] Smuggling was quite ubiquitous, however: low-tonnage American ships came from the Dutch entrepôts on Saint Eustatius, and indeed from Jamaica, to supply the plantations and assure an outlet for their produce. One of the largest centres of smuggling in the Caribbean was represented by the Virgin Isles to the north, where, in 1788, some 1,245 American ships, with a total carrying of 90,000 tonnes, came to load almost 35,000 tonnes of sugar.[68] In 1790, the value of American exports to Santo Domingo exceeded that of exports from the United States to all the other islands in the Caribbean. The French Antilles then took a quarter of the flour, more than three-quarters of the salted meats and more than 60 per cent of the dried fish exported by the Americans.[69]

Even certain French traders did not hesitate to join in smuggling. Thus, immediately after the partial lifting of the Exclusive in August 1784, which the authorities in the Atlantic trade were however unanimous in condemning, Jean-Pierre Labat de Sérène, a Bordeaux shipowner of average means, considered sending ships laden with raw sugar, coffee and cocoa, from Martinique to the United States.[70] Nevertheless, the precaution was taken of disguising the smuggling, and prohibited merchandise was placed down in the hold, covered over with permitted goods, and loads were taken on, as had always been the case, in isolated inlets far from the port. The Frenchman's plan scheduled his ships to reach Charleston at the end of their journey, where they were to take on a cargo for France; he also envisaged having them load tobacco in Baltimore and heading back to Boston as their voyage's destination, judging it to be too far north and less likely to provide a profitable cargo. Although it was not possible to conceal all prohibited products in the hold, this Bordeaux shipowner-turned-smuggler took up the idea of placing them in barrels of rum that would only ever be half-full. It is not difficult to see why one of his ships carried the name *Doctor Pangloss*, and that all this was to be for the best in the world of trade.

The efficacy of the international trade networks thus managed, at least partially, to alleviate the difficulties experienced by the Atlantic community of the French ports in the face of the transformation of Antillean trade. Best placed for this were doubtless the Jewish traders who could make their solidarity with other Jewish networks in London and Saint Eustatius work for them during and after the wars. It would again be advisable, as with the plantation owners, not to let oneself be taken in too much by the barrage of recriminations from traders who, almost complacently, paraded the losses they sustained by being unable to pay back their colonial debts. The growth in the volume of French Atlantic traffic, in both the slave trade and 'honest' trade, remains an indisputable fact, and profit margins remained sufficiently high to enable the costs, delays, and losses accrued by the accumulation of colonial credit to be absorbed. In fact, there had been a particular 'slimming down' that profited the most secure firms. One of Bordeaux's biggest traders, François Bonnaffé, wrote on 12 January 1774 that 'the trade with America is ruining small-scale shipowners'.[71] This proposition, certainly lucid and, at the same time, a hard fact for the weaker traders, captures the reality: the importance of funds and trading links gave a clear advantage to the 70 or so shipowners who dominated shipbuilding in 1789 in the largest French Atlantic port. While the problem of colonial loans certainly existed, for these 'happy few' it must be put into perspective in relation to their enormous fortunes: David Gradis et fils' balance sheet for 1788 showed that credit took up no more than one-fifth of the assets, or 1.2 out of 6 million.[72] Moreover, it is in the future that one must find confirmation of the traders' fears, in a French Atlantic weakened by the ruinous end of the privileges of the Exclusive monopoly, and further weakened by Great Britain's naval superiority. The wars of the Revolution and the Empire were about to make it lose any chance of making good its deficit.

Chapter 6

Men and powers in the Atlantic

Seventeenth and eighteenth centuries

The dominant poles of the Atlantic

In France during the reign of Louis XIV, and on into the reigns of Louis XV and Louis XVI, maritime dynamism shifted the dominant poles of economic space. This had happened earlier in the Low Countries and in England at almost the same time, giving London and then Liverpool, as with Amsterdam or Middelburg, a dominant influence in their countries' economies. New hierarchies were established between towns and regions: those close to the Atlantic seaboard adapted to maritime trades, while the others found themselves marginalized or landlocked.

In England, since the end of the sixteenth century, London imitated Antwerp and provided itself with institutions like the Royal Exchange, built under Elizabeth I by Sir Thomas Gresham on the model of Antwerp's Bourse. But this great English port needed almost a century to prove itself capable of controlling transatlantic trade after the boom it experienced due to the commercial and maritime reforms of the Restoration, and, in particular, with the effects of the Navigation Acts. In the eighteenth century, London was to dominate English trade completely.[1] The volume of its trade and the tonnage of its merchant fleet were higher than those of the other ports put together. On the eve of the American War of Independence, despite a relative weakening of this dominance, London still handled three-quarters of England's imports and 60 per cent of its exports. The human weight of the capital may help to explain this situation. In 1600, one in 20 English people lived in London, whose inhabitants numbered 250,000; in 1700, one out of 10 English people were among the 575,000 inhabitants of the capital; by 1800, when London's population was approaching 950,000, one in eight. London's expansion resulted from the city's undeniable pull: since the end of the sixteenth century, the annual influx of immigrants had been some 3,000; two centuries later, it exceeded 8,000. The importance this large Atlantic port took on fuelled the city's attractions: a quarter of the town's population relied directly on the port's traffic for his or her day-to-day survival. On the other hand, the capital's needs also grew and had to draw from a large, national market.

To dominate this market, London took advantage of its permanent geographical advantages, since the town was well connected to the rest of England and the Gaelic countries, not only by the navigable waterway of the Thames, but also by the excellent network of roads radiating from the capital since the sixteenth century. In 1637, John Taylor's *Carrier's Cosmographia* listed the transporters offering regular services by road from London to the Midlands, Lancashire and Yorkshire. Towards York, Manchester and the distant towns of the north, or towards Exeter in the south-west, lines of carriages left, each able to transport several tonnes. 'Each county produces something to keep London alive', Daniel Defoe remarked at the beginning of the eighteenth century. In London it was above all the presence of the élites constituting an extremely dynamic consumer-led market that explains the attraction exercised over the country's economy. Outside sessions of parliament, a rich clientele were able to spend the revenues from their provincial properties in London, and demanded high-quality products, amongst which the exotic goods coming from overseas were ranked very highly.

In the eighteenth century it is true that there had been a shift of British maritime activity towards the north-western ports, amongst which Liverpool provided the best example. Their westerly position made them well situated for the Atlantic traffic, and during the wars they remained relatively sheltered, whereas London, at the far end of the Channel, suffered the handicap of a position that exposed it to pirate attacks. For exports, however, London, facing the Low Countries and north-west Germany, reclaimed all its advantages due to the effective protection of the Royal Navy.

In the seventeenth century some of London's merchants, as in previous centuries, still benefitted from commercial monopolies taken from a power that had a pressing need for money. This situation, however, largely disappeared in the eighteenth century. One of the companies enjoying such privileges, the Merchant Venturers, also lost its monopoly in the cloth exporting trade and in the middle of the century only the East India Company and the Hudson Bay Company, still based in London, provided their members with the benefits of a fruitful trade. Having certainly seen its pre-eminence in Atlantic shipping in partial decline, having lost the greater share of its privileges, London in the eighteenth century retained supreme control over banking and financial services. It tended to attach less importance to its role as an enormous import and export centre in order to maintain and augment its place as a financial capital, assured by the presence of its brokers, insurers, and its bankers who offered provision of service to firms in 'outports' such as Bristol, Liverpool or Whitehaven: 'London's agents can even go so far as to take from two to three per cent of all the moneys that traders from the outports have invested in their commerce.'[2]

A place such as London certainly owed everything to the undeniable superiority it held in the information networks necessary to trading. Since the beginning of the eighteenth century, its traders could count on seven weekly or bi-weekly business newspapers, for a sum of only £6 sterling per year. These periodicals, brought to their doors, gave the most recent information about ships and their cargoes, the prices of goods and the rates of exchange. The business press network became huge at the end of the seventeenth century, less because of the greater freedom of the press after the Glorious Revolution than because of the effects of the English 'commercial revolution'. The development of information was necessary to the new global commerce to which England opened itself up in the Atlantic. For this reason, publications containing market rates and lists of ships entering and leaving the ports were indispensable. The national postal service distributed the press remarkably well, with three departures a week from London to the largest English towns on Tuesdays, Thursdays and Saturdays; on Mondays and Thursdays there were also two deliveries to Europe, via Dover to Ostende and Calais. Of all these periodicals, it was Edward Lloyd's *Lloyd's List*, appearing twice weekly, on Tuesdays and Wednesdays after 1735, and expanding its columns, that showed the greatest capacity to adapt to the needs of trade. Edward Lloyd, the famous proprietor of Lloyd's Coffee House in Lombard Street, had begun by receiving businessmen at his establishment, particularly brokers for sales of ships, currency and insurance. Since 1692, he provided them with a maritime news publication to consult, listing the ships' arrivals and departures from several of England's ports. From this time on, Lloyd had a network of correspondents in every one of Britain's principal ports. After 1735, his newspaper enlarged its information to include exchange rates, gold and silver prices, the effects of the public debt, the actions of companies and their principal goods.[3]

In the eighteenth century, Liverpool dared to challenge London's hegemony over British Atlantic commerce with Africa, the Antilles and North America, but London's dominance remained intact, a little like Hamburg's did when Bremen, Lübeck and other German ports opposed it, or like Amsterdam when faced with the other Dutch ports. The service network that developed around the business press in Liverpool was by far inferior to London's. Publications of current prices or shipping lists suffered from delays and irregularity.

Nevertheless, in the field of outfitting harbours, Liverpool demonstrated a precocious growth, much earlier than was the case in London. Until the end of the eighteenth century, London's harbours remained faithful to ancient structures that became a genuine obstacle to the proper operation of the port's activities, particularly as regards reducing its operating costs. Until the end of the century, London still lacked proper docks, and in the reduced space of the 'official' quays ranging the 500 metres between the Tower of London and London Bridge, cargoes were loaded and unloaded in precarious conditions, at least as concerns the most expensive products, the colonial goods such as sugar and coffee. Thus, even in the 1790s, a costly and lengthy shuttle had to be moored by the side of vessels that remained in the Thames, in order to unload the shipments of sugar from Jamaica. Liverpool, by contrast, had been equipped with docks since the beginning of the eighteenth century. In 1784, Marc de Bombelles, a French traveller, remarked upon London's inferiority in this regard. Drawing attention to the feverish activity of a harbour swathed in ships from every country in the world, in a forest of masts joining the two banks of the Thames, he continued to protest the absence of real storehouses:

> In vain do the English take as their pretext for not having embellished their capital with quays that commerce finds it far easier to get to the shops lining the riverside. These quays could be built up to a level higher than the surface of the spring-tide water, with the most beautiful vaults where all kinds of merchandise would be stored and well preserved....Some people have claimed that the English aptitude for suicidal behaviour was one of the reasons why one ought not to provide them, in the middle of the city, with a view of the river into which they might throw themselves.[4]

In France, the Atlantic trades had excited a spirited increase in the activities of the maritime seaboards, and traffic in her larger ports rose far more quickly than the country's total volume of trade. The boom in colonial trade was a dominant factor in this development. If one compares the value of trade from France's four principal ports – Bordeaux, Marseilles, Nantes and Rouen-Le Havre – between 1730 and 1788, the same boom can be seen in each, although their respective positions remain different. On the eve of the French Revolution, their colonial trade reached a value of 112, 55, 47 and 52 million livres respectively; little more than a half century earlier, in 1730, it was 8.6, 2.6, 14.2 and less than two million livres. Progress was therefore rather unequal.

The heir to an Antillean tradition created in the previous century, by 1730 Nantes proved to be the principal colonial port and added the profits from its slave trade to its direct traffic with the American islands. However, its growth slowed down soon thereafter: in 1752, colonial commerce reached a value of almost 27 million livres, whereas Bordeaux hauled itself into a position of power by realizing almost 35 million in its colonial trade. Thereafter, in 1788, a sudden boom in the ports of La Gironde and Bordeaux realized more than three times the value of their colonial exchanges in the middle of the century. Marseilles provided a different set of circumstances, since Antillean trade had a relatively lower impact there than in other ports. In Bordeaux in 1788, almost three-quarters of the total trade, 187 million out of 250 million, came from colonial traffic and the re-exports this traffic made possible. Almost half of these French colonial re-exports were sent out from Bordeaux, that is, four times more than from Nantes' sugar re-exports, four times more than Rouen–Le Havre's coffee re-exports. In Marseilles, with 79 million out of a total trade of 230 million livres, these exchanges represented little more than a third of a trade in which the Mediterranean's role had far more weight than the Atlantic's, with almost 149 million in the traffic from Italy, Spain, the Barbary Coast and the Levant. Le Havre returned Rouen to a position it had lost during the previous century: the growth of Rouen-Le Havre as a whole took place fairly rapidly from 1730 to 1750, but only reached full fruition after 1770.

This growth was based on trade with European markets, in particular those of northern Europe, where the sugar trade was concentrated in Hamburg, Amsterdam and Stettin: in 1789, out of 19 ports receiving cargoes from Bordeaux, these ports took in almost three-quarters of the sugar (19,326 tonnes out of 25,865 tonnes). Links with the northern European ports were assured by the presence of some 130 German firms of commissioners in the largest French emporium in Europe. They ensured that colonial goods were re-exported (despite the mercantilist intentions of the monarch) from Colbert until the time of the Revolution, to see the creation of an 'active' commerce with expeditions to Europe under the national flag. In February 1791, Guyenne's Chamber of Commerce still showed its extreme hostility to a project of the Constituent Assembly kind:

> France is jeopardizing its export trade, the outlets for its wines and spirits where foreigners come to buy from us and in exchange, bring us wheat, timber and hemp....There are always disadvantages in going to look for the consumer instead of selling from home.[5]

The Atlantic boom also involved the development of the social economies in the hinterland of these ports, and even in 'deepest' France: flour and wine from the Aquitaine, cloth from Sedan and Languedoc, canvas from western France, lace from Valenciennes or Puy, silk stockings and gloves from Cévennes and Dauphiné; all these riches were absorbed by the colonial trade.

However, this expansion took place in ports that, like London, still lacked modern amenities. We can see Arthur Young's admiration for the opulence of Bordeaux's élites: 'the way of life of the merchants here is extremely lavish'; but we can also feel his contempt for a port apparently left to rot. As in London, the forest of masts in the river impressed the visitor, but he is very aware of the absence of quays and the slowness of the harbour's operations: 'one dirty, slippery and muddy bank with unpaved areas, covered in detritus and stones...clearly shows the dirtiness and the worries of trade without the order, the arrangement and the opulence of a quay'.

The voyager's gaze, aware of the architectural beauty of an Enlightenment city, cannot bear the disorder and uncleanliness of a port that has nevertheless become one of Europe's largest stores, thanks to its predominance in the Atlantic economy.

More and more men

Across the Atlantic, economies and societies took on different forms according to whether a colony of plantations producing the exotic goods demanded by Europe, or a colony for settling people where agriculture, hunting and fishing were the principal resources, was created. The latter, however, linked the colonial economy to Europe's markets, such as those for furs or seafood. Their demand encouraged the inhabitants of French Canada and New England to develop improvements based on a dynamic of the landlocked or maritime frontier. However, the structure of their societies remained relatively close to those back home and, in particular, ignored the slavery that had brought about the triumph of the plantation economy.

The destruction of the Amerindians

Meanwhile, as was the case with the plantation economy, the white settlers had caused a dramatic reduction in the Amerindian population. In both Columbus's America and in that of his successors, the Iberians had already opened the road to a drastic decline in indigenous populations. This decline was due more to the bacterial shock caused by various pandemics introduced by the Europeans, such as smallpox or measles, than to piracy or war on their own. The collapse of the Indian population led Mexico's 11 million inhabitants (in 1519) to fall to a total of only one million at the beginning of the seventeenth century. In Peru, where the Indians had already suffered very severe losses during the first phase of colonization from 1530 to 1570, from this latter date until the end of the century the population fell from 1.2 million to less than 600,000 persons. In the Spanish Antilles, the drama was worse still: in 1492, the population numbered perhaps one million; in 1507, there were no more than 60,000 Amerindians, and by the middle of the century, they were reduced to only 30,000. The 'first and the most important genocide of the modern era' had taken place.[6]

Certainly, in eighteenth-century Iberian America there was a noticeable rise in the Amerindian peoples. The indigenous population had acquired the necessary immune defences, and epidemics proved less fatal. Mexico's Indian population rose by 40 per cent in the second half of the century; according to Alexander von Humboldt, at the beginning of the nineteenth century in Mexico there were almost 3.7 million Indians, that is, three times more than there were at the beginning of the seventeenth century.

However, grafted on to the serious weakening of the Amerindian population, there was also the growth of the new, white, black and half-caste population. European and African diseases destroyed even more of the Indian population in North America. North of the Rio Grande, the North American continent had some two million inhabitants before the conquest, of which the highest density was certainly on the Pacific coast. What is now Quebec had barely more than 100,000 inhabitants, and New England some 30,000.[7] This demographic catastrophe played a major role in the evolution of the colonies in terms of land sales to the colonists, the labour market, the European produce market, and the fur trade, which were all influenced by the spectacular decline in the pre-Colombian population.

In Canada, Colbert had already implored the French and the Indians to become simply 'one people of one blood', and Talon the Intendant wanted to create a new race. However, bringing spirits and smallpox, the Europeans swept through the ranks of the tribes and, moreover, inflicted serious losses after reprisals against the Iriquois and the other Indians allied to the English. The attitude of the English colonists was even more aggressive: since the very beginning of colonization they had needed more land and more furs. In New England and in Virginia, the murderous Indian wars of 1630–1640 and 1670 became wars of extermination.

The booming colonial population

Providing a distinct contrast to this near-disappearance of the indigenous peoples, a spectacular increase in the colonial population took place in English North America. Its scale, and 'a speed probably without equivalent in history', fascinated Malthus.[8] In 1700, the population of the Thirteen Continental Colonies exceeded 250,000 inhabitants, but on the eve of the American War of Independence numbers had increased more than tenfold, having practically doubled every 20 years.

The roots of this boom were, first, the coming of the immigrants from the Old World making their way across the Atlantic. A natural and rapid surplus in the population also played its part, however. The influence of immigration was essential in the beginning of the colonization, but subsequently it slowed down, especially in New England and the Chesapeake in the eighteenth century, whereas it remained extremely strong in the central colonies of Pennsylvania and New York, and in the lower South, the Carolinas and Georgia.

The case of Canada

In French Canada, by contrast, immigration was still very modest. Quebec was founded by Samuel Champlain in 1608, at almost the same time as Jamestown in Virginia, with some 30 colonists. Twenty-five years later, in 1633, New France had no more than 100 inhabitants, whereas in New England, Boston already housed nearly 4,000, and the Chesapeake colonies of Virginia and Maryland almost the same again. In that year, Champlain's arrival with 200 colonists and soldiers marks the point when Canadian colonization took off, although no increase in the population was achieved: in 1659, the Canadian population rose to 2,000 inhabitants; New England's population exceeded 32,000, and 24,000 in the Chesapeake colonies. The last important contribution to French immigration to New France was the arrival of Carignan Sallières' regiment in 1665, when his 400 soldiers settled on their officers' estates.[9] Reaching a total of 6,000 persons through the whole of the seventeenth century, immigration to Canada was intensified from 1740 to 1750, due to the colony's development, with almost 3,600 persons, representing a total of 5,000 immigrants in the eighteenth century. The dream of populating, dear to Richelieu, which Colbert rejected for fear of depopulating the kingdom, did not come to fruition. Only the natural surplus due to exceptional marriage and birth rates managed to quadruple the inhabitants in half a century, reaching 20,000 by 1713.[10]

If we compare the populations of France and England at the end of the seventeenth century, the former some 21 million strong, and the latter with less than 6 million, the disproportion in the number of colonists sent by the two countries might seem astonishing. With the exception of furs, however, Canada offered nothing that France was not already producing, as opposed to the English colonies where exports of tobacco, rice and indigo drew the workforce required to produce them, and the sea and forest life of New England was far superior to Quebec's. Moreover, a prohibition on emigration imposed upon Protestants deprived Canada of the possibility of seeing a growth in its commercial life or in the number of its inhabitants.

Streams of immigrants

It is still the case, however, that the share of immigration to English America remains difficult to discern with sufficient precision.[11] On arrival, immigrants received land rights, either immediately for free immigrants, or in the longer term for labourers under temporary service contracts. This gave them the opportunity to become landowners: in Virginia, some 20 hectares were allocated by the middle of the seventeenth century, at the end of the contracted period. However, taking account of the large number of deaths among indentured servants, who were thus unable to complete a term of service that often extended over seven years, estimating the population on the basis of the actual attribution of land remains dubious. Furthermore, those departures from England of which any traces remain were only a tiny part of the reality: in 1635, London saw almost 5,000 contracted men leave, out of which more than 3,000 were going to North America; from 1654 to 1686 in Bristol, some 2,000 contracted men embarked, half of them for the Antilles.[12] Can we accept the very high general estimate that puts departures for the New World from Great Britain and Ireland at more than 1,700,000 British subjects over the two centuries, as opposed to almost 150,000 Frenchmen?[13]

Due to the significance of streams of emigration from one or more French or British ports, particular but illustrative cases are better able to reflect the intensity of this flow. Thus, in the eighteenth century the port of Bordeaux, with a major role in the emigration of French contracted labour to the American islands, witnessed the departure of a minimum of 6,500 contracted men from 1698 to 1771. In addition, there were numerous passengers: more than 30,000 during the century.[14] On the eve of the American War of Independence, when the boom in Santo Domingo had hardly begun, in only 11 months from 1774 to 1775, some 1,273 passengers could be counted.

During the same period, it was the ports of Northern Ireland that experienced what was perhaps the most intense and feverish exodus for English mainland America. In the middle of the century, the Scots-Irish farmers of Ulster saw their precarious position aggravated by poor harvests and, at the demand of the landowners, tripled rents, so that a large number of them were forced to cross the Atlantic. In 1772–1773, 72 ships loaded with emigrants left Northern Ireland's ports; 49 departed from Londonderry and Belfast, from which ports there boarded 6,000 and 3,451 emigrants respectively. During the months of August to November 1773 alone, out of the 6,222 passengers disembarking in the six North American ports of New York, Philadelphia, Charleston, Halifax, Newport and New Jersey, two-thirds were transported by ships out of Ulster.[15] The total number of emigrants was at least 30,000 in barely three years, from 1771 to 1774. This represented a very clear acceleration of the flow of migration, since for the period 1733–1750 Dickson estimates the number of emigrants at a maximum of 40,000. Together with the Germans, this immigration made it possible to double the white population of South Carolina from 1763 to 1775.

The precariousness of immigration

From its beginnings, as during the greater part of its history, immigration to the New World met with an often hostile nature: swamps in Virginia's James River where the unfortunate pioneers of 1607–1608 settled; terribly harsh winters in the Massachusetts Bay which killed many of the first of New England's colonists; malaria and yellow fever in the Carolinas and Georgia, as well as in the Antilles. Whether due to epidemics such as smallpox and typhus carried by the ships, or to the famines experienced for want of provisions transported from Europe in sufficient quantities in the absence of the first crops, death took a heavy toll on the first immigrants.

A century earlier, this had already happened to the Spanish colonists in Central America, in Golden Castile or Venezuela, and even in Mexico. Out of 170 immigrants who settled in Virginia in May 1607, there remained only 45 survivors by November of the following year; out of the 400 men and women who arrived in July 1609, no less than 390 were dead after the terrible famine of the winter of 1609–1610. In total, in its first three years, the colony lost 550 of its own, while having taken in no more than 570 immigrants. Newcomers arrived every year, while the population remained very low: 10 years later, in 1618, there were still no more than 400 colonists, and in 1625, less than 300. At this time, since the foundation of Virginia, almost 8,000 people had died under assault from a murderous climate, victims of endemic malaria as often as malnutrition. In effect, the colonists had difficulty in seeing themselves as pioneers, and sought desperately to consume produce from England, taking badly to the inhabitants' food which, however, saved more than one.

In 1632, Massachusetts had no more than 2,000 colonists, although twice that number had disembarked there, including some women, over the previous three years. From the very first, with the Pilgrim Fathers' settlement in Plymouth in December 1620, the colony had had extremely heavy losses: half of the *Mayflower*'s 102 passengers perished during the winter through bouts of scurvy, for want of fresh provisions. The remnants survived only with the help of the Indians with their first crops and the fur trade, which they sold on the London market. In 1629, the arrival of 17 ships and some 1,000 people with the Massachussets Bay Company enabled the Puritan community to live self-sufficiently, despite ever higher losses during the winter of 1629–1630, which saw 200 victims.

New England: an unusual case

In the years that followed, however, New England was to find the prerequisites for its boom. The great wave of emigration in the 1630s saw the colonists, escaping Charles I's tyranny and faithful to the Puritans' 'Holy Experiment' that was to create communities of saints worthy of peopling the New Jerusalem, reach Boston and Salem without being destroyed by the epidemics. In a single decade, almost 12,000 immigrants settled in New England. In that same decade, the 1630s, there was a migration from the Massachussets Bay to Rhode Island,

Connecticut and New Hampshire: the land around Boston was almost infertile, and above all, the government of the saints brought about its own tyrannous reign over the conscience, forcing men who loved liberty to go into exile.

In fact, the immigrant Puritans bore hardly any resemblance to the indentured colonists who had already reached Virginia or Barbados in order to develop plantations there. Meanwhile, throughout the whole of English America, the majority of immigrants comprised these engaged colonists who had left Europe in order to serve an overseas master in conditions that were, to all intents and purposes, close to those of slavery. Although these engaged colonists account for almost two-thirds of the total number of immigrants, this proportion would rise to almost 90 per cent of immigrants in the American islands and the Chesapeake colonies. During a period in which the capital markets in England were still imperfectly organized, servitude was an essential means for financing the emigration of persons incapable of settling the cost of a transatlantic crossing. At the same time, it answered the need for a workforce in the plantation economy.

To a large extent, the system of indentured servitude was unknown in New England, where the religious stamp of its founding remained strong. The first arrivals from the *Mayflower*, like the colonists of the Massachussets Bay Company were fleeing a homeland where the structures of the Anglican church, which the Puritans rejected, were being strengthened. In Massachussets, however, exclusion reigned, and undesirable candidates were rejected. Given the miserable amount of cultivable land, there was no pressing need to attract migrants to clear the ground, as was the case in the colonies on the Chesapeake or the Antilles. In addition, the ocean proved more productive than the land: ships built on site were able to export wood, the fruits of the sea and the products of the fur trade. To bring in unworthy migrants would pollute the colony's religious climate. After 1640, and the end of the largest wave of Puritan emigration, there were relatively few attempts to develop immigration.

Meanwhile, New England's population grew larger due to the effect of a natural excess of births over deaths. This increase took on a spectacular aspect, which Franklin underlined in the eighteenth century: 'The population grew proportionally to the number of marriages, which becomes greater due to the tendency to raise a family when families can easily be supported, so that more people marry earlier in life.'

Leaving the strict confines of New England, Franklin was thinking more of the central and Chesapeake colonies that had grown due to the frontier receding into the west. He connected this demographic vigour with the wealth of a country of cheap and abundant land:

These men are not afraid to marry, since if they consider how well provided for in goods their children will be when they are grown, they

177

see that more land will be available at a good price. Thus, marriages in America are more numerous and generally take place earlier than in Europe.[16]

Coupled with America's extraordinarily fertile land, an abundance of material goods encouraged the belief that the growing population would not reduce profits. There was no Malthusian logic since migration towards the virgin lands of the frontier alleviated the pressure on already valuable resources. The natural population surplus that was experienced in the eighteenth century, in Franklin's time, throughout the greater part of English North America, took on a specifically seventeenth-century aspect in New England. The rise of Puritan communities in a forest and maritime environment provided sufficient resources, placed them in the relative security of contact with the larger Atlantic world and enabled them to avoid the constraints that held population growth in check in the homeland. Mortality rates, especially amongst children and infants, fell spectacularly, reflecting improved dietary regimes and disease prevention due to the scattered settlements. Amongst women, the age of marriage was low, and the proportion of those that married was high, due to the preponderance of men and the ease with which young adult couples acquired land and set up farms. Thus, young adults had every opportunity.

These quite exceptional circumstances, however, did not last for long. Land started to seem limited, farms were split and shrank, while land prices rose and a rural proletariat began to appear. At the same time, expectations of life declined, the age of marrying rose while birth rates fell. Only the drive towards the frontier and the diversification of labour prevented a Malthusian outcome. The economy grew in industry and trade, and population pressures were compensated for by the attraction of the markets, especially in the Antilles.

After an interval of a century, Virginia and Maryland experienced a comparable development. The majority of the immigrants in Chesapeake in the seventeenth century, in the Carolinas at the end of the same century, and in Georgia in the eighteenth century, under the dominant system of servile engagement, were men who had low expectations of life. Contracted for five to seven years as indentured servants, they were only able to marry later. Thus, relatively old, they had a lower number of children and growth through natural surplus remained weak. In 1700, the total number of immigrants from the seventeenth century in Virginia and Maryland was largely higher than the total resident population at that date. At that time there were a little under 150,000 inhabitants in these colonies whereas there had been at least 120,000, perhaps 500,000 immigrants over three-quarters of the century. However, the new generations transformed the population's development. Expectations of life certainly remained weaker than in New England, but the 'Creoles' could live longer than their forebears and the sex ratio was tending to balance out. Women married before their twentieth year (that is six to 10 years earlier than their immigrant mothers) and even earlier than in New England, so that a significant natural growth could then begin to show.

Many and different nationalities

Since the seventeenth century in English America, a great diversity in the population was apparent. If New England remained English in the majority, then in Chesapeake, by contrast, at least in the hinterland, Scots and Germans came in ever larger numbers: more than 30 per cent of the Europeans were not English. Immigration of people of many nationalities could again be found in the central colonies of Pennsylvania and New York, where natural growth remained more limited: in the eighteenth century, more than half their population was composed of non-English Europeans; in the 1770s, only a third of the population of Pennsylvania was of English origin, while the rest, in equal parts, were of German or Scots-Irish descent. These groups did not mix but occupied separate areas: the English around Philadelphia, the Germans, to the north and west, and the Scots-Irish, further towards the frontier.

A similar diversity was to be found in the Deep South, in the Carolinas and Georgia, where, under very difficult climactic conditions, and where malaria and yellow fever killed almost as many as they did in the Caribbean, the immigrant death rates were high. Under the regime of indentured servitude, immigration nevertheless managed to increase the population again. It is true that after 1700 the white engaged men left in fewer numbers for the South, even for Virginia and Maryland, whereas they had done so in large numbers during the seventeenth century. By far the greater number reached Pennsylvania and New York where opportunities for work were more attractive.

A certain number of immigrants, called 'free-willers' or 'redemptioners', were not taken on under contracts of servitude. They could be found especially amongst the Germans who migrated as families and settled the fare for their passage on arrival. Abbé Raynal very colourfully described the crowds of 'Irish, Jews, French, Waldensian, Palatines, Moravians, and Salzburgers who, exhausted from the vain political and religious vexations they suffered in Europe, left to seek tranquillity in distant climates'.[17] Highly controversial recruitment procedures were used to attract these people, allowing 'merchants of human flesh' to scour central Europe and Germany in search of candidates for emigration.

The Scots-Irish present one of the most unusual cases. Although they came from Ireland, they were not Irish and were not to be confused with the Scots arriving directly from Scotland. At the beginning of the seventeenth century, King James I (James VI of Scotland), in order to extend the English conquest of Ireland, attempted to people the north of the island with Lowland Scots. These were Presbyterians, very hostile to the Irish Catholics. Some 40,000 of them settled and prospered there from 1610 to 1640. At the end of the seventeenth century, however, London decided to prohibit the export of their fabrics and other products, and, at the same time, to advance the Anglican Church. English landowners demanded even higher rents from their Scots-Irish farmers, even going so far as to triple them. In successive waves, the Scots-Irish embarked across the Atlantic, especially when the terrible harvests of 1729, 1741, 1757 and 1772–1773 created a famine situation in Ulster. In addition, on the eve of the American War of Independence, from 1772–1774, there was a serious crisis in Belfast's linen textile trade. Many were not welcomed in the colonial ports and were sent on to the frontier, at the edge of the lands occupied by Indian tribes. Not understanding the nature of the latters' properties, and believing that it was contrary to divine and natural law that such land should remain wild while so many Christians wanted to work and earn their daily bread, they fought the Indians as they had fought the Irish.

The recruitment of emigrants was accompanied by intermittent publicity campaigns, conducted either in the Belfast or the Londonderry press, or in tours by ships' captains and agents in their pay to announce the departure of their ships in the towns and villages occasionally visited on market days, when crowds gathered.[18] The captains strove to vaunt the virtues and charms of an abundant land for the taking overseas. Their discourse deliberately used devices to attract passing strollers:

> We find people ready to believe in all the expected advantages of New England, not only with the help of letters sent from this colony but also through the intervention of the captains and shipowners of this kingdom. To take advantage of extraordinary cargoes attained on this occasion, they sent their agents to the markets and fairs in order to make public pronouncements to bring people together. They assure them that they can find good land for themselves and their children for very light rents, and even without paying landowners tithes or duties, while entertaining them with tales that they know will be most agreeable to them.[19]

The campaign conducted in 1729 on behalf of New England was subsequently repeated often enough. Merchants from the principal ports controlled most departures. They profited from their Atlantic crossings just as they had from selling goods from their shops, brandy, soaps, indigo, tea and other things. On the indentured servant's arrival at the colony, shipowners could get back from the colonial masters the cost of the crossing and the revenues from the sale of labourers. A few merchants also chartered the necessary ships and sold workers themselves. The cargoes sent were high in value but low in volume, and there were therefore places on board for passengers and indentured servants. The same ship that in spring carried linen textiles and flour from America put into a European port at the start of the summer, returning that November to Ulster in order to load up linen textiles and emigrants for America.

However, on an island where one was always close to a port lending itself to the trade with America, we do not see the same extraordinary publicity that grew up in the Rhenish states through which first the envoys of William Penn and the Quakers, then the American real estate speculators, and Rotterdam's shipowners travelled, sweeping through the towns and villages to the sound of trumpets and deceiving many. No longer was there a surfeit such as was experienced in Scotland prior to and following the defeat of the Jacobites in 1745, during which villagers could be seen expelled by force and driven on board with whips as crews.[20] In Scotland, the power of certain clans was capable, during the 1770s, of raising the necessary monies for emigration and above all for the purchase of American land by sending some of their own on in advance of the community's departure to make the requisite purchases necessary to its settlement.[21] Some were to fear the depopulation of the Scottish Highlands, remembering how the Peruvian and Mexican mines had depopulated Spain.

Irish emigration, which began early in the eighteenth century and accelerated after the mid-century, retained a more stable character at the same time as it brought undeniable profits to its promoters. At the peak of the Scots-Irish departures during the 1770s, a 300-tonne ship transported 300 emigrants, paying £1,050 sterling. With a crew reduced to 12 men, the total cost of the voyage rose to £1,500 sterling, yielding a profit of more than £500. Building such ships brought in almost £2,500, the voyage amounting to 20 per cent of the capital. Emigration was good business for the shipowners. The slave trade seemed to be just as promising, while it was perhaps far less so.

The black majority and the slaves

In Virginia and Maryland, slave trading in African blacks had begun to replace white servitude at the end of the seventeenth century: in 1670, there were only 2,500 blacks for the 38,500 whites in the Chesapeake colonies. One generation later, in 1700, there were 12,900 blacks against 85,200 whites, reaching 53,200 per 171,400 whites in 1730, that is, a ratio of three whites to one black. Although the number of slaves in the Chesapeake tobacco plantations had risen considerably, there was no black majority. On the contrary, this began to appear in the Deep South of the English mainland colonies, in South Carolina at the beginning of the eighteenth century, as it had earlier in the Antilles in the last third of the seventeenth century.

In the West Indies, by 1670, there were already 52,000 slaves for 44,000 whites and in 1710 they reached a number of 148,000 for 30,000 whites, that is, a ratio of five blacks to one white. In South Carolina during the 1670s, at the beginnings of the colony, the colonists used a few Indians as slaves, and the colony also exported them to Virginia. However, this reliance on the indigenous peoples was soon abandoned, since it gave rise to conflict when tribes were raided in search of slaves and damaged the interests of the fur and buckskin merchants who traded with the Indians. In the years 1670–1690, 1,000 slaves were brought from the Antilles with the white immigrants, the majority from Barbados.[22]

After the 1690s, the production of rice for export to southern Europe and the Antilles arose. It was then that in South Carolina a black majority emerged as the new plantations prospered. Slaves were imported from the Ghana coast in Africa who were familiar with rice cultivation and immune to the malaria and yellow fever that destroyed the white colonists; the Antillean slaves were also immune. In 1710 there were 5,000 slaves against 4,800 whites, and, 20 years later, slightly more than 20,000 slaves. Producers of rice, as well as those of the naval stores of the tar and oil of turpentine drawn from the vast pine forests on the western frontier, profited from a boom in these products. In England's shipbuilding yards, their importation benefitted from the protectionist legislation set up in 1705, during the Spanish War of Succession, when the transportation of Scandinavian products became more difficult. Rice planters and producers of naval stores were encouraged, as they were in the Antilles, to increase their production and the number of their slaves. The intensification of the plantation system diminished the slaves' life expectancy and the stability of black families, leading to an increasing reliance on the slave trade. Already, during the 1720s, some 9,000 captives arrived in Charleston and the other Carolinian ports from Africa; from 1734 to 1740 a further 15,000 slaves were imported. On this latter date in South Carolina the number of slaves was nearly double that of whites: 38,000 against 20,000.[23]

Of all the European colonies, however, it was Santo Domingo that saw its slave population rise most rapidly. Throughout the entirety of the French islands, slavery amounted to almost 10,800 blacks in 1670; in 1710, their number exceeded 74,000 and they were more than 167,000 in 1730 against, respectively, 8,200, 21,100 and 29,800 whites. Still timidly entering the age of slavery in 1670 with some 600 slaves, Santo Domingo witnessed an increase that could already be perceived in the first half of the eighteenth century: there, blacks numbered 43,000 in 1710 and 94,300 in 1730, whereas during this same period, there were only 8,000 and 10,400 whites. The island therefore had almost 10 slaves to every white in 1730; the pearl of the Antilles was even to reinforce the disproportion between the colours by 1770, with more than 241,000 slaves for less than 19,000 whites, approaching 500,000 slaves while there were still only 30,000 whites in

1790. At the beginning of the French Revolution, there were more than 16 blacks to every white on Santo Domingo.

Following its appearance in the Antillean and Virginian plantations, slavery presented significant advantages over white servitude. According to the possible length of working hours, the price of African captives became less expensive, especially after 1697 when prices in the slave trade began to fall. The Royal African Company's monopoly in the slave trade in England came to an end and trade in both the West Indies and in English North America opened up to English and colonial merchants. In Utrecht in 1713 they were also able to benefit from the advantages Spain granted to England in agreeing the *asiento* contract in the slave trade that was to last into the middle of the century. Jamaica became a large entrepôt for selling on slaves to both the Spanish possessions and the French colonies that their national trade did not sufficiently provide for.

Of course, in the eighteenth century the spectacular boom in sugar, and then coffee, not only in Santo Domingo, but also in Jamaica and islands occupied by the English after the Seven Years' War, such as Dominica, or by the French in Tobago after the American War of Independence, brought with it a considerable increase in the investments necessary to prepare the way for new wars and to increase production.[24] In Jamaica, the proportion of capital allocated for slaves rose according to the scale and the quality of agriculture: on a plantation of average size, 150 hectares, with extensive agriculture, the work-group was reduced to only some 30 slaves and absorbed 30.4 per cent of the capital; over the same area, but with intensive cultivation with many more canes planted and renewed, 100 slaves were required, with 36 per cent of the capital given over to them. With intensive cultivation, a larger plantation of 450 hectares needed a workforce of 300 slaves, worth more than £10,700 sterling (267,750 *livres tournois*) and absorbing 38 per cent of the plantation's value (£28,039 sterling or 700,975 *livres tournois*). On Santo Domingo, Jean Rabel's Foache plantation, one of the largest, owned by the great trader of Le Havre, worth 4.4 million *livres tournois* and employing more than 800 slaves estimated at 1.6 million *livres tournois*, we find an investment in the workforce close to that seen in Jamaica.[25] Plantations less given to such a gigantic scale, such as the Fleuriau, close to Port-au-Prince, contained some 250 slaves, making this investment proportionately lower but still above 30 per cent of the colony's capital.[26]

To respond to the demands of the sugar boom, the purchase price of captives rose strongly on the eve of the French Revolution: an adult African in peak condition was worth more than 2,000 *livres tournois*. Bought with loans, the plantation owners had to put themselves heavily into debt to keep the workforce constant. The new arrivals suffered heavy losses: one-third of the blacks who disembarked died during the first three years of their acquisition, and half after eight years in the colony.[27] The workforce had therefore to be replenished quickly: an owner of

100 slaves had to buy eight to 10 a year in order to keep production up, which was the only way he could pay off the debts he had incurred.

Did these black majorities represent a real danger for their white masters, whose numbers were very much lower? It would appear that cases of actual revolt remained exceptional. Of all the American islands, Jamaica was the one that witnessed the largest number of slave revolts from 1720–1730, but the island that had the highest number of blacks, Santo Domingo, suffered only one, in August 1791, which, it must be said, was by far the most violent and had the most decisive consequences for the plantation economy, contributing to its ruin.

In contrast to the white engaged labourer, the black slave was identifiable by his colour, and could only with difficulty escape and lose himself amongst the crowds of free men. It was, however, possible for him to take flight and reach a foreign colony ready to accommodate him due to its hostility to the colony he had left, as was the case in Florida regarding South Carolina, or the Spanish part of Santo Domingo for those in the island's French colony. Most often, even in the little islands like Antigua or Montserrat in the West Indies, relatively deserted mountainous regions provided shelter for the fugitives. The mountains in the interior of Jamaica sheltered runaways just as often. In the beginning, in Jamaica, the Marrons were the black slaves of the Spanish colonists; taking refuge in the island's interior, they were joined, following Cromwell's conquest of the island, by slaves from the British plantations. They launched raids on the plantations on the 'frontier'. The rebellions reached their height in Jamaica in the 1730s. In 1739, a peace was agreed between the Marrons and the English, in which the rebels saw the recognition of their autonomous territory and, in exchange, agreed to return new fugitives to the plantation owners. In effect, 30 years later, they helped the colonists to put down a revolt.

Repression alone would not have been sufficient, despite being supported by the rigours of colonial legislation – death was the only sentence handed down to a slave guilty of rebellion, if it had not also been for the help of a mentality amenable to perpetuating the institution of slavery.

A single example will be enough to demonstrate the vigour of these repressions: in Antigua in 1736, where there were some 24,000 blacks to barely 3,000 whites, a plot was discovered before a revolt brewing amongst the slaves burst out. 'We have many troubles on our island: blacks are burned, others are hanged on gibbets, still others are tortured on the wheel, and this takes up all our time.' Writing to his brother in London, Walter Tullidelph, one of the plantation owners, could not have exaggerated the cruelty of a repression that put almost 80 slaves to death.[28]

With emancipation freeing some from their condition of servitude, there were some 30,000 mulattos on Santo Domingo in 1789, free men of colour who became slave-owners in their turn and intended to maintain servitude for their own profit. 'United with the coloured people, we are sure of submissive slaves and the conservation of our property', one of Moreau de Saint-Méry's correspondents on Santo Domingo declared, only two months prior to the revolt of the Cape plain. He was certainly wrong, but during the eighteenth century the whites were quite constantly in solidarity with the mulattos in defending the order of slavery.

Could the racial disproportion have been accepted until these revolts because of 'the Africans' system of magical thought, which gave rise to resigned behaviour and a fearful obedience to reality'?[29] Servitude would have belonged to the traditional social organization of the dark continent, so that the negro would believe himself to be the victim of a fate over which his will had no control. In 1791, the mulattos intended to protect the shared interests of the slave-owners – amongst the plantation owners, they were the most dynamic in the coffee growing South – through the mixing of blood and equality of rights. There was no question for them of questioning the institution of slavery which had been condemned by Enlightened Europe. It is true that Montesquieu could condemn servitude in the name of law and morality, and yet maintain, without irony, its economic justification: 'sugar would be too expensive were the plant that produces it not worked by slaves'. Although in France the voices of the Friends of the Blacks were to be heard at the end of the *ancien régime*, and Condorcet could thus address himself 'to the Electoral Body against the slavery of blacks' during the preparations for the Estates General, it was in Great Britain that the largest mobilization of public opinion took place at the end of the 1780s. In 1787, a national Anti-Slavery Committee was founded in London under the influence of Quakers from America and England. Wilberforce and Pitt extended its influence to parliament, but fears raised by the French Revolution and the radical movement in Great Britain held up the passage of an act. Pressure was renewed in 1805–1807, ending with the British suspending the trade in 1807. This measure was passed although the seas had belonged to England for more than 12 years. Buttressed by a hitherto unrivalled sea power, the United Kingdom had extended its grip over the networks of foreign colonies, Dutch, French and Danish, and considerably increased her imports of colonial goods. This expansionist politics was equally denounced by the abolitionists and the plantation owners in the West Indies, who feared increasing competition from foreign production or from that obtained by the British in countries only recently open to plantation, such as the colonies of Berbice or Demerara in Guyana, or the island of Trinidad where sugar, but above all cotton, were at the height of their boom.

The decision for abolition was not taken at the time of the decline of the sugar isles – in 1792, William Pitt had presented the justification for the measure to the House of Commons, citing the decline of the colonial sugar economy – but was taken while new 'frontiers' were attracting investment in the form of a slave workforce in Cuba, Guyana, and some of the Antilles. Following the fall of French Santo Domingo, a renewed dynamism appeared in proportion to the new markets the Iberian empire was opening to slave-traders. In the shorter term, however, the Napoleonic blockade measures and their British replicas appeared to be a serious threat to trade due to the closure of the European markets. The abolition of the slave trade could therefore appear as responding to economic imperatives.

Black cargoes in the Atlantic

The full weight of the slave trade, the largest ever deportation of humanity, can only be appreciated within the four centuries of its history and in all the shifts in the African slave trade. From the tenth to the fifteenth centuries, the Saharan slave trade managed to seize more than seven million captives, while from the Middle Ages to the nineteenth century, the Indian Ocean trade took some five million. We can estimate that, from the middle of the fifteenth to the end of the nineteenth century, the Atlantic trade encompassed a few more than 12 million slaves, more than three million of them in the nineteenth century alone. Thus from 1450 to 1800, more than eight million blacks crossed the Atlantic to reach the New World. The eighteenth century took by far the largest proportion of them: more than 6 million slaves then reached the American plantations, that is, almost three-quarters of the trade realized in the Atlantic before the nineteenth century. In comparison, the respective contributions of the sixteenth and seventeenth centuries, despite the development of the Iberian and other European colonies, seems modest: 367,000 captives were transported between 1450 and 1,600, and 1,860,000 from 1601 to 1700. The progress of shipments in the eighteenth century was highly irregular: from 1701 to 1770, a little more than three million slaves left Africa to cross the Atlantic, whereas the last third of the century saw the transportation of negroes escalate significantly, when more than two million captives were transported.

The number of slaves taken from Africa by British, French and Portuguese traders may have been more than five million, of which a little more than half were carried by the most powerful of the slave-trading fleets, that of Great Britain. Although difficult to measure, the Iberian markets were undeniably attractive to the European slave trade. To satisfy the demand of the Minas Geraes mines, as well as the plantations of Pernambuco during the revival of sugar and cotton in the second half of the century, the total number of captive entrants to Brazil was almost 1.7 million.[30] In Bahia, it was a boom in the sugar plantations in the last years of the century after the Santo Domingo revolt; almost 600,000 slaves were imported into Brazil from 1761 to 1800.[31] In both La Plata and Cartagena, the slave-traders, first the South Seas Company and then ordinary individuals, holders of supply contracts granted by the Spanish Crown known as *asientos*, found markets with a high demand for a workforce for both the Potosi mines and those in New Grenada, where gold production in Popayan had developed in the last 20 years of the eighteenth century. From 1736 to 1789, 'legal' entrants in Cartagena alone, under the *asientos*, climbed to more than 40,000 slaves. At this latter date, the removal of the Bourbon monarchy's import monopoly raised the number of entrants. This can be seen in Cuba, where, according to Humboldt, the emergence of large sugar and coffee plantations during the same period brought about the import of more than 50,000 slaves from 1790 to 1799.[32]

In addition to these legal imports into the Iberian colonies, sales of smuggled slaves from the Curaçao entrepôts and Jamaica ought also to be considered. Regarding the latter, England legislated against fraud: the 1661 Navigation Act excluded foreign ships from trade with English colonies, although several thousand slaves transported by the Royal African Company were 'misappropriated' by the *asientists* ships in the decade following 1670. In 1685, the Lords of Trade exempted from seizure Spanish vessels that came to buy blacks in English Caribbean ports, since the Spanish paid high prices in a strong currency, the piastre. When the slave trade was just beginning in Liverpool, the town devoted itself to smuggling blacks in the Spanish colonies, since it would have been difficult for its traders to challenge London and Bristol in the West Indian or Chesapeake markets.

The growth of plantations in the Antilles and English mainland America provided the greatest impetus to the slave trade in the eighteenth century. The total number of slaves imported in the West Indies exceeded 1,200,000, and from 1655 to 1787, almost 700,000 entered the colony of Jamaica alone. Some new markets in English North America, such as South Carolina, exerted a particularly strong pressure at the time of the boom in their plantations: in only five years, from 1735 to 1739, the colony imported almost 12,000 slaves. Practically doubling the servile population, the arrival of these new slaves in the plantations' workforce caused whites to fear that the black majority might consider opting for freedom, which some slaves, admittedly a low number – only a few hundred – attempted to do in the Stono revolt of 1739.

The importance of the French markets remains difficult to determine precisely. According to Calonne, from 1768 to 1777 the French slave trade transported 14,365 slaves each year to the colonies, which in 10 years would amount to more than 143,000 slaves. Just as after the American War of Independence Versailles politics supported the slave trade through a system of subsidies granted to shipowners, and because the demand in Santo Domingo due to the boom in coffee and cotton demanded a sharp rise in its workforce, the slave-traders increased their shipments to more than 20,000 slaves a year, reaching a record number of nearly 30,000 on the eve of the Revolution, with Santo Domingo alone receiving more than 28,000 slaves in 1789. Between the Seven Years' War and the French Revolution, the French slave trade's sales managed to exceed 400,000 slaves, and over the whole century French markets in the Antilles absorbed more than a million captives. Since the national slave trade was far from sufficient for their needs, foreign slave traders, especially the English and the Americans, unloaded their cargoes in the Windward Isles or in the southern part of Santo Domingo. They sold their slaves most competitively, and less expensively than French traders. Thus, on Martinique, official French sales on the eve of the American War of Independence amounted to some 180 slaves a year, an estimate lower than it was in reality, since in the year 1776 alone almost 20,000 slaves were sold.

The centres of the European slave trade

In England, the slave trade made the fortune of the world's largest slave-trading port in the eighteenth century, Liverpool. From 1699 to 1807, the traders of this port transported 1,364,930 African captives in 5,249 voyages. In the same period, London, England's second slave-trading port, transported 744,721 captives in 3,047 voyages. Bristol, which over several years, from 1728 to 1742, held first place in slave-trafficking, fell back considerably in the second half of the century, transporting a total of 481,487 captives in 2,126 voyages.[33] More than half the slaves sold by English traders were therefore sold from Liverpool; London's sales remained less than a third of this total and Bristol's slave-traders did not sell a fifth of it.

After the 1740s, Liverpool began to dominate the English slave trade, already accounting for more than half the slaves shipped from 1743 to 1747, whilst its port managed to hold on to the overwhelming proportion of the traffic after the American War of Independence, when it controlled more than two-thirds of the slave trade. From 1783 to 1807, its voyages and shipments of slaves were as shown in Table 6.1.

Table 6.1 Voyages and shipment of slaves, 1783–1807

Liverpool	1783–1787	1788–1792	1793–1797	1798–1802	1803–1807
Total voyages	405	475	415	675	515
%	68.06	68.34	80.58	85.98	88.00
Slaves	131,300	147,935	126,380	185,430	129,765
%	70.29	71.76	82.08	86.18	86.5
England					
Total voyages	595	695	515	785	585
Slaves	186,795	206,150	153,955	215,160	149,865

Liverpool's boom was all the more spectacular because, until the end of the 1730s, its port contented itself with sending products from Lancashire across the Atlantic, linen textiles and cotton fabrics from Manchester, sold especially as contraband in the Spanish islands, which also bought slaves from Liverpool's traders. Smuggling, however, became more difficult when, in 1739, war broke out between England and Spain. The privilege of the *asiento* was withdrawn in 1750 and Liverpool's traders had to turn to the slave trade and challenge their competitors on the markets of English America. In 1768–1772, they showed their overall superiority with a total of 460 voyages in five years, while London made do with 205 voyages, and Bristol with 135. During the 1780s, these two ports' share was reduced even further: after 1783, Liverpool accounted for almost two-thirds of all voyages, and at the end of the century, was close to exercising a monopoly over the slave trade, with more than 85 per cent of the voyages and 86 per cent of the captives belonging to the Mersey shipowners.

Liverpool's principal advantage was having immediate local access to the goods that the traders of Guinea and Angola wanted: cheap textiles, copper, hardware, iron, knives, firearms, products from Manchester, Birmingham and Yorkshire. On the nearby Isle of Man, in Great Britain's largest centre of smuggling, shipowners also bought themselves brandy, armaments and powder for rifle shot unloaded by Dutch ships.

Before the appearance of schooners from Baltimore towards 1800, the fastest ships were built in Liverpool. Traders managed their voyages remarkably tightly – crews' salaries were low, captains were kept under control and provided with few privileges: whereas a Londoner, when putting into port, received a bonus and went ashore to dine with a good bottle of Madeira, a Liverpool captain was more competitive in the island markets and lowered the price of slaves by £4–5.[34]

In the face of this trading giant, foreign competitors paled even before seeing their ships chased from the ocean by Her Majesty's frigates. France's first port, Nantes, launched 1,427 voyages, 42.4 per cent of those of the French slave trade in the eighteenth century, and transported from 350,000 to 360,000 captives from 1725 to 1792. With 411 voyages, Bordeaux took more than 12 per cent of the French total despite coming late to the trade. A certain enthusiasm gripped Bordeaux's shipowners after the American War of Independence for doing more trade in the new sites of the Indian Ocean than in Guinea and Angola.[35] For a long time, the Bordelais kept their reserve as regards a costly trade that seemed less profitable to them than direct expeditions to the Atlantic. The total number of captives transported by them as late as 1792 reached more than 150,000. Their trade thus remained Lilliputian in the face of the Leviathan that was Liverpool. The two other French ports of notable activity were La Rochelle (427 expeditions) and Le Havre (399).

The Bordelais' fears were not unfounded, since the slave trade entailed grave risks. First, there was a long immobilization of capital due to the longer journey time, which more often than not was double that of a direct passage to the Americas. During the long halts on the African coast – where the Bristol slave-traders remained on average for 100 days – crews were struck down by fevers. Immobilized for a long time, ships were damaged and the means for repairing them were limited.[36] In selling the products of this trade, there were frequent miscalculations, and it was sometimes difficult to gather enough slaves: hence, anchored off the coast of Gambia in 1764, four ships from Bristol could only procure 289 of the 440 captives they wished to purchase.[37] Intense competition with other traders, difficulties in supplying the coast's trading posts: these were all reasons for viewing a cargo of blacks as extremely difficult to load. When selling this cargo in the Antilles, one might also meet with several obstacles: saturation of the market, and especially the poor state of the cargo if the ship had been delayed by calm while crossing the equator, or a capricious trade wind on approaching the Caribbean. Losses could also be sustained during this crossing: from 1748 to 1782, Nantes' shipowners bought 146,799 captives in Africa; there were 19,666 deaths on board their ships, a rate of loss of 13 per cent. Higher rates could arise, as much amongst the ships' crews as in the cargo of slaves, due to the effects of dysentery and deadly fevers or lack of nourishment. Finally, there were some cases of rebellion. Reaching the Antillean ports, captains seldom avoided having some captives in poor health which even a week of 'refreshment' did not succeed in alleviating. They could only sell them as 'the bottom of the barrel', at half price.

The slave trade was therefore not the Eldorado that some painted it, and, at least in the French ports, average profits of the order of six to ten per cent were more realistic than the 20 to 30 per cent sometimes made. 'It is a precarious trade', declared James Jones, a Bristol trader, before a Commons Commission in 1788, in which 'profits are sometimes good, and sometimes not'.[38] Perhaps due to its ships' successes, Liverpool's profits had been much higher, according to Mannix, reaching 30 per cent in 1786.[39] The traders of the slave trade's first port were apparently able to enjoy more favourable conditions: they were past masters at reducing costs, in manning the slave ships and in buying the goods of the slave trade at the lowest prices, whether in Holland or in the entrepôt of the Isle of Man, and in securing attractive credit terms from the merchant manufacturers of Manchester, obtaining almost two years of credit from them. They also knew how best to negotiate the bills of exchange accepted as payment for the sale of their cargoes of slaves in the Antilles. Of course, this estimate, from 1786, was made before the vote in parliament in favour of the Dolben Law in 1788, which, with humanitarian goals in view, forced shipowners to reduce the number of slaves loaded onto their ships, in order to assure the captives of the best conditions of transport. In Bristol, some claimed that through this they lost up to a quarter of the slaves they used to transport, so that they had to endure a large loss to make good.[40]

The real rivals to Liverpool's trade at the end of the eighteenth century were not found in Europe but in America. In the ports of the new United States, Yankee slave-traders leaving Newport or Bristol in Rhode Island, Boston, Salem, Charleston and Baltimore were more and more numerous on Africa's coasts.

The American slave traders

Before independence, the slave-trading ships of the Thirteen Colonies already supplied the English Antilles with slaves, along with the other European possessions in the Caribbean. This trade, however, acquired new proportions after the American War of Independence, while the legislation of the Union and the states was being enforced to prevent the Americans' participation in the slave trade. Shipowners developed the practice of sending their ships, loaded with provisions, wood and other products, to the Antilles in order to set sail from there for the coast of Africa, thus disguising their slave-trading destination. Returning to the islands with their captives, the ships then reached the American ports with the colonial goods without which the authorities might have been suspicious of their trading.

In 1753, the Board of Trade in London estimated that some 20 North American ships were employed in the African slave trade.[41] Eleven years later, the governor of Rhode Island confirmed that for more than 30 years, some 18 slave carriers had left for Africa, principally from Newport. These ships were generally smaller in size and carried little more than 100–120 slaves. Thus, from 1761 to 1768, the American slave-traders took cargoes from the Gold Coast to their destination in the English Antilles as shown in Table 6.2.

Taking account of the other ships loading up on the African coast and returning to the French and Spanish colonies, Anstey raises the annual average number of American expeditions to almost 30 during the years after the Seven Years' War: more than a third of Liverpool's slave-carrying traffic, although far lower in cargoes of captives – not even a fifth, since the American total rose to 3,300 slaves transported each year, as opposed to almost 17,000 in Liverpool.

After the American War of Independence, despite the swelling abolitionist tide in American opinion, the ports of Rhode Island, Boston and Salem, and even

Table 6.2 American slave-traders' cargoes, 1761–1768

Antilles	1761	1762	1763	1764	1765	1766	1767	1768
Ships	12	9	12	8	2	5	8	12
Slaves	1,322	980	1,340	1,075	300	430	1,060	1,697
Average cargo	110.5	108.8	111.5	134.3	150	86	132.5	141.4[42]

Philadelphia, the Quaker town that was at the centre of the anti-slavery propaganda, took up their trade again. The opening of a large number of Spanish ports in the New World, after 1 January 1790, to foreign traders was an essential influence: Cuba began to receive slaves in increasing numbers for working the sugar and coffee production that benefitted from the fall of Santo Domingo in 1791.

In 1789 and 1790, American cargoes climbed to almost 4,000 captives per year. The introduction of slaves onto American land was, however, illegal in the vast majority of the states of the Union: in 1785–1786 only three states allowed it, and from 1786 to 1790 only Georgia did. From 1790 to 1793, North Carolina joined Georgia but closed its ports in 1794, and, from 1798 to 1803, not one state could receive slaves. On this latter date, South Carolina lifted the prohibition until the intervention of a federal law that totally suspended the trade in 1808. Similar legislation had outlawed the slave trade from the United States to any other country as American participation in foreign trade.

In fact, these laws were not applied despite the activities of the abolitionists. Legislation was violated with total impunity: thus, on Rhode Island, Charles Collins, the head administrator of customs in Bristol, the state's largest port, called to office in 1801 by Jefferson, was the brother-in-law of one of the largest slave-carrying shipowners in the town and himself took part in the slave trade. The day on which he was ready to swear allegiance to the Constitution and to take possession of his office, one of his two ships unloaded 150 slaves in Havana; two years later, he himself delivered a cargo in Georgia. The import of slaves into the United States could be slowed down, but the activity of the American slave-traders carried on.

The Americans profited from the new activity of the Iberian merchants: no fewer than six Yankee slave carriers entered Montevideo on a single day in February 1806. It was above all, however, the effects of the war that broke out between England and France in 1793 that stimulated the trade. France became completely dependent on foreigners, both for supplying her colonies with slaves and for colonial trade.

After the end of the protected market that had existed until independence, benefitting from the services of the British fleet and market, the United States was obliged to provide itself with a new merchant fleet and to open new markets. They met the challenge this posed in less than 20 years, and became the new great power in the Atlantic: from 1789 to 1806 their merchant fleet became the second largest in the world, its tonnages increasing by more than eightfold. The slave trade from the ports of Rhode Island and the other states profited from this boom. Their ships completed a triangular traffic between America and Africa: the molasses produced by the plantations under American possession in Cuba were sent on their ships to Bristol and other American ports, where they were converted into rum which the slave ships dispatched to Africa in order to acquire new slaves to be transported to Santiago and Havana in Cuba. From 1791 to 1810, American exports of slaves to the New World can thus be given as shown in Table 6.3.

Table 6.3 American export of slaves, 1791–1810

Cuba	Spanish America	Guadeloupe and Martinique	United States	Total
41,730	18,720	12,120	108,273	180,843

Despite the prohibition decided upon by the federal government in 1808, it was extremely difficult for the shipowners of Rhode Island and the other states to give up the profits available, due to the increasing needs of Cuba and Brazil. The famous Baltimore schooners were built for the fastest possible Atlantic crossing. Their speed had to minimize the number of deaths in crossing, and having adequate steerage for slaves, although on a small scale, was appropriate; for a slave ship in an illegal trade that had to avoid British cruisers, a reduced capacity as regards the cargo was unimportant. On the other hand, it required a larger crew: painted scuttles on each side hid solid cannons since these weapons were desirable on a ship anchored in a West African river where it was exposed to the danger of attack. The rake of their masts and the trim of their yards were signs of these schooners' speed, but their construction sacrificed cargo-carrying capacity.

British subjects convicted of being engaged in the slave trade could be hanged and their ships confiscated; but captains of ships that flew the American flag refused to bring to and allow themselves to be inspected on the high sea. Eloquent defenders of the Anti-Slavery Society in England and their powerful support in the two houses of parliament forced their government to put down this shameful and illegal trade. The slave trade was a partial cause of the war between the United States and Great Britain in 1812. America dared to go to war against the greatest maritime power in the world, which had permanently secured its empire on the seas in the eighteenth century, emerging victorious from long naval wars as France's opponent.

The Atlantic powers

In 1749, Bolingbroke, a friend of Voltaire's and a signatory of the Peace of Utrecht, who had for many years been engaged in England in forming a patriotic party, gave lively expression to the indestructible bond between the sea and the British:

> Like other amphibious animals, we must sometimes climb onto the bank, but the water is very much more our element and, in the sea, we find our greatest security. It is at sea that we exercise our greatest strengths.[43]

The words of this Tory leader clearly show a consciousness of English naval superiority acquired over more than half a century through the victories achieved
during the wars against Louis XIV. Previously, despite the exploits of the mariners
of Elizabeth I and the efforts made under Cromwell and the Stuart Restoration,
England had not yet managed to regain mastery of the seas. Beforehand, it had
had to bring down the strongest maritime power of the seventeenth century, that
of the United Provinces, at the cost of three successive wars, and then successfully
remove the French threat posed by Colbert. After the peaceful intermission of
Walpole's era, from Utrecht to the War of Jenkins' Ear against Spain in 1739, it
still took 60 years for Great Britain finally to seize this superiority by chasing the
French flag from the seas. It did this first by winning the Seven Years' War, and
then, in an even more spectacular manner, with the great successes of the French
Wars, under the Revolution and the Empire. In 1815, the English established a
Pax Britannica over the Atlantic that allowed them to exert their predominance
throughout the nineteenth century.

The importance of this naval power, gained after long conflicts between the
Europeans, must not however be overestimated, at least as regards the seventeenth century. Certainly, men of state such as Richelieu had wanted to claim it
for their own countries, not to put paid to England, which was still only a small,
sparsely populated and somewhat marginal kingdom in the north,[44] but primarily
in order to free themselves of the hegemony of a Spain that still spearheaded
European affairs, by attacking it on the other side of the Atlantic, in its wealthy
colonies: 'The uses that the Spanish…make of the Indies, requiring them to be
strong on the Ocean Sea – a wise politician's reasoning cannot tolerate any weakness in it.'[45]

In the middle of the seventeenth century the attention of the European powers
was turned far more towards Continental affairs than to those of the Atlantic. The
Turkish conquest of Hungary and the lifting of the threat to Vienna following the
striking victory of the Christian army at Saint Gothard on 1 August 1664 were far
more important than establishing colonies in the New World. Moreover, beyond
the Spanish colonies of Peru and Mexico, on the American continent the influence
of Europeans barely extended beyond a narrow coastal fringe.

It is also necessary to take stock of the character and the extent of the naval
domination that the British acquired. In the first place, it had to ensure free trade
on the seas, but – an equally essential objective for England – it also had to guard
the country from an invasion that was constantly feared until the Napoleonic
period. The memory of Philip II's armada and the French attempts during Louis
XIV's and Louis XV's reigns were still remembered on the other side of the
Channel until late into the nineteenth century.

The resources of British sea power

The means for this domination were provided by the commercial mastery of both the markets of northern Europe, where England successfully challenged the Dutch, but could not remove them altogether, and on the other side of the Atlantic. The markets of northern Europe were rich in the 'naval munitions' of wood, hemp, tar and iron that were indispensable to the construction of the proud vessels of the navy's line. However, in the eighteenth century, they were replaced by the English Continental Colonies of America. In fact, at the end of the eighteenth century, England was still drawing resinous products as well as the masts, yards and planking from the Baltic countries from Lübeck to Riga. The needs of the navy were to increase during the wars with France, prices in northern Europe rose, and it was often necessary to pay with a relatively rare currency. In 1699, the great War of the North broke out between Sweden and Russia; it lasted more than 20 years and the English were excluded from the Baltic trade. In 1705, parliament passed a law to encourage production of 'naval munitions' on the other side of the Atlantic, offering subsidies of £4 sterling per tonne of tar and pitch, and £3 sterling per tonne of terebinth. Despite the war, the traffic in these products, essential for the construction and repair of warships, rapidly increased between the colonies and the home country. With the peace, the subsidies were renewed and, in 1715, America already covered half of England's needs for tar and pitch.

These colonial resources were an essential element of the great English capacity for naval mobilization in time of conflict. As the navy's vessels were almost all disarmed in peacetime, since the wartime mariners of the *ancien régime* were not permanent, when war broke out it was necessary to be able to count on sufficient stocks and to dispatch the necessary supplies as quickly as possible. The naval yards had to demonstrate their capacity to repair with great speed the numerous vessels that had been laid up for many years, and to begin construction of new ones. Of course, France was also able to mobilize her resources from northern Europe in the arsenals constructed since Colbert's time in Brest, Toulon and Rochefort. In wartime, however, her fleet met with great difficulties in obtaining supplies, due to the English mastery of the seas. Only a massive appeal to neutral countries allowed her to maintain vital imports for the construction and maintenance of ships. Here lay a vital component of Great Britain's superiority.

In the eighteenth century, Great Britain also experienced a mobilization of the human resources necessary for manning the squadrons.[46] There was no shortage of difficulties, however, as much in providing competent officers as crews, and the naval powers, even Great Britain, encountered many problems. With warships decommissioned following the onset of peace, the majority of the officers were unemployed in peacetime: in England, they were put on half-pay (which happened even during a conflict if they had no ship to board); they remained on land and were unable to continue to acquire experience of being aboard ship at sea. The only solution for them was to serve on merchant ships. The command of the English squadrons at the outbreak of war was in the hands of senior officers who had not been to sea for 10 or indeed 15 years. Several months were always necessary to relearn the principles of handling vessels in manoeuvres demanded by current tactics.

Recruiting sailors was never easy. During peacetime they could only serve on merchant ships or fishing boats. However, the proportions her commercial navy had assumed gave England a great superiority. The total number of seamen employed by the navy approached 130,000 during the Seven Years' War, and more than 150,000 during the American War of Independence.[47] In these same conflicts, the number of sailors enlisted through the French class system was no more than 60,000. The only advantage to the class system created by Colbert and admired by the English was to mobilize men more quickly: 'It has provided us with the means to get our fleets out well before the English can, an important advantage and one that is even difficult to evaluate.'[48]

However, France had only a passing advantage, since, although slower, the British could appeal to a population of seamen much larger than France had available, and was therefore capable of arming many more ships. Furthermore, although having larger financial means at its disposal, Britain was always attached to arming a maximum number of ships, thus realizing a complete mobilization, whereas France, like Spain, only armed particular squadrons and therefore only really brought some of their ships and the available men into service.

To understand the naval mobilization thus achieved, it is necessary to emphasize that a relatively lower number of 'professional' sailors was recruited:

> What proportion of men in relation to the entire crew excel in the genuine profession of the sailor, or are at least of a cast ready to chance every wave, to take any risk, to trim the sails in the worst of weather?[49]

In 1791, Minister La Luzerne estimated that there was no longer one man in five who could exercise 'the genuine profession of the sailor'. Remarking that many spent their lives at sea without climbing a yard, he recalled the distinction the English made amongst their crews between 'able seamen', 'ordinary seamen', and 'landsmen'. It was the landsmen who heaved at the capstan, drew in the rigging and above all provided the numerous servants necessary to manoeuvring cannon: nine men for a cannon of 12, 13 for one of 24, 15 for one of 36.[50]

These landsmen were the largest number to respond in Cornwall and Devon, in the countryside around Plymouth and Portsmouth, to appeals by the captains of ships of Her Royal Majesty's fleet posted throughout dozens of towns. Lieutenants, each accompanied by half a dozen men, waged a campaign for recruits. For every professional sailor, four to five landsmen had to be found, and men of the ports, the majority carpenters, riggers or warehouse porters employed in the naval yards, could not be counted on. It was not rare to see columns advancing towards the ports of some 30 men each, their ankles in irons, coming from the Crown Courts in towns such as Exeter, caught for poaching, stealing cattle or setting fire to mills. They preferred service at sea to the gallows, deportation or prison. These, however, were potential mutineers, often in a pitiable physical state, and it was not certain that the squadrons had made a good acquisition; but they were pairs of arms that the captains needed to get their ships to sea.

This was the famous press-gang system that many deplored, but that remained unaltered until the beginning of the nineteenth century in every British naval port. The poor quality of these men and the often forcible conditions of recruitment explain the large number of desertions: in the course of the Seven Years' War, there were perhaps as many as 40,000 deserters in the navy, in particular in the American islands, where deserting the ship was easiest.

In France, the class system, which trained men and offered assistance to their families, made the king's service more bearable. Moreover, in wartime, at least in the ports of Ponant, trade and fishing collapsed. Even with delays, the royal fleet paid, and the years of service added up to allow access to a pension. Desertions were less frequent in the French squadrons. However, in the Antilles, there was a situation comparable to the one the British were familiar with. Loyal to the kingdom's class system, the French were not afraid in the American islands, where desertions were frequent, to use press-ganging themselves. Great Britain's colonies in the Caribbean, however, most frequently experienced critical situations. Indeed, Christian Buchet shows 'frightening' losses not only because of desertions but also a higher mortality rate due to the effect of fevers and typhoid epidemics, so that it was necessary to practise a mass levy of new sailors.[51]

Confronted with the demographic paucity of the English Antilles, with the competing needs of sailors, merchants and corsairs, the requirements of flag officers were extremely difficult to satisfy. Only the human potential of New England enabled this need for men to be met, at least during the Seven Years' War and, after the beginning of the century, they were not afraid to press from merchant ships belonging to the mainland colonies.

This power of British naval mobilization was itself supported by financial means far superior to France's. While in 1760, Berryer, the Secretary of State for the Fleet had some 30 million *livres tournois* at his disposal, on the other side of the Channel the navy's budget rose in the same year to almost 150 million *livres tournois*, £6 million sterling). Fuelled by massive borrowing from the markets of London and Amsterdam, on the eve of the Seven Years' War England's naval budget was already at a greatly heightened level: some 100 million *livres tournois*. In 1762, the year in which Havana and Manila were taken, England devoted more than 175 million *livres tournois* to her fleet. Of course, French finances had dried up after 1759, due to the heavy engagements they experienced on the European continent.

The situation became more favourable to the French naval budget in the reign of Louis XVI, and during the American War of Independence the fleet was able to obtain credit that had never been attained until then: 169 million *livres tournois* in 1780, and 200 million in 1782.[52]

In 1760–1763, during its triumphant period, these means allowed the navy to equip more than 120 ships of the line, 40 of which had been built during the war. The French fleet could count on no more than 50 ships of the line in 1760.[53] In 1775, the French deficit was partially made up with a total of 75 ships of the line, but the navy, with more than 110 ships, retained her superiority. On the eve of the wars of the Revolution and the Empire, Great Britain's predominance was beyond dispute. Estimates made for 1790 by Robert Fulton attributed almost 200 ships of the line to the navy, but Jean Meyer remarks that this figure was reached by placing the 'numerous 50 cannon ship used as large frigates in distant seas and the protection of convoys' in this category.[54] By this date, Britain's capacities extended solely to swift frigates designed either for exploratory missions or for protecting trade; in 1790, again according to Fulton, Great Britain possessed 210 of them. France then came in second place both for ships of the line and for frigates, respectively 81 and 69 ships.

Again we must emphasize that these numbers were theoretical: they represented the maximum that a power was capable of mobilizing during a conflict. If England, thanks to almost perfect logistics, managed a complete mobilization, other countries did not, since the costs of rearming the high number of ships disarmed during peacetime exceeded their financial, and even their human, resources.

Strategic choices

Dominating the seas does not ensure the mastery of the entire space of the oceans, since this was physically impossible and was not strategically necessary. It means gaining control of the maritime routes followed by the ships of other nations leaving Europe, after leaving the Channel and in the Gulf of Gascony, then in the Atlantic crossing around Madeira and the Canaries and at the entrance to the Antillean arc, whether to the south of the Tobago Straits or by way of the islands of Dominica or Guadeloupe, or further north, by the Leeward Islands and Puerto Rico. On returning from the Caribbean to Europe, between Cuba and Florida, the Bahamas Channel was the most frequent route, incorporating the indispensable stopover of the Azores in European waters.

In order to gain this control, one could attempt to lay hold of the naval bases on the other side of the Atlantic. In this regard, in the eighteenth century, England discovered the possibility of using two bases, which France had never undertaken: English Harbour in Antigua and Port Royal in Jamaica. From these bases, where careening facilities and supplies of provisions and weapons were available to them, English forces protected Great Britain's trade from the piracy that was still raging in Caribbean waters in the years 1710–1720, where it was an inheritance from the buccaneering of the previous century and of Spanish attempts to suppress illicit English trade with their colonies. A handful of frigates based in these two ports could suffice.

However, the aim of these stations was to answer the requirements of trade in peacetime, rather than to satisfy the pursuit of more extensive naval operations during wartime. However, their bases were not well placed for this purpose: English Harbour was ill-suited for offensive operations against the French Windward Isles, situated further south, since it had to be reached by struggling against the trade wind from the south east; similarly, Port Royal, which had the most powerful squadron at its disposal, lay much further west of the Leeward Islands, for protection. On the other hand, it was a good base for frigates keeping watch on the Yucatan Channel that ships were obliged to take on their way from the Gulf of Mexico and going to Tierra Firme or the Antilles, just as they must on their ascent to the Bahamas Channel to meet up with the route for returning to Europe.

Beneficial on the commercial level for protecting or attacking merchant ships, this situation did not lend itself at all to conquering foreign colonies. It is true that the English knew how to provide their bases with the provisions and arms that were, on the whole, sufficient, thanks especially to the irreplaceable aid of provisions gathered from the nearby mainland colonies. By contrast, on the French side there were more often than not insufficient supplies: soldiers, provisions and munitions had to cross the Atlantic in expensive convoys that were utterly exposed to enemy attack. Canada was in no position to play the role of a rear base for the French Antilles that New England played for the West Indies. Indeed, merchants from the continental colonies did not miss an opportunity to smuggle their supplies onto these foreign islands, and their shipments did much to reduce French logistical weaknesses.

On the French side, supply missions for provisions and arms for her Caribbean possessions, entrusted to the quartermaster at the end of the seventeenth century, were never satisfactorily fulfilled.[55] Although the Windward Islands had been able to play the role of an English naval base, for want of receiving regular supplies by convoy, as the English bases received theirs, French bases were never able to provide the squadrons sent to the Caribbean with the necessary naval materials. On the islands, the most terrible heat alternated with torrential rains; woodworm that attacked hulls proliferated in tropical waters, so that the damage the ships thus suffered had to be repaired. Squadrons lacked replacement masts and yards in the aftermath of battle, and the lack of tar made planking and rigging wear out early. 'Generally speaking, we must pay six times more for things than they would cost the King were we to receive them from our arsenals in France', asserted Commissioner Lambert in 1758, on Santo Domingo.[56] The ever higher costs of supplies became the most notorious block to maintaining the ships properly. As provisions had gone the same way, commanders were advised not to prolong their stay in the Antilles, which impaired the proper protection of trade.

The same high prices were found back in France, where naval equipment, provisions and munitions had to be dispatched from Bordeaux, Rochefort, La Rochelle and Nantes to Brest, where they were stockpiled. To equip a squadron for Canada and the American islands became increasingly expensive from 1757 to 1762. In England, by contrast, needs were properly satisfied, with frequent and regular deliveries to America, since the naval bases of English Harbour and Port Royal were replenished by the private enterprises of contractors, who in the main were important North American merchants. Back in England, numerous contracts issued port by port, and product for product, enabled costs to be lowered by putting the various contractors into competition with each other.

The greatest control over ships arriving in or departing from Europe during wartime was gained by setting up a highly mobile force, primed to attack or defend. It was the western squadron that enabled England to ensure her mastery over the Atlantic. Of course, British naval power made its influence felt over all the oceans, but it was above all in narrow seas, at the nerve centres, that the decisive events unfolded. Windward of the entrance to the Channel and the most important English and French Atlantic ports, the western squadron played an essential part in ensuring that the Atlantic belonged effectively to England.

In order to realize the strategy of controlling the Channel and the Gulf of Gascony, of all the points on the globe it was Ushant that took pride of place in English naval history, where Hawke, Boscawen and Rodney found fame. Three-quarters of England's outward- and homeward-bound merchant shipping rounded Ushant. British sailors spent long, uneventful days in sight of the island during the blockade of Brest, the largest French port, from where squadrons could set sail for the Atlantic. This position also made the squadron able to intervene quickly in the Channel in case of an attempted invasion, as well as to prevent the arrival of a fleet from Rochefort or Toulon in the south of France. English coasts under threat were to be found leeward of Ushant, and ships would reach them running fast under full sail before favourable west winds.

South of Ushant, the squadron could support English landings on the French coasts, as at Rochefort in 1757. It could also protect the movements of English convoys in the Channel, as well as those using the Bristol Channel and the Irish

Sea. Descending into the Gulf of Gascony, in the direction of the coasts of northern Spain, as far north as the Cape Finisterre, it blockaded their ports from San Sebastian to Ferrol, as also on the French coast, from Bayonne to Nantes.

This squadron was supported by installations in Plymouth, where important naval yards were built in 1696, and further developed in the eighteenth century. Here, the squadron's supplies were gathered from construction and careening yards: supply stores for powder and provisions, rigging, masted ships and sea-biscuit manufacturers, were all vital installations for rapidly fitting out a fleet that was not permanent and that had to be put back on its feet at the start of every war and to be maintained during the conflict.

Serious difficulties on the nautical level lay in store for the ships of the western squadron, however, since, off the Ushant coast, the presence of dangerous reefs could lead to the loss of their most experienced sailors. Meanwhile, these ships ensured many English victories in the Seven Years' War. Their blockade of the western coasts enabled them to isolate France's colonies from the rest of Europe. The departure of squadrons from France's Atlantic ports became practically impossible. Since provisions had to be stockpiled in Brest during the Seven Years' War, supplying the squadrons took an increasingly long time since provisions, equipment and munitions could never be delivered from there on time. In 1759, more than six months had to pass before a squadron commanded by Bompar managed to turn up in Brest; this delay was one of the factors that lost Guadeloupe for France. Similarly, in 1760, the Blénac squadron saw its armaments significantly delayed due to the difficulties experienced in carrying provisions from Bordeaux to Brest.

The permanent presence of the western squadron also ensured the safety of Britain's merchant fleet, particularly those ships that supplied England's possessions in America. Unless England's most important fleet had to cross the Atlantic, the security of the blockade enabled England to control Caribbean waters for as long as they remained an important theatre of naval operations. During the American War of Independence, when, forced to provide enormous supplies to the troops fighting the insurgents, the English were unable to continue to maintain this squadron to blockade French ports, especially Brest, the Caribbean once again became an important theatre, with the presence of French squadrons capable of conquering English islands such as Grenada or Tobago.

The battle of the Atlantic

The British were not caught up in this battle until relatively late: since the end of the sixteenth century, the Atlantic had become a closed field where European ambitions confronted each other. It was not until the beginning of the eighteenth century that Great Britain acquired its naval pre-eminence.

The relatively slow progress of the English

Despite the defeat of the Armada, the new naval forces acquired by Philip II in 1580 when he captured Portugal – which included Lisbon, an important base in the Atlantic, and, above all, Portugal's fleet of heavy galleons of extraordinary firepower – enabled Spain to maintain its treasure route. In the first half of the seventeenth century, England was unable to prevent the Dutch and Spanish fleets from confronting each other on her coasts when, in 1639, Tromp had just defeated the Spanish in the Dunes. Algiers pirates also managed to go unpunished when they captured some English sailors in the Channel and made them slaves.

However, after the fall of Charles I, the era of Cromwell's Protectorate saw the beginning of a new Atlantic era for England, in the course of which she began to prepare the ground for her maritime hegemony. Penn in the Caribbean, with the Jamaica expedition, Blake in the Mediterranean and Goodson in the Baltic, demonstrated their ability to protect English merchants and above all, to deploy an offensive capacity, to the detriment of the Dutch and the Spanish. In the first Anglo–Dutch war, numerous English corsairs dealt severe blows to the Dutch merchant fleet, making more than 1,000 seizures. Blake pitted his confidence at sea and English primacy in the national waters of the Channel against Tromp, when he made the Dutch admiral salute the English flag. In the Three Days' Battle of 1653, which pitted Blake's 80 ships against Tromp's 60, the adversaries inflicted heavy losses on each other. With the Westminster Peace in 1654 the Dutch capitulated over saluting in the Channel and recognized the Navigation Act. In the same year, relying on an initial alliance with Portugal, the English gained important commercial concessions in Brazil and West Africa, and thus became capable of developing a global strategy.

The war against Spain saw Blake destroy the *flota* at Santa Cruz in the Canaries, there seizing a treasure of £2 million sterling. In 1657, with Dunkirk, Spain lost the privateering port most feared by English commerce. Thanks to supplies of men and provisions obtained in Barbados and the Leeward Islands, Penn was able to transform an expedition that began in failure off Santo Domingo and Hispaniola into a success, taking Jamaica in 1655.

The principal enemy, however, was still Holland, and after the Restoration, England suffered some defeats during the second Anglo–Dutch war: in 1666, the Four Days' Battle, and Ruyter's raid on the Thames in particular, caused panic in London. Already, however, a new enemy was emerging, with the France of Louis XIV and Colbert capable of threatening the English and Dutch Antilles and, most importantly, of launching a commercial challenge in the tariff war of 1664–1667. A remarkable development in the navy took place in France, where the number of ships rose from only 30 at the beginning of Louis XIV's personal reign, to 70 in 1666, and 97 on the eve of the war with Holland. Several had been bought in the

United Provinces, and the quality of some was doubtful, but the effort was evident.

Meanwhile, Dutch superiority made itself felt once more when Ruyter managed to block the attempts of the French and English allies against the Republic at Solebay and Texel in Europe, as well as in the Antilles. The great Dutch sailor executed an astonishing naval performance off Saint Pierre de la Martinique on 20 July 1674, with his 40 vessels manned by 8,000 men. However, lacking sufficient Antillean bases, his crews were seriously affected by dysentery and fevers, and he had to turn back. The Frenchman d'Estrées, aided by the buccaneers of Martinique and Santo Domingo, was able to come and take Tobago, but was wrecked off Curaçao, the great Dutch entrepôt in the islands.

During the French alliance, Charles II's England had suffered defeats at sea. After the Glorious Revolution of 1688, the British took greater stock of the basis of their control of the Atlantic. The 'blue water' strategy proved increasingly suited to colonial conquest as well as commercial power and naval victories. Meanwhile, during the Nine Years' War, France struck rapidly in 1689, since its incipient class administration mobilized faster than the English Admiralty which had just enjoyed 10 years of peace. However, with the aid of Baltic supplies provided by the Dutch, England gained decisive advantages. Following the victory of Tourville's 75 ships in 1690 at Béveziers over Torrington's Anglo–Dutch fleet, the Allies strengthened themselves in the Channel, and in 1692 inflicted the defeat of La Hougue on Tourville: 15 French ships were destroyed and the threat of an invasion of England was removed. Grappling with an increasingly demanding Continental war opened on three fronts – the Low Countries, on the Rhine, and in Italy – France had to abandon the expensive war-fleet. In 1693, Tourville's victory in attacking the Smyrna convoy, dealing a mortal blow to the English Levant Company, had more to do with privateering than with regular naval operations. Resultant English losses were heavy, totalling some 4,000 ships captured between 1693 and 1697.

The French threat was renewed in the Spanish War of Succession. At the beginning of the conflict, Daniel Defoe set out the issues:

> What is England without trade? Without her colonial trade, her trade in Turkey and Spain? What will become of her when a French garrison is installed in Cuba, when a French fleet returns with Havana's silver? What would be the value of the colony of Virginia were the French at liberty to trade from Quebec to Mexico?[57]

Meanwhile, without being able to completely blockade France's Atlantic coasts, supplied by the Dutch and the Hansards, and without being able to halt the new successes of piracy or the traffic in American precious metals foreseen by Defoe, the navy managed to win some striking victories. Since 1702 at Vigo, Rooke sank the *flota*, destroying 15 vessels. Following the Methuen Treaty of 1703, which ensured England's control over Brazilian gold and the base at Lisbon, the taking of Gibraltar in 1704 opened new strategic possibilities for the Admiralty in the Mediterranean. Apart from a few raids in the Antilles, there were no notable gains in the colonies and, in 1711, the British were thwarted at the entrance to Quebec. The principal success was still commercial, however, and the number of ships leaving English ports demonstrated the primacy of the overseas trade: in 1710, there were 3,550; in 1712, 4,267; in 1713, 5,807. At Utrecht, to maintain the balance of power in Europe, the Low Countries had gone to Austria, a non-maritime power, and with the Hanoverian accession in 1714 England became the principal sea power.

The British conquest of the Atlantic in the eighteenth century

After a long interval of peace under Walpole that witnessed the rapidly growing threat of French colonial trade, and Spanish reactions to illicit English trade in the Americas, the War of Succession in Austria was the first conflict in which Great Britain asserted its new claim to hegemony in the Atlantic. The imbalance of powers was huge since, against the 100 ships of the line the navy had at its disposal in 1744, France could only muster fewer than 50 vessels, 18 of which were more than 20 years old, with 11 others being 60-gun ships of an outdated type.[58] The royal fleet was the chosen victim of the politics of peace of the Regent and Fleury: the fleet's budget had fallen and the number of ships had dropped dramatically since 1715, when France still had 80 ships of the line at its disposal. From 1725 to 1738 Rochefort remained without a commander, and from 1718 to 1733 there were only two ships under construction in Brest. Of course, the quality of these ships improved, and the *Terrible* was the first vessel with 74 cannon, much admired on the other side of the Channel. It left the yard in 1737, but France still had no bases in the Antilles comparable to those the English had, although the colonial governors had asked for them.

Maurepas, the Secretary of State for the fleet since 1718, under a great deal of pressure from traders worried about their protection, began at the onset of war by sending ships to survey the strategic routes of the Iberian Capes of São Vincente and Finisterre, the Azores, and the islands themselves. The results lacked detail and, before the seizures made after summer 1744, there was great disarray amongst the shipowners:

> Of the twenty ships that left you [from Cap Français] on the 2nd and the
> 31st of July, only the *Aigle* has arrived; all others were captured, several

taken to New England, others to La Vieille. In November 1744, the Bordeaux shipowner Philippe Nairac gave vent to his discontent in the face of the attacks that trade had suffered.[59]

Some, meanwhile, accepting the risk, did not hesitate to send their ships out before a convoy was established:

> If God has the grace to lead me into a safe port, I have every reason to hope for a good journey, for not one vessel has left since, and none will leave except with the convoy which, it would seem, will not be able to set sail for the Island of Ré where the rendezvous will be, before June next year, resulting in a delay of more than two months. Thus my captain will have time to sell his cargo and to buy one for his return before the arrival of the vessels escorted by warships.

Getting his ship under way on 26 April 1745, the shipowner Pierre Desclaux, again from Bordeaux, combined speculative daring with realism, since he insured his ship through his father-in-law, Griffon, a London trader.[60]

For these convoys, Maurepas again took up the legislation of 1690: traders were charged to finance the escorts, due to the paucity of the fleet's budget, through a tax levied on the products of the outward and return journey. Its implementation, however, proved difficult: theoretically, merchant captains ought only to leave under escort and apply for approval to leave. In fact, this did not stop them going without doing so. However, the results were far from insignificant: in 1745, three large convoys left, with the September departure comprising 123 ships, 59 of which were bound for Martinique, and 64 for Santo Domingo; in 1746, there were two convoys, a first in April, of 196 ships, and a second in October of 80 ships.[61]

However, under the leadership of Admiral Anson, the British reacted: the powerful western squadron managed to delay considerably the sending of supplies to North America and the Antilles. In May 1747, off Cabo de Ortegal on the north coast of Spain, Anson, with 14 ships, attacked a convoy of 40 ships destined for Canada, protected by the nine ships of Jonquière, who sacrificed himself so that the majority of the convoy reached Quebec in July. Of the two convoys bound for the Antilles in 1747, the July departure lost 47 ships out of the 100 that composed it; in October, 252 ships escorted by eight vessels were attacked by Hawke off Cape Finisterre, but managed to reach the islands by sacrificing the escort. The year 1747 saw British naval superiority clearly established. Meanwhile, with the exception of the fortress at Louisbourg, which was ceded with the peace, French colonial property was preserved. Against the Spaniards, after having taken Porto Bello, Vernon had suffered a serious setback off Cartagena.

The English zenith was to be reached during the Seven Years' War. However, the French made an enormous effort: 33 vessels were under construction from 1749 to 1755, and 23 had been lost during the war. In 1755, the *Royale* fleet numbered 59 vessels and 35 frigates, but 34 vessels carried 54 and 64 cannon, and were thus outdated models. In theory, the British had a complement of 136 vessels at their disposal, and the navy, under Anson's impetus, had constructed 100 ships of the line, and as many frigates. Its superiority was overwhelming.

The Englishman Boscawen's act of maritime piracy in November 1755, before the declaration of war, seizing several ships coming from the Antilles, 155 of which came from Bordeaux, was a 'commercial Pearl Harbour'.[62] Six thousand men were lost, 10 per cent of the French fleet's human resources; the insecurity of the merchant fleet grew for the duration of the war. Under the leadership of Pitt the Elder, Great Britain was going to conquer the seas, mirroring Frederick the Great's military glories in Europe. The French forces were only going to be seen occasionally in the Antilles, where in 1757, supported by the logistics of their naval bases, the British had 23 vessels and 11 frigates at their disposal. In 1759, only Bompar's squadron managed to take advantage of a certain relaxation of English surveillance in the islands. So unremitting was the situation off the French coasts, that in 1758, Anson prevented French reinforcements from crossing the Atlantic while Boscawen, with 23 vessels, supported the 11,000 men of Amherst against Louisbourg.

For the British, 1759 was the *annus mirabilis*, with victories for Hawke and Boscawen. To measure its scope, it is appropriate to recall the constraints imposed on the cruisers of the western squadron, on which the essence of the English strategy rested. Blockading aid bound from Brest to the colonies, it found itself in the grip of a plague of scurvy that severely reduced its crews. After several weeks, or months in some cases, it was necessary to break the blockade of Ushant for want of fresh provisions. This was what Anson had to do in 1758 when he returned to Torbay. In May 1759, when Hawke set sail from Torbay for the waters of Ushant, concern over supplying the squadron was still acute, and his orders were to return to Torbay after only 15 days of cruising. Now, in Brest, the feverish efforts of Choiseul had produced a powerful fleet, an army of invasion was centred in Morbihan and, in America, the battle's outcome was being decided. On 27 May, rather than returning to Torbay, Hawke decided to 'cling' to his station in Ushant so as not to leave the French ships' masters to their own devices or to leave Brest unguarded. Led by Anson, the English Admiralty had taken the remarkable initiative of then providing Hawke with supplies of fresh provisions, livestock, vegetables and beer. Thus supplied, Hawke, with his 27 vessels, was able to inflict an irreversible defeat upon the fleet of Brest in the Bay of Quiberon on

20 November 1759. The majority of the 21 ships under Comflans, who demonstrated his incompetence, were sunk or forced to run aground.

Hawke's victory brought about the fall of Quebec, deprived of all reinforcements, and the threat of invasion was finally removed. In August of the same year, Boscawen had crushed Laclue's squadron at Lagos, in the south of Portugal, and in the Antilles, Guadeloupe was conquered. The total mastery of the seas was to ensure final victories for the English over Spain, in Havana and Manila, and over France in Martinique.

In 1763, in the Peace of Paris, France's naval power seemed utterly defeated: her fleet numbered no more than 40 vessels and a dozen frigates. However, with the support of commercial bodies and provincial states, from 1762 to 1768 Choiseul inspired a remarkable reconstruction: 22 new vessels were launched, 13 of which were 74-guns and of the most up-to-date design. At the beginning of the American War of Independence, there were 52 armed French vessels against 70 English.

In this new conflict, England no longer had, as was previously the case, allies available to her on the Continent, and one might think that the Duke of Newcastle's prophecy, made before the Seven Years' War, had come true: 'France will chase us from the seas when she no longer has anything to fear on land.' In fact, France did not manage to gain such a result, but England was unable to maintain control of Europe's waters as it had hitherto, and great naval battles were unfolding in the New World.

In fact, the imbalance between the fleets was reduced: from 1776 to 1783, the French launched 40 vessels and 47 frigates. In April 1781, the year of the French victory on the Chesapeake, there were 70 French against 94 English vessels. The support of 54 Spanish vessels even created a numerical superiority for the Franco-Spanish allies. These latter ships, however, were of very average quality, and cooperation between France and Spain remained minimal.

Atlantic communications were therefore far more secure for the French: from 1778 to 1782, 31 convoys left for the Antilles, and 29 returned. Tactics were perfected: frigates preceded the convoys as scouts, and the bulk of the squadron followed them, remaining windward of the convoy. Enemy seizures fell from 110 in 1778 to only 20 in 1782. By contrast, the English were suffering, and 1,000 of their ships were captured by privateers, 800 ransomed, and 900 taken by the Royal Fleet. The battle of Atlantic transport saw a French victory that must be linked with the victory on the Chesapeake in September 1781.

The English navy's failures in the American War of Independence can be blamed on a decline in the political leadership of the Admiralty and the government. North and Shelbourne were not Pitt, and factional conflicts weakened power. Anson had protected the navy from the abuse of patronage. There were thus disagreements between the Admiralty and the opposition's senior officers.[63]

Some of the latter, such as Keppel, were against the suppression of the American rebellion by force. Hawke and Boscawen had no equals; Rodney and Kempenfelt were their inferiors. The latter especially always feared the damage caused to his ships by winter campaigns and the French squadrons in the Atlantic were consequently allowed a degree of freedom. Economizing on the navy in European waters, they attempted to establish naval control in distant seas and therefore their forces were dispersed. Endeavouring to remain in the four principal theatres of operation – the Channel, Gibraltar, the Antilles and the American coasts – England bowed before the superiority of enemy forces. In North America, the expeditionary corps' 50,000 soldiers had to be supplied across 3,000 miles of ocean. English ships suffered a decline in their maintenance due to a fall in the fleet's credit. Out of the 35 vessels assigned to the Channel, Keppel found only six in good repair. Above all, there was a lack of the naval stores that had until then been imported from America at very high cost, so they had to turn to Russia for supplies. Thousands of sailors were also missing, taken to gain an additional advantage by the 136 American corsairs who lay in wait in the Caribbean.

The results of the naval war were nevertheless undecided for a long time due to French failure to exploit their successes sufficiently. In the Antilles, since the end of 1778, the French had seized Dominica and, in the summer of the following year, d'Estaing occupied Saint Vincent and Grenada. After this island was seized, the principal English base at Santa Lucia was surrounded, but with his 24 ships d'Estaing was unable to exploit his victory to chase the navy from Santa Lucia and to go on to Jamaica, England's principal sugar colony.

In spring 1781, De Grasse managed to leave Brest for Martinique, from where he attacked Tobago and Santa Lucia, but these successes were compensated for by Rodney's raid on the Dutch entrepôt of Saint Eustacia. The English loaded a fortune onto their ships. The major French success was finally won in the Chesapeake in September 1781, when De Grasse blockaded the bay, demanding that the English fleet withdraw, removing any support from Cornwallis and forcing him to surrender. If Yorktown made the English decide to negotiate with their rebellious colonies, arms were going to decide the fate of the French in the Caribbean.

To give the French the greatest possible opportunity before discussing the inevitable peace treaty after the surrender at Yorktown, Castries, the new Minister of State for the Fleet, ordered De Grasse, who up to that point had remained rather prudently in the Caribbean after his victory, to attack Jamaica. However, at the same time, Rodney, the English Admiral, had to avenge the honour of His Majesty King George III, who was not happy with defeat. He demanded that he retake Grenada or attack some other island in the Windward Islands or Santo Domingo. De Grasse also had to protect the convoy of 150 sails that he had to despatch from Port Royal in Martinique via Santo Domingo, from where these and other ships would return to France. The two squadrons kept a check on each other, and in order to protect one of his ships that was lagging, De Grasse accepted battle on unequal terms on 1 August 1782. The English suffered badly, but De Grasse had the heaviest losses and was himself taken prisoner. His sacrifice nevertheless enabled the convoy to reach Santo Domingo.

This defeat at least partially restored British naval power in the Antilles, although their North American colony had been lost in the American War of Independence.

Trafalgar: England rules the waves

A final challenge was posed to Great Britain during the wars of the Revolution and the Empire. In fact, the French never ceased to hope to undo England's hegemonic designs: 'Holding back the pride that inspired the British Nation to the ambitious project of being the despot of the seas and of seizing, by way of consequence, all the world's trade.'[64]

In 1762, Jacob O'Dunn, Louis XV's ambassador in Lisbon, denounced Albion's ambitions while attempting to compel Portugal to abandon the British alliance. Such thoughts had always filled the minds of governments, whether those of the *ancien régime* or the Revolution.

After the American War of Independence, a remarkable effort was made to provide France with a strengthened naval capability. At the tribune of the Assemblée des Notables, Calonne had just argued that France's annual budget deficit from 1783 to 1787 was due primarily to the reconstruction of the fleet. In fact, in 1783, 28 new vessels and 23 frigates were launched, that is, 40 per cent of the fleet's ships of the former type and 50 per cent of the latter.[65]

In the first years of the Revolution, from 1789 to 1793, this effort was maintained: in 1793, France's navy had a greater potential, with 88 vessels and 73 frigates. Copper sheathing on the planking beneath the water line cut down on repairs; careening and caulking, largely introduced by the English, began to be practised and, thanks to all this, a squadron could remain at sea for far longer. Meanwhile, these policies did not cause any fear among the English because, on that side of the Channel, there reigned a feeling of profound security, born of the real superiority gained at the end of the previous war. The navy was still double the size of the French and the English launched no large-scale naval construction projects, while other powers, such as Spain and especially Russia, were clearly adding to their fleets. Conscious of English superiority, France's *ancien régime* drew back on two occasions in the face of new large-scale wars; at the time of the Dutch affair, on the one hand, and, on the other, during the Anglo–Spanish incident in Nootka Sound in 1791, on the coasts of British Columbia.

France's declaration of war on England in January 1793 was not made with a reduced fleet, at least as regards ships. It was not doing so well for naval supplies, and still worse for men. Of course, large stocks of wood had been established, but revolutionary disturbances had broken out in the arsenals. Above all, indiscipline was rife amongst the crews, with numerous incidents in Brest and Toulon. In 1792, Pitt judged that the French fleet was already in such disarray that he risked reducing the navy's strength. In fact, emigration amongst the officers had reached two-thirds of the corps at the end of that year, and the sailors' mutiny led to the fleet being seriously weakened.

There was the same need to protect trade as in previous conflicts, but it was now even more important since both the Antillean convoys and those coming from the United States to deliver grain to a destitute country had to be taken into consideration. In fact, transatlantic commerce had collapsed since the end of 1792 or the beginning of 1793; only the support of neutral countries enabled the traffic to continue. Ports chose to swap piracy for trade.

France's real resources had diminished since summer 1793, when the Toulon squadron, retaken by the Royalists, was in part delivered to the English. We can understand this under the circumstances, since, on the 'Glorious First of June' 1794, off Ushant, Howe had had his first great victory. Meanwhile, Villaret-Joyeuse and the Brest squadron, which lost seven ships, including the famous *Vengeur*, enabled the 117 ships of the convoy of grain and flour coming from the United States to get back to French ports. Here, the French lost 7,000 men, one-tenth of the fleet's complement of sailors. On the other side of the Atlantic, Martinique and Guadeloupe were lost in the same year, and the English also settled on the south coast of Santo Domingo, where the slave revolt three years earlier had already seriously damaged the economy.

The effort made in 1794, during the Terror, under the impetus of Montagnard Jean Bon Saint André, did not last. The following year, in engagements on the south coast of Brittany, the fleet lost three more ships at Belle Isle and Groix. It was under the Directory that France experienced its worst naval disasters while, however, the daring mariners of the privateering wars in the Antilles, in the Indian Ocean, in the Gulf of Gascony and the Channel scored an overall victory to the detriment of the English merchant fleet. Of course, England retaliated, whether by protecting her convoys or raids by the navy; warships were even disguised as peaceful merchantmen operating along the English coasts to ambush the privateers. Expensive convoys of 200 to 500 merchant ships crossed the Atlantic protected by entire squadrons. Only the ships of the East India Company and the Hudson Bay Company were exempted from sailing in these formations. Lloyds experienced a dizzying rise in insurance costs, and the English employed neutral ships. In total, from 1793 to 1800, Great Britain lost almost 3,500 ships. Often tragic for shipowners, these losses were a negligible blow in commercial terms. Under the Revolution and the Empire, British foreign trade experienced an unprecedented boom, climbing from £78.2 million sterling to £114 million from 1796 to 1800, and rose again to £151 million in 1815.[64]

Of course, the effort demanded of the navy was also unprecedented, and its expenditure increased tenfold from 1793 to 1814, rising from £2.4 million sterling to £22.8 million. It proved effective, however, since a 'galaxy of talents' was at the head of the fleet, from Nelson to Jarvis, Howe, Collingwood and Keith. Each of them applied themselves to inculcating in their crews the skills that were necessary for defeating the Channel's fogs and the Atlantic's gales as well, that is, as destroying the enemy's forces in the coming battles.

Meanwhile, the exhaustion that blockade cruising and the constraints of escorting convoys caused in the crews is one of the explanations for a lowering of their morale that led some sailors to one of the most serious mutinies, at Spithead and the Thames estuary in May and June of 1797. However, facing a Franco-Dutch-Spanish naval coalition, decisive victories had to be won. In February 1797, the first opportunity to do this fell to Admiral Jarvis, who had long since declared 'England needs a victory'. A Spanish attempt to bring the Cartagena squadron back across the Atlantic to Cadiz, in order ultimately to be able to join in the movements of the French squadrons, allowed the English to demonstrate their tactical skills. Admirably assisted by Nelson, with only 15 vessels against Spain's 27, which had, ill-advisedly, been split into two groups, Jarvis managed to break the enemy line. Nelson was able to attack the world's largest vessel, *La Santissima Trinidad*, a four-decker with 130 cannon. Well supported by his friend Collingwood who followed behind, the future conqueror of Aboukir Bay and Trafalgar took on four vessels by himself. However, with a certain pugnacity the Spanish managed to rebuff him a few months later in July 1797, when he attempted to disembark at Santa Cruz in Tenerife, where he hoped to capture the silver fleet on its return from America. This, moreover, was an attempt of the same type as had provoked a rupture between England and Spain.

Almost a year later, at Aboukir Bay, the fate of the French fleet was sealed for a long time to come. Although it was in fact nothing but luck that enabled Bonaparte to avoid Nelson's cruisers from Toulon to Malta and on to Alexandria, it was not going to go the same way after his landing in July 1798. By a rare piece of daring on the part of their leader, Nelson's 14 ships managed to break up and disorient Bruix's line of 13 vessels and four frigates. The 'brotherhood', the captains of the vessels serving under Nelson's orders, had astonishingly managed to complete a manoeuvre that surrounded the French in small groups, wearing their crews down with cannon shot.

Despite last attempts by the Brest squadron to rescue the Egyptian army with Spanish aid, England's mastery of the seas had already become absolute. After breaking the peace of Amiens, when Napoleon took the English invasion plan back to the Directory, England's mastery was to be confirmed across the entire Atlantic. At the beginning of 1805, Napoleon had prepared an invasion army at the camp of Boulogne. To gain the few hours that the flotilla required to cross from Boulogne to England, the navy had to be dispersed far from the Channel throughout the Atlantic. In March 1805, Villeneuve succeeded in leaving Toulon, and was met in Cadiz by six Spanish vessels, and by mid-May he was in the Antilles. Nelson followed two weeks behind him. Advised of the English arrival, Villeneuve headed back towards Europe and the English Admiralty strengthened its blockade of Brest and Ferrol. Villeneuve lost a first battle against the squadron blockading the port, taking flight and reaching Cadiz. Already Napoleon's Boulogne plan had become impossible. Pressed by the emperor to fight, Villeneuve, with his 33 ships and 30,000 men, confronted Nelson's 27 ships and 20,000 men at Trafalgar.[67] The defeat was crushing: in two columns, his own and Collingwood's, Nelson broke the Franco-Spanish line; the allies lost 18 ships, with 2,500 dead and 7,000 taken prisoner. England totally dominated the seas.[68] Liverpool and London could name their streets and their squares after their sea-going heroes who had done so much to protect Great Britain's trade: Duncan, Nelson, Jarvis and Collingwood had defended trade well. Ports built their new docks (London) or enlarged their old ones (Liverpool), and their ships flourished in the most distant corners of the earth, from India and the southern lands to the New World. Jostling masts made these docks into the crossroads of a global trade upon which England was to impose the Pax Britannica.

Chapter 7

The Atlantic in the nineteenth century
Tradition and change

An age-old but always changing transatlantic trade

Before the middle of the nineteenth century, trade in the Atlantic underwent no major change. In fact, global commerce covered this maritime space as it had any other, with characteristics similar to those it had in the previous century: the goods were the same, the movements of trade were identical, and the sailing ships that kept them thus were fundamentally no different. What had changed was the volume of the quantities transported, as the case of cotton from America for supplying Lancashire's textile industries shows, as well as North America's increasing importance due to its trading links.[1]

By contrast, the second half of the nineteenth century, with the development of a traffic in heavy raw materials, especially foodstuffs from the temperate climates such as cereals (wheat, maize), meats, butter and cheese, fresh fruit and preserves, exported to Europe in growing quantities from North America, Argentina and Uruguay as well as from Australia and New Zealand, marked a genuine change in large-scale overseas trade. The Atlantic, particularly the North Atlantic, became the privileged area for inter-continental trade, since a global market for these goods sprang up. The cereal market was the most important. In addition, an increasing amount of raw materials was transported: metals and non-ferrous minerals, nitrates, petrol, rubber, oil-producing plants and coal, since boiler coal from Wales was exported to coal depots in Africa or America, where steamships were re-fuelled. Larger and larger quantities of new manufactured goods, such as the materials for the railway networks that enabled products from the western United States or Canada to be sent to port, also began to appear in cargoes. These same railways enabled ever greater numbers of immigrants to be transported across the ocean to the 'frontiers' of these new countries.

Thus a change occurred in men's relation to the seas, where, after the end of the 1840s and during the 1850s, they were often chased from their native lands by hunger and political persecution, drawn by the appeal for a workforce in the industrial towns of the eastern United States, as well as by the receding frontiers of North and South America. The ships that transported them increasingly belonged in the service of the regular transatlantic shipping lines that had appeared since the 1820s, but improved enormously during the steam age. Their departures were set for precise dates and they were the property of limited companies, sailing firms in bitter competition over the most profitable human freight to transport from Europe to America, as well as wheat and other products on their return. Fierce competition caused freight and transport costs more generally to fall. It saw German and, to a lesser extent, French companies successfully challenge the British and the Americans over the Atlantic traffic.

There were also changes in the recruitment of sailors and their relation to captains and shipowners. Previously, the particular characteristic of sailing ships, in almost every European and American port, was the connection between captain and crew lasting only for the duration of a voyage. After that, the whole complement was dismissed with the exception of the captain. In Bordeaux in the eighteenth century, this same practice of temporary associations could be seen in making preparations for the Antilles, and extremely diverse crews frequently changed.[2] A ship's boy on the *Highlander* in 1837, Herman Melville managed to escape his miserable comrades on the ship's arrival in New York. His comrades, sharing a 'cordial antipathy' towards a captain despised for his severity, were able to calm themselves sufficiently to say a collective farewell 'to an old lord and master' they did not revere. Like 'rootless seaweed', the sailors went this way and that.[3]

Despite being a simple anecdote, such behaviour reveals a general rule that contracts of labour between sailors and shipowners' firms were only to become permanent with the introduction of steam and shipping lines. Creating large companies, their directors maintained a permanent workforce that henceforth sailed under a flag noted for its consistency – and its ambitions.

At the same time, the new Atlantic era saw the reinforcement of the predominance that had, it is true, been acquired from the beginning of the century, by ports that dared to challenge the hegemony of the largest – London. Still unrivalled at the end of the eighteenth century, London saw Liverpool challenge its role and successfully compete for its traffic, even clearly outdoing it in the North Atlantic. This was also the era of the spectacular growth, on the other side of the Atlantic, of a port like New York, whose activity complemented Liverpool's remarkably well. In Europe, Hamburg, to a certain extent dependent on London for capital at least, also developed more and more while the great centres of the previous century such as Bordeaux, Cadiz and even Amsterdam, declined.

English advantages and American successes at the beginning of the nineteenth century

British commercial supremacy in 1815

At the close of the wars of the Revolution and the Empire, Great Britain's naval and commercial supremacy seemed beyond question: in 1814, the United Kingdom possessed more than 21,000 merchant ships having a capacity of 2,400,000 tx.[4] As regards ocean-going ships alone, in 1816, the ports of London and Liverpool possessed 6,198 and 2,946 ships respectively, with a capacity of 1,250,000 and 640,000 tx.[5] However, well beforehand, from the American War of Independence to the French Revolution, the sudden boom in British trade raised England to a new rank: in 1785, the British fleet comprised almost 12,000 ocean-going ships with a capacity of 1,200,000 tx, that is, considerably more than double the French merchant fleet, which then comprised more than 5,000 ocean-going ships with a capacity of 729,000 tx.[6] Naval war under the Revolution and the Empire created a period of 'splendour' for British foreign trade, although it was uneven, since its growth slowed after 1802.[7] Moreover, Great Britain owed this growth more to the spectacular improvement in its exports of cotton fabric than to the mastery of colonial traffic made possible by the war. In fact, it left the neutral countries, especially America, with a reasonably firm hold on this traffic. While it certainly became the world's entrepôt for all exotic products, thanks to its naval power, Great Britain nevertheless came up against the far from insignificant effects of the Continental blockade that closed Europe's markets, and had then to face up to a conflict with the United States. To offset this situation, Britain had to turn towards the new Atlantic markets in an Iberian America that was seeking its own independence. In fact, although speculative sales could be made there, they were far from offering the desired Eldorado.

After withdrawing from Europe's markets, the British had found their best clients in the United States which, in 1806–1807, took 27 to 28 per cent of their manufactured goods and was to hold a privileged position after the peace.[8] The Americans, however, had also become Great Britain's rivals.

The advantages of America's neutrality

Remaining outside the naval war even in 1812, and with the war with Great Britain lasting no more than 30 months, the United States profited from France's maritime decline. Their neutrality ensured them an exceptional advantage throughout the several years of conflict. In the days following the American War of Independence, in 1784, America's trade with Europe employed almost 1,220 ships with a capacity of 200,000 tx.[9] In the Caribbean, United States ships profited considerably from the European powers having abandoned their commercial monopoly, creating free ports, beginning in the days following the Seven Years' War, and accelerating on the eve of the French Revolution.[10] In 1789, the slave trade was opening up to foreigners in the Spanish colonies; in 1794, by the Jay Treaty between the United States and England, the West Indies' ports were open to American ships. It was above all, however, during the maritime war of the revolution, after 1793, that American neutrality became valuable, enabling it to enlarge its trade considerably: the French and Dutch Antilles had no choice but to turn to neutral ships, and the Americans were more numerous, for delivering manufactured goods and provisions and carrying colonial goods. There was a huge expansion of American trade in the Antilles and the Spanish mainland colonies (Central and South America). These markets absorbed almost a third of all American exports from 1792 to 1812, that is $383.8 million out of $1,234 million. Even in the English Antilles, whose ports received foodstuffs and wood imported by Yankee ships, the Americans took the advantage: in 1803–1805, these colonies received two-thirds of their imports of provisions, and almost the entirety of their wood, from the United States.[11]

By the Council Order of 6 November 1793, London ordered the navy to capture all neutral ships trading with the French colonies; however, two months later the English gave in to the protests of the neutral countries and only prohibited direct trade between France and her colonies. This tolerant attitude was maintained until the blockade was more stringently enforced in November 1807. Colonial cargoes travelled through United States' ports and ships experienced a fictive interruption in their voyages since, without charging, American customs delivered certificates of payment of duties for captains to show in case of British arrest. In 1807, 40 per cent of the Antillean trade was in American hands, and the French islands provided their privileged market. From 1793 to 1797 they took from 39 to 44 per cent of American exports to the Antilles and Spanish America.[12] The annual value of United States' sales in the French colonies thus reached almost $8 million.

Meanwhile, Spanish America also turned out to be a highly attractive market: in 1799, the United States made sales of $9 million there, because its colonies had been freely opened to American ships and products. Although this decision was then rescinded, the complicity of the colonial authorities kept trade at more than $8 million in 1800 and 1801. Throughout the decade of the 1800s, this market took at least 40 per cent of America's exports in the Caribbean. In 1807, Spanish America received more than $12 million-worth from the United States. The British did not hide their annoyance at seeing American trade reducing the capacities of a market that had turned into one of the most attractive by Napoleonic Europe's being closed to their products.

It was with Cuba that the volume in American trade developed most. From

1792 to 1817, the colony's population doubled due to the arrival of new slaves for a sugar economy in the midst of expansion. The example of Philadelphia best brings out America's interest in Cuba: in its port, the majority of the ships that came from Spanish America from 1798 to 1809 departed from Cuba, as shown in Table 7.1.

Table 7.1 America's trade with Cuba, 1798–1809

Arrivals in Philadelphia	1798	1801	1807	1809
From Cuba	58	98	138	91
From Spanish America	75	137	200	184

At the time of the colonial revolt, the Americans hurried several of their ships to Rio de la Plata (42 in 1806), to Montevideo and Buenos Aires (30 in 1810), and to Mexico, where Vera Cruz received 47 Yankee ships in 1806.

Meanwhile, owing to the wars, American progress in the Caribbean and Spanish America served the interests of the colonial cities. Neutrality provoked an expansion in the transit trade that practically ceased at the end of 1807 with the American embargo, and in its entirety with the peace in 1815. This 'ephemeral' trade had seen its value increase very quickly, rising from $1.8 million in 1792 to $47 million in 1801 and $60 million in 1807, that is, 32 times higher than in 1792. On the other hand, when the Americans exported more and more cotton to the British Isles, they developed a trade destined to grow further after the peace: on the eve of the blockade, they were far and away Great Britain's principal providers, their cotton covering slightly less than half her needs, 27,038,000 pounds out of a total of almost 60,000,000 pounds per year.[13]

British ambitions and initial disappointments

While in Europe the Napoleonic blockade was reducing English sales, and while, after 1808, the United States also closed its ports, the markets in America's foreign colonies – Portuguese and Spanish – seemed to be capable of supplying the outlets the British needed. The combatants respected American neutrality less and less, and numerous incidents pitted the Americans against the British, not the least of which was the capture of American sailors or deserters from the navy on board American merchant ships by the English. President Jefferson decided on an Embargo on 22 December, 1807, refusing to trade with Napoleon as well as Great Britain.

Since 1806, there had been massive expeditions to Buenos Aires, by the English who took advantage of the colony's rebellion against Spain. English exports of manufactured articles at this time reflected a sophisticated speculative ability on the market of Rio de la Plata, with those made to foreign colonies rising from £162,000 sterling in 1805 to £318,000 sterling in 1806.[14] Two years later, Brazil saw an improvement in English sales that was just as unexpected: England sent almost 10 per cent of its national product there, with foreign American colonies then receiving £3,416,000-worth of manufactured articles.[15]

However, disappointments were not long off: sales were to a large extent at a loss, since they had sent far higher quantities of products than these markets had the capacity to absorb. Several adventurers were left with packages of poor-quality goods bought at rock bottom prices; firms thought that they would be able to get rid of unsold stocks of articles made more for the North American market than for Brazil: ice skates or warming pans were ill-suited to the tropical climate. Already at the beginning of 1809, two-thirds of the cargoes received in Rio de Janeiro remained unsold. The trader Antoine Gibs decided that to send goods to Brazil was 'to throw money out the window'.[16]

Exchanges were often made with cotton, which was much in demand since the Americans had suspended their shipments; however, stocks piled up, and, due to the industrial crisis of 1810 in England, sales were difficult. At the beginning of 1812, London and Liverpool held stocks of 110,000 bales of Brazilian cotton in the former port, and 300,000 bales of American cotton in the latter, brought back by expeditions in 1811.[17] The value of English exports to the United States rose in 1812 to more than £4 million pounds sterling, and was improving again in Europe.

The disappointments the English suffered in Brazil and Rio de la Plata did not prevent Great Britain, after the peace, from hoping to achieve success through large commercial and political projects in a Spanish America that had attained independence, thus finally being able to find some stability. Exporters thought that in Latin America they could find an alternative to the traditional colonial system within an 'informal' empire that was easy to build up due to the total elimination of French naval power. In so doing, however, England was heading for confrontation with the Americans.

Anglo–American rivalry in Latin America

After 1815, Castlereagh and Canning in England believed that the liberalization of trade with new partners, in particular the Latin Americans, would further British influence beyond solely commercial effects. The City of London could develop large investments there, British advisers would be consulted on constitutions to establish new states. In so doing, they hoped to find agreement with Great Britain's major competitor in these markets, the United States. Turning away from crossing the Atlantic towards Europe, since the transit trade that had been the principal cause of the Yankee boom during the Napoleonic wars had come to an end, the Americans were tempted to turn again to the Latin American continent.

In the face of the success of independence movements in the Spanish colonies at the beginning of the 1820s, Canning proposed to the American government that they sign an agreement by virtue of which London and Washington would guarantee the independence of the new states against all military intervention from Spain, France or the Holy Alliance acting together. Welcoming an American diplomat to Liverpool, the English Minister had this to say:

> a common language, a common spirit of commercial enterprise and a common respect for properly governed liberties should force our two countries into an understanding. Old quarrels forgotten, mother and daughter will join together to face the world.[18]

These propositions received a very cool response since they arose while London was conducting gunboat diplomacy, the already declared the law of the Pax Britannica in Caribbean waters. British merchants suffered there from the anarchic situation created by rebellion. For the French Minister Villèle in December 1822, when London launched an expedition against Cuba, the 'island traders' were playing a new role when they profited from a police action that was supposed to reach the pirates in their lairs.

Facing squarely up to this, the United States found confrontation difficult due to the crushing superiority of the British navy. However, the privileged character of US relations with the rest of the American continent had already been recognized for almost a generation. At the beginning of the American War of Independence, on Saint Eustacius, the great Caribbean entrepôt, the Dutch governor had honoured the star-spangled banner of the American brig the *Andrew Doria* with a cannon salute.[19] In 1781, Vergennes feared that the Americans were forming a naval power capable of becoming master over the whole immense continent. However, although the American frigates had inflicted important losses on the Royal Navy at the time of the war in 1812, it was not for all that a matter of challenging English sea power.

Meanwhile, the Americans worked to realize their ambitions. In 1819, they purchased eastern Florida from Spain for $5 million after having cleared it of bases for pirates such as the Frenchman Jean Lafitte, as well as the anti-Spanish rebels. In the same year, President Monroe sent a squadron to Buenos Aires in pursuit of the pirates who were attacking American ships on the Rio de la Plata. In Venezuela, the same expedition forced Bolivar to abandon his pirate operations against the Americans. The instability of the Spanish colonies favoured the explosion of piracy in the Caribbean where trade needed to be protected, since the Yankee traders occupied strong positions there. This was particularly the case in Cuba where, in 1820, American exports accounted for more than two-thirds of all the United States' exports to Spanish America. A law was voted in by Congress to protect trade, and three years later the American squadron in the Antilles comprised two frigates, a corvette, a sloop and two schooners charged with protecting American interests from West Africa to the Gulf of Mexico. At the same time, however, Monroe supported the rebels against Spain, and the American navy was not allowed to assist Spanish officials in Cuba and Puerto Rico, where the pirates had their bases.

When, at the end of 1822, Canning proposed to the United States that they be the 'second light' enforcing English initiatives for stabilizing the Caribbean, President Monroe's response, on 2 December 1823, was that the American continent should avoid all future colonization. America should not get involved in European affairs. The American government alone took on the commitment to protect the continent of the two Americas against all European intervention. The Monroe doctrine became: 'the Rock on which American politics remained standing for more than a century'.[20]

In the immediate term, the Americans pursued their mission to protect trade: 16 ships carrying more than 1,500 men and 133 cannon cruised off Puerto Rico, Hispaniola and Cuba in February 1823. Numerous pirates were destroyed but yellow fever struck down the American forces and calm was not to return until several years later, once Madrid had recognized the independence of the republics in 1827.

When London wanted to enforce the decision, taken in 1807, to abolish to slave trade, the United States had no intention of recognizing Great Britain's right to police the seas, either in the waters off the American mainland, or on the other side of the Atlantic. American slave-traders were one element of this trade, and England wanted to persuade or force the other maritime powers to negotiate treaties allowing them to seek out and arrest slave-traders sailing under a European flag. Cruising off Africa or the Antilles, American ships might arrest ships of their own, but they did not act against other flags, and their actions turned out to be somewhat limited: there was rarely ever more than one ship stationed off the West African coast, although numerous slave-traders flew the star-spangled banner.

An impossible Eldorado

Confronted with the very firm intentions of the Monroe declaration, Canning wanted to react: on 3 February 1825, the Speech from the Throne announced that His Majesty George IV, who until then was opposed, in the name of the principle of monarchy, to recognizing the independence of the Spanish colonies, took measures to confirm, by treaties already existing, commercial arrangements between his country and the American nations that appeared to have consummated their separation from Spain. 'Spanish America is free and, if we manage our affairs well, it will be English', the minister announced on 17 December 1824.

The hopes that England placed in the markets of Latin America, stabilized at last by independence, were to be quickly disappointed. The violent crisis of 1825 revealed the absurdity of hopes founded a short while before on the future of the American republics. In September 1825, in the face of the market's expansion, the Lancashire cotton trade collapsed and panic broke out on the London Stock Exchange at the end of the year. Foolhardy commitments made in Latin America would appear to be one of the major causes of the crisis through which England was passing. The surplus in manufacturing production had been dumped there without taking sufficient account of the market's real capacity, and banks had agreed to make heavy loans to the new governments: in 1822 and 1824, Barings lent more than £3 million sterling to Colombia and Argentina; in 1825, Barclays had lent Mexico more than £3 million; in Brazil, Rothschild lent £2 million in 1825. Firms had been established for mining the mineral wealth of Peru and Mexico, with some 29 companies from February 1824 to September 1825.

But the new states were not credit-worthy, the mining companies were not viable, and exports could not find buyers. Traders were fortunate when they were paid in silver, which the capital holders had simultaneously exported there, for some of the products sent across the Atlantic. The independence of these countries had limited economic and social effects, and they neither enhanced the market's needs, nor provoked a redistribution of wealth, nor improved inland transport.

It nevertheless remains the case that once the crisis was passed, British predominance was long lasting in all these countries, with the exception of Cuba and Mexico, where the Americans occupied strong positions. In Salvador de Bahia and Rio de Janeiro in Brazil, English traders, still few in number in 1815, occupied an important position 10 years later. In 1828, a boom again began to take shape in English exports, and British goods were sold more cheaply in Rio than in the City of London: 'handkerchiefs, cotton fabrics in all colours, silks, hats, shoes and stockings; all these articles hung from shop fronts, covered doors and windows with their finery'.

The British kept the lion's share in the Brazilian trade where, in the middle of the century, they provided half of the country's imports, and their sales improved noticeably,[21] occupying first place in the provision of manufactured articles. It is still true that, with the exception of the cotton fabrics, these were reserved for the leisured classes: table linen, porcelain, glassware and silverware crossed the Atlantic and took their place in every wealthy house in Rio, Salvador and Recife, the three large ports that absorbed the majority of the imports. In the rest of the country, a very low purchasing power and poor transport explained why these articles were stationary products. The same observation could be made of the whole of Latin America.

Brazil in particular, having made a considerable contribution under Napoleon to supplying England with cotton, withdrew its sales while the United States controlled the British market. Brazilian sugar and coffee were also barred from England, at least until the middle of the century, when the produce of the English colonies enjoyed imperial favour that for coffee did not end until 1851, and for sugar until 1854. It was no longer possible to sell these goods to France for the same reason. Countries without colonies, such as Germany, Austria and the United States – although the latter favoured Cuba – were certainly able to absorb some proportion of this produce, and the Hanseatic towns therefore developed an Atlantic trade with Brazil: the number of ships arriving in Hamburg from Brazil climbed from four in 1815 to 137 in 1824.[22]

An old colonial structure persisted between England and Brazil: the former sold a relatively large amount and bought little, so that the latter's trade deficit was considerable and had to be regulated in a multilateral system of payments, due to the surplus in its trade with North America and the countries without colonies. This was indeed the 'informal' empire on the subject of which the Brazilian minister in London showed so much bitterness in 1854: 'Trade between the two countries is conducted with English capital, on English ships, by English companies. The profits…interest on the capital, insurance payments, commissions and dividends, all goes into English pockets.'[23]

Despite an initial infatuation, relations remained strained, and Brazil – like Argentina with its skins – still had something to offer the market, while the other Latin American republics had nothing, with exports of guano from Peru only beginning in 1840, and Bolivia and Colombia exporting only gold and silver. There were serious handicaps: the extremely high costs of transport in the age of the sail, even along the Atlantic coasts, and all the more prohibitive for reaching the Pacific coasts by navigation around Cape Horn; costs and total credits were both increasingly burdensome, requiring more than substantial profits. Meanwhile, cargoes fell after the end of the 1820s, while traffic remained just as irregular. A single cargo could fill a port's shops for months or even years, and it was crucial to calculate precisely the date of arriving at the stopover, or ships would run the risk of being left with unsold goods. Contrary winds from Europe to America could make a ship wait in Liverpool's docks for weeks or even months: a cargo of winter textiles that was supposed to reach the market in autumn might be unloaded in Valparaiso in Chile in the southern spring, when the wintry weather had disappeared.[24]

The same handicaps on sailing were also found in the North Atlantic on the route from Europe to the United States, although here market relations were quite different, due both to the European demand for American products and the spectacular growth of consumption on the other side of the Atlantic.

New York and Liverpool, the new Atlantic of the liners

In the eighteenth century, the principal entrepôt ports on the European Atlantic front, from Cadiz to Hamburg, knew huge prosperity. London already dominated British trade by a long shot, and it retained first position in 1800, when it took in two-thirds of Great Britain's foreign trade. On the other side of the Atlantic, despite the sudden explosion in the population of the United States and the Antillean boom, there had been no comparable growth of the ports. In 1815, in the aftermath of the Napoleonic wars, the French and Spanish ports still felt the consequences of long naval conflict very keenly. In Spain, neither Cadiz nor Barcelona could regain the wealth of the previous century, and in France, neither could Nantes, La Rochelle or Bordeaux. When peace returned, there was certainly a desire to return to the golden age of the past, but the plantations of the largest Antillean island, Santo Domingo, the flower of French Atlantic wealth, had been partially destroyed by the slave revolt of 1791 and the maritime war had unsettled its markets. There were efforts on behalf of French Atlantic trade even in the midst of the conflict, and even more under the Restoration, to reconstitute a commercial empire that was still held in living memory. Huge fortunes were made, particularly in farming the new sugar islands like Cuba, or in the traffic from India. However, they were never comparable to those created in the new trading giants of the nineteenth century, Liverpool in the British Isles, and New York in North America, which were indisputably the dominant poles of exchange. We could add, off course, Le Havre in France, or Hamburg in Germany; and London remained a large metropolis, especially in financial terms as well as in its trade in Asia and the Antilles. As regards relations with the United States and the other Atlantic countries, however, Liverpool took on a far greater importance and New York was to dominate trade in America.

The age of King Cotton

Before the wars of the Revolution and the Empire, the signs of a spectacular boom in Liverpool were already emerging. In 1791, one commercial directory saluted its port's success in trade and business in the islands: 'The merchants here trade throughout the entire world except Turkey and the East Indies, but the most profitable trade is that of Guinea and the Antilles that has enabled many to build large fortunes.'[25]

After the end of the eighteenth century, however, striking improvements in the Lancashire cotton industry turned out to be an incomparable contribution to the boom of the Mersey port. Following the peace of 1815, Liverpool was able to play a full role as an intermediary between the adjoining area, with industrial

Lancashire in full growth, and the other side of the Atlantic, for the supply of cotton and for the available outlets.

In the United States, at first in South Carolina and Georgia, then in Alabama and Louisiana, the use of machines for cleaning cotton fibres allowed production to be handled much more quickly: in a single day, one man could clean 300 lbs as opposed to 10 lbs when the work was done by hand, particularly when Whitney's machine, invented in 1794 but only generally available around 1820, was used. On this date, cotton was grown in an area 1,000 km across and 1,620 km long. Liverpool became the primary port for importing it into Great Britain: in 1833, 840,953 bales of cotton were unloaded there as against 40,350 in London and 48,913 in Glasgow, and Liverpool thus covered more than 90 per cent of the needs of British industry.[26] Its port kept this role until the American Civil War, while the United States remained the primary provider. On the eve of the war, Great Britain used some 2 million bales of cotton every year, of which Liverpool imported from 80–90 per cent. To deal with these imports, its port possessed more and more ships: in 1816, there were 2,946, with a total tonnage of 640,000 tx. London had 6,198 ships with a tonnage of 1,250,000 tx. However, in the middle of the century, Liverpool's tonnage exceeded 3,600,000 tx over 9,338 ships, while London then reached only 3,290,000 tx over 16,437 ships.[27]

In the 1840s, at the same time as the cotton trade was developing and, in exchange, exporting manufactured goods to the United States, a new element intervened that strongly favoured the traffic between Liverpool and New York. This was the massive immigration of Europeans, with waves of immigrants pouring in to the United States as Europe began to 'burst in large numbers into America'.[28] The Irish famines, the economic difficulties on mainland Europe and revolutions were many of the causes of the more and more numerous crossings. This ever growing flow, transformed into a tidal wave at the end of the century, enabled the United States to receive 10 million immigrants from 1880 to 1914, when Slavs and Italians from central and eastern Europe followed immigrants of Nordic origin, Irish Catholics, Germans and Scandinavians.

The crossroads of New York

For receiving immigrants as well as manufactured goods, New York was particularly well placed for its exceptional vocation as a crossroads. Its port opened onto the greatest variety of horizons: the Great Lakes to the west, more easily accessible after 1825 following the digging of the Erie canal; to the south by inshore navigation (although this was not without its dangers) towards the ports of the Carolinas and Georgia, and further on, Florida, the Gulf of Mexico, towards the Alabama port of Mobile, and New Orleans, the port of Mississippi and Louisiana. From New York, one could also head further south towards the Caribbean, where

Cuba turned out to be an excellent market. To the north-west, the utterly safe shelter of the waters of the Sound, beyond Long Island, opened onto some 200 kilometres of inshore sailing in the direction of New England.

As well as men, New York received manufactured goods and equipment, especially materials for the railroad that was indispensable to pushing back the frontier, and distributed them inland. However, its port also played a very significant part in the wealth created by the export of American cotton. A *cotton triangle*, established over the voyage across the North Atlantic between the American Atlantic façade and Liverpool, gave New York an essential role.[29] In fact, ships entering New York were often headed for ports further south in order to take on cotton and carry it back directly to Europe. For this reason, departures from New York for the European continent were lower in number than arrivals. However, there existed a very important inshore navigation traffic from New Orleans, Mobile, Savannah and Charleston headed for New York, taking cotton there to be exported from the Hudson port and to bring back the foodstuffs, such as wheat and flour, that the South needed. In fact, a monoculture reigned in the cotton fields, and foodstuffs had to come from the north or the north-west. Initially transported by way of the fluvial axis of the Mississippi, flour and meats from Cincinnati and other markets in Ohio and the west were, after the 1830s, rerouted through New York via the Erie Canal to be shipped as before in their totality to New Orleans.[30] This trade was conducted in exchange for the import of European manufactured goods, which New York stringently controlled. The sale of these products in the western and southern United States was conducted through the intermediary of large commercial firms, whose head offices were in New York, supported by the banks and the shipowners of that city, and that sent their agents to buy cotton and finance the loans that enabled plantation owners to purchase the foodstuffs and textiles they required. The key to New York's success lay in the exceptional ability that the city's trade had to supply the credit needs of the South. As previously in the Antilles, the plantation owner was likely to commit himself to at least a year's credit, corresponding to the maximum value of future crops, with a view to being able to buy more land and slaves.[31] New York was better placed than anywhere else to make increasingly large profits from this situation.

Under the commercial dominance of New York, the South received far less from Europe than it sent by the direct maritime route. In 1822, exports from South Carolina, Georgia, Alabama and Louisiana rose to almost $21 million, whereas their imports were no higher than $7 million.[32] One of the principal activities in the New York market, at the beginning of the summer, was the arrival of traders from the South to replenish their stock for the coming season. They did not hesitate to spend several weeks in a city that was already highly attractive, with lively theatres and clubs, and often returned in the same ship that carried the goods they bought.

Profiles of the ports of New York and Liverpool

Drawing in the best part of the boom in the transatlantic traffic in the first half of the nineteenth century, these two ports experienced continued growth. In Liverpool, from 1816–1818 to 1843–1845, measured by tonnage, arrivals and departures were more than tripled; average annual arrivals rose from 390,073 tonnes to 1,214,794 tonnes, and annual average departures from 317,476 tonnes to 1,300,632 tonnes In New York, from 1821–1823 to 1843–1845, growth was less powerful: average annual departures rose from 195,600 tonnes to 488,600 tonnes, and arrivals from 212,000 tonnes to 555,000 tonnes After 1845, the boom accelerated in the two ports. In Liverpool in 1850, departures exceeded 1,483,000 tonnes, and in New York, during the years 1851–1853 and 1858–1860, saw arrivals rise to an annual average of 1,634,000 and 1,852,000 tonnes, and departures to 1,297,600 and 1,538,000 tonnes. On the eve of the War of Secession, the port of New York had tripled its traffic since the 1840s and multiplied it by seven to eight times since the beginning of the 1820s.[33]

This statistical measure of the boom leaves the particular characteristics of the two ports somewhat obscure, and it is essential to illuminate these since they represented the foundation of their Atlantic dynamism.

In relation to the European ports, New York enjoyed the enormous advantage of not experiencing, as London, Liverpool and Le Havre did, enormous tidal swells. There was no point therefore in fitting out expensive floating docks; they could content themselves with building wharves perpendicular to the banks of the East River and the Hudson so as to enable ships to come alongside at any state of the tide. The coast itself, however, comprised long cordons of sand scattered throughout the Hudson estuary, and did not provide very favourable access. Towards the north, Long Island's coast extended over almost 160 kilometres, while the sandy coastline of New Jersey was spread over 150 kilometres. Via Long Island, ships could take the maritime route for Europe by ascending towards the Gulf Stream in the direction of Newfoundland, where, in winter, fogs and icebergs represented a real danger. Via New Jersey, there was the southern route through the Caribbean.

Some 25 kilometres from Manhattan, Sandy Hook formed the edge of the port. Sandbanks stretched between Sandy Hook and Long Island, and ships had to navigate the pass at Gedney Channel with the aid of pilots, in order to leave or enter the bay of New York. This was split, by the 'straits' of the narrows between Brooklyn and Staten Island, into two parts, the Lower Bay and the Upper Bay. From the latter, vessels passed Governor's Island in order to gain access, via Manhattan, to the Hudson or the North River and the East River. Long lines of boats, quays and docks lay stretched out there, creating the feverish life of the port.

After the 1830s, steam tugs helped ships as they left, and a pilot would climb aboard before departure. In the Upper Bay, several ships lay at anchor, before passing the green coasts of Staten Island to gain access to the entrance to the sea from New York harbour, in the narrows. Here, they had the impression that the port was closing in on itself, already constituting its limit, beyond which, in the Lower Bay, the immensity of the ocean unfolded. Nevertheless, they still had to clear the straits in order to reach the Atlantic, and sails were unfurled and filled upon reaching the Lower Bay, allowing the tug's pilot to return. Right up until the beginning of the 1880s, sea-going sailing ships and steamers could enter and leave from Sandy Hook without waiting for high tide, the 7.30 meters of low tide sufficing for a sailing ship of 2,500 tx or a 5,000 tx steamer. By contrast, in 1885–1890, the departure of the new, much larger, much lower-lying steamers, laden with cotton, cereal and meats, had to await high tide to move into a depth of 8.5 metres.

Space soon turned out to be limited and expensive, bribes had to be paid for wharves, for making use of the services of the tugs that depended on the port's masters, because thousands of sailing ships, and then steamships, were crowded into the Bay. In 1824, James Fenimore Cooper provided a realistic picture of this – a port of intense activity with still rudimentary installations:

> The time has not yet come for the construction of massive, permanent quays in New York Port. Wood is still too cheap and labour too expensive for so large a capital investment. All these wharves are still very simple, a frame of posts covered in stones and recovered in a hard-packed surface. The front of the port takes up some seven miles...only the Battery, the Post office, is protected from the Bay's waves by a stone pier....New York's wharves form a succession of little docks, sometimes quite large, for sheltering thirty to forty sails, sometimes much smaller.[34]

Remaining provisional, the wharves were only built for 30 years and gave the impression of incompleteness and disorder. Waste from cargoes of molasses, oil, tea and cotton were strewn over the quays of some 60 wharves in the East River and the 50 in the Hudson around 1840. But the activity did not stop there: in a single day in spring 1836, up to 921 ships could be counted in the East River and 320 in the Hudson. Three-masted square riggers, brigs, schooners and cutters came in great numbers to New York's port because its costs were the lowest on the entire American Atlantic coast, and loading and unloading were very quickly done: in 1852, two and a half days were enough to unload one of the 1,700 bales of cotton from a packet out of New Orleans, on a wharf in the Hudson. Moreover, this cost less than $5, whereas in Baltimore it would have cost $50, and $68 in Boston, Charleston and Mobile.[35]

At Liverpool, the Mersey estuary provided a clear route for navigating, at least at the entrance to the port, since on leaving, contrary westerly winds frequently delayed departures or required much tacking before being able to reach the open sea.

To land here after a crossing lasting, on average, 30 days from New York for traditional sailing ships, or less than 20 days for ships following the transatlantic lines, it was necessary to round Holyhead and Anglesea in Wales, after having passed Ireland. Often the westerly breeze that until that point blew regularly, had just dropped, and ships had to start to tack. It was only when a strong following wind filled the sails that they started to get under way again, arriving in the Irish Sea to pick up one of the pilots cruising there on light sloops, looking for ships heading for Liverpool. The ships had to moor at the mouth of the Mersey and wait for the flood tide to carry them, with a favourable wind, into the great arms of the estuary's waters. After a few kilometres, the river narrowed and they could anchor off the city. The most important thing, however, was still to be accomplished: to reach the dock where they would find a mooring quay. It was necessary to leave anchorage, then under pilot's orders, manoeuvred by a tug, bumping against other ships, the ship would thread its way into a lock before the tide carried it back. Having managed this, the ship found its mooring at a quay in one of the docks that were built in Liverpool since the eighteenth century, and that subsequently multiplied.

It took a patient and long-term effort, leaving nothing to chance, to make Liverpool ready to exploit Atlantic traffic by building installations to ameliorate the natural inconveniences of an estuary open to the tides. In 1710, the first closed dock for accommodating ships was built, and at the end of the century Liverpool already possessed a complete system of docks, while London was still vacillating over building its own. By 1771, George's Dock had been built for receiving ships from the Antillean and American trade, fitted out with 17 warehouses. The King's and Queen's Docks were opened in 1788 and 1789. Herman Melville could compare Liverpool's docks with the Egyptian pyramids or to genuine Chinese walls, when celebrating their monumental scale. With the peace of 1815, the available area amounted to 7 hectares. In 1821, the Prince's Dock, the largest yet constructed, added 4.5 hectares to this, its two locks 15 metres in size, and cost £650,000 sterling, whereas the docks of the eighteenth century cost no more than £150,000. Brunswick Dock was added to these in 1832, and in 1834–1836, Waterloo, Trafalgar and Victoria Docks. By 1836, the available area was close to 37 hectares. Almost 30 years later, when the steam age was at its height, it exceeded 100 hectares.

Liverpool's docks were closed off from the city by railings, ensuring security for the merchants that New York's quays could not provide. Men were often searched on leaving, as there were so many thefts perpetrated on board the docked ships. Metal sheds stretched along the quays for protecting unloaded cargoes.

This remarkable effort of fitting out, completed around the middle of the nineteenth century by extending the docks over to Birkenhead, on the other bank of the Mersey, benefitted from the first railways being set up, after the 1830s, linking Liverpool to the rest of Lancashire and the Midlands. In 1837, the Great Junction Railway joined Liverpool to Manchester and Birmingham. Around 1850, via the London and North Western Railway, the transportation of goods had already risen and the predominance of the link with Manchester was quite clear: with almost 125,000 tonnes a year of goods sent from Liverpool to Manchester, 52 per cent of the traffic went on iron wheels, and two-thirds of this was the cotton imported by Liverpool. The remainder was sent to Birmingham (25,000 tonnes), the Black Country (35,000 tonnes), Sheffield (29,000 tonnes) and London (27,000 tonnes).[36]

A port providing an essential service to its surrounding industries – textiles and metallurgy – Liverpool also profited, around this time, from the extension of railway lines in the north of England. Immigrants coming from northern Europe and disembarking in Hull then reached the Atlantic coast by train.

All this explains why Liverpool had managed to dominate so many of the Atlantic routes in the middle of the nineteenth century. In 1850, the United States came at the head of the list of purchasers of manufactured goods, taking 852,500 tonnes out of a total of 1,483,000 tonnes exported by Liverpool, that is, almost 58 per cent, followed by Canada with 187,500 tonnes, Brazil and Argentina with 76,100 tonnes, and the Antilles with 71,000 tonnes. In total, the New World received more than 80 per cent of Liverpool's exports.[37] In 1857, Liverpool occupied first place amongst Great Britain's exporters, with more than 45 per cent of this trade, ahead of London's 23 per cent and Hull's 13 per cent.

However, there were also unfavourable aspects. Inclined to demand total freedom for its exports to Europe, the United States intended, from the 1820s, to protect its young, north-eastern industries. There was a gradual increase in import duties for European products: with the tariff of 1828 they reached a rate of 35 per cent on English woollen textiles, and in 1832, on the same product, the rate was 50 per cent. In 1842, certain goods were taxed as high as 100 per cent *ad valorem*. The South, which needed machines and manufactured goods that were sold less expensively in England than in the United States, reacted against these taxes that favoured the north's industries, and this was an important aspect of the differences that contributed to creating the tension between north and south leading to the crisis of the War of Secession.

These policies could cause immense harm to firms of traders. Thus, in 1828, the ship *Franklin*, leaving Liverpool on 18 May, did not reach New York until 6 July, after a crossing of 49 days. It bore a total tax burden of $70,000 on its cargo of fine textiles and cheap cotton fabrics. Another ship, the *Silas Richard*, more fortunate, left Liverpool six days later and reached New York on 29 May, some hours before the application of new taxes. Its crossing time of only 42 days allowed it to avoid the tariff. The *Franklin*'s cargo had to be re-exported to another market.

Moreover, Liverpool could not struggle against competition from Le Havre for the finest goods. These articles, the most recent of fashions coming from Le Havre and Paris, already created a vogue for luxury goods, the finest gauzes, birds of paradise, pearl necklaces, 'Hernani' scarves, fine boots, handkerchiefs 'à la paysanne', and small bottles of perfume. The majority were re-exported from New York through the ports of the South. The regular shuttles of the new transatlantic lines enabled stocks to be replenished rapidly.

The Mersey port was also endowed with a powerful commercial network for selling in the United States. In the first half of the nineteenth century, one of the most characteristic cases was that of the Quaker firm Cropper, Benson and Company, agents in Liverpool for another Quaker, Jeremiah Thompson, who emigrated from Yorkshire to America in the eighteenth century and in 1818 founded the first regular sailing line from New York to Liverpool, the Black Ball Line. The importance of Cropper, Benson and Company's role is shown in the part played by the speculation on cotton that preceded the crash of 1825. It had regular shipments at its disposal, made by the packets of the Black Ball Line. An orgy of speculation developed at the end of 1824 when it was announced that Liverpool's stock was one-third lower than normal stock. Prices soared. Cropper, Benson and Company, and a few other traders, stocked up to the maximum. In New York, they only learnt of the situation some weeks later, and Jeremiah Thompson dispatched a messenger to New Orleans to give his agents the order to buy as much cotton as possible. There was a race to buy in Liverpool, New York and New Orleans. In Liverpool, the crash began in April 1825, when a Scotsman threw a small quantity of low-priced cotton onto the market as enormous quantities of Brazilian cotton were arriving. Manchester cut back stringently on its purchases and prices collapsed in Liverpool while remaining high in New York as the speculators carried on putting in their orders in the South. On the arrival of the Black Baller, the *Florida*, in New York in May, announcing the collapse in prices in Liverpool, there was a rapid collapse. New Orleans still did not know this, and Thompson's agent, ascending the Mississippi, bought even more at the highest prices. By mid-summer, all the ports in the South were aware of the crisis and its trail of bankruptcies. The crisis was very serious for Liverpool, since British credit underwrote these exchanges: Jeremiah Thompson's numerous bills were drawn on Cropper, Benson and Company, and were very expensively discounted in New York.

The capital of these Liverpool firms remained quite low, so that Cropper,

Benson and Company had £60,000 sterling available to them, and Browns £125,000. Highly dynamic, however, these traders tried to take advantage of the manufacturers of Manchester and Yorkshire in controlling foreign commercial networks.[38] In the second half of the nineteenth century these trading firms carried themselves to the forefront of Liverpool's shipowners. This was the case with the Harrison brothers, who created the Charente Steamship Company, and Alfred Holt, with the Ocean Steam Ship Company. Just as Cropper, Benson and Company had done, the Harrisons had an excellent agent in America at their disposal, one Alfred Le Blanc, who had representatives in the cotton belt and the cereal states, the products of which were now the object of highly important exports. These traders made purchases by taking advantage of profitable freight agreements signed with the railway lines that transported wheat and cotton to New Orleans to send them on to Liverpool. The Harrisons, like Liverpool's other large firms, such as the Rathbones, managed to diversify their traffic. The Harrisons' American agent, Le Blanc, thus switched to Mexican fruit while American cotton was depressed. Following their associations in the Antilles, the Harrisons also worked on Brazilian cotton.

Due to the seasonal aspect of these trades, it was best to organize the turn-around of their ships to get the best ships in the most appropriate areas to secure profitable freight levels to compensate for the general tendency of freights to fall. Those who could call on the Forsytes of Liverpool, the Rathbones, the Holts or the Harrisons, whose role was cultural as well as commercial, could struggle against increasing foreign competition, in particular from the Germans of the Hamburg Amerika Line, by making an effort to concentrate their exports of coal, salt and manufactured goods from Manchester, in exchange for imports of American wheat and cotton, Brazilian cotton, African palm oil and Chinese tea, to Liverpool's advantage. For this, they made use of 'on the spot' agents able to prepare the best loads for their sailing and steamer fleets, taking advantage of the new rapidity in the transmission of market news due to the installation of undersea telegraph cables.

The Atlantic of the liners

Liverpool and New York profited more than any other ports from the establishment of the liners, packet sailing boats that could complete the fastest crossings of the Atlantic, offering traders a punctual service. Freights of high value, couriers and cabin passengers were the first clients of the new shipping lines that reduced the uncertainties of business.

For over 30 years before the middle of the century, before the steam age took shape, great sailing ships were used. Their departures on fixed dates along the Gulf of Mexico line from New York to Vera Cruz and then to New Orleans, and on the North Atlantic line from New York to Liverpool, constituted a major innovation. In 1818, the Black Ball Line opened, the first regular line between New York and Liverpool. Up until then, charterers had to depend on shipowners sending their ships out, the 'occasionals', when they considered them sufficiently full, after longer or shorter delays. They did not disappear altogether, but continued to be attached to Liverpool or New York, leaving on dates they set in accordance with when they expected their freight, and sailing when it suited them, provided that their destination was always either Liverpool or New York. The same services existed, although more sparsely, between other European ports such as Le Havre, Hamburg or London and the Atlantic coast of the United States, in the same ports in which the liners were about to appear.

Regular liner services for courier traffic first sprang up in the American North Atlantic, from Newfoundland to Halifax and Boston. It was again for the courier traffic that liners began their crossings between Europe and America. The crews on these ships had a very tough job because of the amount of sails they carried in order to make as quick a crossing as possible and to maintain their reputation for speed. Favoured by westerly winds, they could complete their Atlantic run from New York to Liverpool in less than 18 days, whereas other ships needed 30 days. From Europe to America, contrary winds delayed them and they required at least five weeks, or up to eight in winter. A few years of running before the wind were enough to damage them, and they were then sold to traders in Nantucket or New Bedford who repaired them and fitted them out for whaling.

The ocean-going ships provided their passengers with great comfort, with salon cabins in mahogany and maple, furnished with rosewood tables with fine silverware, an enormous quarter-deck where the gentry – their clientele consisted of rich businessmen and wealthy English aristocrats – took the air. The fare on board was sophisticated, and passengers drank champagne, fine wines and prize cognacs. When the first liners appeared, shipowners, in advertising their voyages, emphasized the quality of their construction, the speed and the regularity of the crossings, as well as the comforts of these ships, 'built entirely in New York from the best materials, covered in copper, with extraordinary sailmakers, thoroughly experienced commanders, offering regularity underway and prompt delivery of goods'.[39]

When the first departures of the Black Ball Line took place – the *Courier* from Liverpool and the *James Monroe* from New York – the quality of their ships justified the publicity. On 5 January 1818, an inquisitive and sceptical crowd gathered at the foot of New York's Wall Street to see if the departure lived up to the publicity that had already been created. With her seven cabin passengers, a valuable cargo, albeit low in volume, and above all, her postbag, brought on board from a nearby coffee house at the last minute, the *James Monroe* left her moorings at the appointed time and sailed down the port in a snowstorm. She had to go through the seas off Newfoundland, where fog had turned its shores treacherous and, to make sure of her position, the ship often had to make use of a sounding line. Despite these obstacles, the crossing took only 25 days. Leaving Liverpool on 4 January, the *Courier* took 49 days to reach New York.

In 1822, the Red Star Line was the second line to be opened from New York to Liverpool, with the departure, again in January, of the *Meteor*. The Black Ball Line then worked with four ships and responded by doubling the number of its vessels. A third line, the Blue Swallowtail, was created in September of the same year. At the end of 1822, there were four departures a month from New York, and just as many from Liverpool, and they were already enormously successful. In 1819, the New York firm Leroy, Bayard and Company opened a line to Le Havre. At the end of the 1820s, the number of liners from New York was nine times higher than it was in the first year, since there were 36 of them, and in 1845 they passed the 50 mark. Similar attempts were made in Boston and Philadelphia, although they were in no way comparable. The *Amazon*, the largest ship in service in the middle of the century, was almost 71 metres long and 19 metres wide with a tonnage of 1,771 tonnes, whereas, in 1816, the *Amity*, the first liner from Newfoundland, was 35 metres long, less than 10 metres wide, and had a tonnage of less than 400 tonnes. Their dimensions grew towards the end of the 1820s, and the *Charles Carrol* from Le Havre, which carried Charles X into exile in England in 1830, was 40 metres long and had a tonnage of 411 tonnes.

The steam age

On 22 April 1838, 20 years after the departure of the first liner of the Black Ball Line, New York welcomed the first two steamships on a regular line to have crossed the Atlantic from Europe to America:

> News of the *Sirius*' arrival spread through the city like a powder trail and the river was completely filled with boats carrying onlookers. A universal joy reigned, every face beaming with happiness.... While all this was unfolding, suddenly a large cloud of black smoke streaming into the sky came into view over Governor's Island. It all happened very quickly and in three hours the cause of the phenomenon became clear: it was the steamship the *Great Western*, whose immense bulk was propelled at high speed across the bay. It passed quickly by and, next to the *Sirius*, graciously exchanged salutes with her before coming to anchor in the East River. If public opinion was excited at the arrival of the *Sirius*, it became intoxicated with joy at the sight of the superb *Great Western*.[40]

The *Sirius* had left Cork on 4 April, and the *Great Western* left Bristol on 8 April, that is, a 19-day crossing for the former, at 6.7 knots, and 14 and a half days for the latter, at 8.7 knots. Each ship used steam continuously, burning 400 tonnes of coal. With its shorter crossing, the *Great Western* had enough to burn, but the *Sirius* had to burn some of its wooden superstructure.

The steam age had, in fact, begun earlier, with a crossing in May 1819 from Savannah to Liverpool in 27 days on a steam sailing ship using steam over 80 hours in alternating 10-hour days. On the Irish coast, sighting the funnel spitting out its smoke, a cutter from the Irish customs thought that the ship was on fire and raced to her aid. However, for many years steam was only used in coastal voyages around the American Atlantic. The successful crossing of April 1838 unleashed a 'rush for steam' in New York throughout the rest of the year. In July and November, Liverpool dispatched four more. After 1840, steamships could make six voyages per year, twice more than sailing ships, and two steamers provided the same monthly service as four packet sailing ships of the traditional line.

The entry into service of Cunard's vessels, first on the line from Liverpool to Boston via Halifax in 1839, and then from Liverpool to New York in 1847, marked a new stage. Originating from Halifax in Nova Scotia, where his Quaker father from Philadelphia had taken refuge after the American War of Independence, Samuel Cunard took an initial interest in the postal service from Halifax to Liverpool by traditional liner. When London considered subsidizing the postal service in 1838, Cunard managed to obtain the subsidy for a thrice-monthly Liverpool to Boston line by steamships. He hired excellent crews, placed them under an iron discipline, safety being the primary objective, in order to beat fogs, icebergs and storms. In 1847, his son Edward set up in New York, where he obtained a postal grant twice as large as the preceding one. Samuel Cunard then doubled his fleet, using his eight ships every fortnight from Boston to Halifax to Liverpool and from New York to Liverpool.

'Drive the Cunarders off the ocean!' — crushing the Cunards was the dream of many an American, the most aggressive of which were the ships of the Collins Line. Collins was a shipowner who, over a period of 20 years, had sent packet sailing ships to Vera Cruz and New Orleans. In November 1847 he obtained a large subsidy from the American Mail while starting to build four fast ships that could beat the Cunarders. The United States Mail Steamship Company could offer the best crews and most comfort for passengers. Its first steamer, the *Atlantic*, began its crossings from New York to Liverpool in 1848 and in 1850, three more ships, the *Pacific*, the *Arctic* and the *Baltic*, with a tonnage of some 2,800 tonnes, that is, 100 tonnes more than the average Cunard ship, of 35 metres in length, were put into service. Speed was to be the new company's major advantage. However, despite the immense resources the Americans put into it, Cunard maintained its top ranking for the postal service and in 1851 its ships transported three times more courier traffic than Collins. For passenger transport, however, the Americans' speed and comfort pleased many: in the first 11 months of 1852, Collins transported 4,306 passengers, and Cunard 2,969.[41]

Daringly taking great risks to increase his ships' speed, and enduring very high operating costs, Collins was to suffer a serious set-back when, on 27 September 1854, his ship the *Arctic* collided with the *Vesta*, a small French steamer, in thick fog off the Newfoundland coast; the ship sank, and there were more than 300 deaths. Less than two years later, crossing from Liverpool to New York, the *Pacific*, having struck an iceberg in fog, sank with all hands and cargo. The tragic disappearance of this steamer, prefiguring that of the *Titanic*, the giant of the White Star Line, in April 1912 in these same coastal waters off Newfoundland, dealt Collins an extremely heavy blow. His largest ship, the *Adriatic*, 116 metres in length with a tonnage of 4,114 tonnes, costing $1.2 million, that is, 6.6 million gold francs, completed only two voyages and had to be sold in 1858.[42]

The loss of two of the best ships in his fleet hit the American shipowner hard, whose new ship, the *Adriatic*, under construction after the wreck of the *Arctic*, was not yet ready. He had to use old ships and was unable to keep up the twice-monthly crossing on the basis of which he had secured a grant from Congress. To pay his creditors, the *Atlantic* and the *Baltic* were sold, just like the *Adriatic*. Enabling the entire company to maintain challenging speeds turned out to be very costly: the engines were extremely heavily used and had to undergo major repairs between voyages. Cunard's gains between 1850 and 1855 were more than 50 per cent of the Americans' (£1,202,885 sterling as against £801,420).[43]

Cunard's prestige came out of this battle of the North Atlantic greatly strengthened. Charles McIver, an associate of Samuel Cunard's, was fond of emphasizing how his company's success was based on disciplined crews and regular services, announcing to his captains that 'we are counting on you to maintain loyalty amongst everyone connected with your ship, officers and crewmen, through the firmest discipline and efficiency'.

Approaching the coast always turned out to be a delicate operation, and particular care had to be taken in navigating, and it was always necessary to use sounding lines to confirm the ship's position, even if this meant reducing speed. Similarly, captains had to concentrate on avoiding what was the most feared of hazards, the numerous icebergs in winter and spring along the coasts of Nova Scotia and Newfoundland.

The duration of crossings was notably reduced due to the struggle between Collins and Cunard. In 1848, Cunard's *Europa*, averaging 12 knots, made the crossing from New York to Liverpool in 11 days and three hours; three years later, Collins' *Baltic* proved faster, reducing the journey time to less than 10 days at an average speed of 13 knots over the same route.

Around 1880, when steam finally took over from the sail in rapid transatlantic crossings, Cunard's progress was again confirmed. Whereas in 1840 the company had four ships displacing 8,200 tonnes, 40 years later his fleet possessed 28 ships, displacing almost 137,000 tonnes, Cunard, however, was far from monopolizing the transportation of emigrants, the steerage-class passengers who proved to be the most profitable; its share of the passenger trade in the North Atlantic was no more than 15 per cent in 1880, and the ships assigned to this trade were of only average tonnage, less than 3,000 tonnes, fitted with low-output engines. The crisis of 1873 had proven the status of the company, which had had to face increasing competition. Efforts were made to increase the capacity of its liners: the *Bothnia* and the *Scythia*, entering service at the end of the 1870s, could each transport 300 cabin-class passengers and 1,200 steerage, displacing more than 4,000 tonnes.

In fact, competitors multiplied, initially in Great Britain, where three rival companies sprang up from 1850–1860: the Inman Line, the White Star Line and the Guyon Line. Although the last of these disappeared after a few years, the other two led a bitter struggle for the conquest of the North Atlantic. William Inman, the creator of the Inman Line, began with the London to Philadelphia line in 1849, where he undertook to make a fortune from his fleet by increasing his share in the transportation of emigrants, which was then in full swing. Understanding the financial interest they represented, he gave them better transport conditions, offering berths and light meals, while his competitors held onto traditional transports, cramming their passengers in without hygiene or comfort.[44] His profits enabled him to offer a weekly service on the New York line, opened in 1857, and in 1869, to bring in liners capable of worrying Cunard: the *City of Brussels* and the *City of Berlin*, followed later by the *City of Rome* and the *City of Paris*, steam sailing ships with iron propellers and hulls. Cunard's most serious rival, however, was Thomas Ismay, owner of sailing ships; he founded the Oceanic Steam Navigation Company by taking over the White Star Line that had undergone expansion around 1851, during the time of the gold rush in Australia. His first transatlantic vessel, built in the Belfast dockyards, was the *Oceanic*, for the Liverpool to New York route completed in May 1871. He made rapid progress, and the following year Ismay had six ships at his disposal in the North Atlantic. The White Star Line – the shipowner had adopted the name of the company he took over – stood out by virtue of its comfort, a highly valued innovation: cabins were fitted with running water, heated by steam; the great hall, magnificently decorated, occupied the entire width of the ship, opening onto the seaport and starboard.

The ships of the White Star Line set about challenging their rivals in high speed runs. In fact, after 1869, Cunard no longer figured among the medal winners in the Atlantic, preferring security to speed, to which policy it adhered until the beginning of the 1880s. Around 1880, speeds reached 15 knots; then, at the beginning of the 1890s, they reached 20 knots. The White Star Line then brought new ships into service, the *Teutonic* and the *Majestic*. The Inman Line responded with a new series of the *Cities*, built in Glasgow, and Cunard was obliged to follow in the dash for speed with its two new ships, the *Luciana* and the *Campania*, also built on the Clyde. At 189 metres long, sailing at 21–23 knots, displacing 13,000 tonnes, and carrying 2,000 passengers, these transatlantic vessels gave Cunard back its predominant position. In 1880, the company was restructured with this in mind, increasing its capital, and by 1885 it had already taken the record, the Blue Ribbon, for the crossing, with the *Etruria*, in six days and two hours, four days less than in the middle of the century. The *Etruria* was the last steamer to be fitted with auxiliary sails.

At the same date, the efforts made by Cunard and other British companies to maintain their control over North Atlantic crossings met with increasingly severe competition from shipowners on the German side of the Rhine. Two companies from Hamburg and Bremen appeared on the North Atlantic in the middle of the century and took on an important position in the link between Europe and America. Until the end of the 1840s, the sailing ships of the Hamburg Amerika Line sailed for New York; after 1865, this company turned to steamers, and was imitated by its Bremen rival, the North German Lloyd, in 1858. From the 1860s their ships occupied an important role in the transatlantic transport of North European immigrants to North America, as well as Latin America. It was at the end of the century, however, that, under the impetus of Albert Ballin, with the Kaiser's support, the Hamburg Amerika Line turned out to be increasingly threatening to the British. 'Our future is at sea', Emperor Wilhelm II could declare in 1896, and Ballin enlarged this ambition still further, setting vast horizons for his company: 'the world is my kingdom'. It was the Bremen company, however, that in 1898 was the first to assert the new German ambitions. The *Kaiser Wilhelm der Gross*, with a tonnage of more than 14,000 tonnes, capable of transporting 1,725 passengers, and with a crew of 480 men, offered baroque splendour in its cabins as well as speed. In 1898 it took the record for the crossing between Bremen and New York, calling at Southampton and Cherbourg in less than nine days. In 1900, the Hamburg firm launched the *Deutschland*, but Albert Ballin then abandoned the dash for pure speed that put management at risk, preferring to give his liners the advantage of the most splendid comfort. At the same time, he was willing to side with the Americans when Pierpont Morgan, the steel magnate, wanted to lead the struggle against Cunard to reconquer these maritime routes.

For a long time during the age of the liner, the French rather paled. At the beginning of the opening of the transatlantic route the French – who had showed great reticence regarding railways – were even more reticent about the use of steam in maritime transport. At the opening of the initial debate in 1840 in the Chamber of Deputies, where the creation of three steamship lines, Marseilles to the Antilles to Mexico via Bordeaux, Saint Nazaire to Rio de Janeiro, and Le Havre to New York, was being discussed, Lamartine stated: 'Fire is a thousand times more expensive than wind, the wind that God gives freely to every sail.'[45] Despite the irritation of traders in Le Havre and other ports, they had to wait for almost seven years to see the state support the creation of the *Compagnie Générale des Paquebots Transatlantiques*.

In 1847, the *Union* was the first steamer with a paddle wheel to leave Cherbourg for New York. The administration and operation of the line, however, were very poorly handled. Only the first voyage was completed in a satisfactory manner. Boat after boat ran out of coal, and the crossing had to be finished by sail, and even the sail liners of New York harbour outran them. In New York, not understanding English, the helmsmen did not follow the pilots' orders, giving rise to clumsy accidents and numerous jokes on this topic that injured French self-esteem.

It was the creation of the Compagnie Générale Maritime on 25 February 1855, by the Pereire brothers, that marked France's real entry into the transatlantic routes. The Pereire brothers bought up ocean-going sail ships for the first commercial service to the Antilles and California, and on 20 October 1860 the Compagnie Générale Maritime became the Compagnie Générale Transatlantique for postal transport. Three ships were under construction in Greenock in Scotland: the *Washington*, the *La Fayette* and the *Europe*. The *Washington* made the first departure, giving the opportunity for a sumptuous feast in Le Havre on 15 June 1864. At 105 metres long, with paddle wheels and sails, the packet boat was luxurious and richly decorated, with salons, a library, a smoking room, and 10 bathrooms, while the cabins were fitted with toilets and dressing rooms for the ladies. On its rear mast the white flag with a red globe of the Transatlantique flew for the first time.[46] In the same year it reached a new stage with the foundation of the Penhoët shipyard in Saint Nazaire which was destined to experience a great boom, with five ships built there and three others ordered from British yards. The return of peace in the United States after the American Civil War created a favourable opportunity, and in 1867, 9,100 passengers were transported to New York while the Compagnie benefitted from a postal subsidy.

Meanwhile, the Transatlantique was to go through a difficult period when competition was fierce: in 1872, there were up to 39 departures a month for the United States, that is, 468 a year, in place of the 100 in 1861; from Le Havre alone there were 130 departures a year for New York, 104 of which were foreign.[47] The German companies, having no postal service to ensure, took the majority of the market. The split between the Pereire brothers in 1868 was an initial blow for the French company, after the collapse of Crédit Mobilier the year before. This was followed by three catastrophes: on 21 November 1873, the *Ville du Havre*, rammed by an English three-master with 226 lost; the *Europe*, abandoned at sea on 10 April 1874 with 18 feet of water in the engine room and the holds; and finally, on 15 April 1874, the *America*, deserted by its crew 80 miles west of Ushant, after transferring passengers to other ships, was towed into Plymouth by the English. This last incident unleashed furious criticism of the sailors, whom the public suspected of giving in to panic and abandoning the passengers.

In the same year, however, Isaac Pereire's return led to a new boom, and the number of passengers doubled and freight tonnage tripled by 1880. Isaac Pereire immediately strengthened the other maritime routes operated by his ships, in particular that to Central America, where the Le Havre to Bordeaux to Colón and Marseilles to Colón met with great success. The Marseilles line was opened by Ferdinand de Lesseps, who was making ready for the opening of the Panama Canal on 7 August 1886, serving Genoa, Naples, Cadiz, Madeira, Tenerife, Martinique, Venezuela and Colombia. On the North Atlantic four new liners, the *Bretagne*, the *Champagne*, the *Bourgogne* and the *Gascogne,* laid down a challenge to other companies. The *Bretagne*, with a speed of close to 20 knots, managed to better Cunard's *Etruria* to take the record for the crossing in 1888. A dazzling liveliness on board and a lavish table made the French line renowned. They were, strictly speaking, the preserve of a wealthy clientele, 5,528 first-class passengers transported by the four liners in 1888, whereas, in the same year, there were 1,881 second-class passengers and 23,124 third-class, or steerage, passengers. On the other hand, a section of the steerage where the immigrants' quarters were located could be dismantled and filled with goods.[48]

Despite the launching of a new packet boat, the *Touraine*, in 1890, with a steel hull and two propellers, capable of reaching more than 21 knots, the Transatlantique was again to go through an eclipse relative to the successes of the German giants and Cunard's fastest ships at the end of the 1890s and the very beginning of the twentieth century. Four other liners put into service from 1890 to 1914, the *Lorraine*, the *Savoie*, the *Provence* and the *France*, did not look for spectacular success in a dash for speed which, moreover, was considered passé, while people were looking for comfort and luxury through increased tonnages. The *France*, which made her maiden voyage to New York on 20 April 1912, was not concerned to take the Blue Ribbon from Cunard's *Mauritania*, which had stolen it from the *Deutschland* and was to keep it for 20 years. For a crossing of six days from Europe to America, at a speed of 23 knots, the use of turbines enabled more space to be made in the steerage decks, and led to more passengers being carried. With 27,300 tonnes displacement, the *France* could carry almost 1,900 passengers in comfortable or even luxurious conditions, so that the American press could define it as 'a floating Paris'.

The Americans who, after the Civil War and Collins' failure had left the initiative in the North Atlantic first to the British, and then to the Germans, began to take it back again in the 1880s. They got their opportunity when the Inman Line was experiencing difficulties in 1881, and American capital took over the British company, bearing the name of the Inman and International Line. It became the American Line in 1893, and was sufficiently powerful to incite Cunard and the White Star to join together to negotiate with the Americans, resulting in their choosing Antwerp, rather than a British port, as their European terminal, with Southampton becoming their English port of call.

It was with the intervention of Morgan, the fabulously rich American banker and industrialist, that the British were led to fear the worst. For $25 million, Morgan made himself master of the White Star Line in 1902 and managed to unleash a price war in the North Atlantic for transporting immigrants. At stake was the transportation of new waves of European migration – Latins and Slavs – to the United States and the rest of the Americas. Since the 1880s there had been price wars pitting the White Star Line against Cunard, then English companies against German ones, but Morgan's offensive aimed to sharply reduce, if not to eliminate, the share of his only two competitors, the French Transatlantique and Cunard. In fact, he had allied his group, International Mercantile Marine, with German companies, this alliance aiming to eliminate Cunard from transporting emigrants from Mediterranean Europe. At the beginning of 1904, Morgan lowered his prices for steerage passengers to only £2 sterling for the crossing from London to New York. Cunard, which then charged prices ranging from £2.10s to £3, had to revise its fares downwards, but Morgan went further in order to beat these prices, reducing his fare to 30 shillings.[49] At these levels, losses were inevitable. To avoid a price collapse that would hurt everyone, especially the German lines that were still supporting Morgan, a conference was held in Frankfurt in August 1904 that brought Cunard and the continental European companies together again. As Cunard was trying at that very moment to take its share of the transportation of Hungarian and Austrian emigrants boarding in Fiume for the United States, an emigration that had until then been dominated by the German lines, a compromise could be reached. Cunard undertook to put a sharp limit on its presence in Fiume, the English having to make no more than 26 annual departures, that is 5.2 per cent of the trade taken on by the continental European companies. In exchange, the price war came to an end.

After further episodes, with Cunard continuing to challenge the Germans in Fiume, strengthened by their technical superiority – the company held the speed record for crossing the North Atlantic – its prestige was strengthened in January 1908 when, at the London conference, Cunard accepted an agreement with its rivals. The English company could cover 13.7 per cent of the traffic between Europe and America and was free to transport Hungarian passengers from Fiume.[50] Despite the opposition of a hostile American government, in the name of the anti-trust legislation against all price agreements between companies, this agreement would govern transport on the North Atlantic right up until the First

World War, each company agreeing to respect fixed quotas for transporting emigrants to North America.

Tensions arising between the transatlantic companies and governed by agreements like the London accord, looked more like truces than final rulings: in 1906, an English commission declared that 'in the ocean-going business, there is no middle ground between war and peace'. There were also more profound phenomena marking new life on the Atlantic. First among these was the preponderance of the regular lines, originally created for postal services, such as the English firm Cunard or the French Transatlantique, over the 'tramps' – the charter ships not tied to a regular line, that sailed whenever their holds were full. These tramps, of which there were several in New York for trade with the Caribbean and Central America, maintained a sailing tradition born of the seventeenth century. They continued to cross the seas, but their share was reduced: in 1914, it stood at less than half the world's traffic.[51]

The tendency of falling freights that became manifest during the first third of the nineteenth century, was also strengthened and proved to be compatible with the consistent operation of the lines. The maritime conferences that established a minimum discipline and 'fair play' between the operators attempted to find solutions, without genuine success, for what was a real collapse of the price of transport that favoured the giants and concentrated resources. Thus, in 1913, the Hamburg Amerika Line had 48 liners as opposed to only six in 1886; it gathered available traffic in European ports; its liners and its cargoes leaving from the North Sea and the Baltic took it largely from the national shippings.

These commercial rivalries led to severe confrontations in which nations' grievances came out more and more. Imposing their laws on the Atlantic for almost a century, the British did not take well to the claims of Wilhelm II to develop his naval forces so as to be better able to put the ambitions of his merchant fleet into practice. They were entering a new age of the Atlantic, the twentieth century. The 1914 war brought to an end a long period during which the Atlantic had known the Pax Britannica. This Atlantic had built its wealth on industrial growth first in Great Britain and then on the Continent, as well as an ever healthy exploitation of the wealth of the New World. The appeal of a still-virgin continent in which to prosper, and the hope of finding a freedom in America that old Europe often denied, encouraged Europeans to cross the Atlantic in an unprecedented flow of immigration.

Europe crosses the ocean: immigrants in the New World

From 1840 to 1914, almost 35 million Europeans left the Old Continent to fill the rest of the world. The New World attracted them in the greatest numbers: the United States alone, between 1840 and 1890, welcomed some 15 million immigrants, whereas, in the 40 years between independence and 1840, there had been no more than a million. This unprecedented flood of migration accelerated again at the end of the nineteenth century: from 1890 to the First World War, more than 14 million Europeans landed in the United States. The peak of the wave of immigration was reached in the 1900s, with more than six million immigrants.[52] From 1815 to 1914, Canada saw the arrival of more than 4 million immigrants, coming principally from Great Britain, more than 2.5 million of which settled after 1880.[53] It is true that in Canada, 'a reservoir with two taps', many were only passing through to go on to the United States.

Immigration in Latin America, derisory before 1850 and still low as late as 1870, suddenly exploded,[54] because, in the less than half century from 1871 to 1914, 9–10 million entrants were counted. In Brazil alone, from 1891 to 1900, there were more than a million immigrants. Exercising a relatively stronger influence than in the United States, due to the low population of the states in Latin America to begin with, immigration contributed strongly to a rise in the number of inhabitants. Thus, Brazil and Argentina rose from 3.2 million inhabitants in 1800 to 26.6 million in the former in 1914, and from 400,000 to 7.6 million in the latter. As in the United States, the pull exerted by development on pioneering fronts, such as coffee in the Brazilian state of São Paulo, cereal crops and cattle-farming in the Argentine Pampa, made immigration all the more important. In Europe, however, demographic pressure and changes in the economy also played an essential role.

Old and new immigration to the United States

In the United States the immigrants' origins were of two clearly opposed kinds: the old and the new, the first dominating entrances up until 1890, while the second was growing stronger right up until 1914. During the 1880s, 'old immigration' still accounted for almost two-thirds of the arrivals, but amounted to less than 40 per cent of them at the end of the 1890s.[55] Western and northern Europe provided the majority of the immigrants, with a predominantly British contribution in the beginning, after which a larger and larger place was taken by Germans and Scandinavians. In the 'new immigration', Austro-Hungarian elements, Italians and Slavs largely took over, coming from southern and eastern Europe.

Set apart by their origins, these two currents also differed in the types of reception offered to immigrants, as well as in their reactions. Regarding the former, the immigrants were welcomed with the greatest favour. Vast spaces to clear, fertile land, a variety of natural resources and the lack of a workforce were among the factors that attracted new immigrants. In the land that received them, they themselves felt satisfied at discovering a freedom that until then they had not known. Economic, social and political crises struck north-western and central Europe between 1845 and 1853, and the same conditions were reproduced again and again thereafter, prompting a large number of Europeans to leave the land of their birth. Having generally suffered in Europe, the immigrant 'shook off and repudiated his past, leaving for a new life in a new environment on another continent'.[56] With a certain pride, he acquired a new dignity and Siegfried cites the case of the Welshman, Stanley, who came to settle in Louisiana, where he was adopted by a New Orleans trader:

> A few weeks after my arrival in New Orleans, I had become utterly different in character and in mind. My new feeling of dignity made me stand up straight to my full height, and plunged me into a kind of ecstasy. Here, poverty and inexperience were nothing diminishing, they were not exposed to the scorn of the wealthy or the mature. It would take me centuries to extinguish the affection I feel for the town where it was revealed to me that a child may become a man.

Doubtless very fortunate, Stanley was not however the only one to be happily absorbed into the American 'melting-pot'. Numerous British artisans and their families, coming from the valleys of the Mersey, the Clyde or the Tyne, also managed to find a new pride on American soil. The exemplary success of Andrew Carnegie, the magnate of the iron and steel industry, is testimony to this. His father, a master-weaver from Scotland, felt the destructive impact of the industrial revolution.[57] Rendered redundant by mechanized industry, on 17 May 1848 he and his family boarded for Pittsburgh to meet his parents, who had already settled there. Although the elder Carnegie could not turn to another kind of work, Andrew Carnegie, aged 13 at the time of his crossing, erstwhile bobbin winder in a cotton factory at $4.80 cents a month, learnt to adapt, and managed to become a telegraph operator. At 18 years of age, he entered the Pennsylvania railroad, which paid $35 a month, and at age 24 became one of its directors.

At the end of the nineteenth century, the conditions of welcome had changed a great deal: there was a reduction in social mobility, the price of land had grown increasingly higher, and the immigrant was no longer welcomed as a pioneer coming to clear new spaces: the final frontier had disappeared. Increasingly important after 1880, the Latin and Slav presence also represented another social stratum, quite different from that of the British, German and Scandinavian agriculturists and artisans. Chased away by overpopulation and lured by the bait of better salaries, shamelessly recruited and lulled with illusions by the agents of maritime transport companies competing with each other for passengers, the new arrivals were crushed into the poorer districts of the large towns on the east of the United States, grouped by nationality, which made it very difficult, if not impossible, for them to assimilate. The problem of the American soul being endangered by the admission of foreigners was exacerbated.

Of course, similar fears had come up since the beginning. Before 1840, in his newspaper, Philip Hone had exclaimed:

> All of Europe is crossing the ocean....All those who cannot live at home. What are we to do with them? They raise our imports, eat our bread, fill our streets and not one of their twenty year olds is able to fend for himself.[58]

However, on reaching economic maturity at the end of the century, America became more conscious of its national identity. Inhabitants and new arrivals alike shared this sentiment, believing that Europe was increasingly using America as a dumping ground for its poor, its homeless and its criminals. The future of the Union would be threatened if immigration were not controlled. The Atlantic had to become an unbreachable barrier once again. The politics of immigration quotas, decided in 1924, was already in outline before the First World War, and fairly early on voices were raised in Congress for putting these measures into effect. Since 1882, when the first federal law on immigration was passed, a tax as well as penalty measures against criminals were established; then there was a law against undesirables – anarchists, prostitutes and polygamists – but there was as yet no funding debate in Congress. The only one, at the highest point in the wave of immigration, was concerned with the registration of migrants, since one-third of the immigrants from southern and eastern Europe did not know how to read. As late as 1917, the White House opposed a resolution in Congress imposing a reading test. Given tangible form by the Statue of Liberty lighting the world, erected by Bartholdi at the entrance to the port of New York in 1886, the American tradition turned the country into a land of refuge for the oppressed of the Old World.

Why emigrate?

Conditions reigning on the Continent and those existing on the other side of the Atlantic held sway over leaving Europe: Europeans were subject to a 'push' effect inciting them to leave their country and a 'pull' effect that drew them to America. Demographic pressure certainly represented the strongest element driving towards emigration, and Ireland presents an illustrative case.

From 1781 to 1841, its population rose from four million to more than eight million, an extraordinary excess of births over deaths, during a period of relative prosperity that lay at the root of this exceptional boom. However, after very poor potato harvests, the basic diet of her inhabitants, Ireland experienced a terrible famine from 1845 to 1848. The number of emigrants leapt from 20,000 in 1843 to 220,000 in 1851. It reached 105,000 in 1847, and in total, in the nine years from 1847 to 1855, 1,187,000 Irish crossed the Atlantic, whereas, in the previous 60 years from 1781 to 1841, 1,750,000 had reached Great Britain and North America. At this point, there were less than 20,000 a year, but this number rose to slightly less than 130,000 a year during the 'hungry years'.

Driven out also by the Malthusian effects of the famine that afflicted their native land after the first demographic boom had also taken place there, the Germans of Saxony and the Rheinland were forced by poverty to cross the ocean: from 1847 to 1855 there were 919,000 of them, slightly more than 100,000 a year; in New York the number of arrivals from Germany exceeded even those from Ireland, and from 1853 to 1854, 176,000 Germans landed there. Added to the demographic pressure in both countries was the effect of changes in agriculture that produced an overabundant workforce: concentrated properties drove small farmers out.

In America, the attraction was essentially caused on the one hand by new transport facilities that enabled immigrants to reach the lands in the west; and on the other, by highly specific factors, such as the discovery of gold in California. Until the decade from 1830, once they got clear of the Appalachians, immigrants found themselves in the west. Digging on the Ohio canal from Albany to Buffalo came to an end after 1825, and considerably enlarged New York's hinterlands, but had progressive effects: the tonnage of goods transported rose from less than 40,000 tonnes in the 1830s to almost 262,000 tonnes in 1853.[59] The extension of the railroad was another factor that played a fundamental role. Effected during the 1830s, it came to an end in 1835, and the line from Philadelphia to Pittsburgh aspired to challenge the main line of the Erie canal, and by 1840 the American network was the largest in the world. However, rail did not reach its height until later, and we can recall the stages in its growth by the number of miles constructed from 1831 to 1890, as shown in Table 7.2.

At the same time as these transport facilities, created by the progress of the railroad (the completion of the first transcontinental service in 1869 should also be highlighted) came into being, technological changes that enabled industries to create positions for the immigrants also occurred. The case of Boston is especially illuminating here. Isaac Merritt's sewing machine, modernized by Singer in 1851,

Table 7.2 Growth of the railroad, 1831–1890

1831–1840	1841–50	1851–60	1861–70	1871–80	1881–90
2,795 miles	6,203 miles	21,605 miles	22,096 miles	40,345 miles	73,929 miles

revolutionized the manufacture of textiles, and labour costs fell dramatically. This mechanical manufacture could absorb the flood of the unskilled Irish workforce, men, women and children, and Boston managed to become the fourth largest industrial town in the United States at the beginning of the 1860s.[61] The industries in the east then absorbed an increasing number of immigrants, and at the beginning of the twentieth century, in 1911–1912, east of the Mississippi and north of the Ohio and the Potomac, 60 per cent of salaried workers were originally foreign.[62]

It is true that the dynamic that enabled the European workforce to be absorbed into a developing economy was created by numerous exports of capital, mostly British. In Great Britain, a rich land-owning class, lightly taxed, sought to place their capital overseas. By 1851, $225 million had been invested in state federal funds, towns and above all, the railroad.

The discovery of gold in California represents a particular case in point. In 1849, many ships crossing the Atlantic were filled with speculators, their imaginations ablaze with visions of the unbelievable wealth waiting for them in Sacramento. On 24 January 1848, in the valley of the American River, James Marshall, overseeing the construction of a sawmill for John Sutter, discovered gold by the banks of a stream. Less than six weeks later, the gold fever had spread and Marshall's workers abandoned him. On 15 June, San Francisco was a ghost town, deserted by its inhabitants who had left for the Sierra where prospectors rushed in search of nuggets or alluvial river beds. The Atlantic coast learnt of this only later, on 19 August, and had to await confirmation, which was provided, in his message of 5 December, by President Polk in order that the real rush to Eldorado could begin, with more than 80,000 migrants in 1849, 25,000 of whom came via Panama or Cape Horn, the rest across the Union's interior, over poor tracks across deserts and mountains. Production in the United States was to rise from less than two tons of gold in 1847 to 127 in 1852.

In Latin America, too, similar factors can be found to explain immigration. As in the United States, the effect of Europe's population boom played its part in driving up departures. The attraction of the pioneer frontiers in Latin America also made itself clearly felt: these were the coffee boom in Brazil, from the 1870s to the 1890s, and the cereal boom in Argentina in the same period. To reach virgin lands for clearing, as for transporting this new produce, the railroad was also an essential resource. The example of the Brazilian state of So Paulo makes this quite clear: at the request of the Paulists, a line was built from the port of Santos in 1867 towards the 'frontier', reaching Campinas in 1872. At the end of the century, several Italian immigrants managed to take advantage of these transport facilities, and in 1910 one-third of the state's population was originally from Italy. The same phenomenon took place in Argentina, where in 1895 the Italians constituted one-third of the population. The railroad companies turned themselves into immigration companies, bringing new colonists into the state's interior.

A form of seasonal immigration developed in Latin America and was also present in North America, although in a less obvious manner. Departures of these *golondrinas* or 'swallows' from Italy to Argentina belonged to this kind of immigration. Seasonal work such as harvests demanded an exceptional reinforcement of the labour force from countries that were still very sparsely populated, and lay at the root of these voyages of 'birds of passage'. Thus, after the harvest in their own country, peasants left Italy to reach Cordoba and Santa Fe in northern Argentina, where they harvested wheat; similarly, for the maize harvest they moved again from December to April–May to reach more southern regions, the hinterland of Buenos Aires. At the end of May, they travelled back to Piedmont to sow seed in spring. This voyage represented a crossing of the Atlantic in two senses.

This practice can also be found, in the United States this time, by the masons of Venice arriving in March and leaving again in October. For seasonal labour, however, the United States appealed more to the Mexican workforce, and the Mexican harvesters thus left for the wheat fields of Montana and California.[63]

For immigration to North America, departures could be facilitated in Europe by apprenticeships in professions prized on the other side of the Atlantic. Thus, the Jewish tailor from Dublin or Poland, or the cigar maker from the same country, learnt their profession in the East End of London. A first emigration paved the way for another. In the same way, the Italians left to dig the Suez Canal before coming to work on the Panama Canal.

Crossing the Atlantic

It is indubitably the case that the multiplication of regular liners capable of crossing the ocean at sufficient speed, if not sufficiently comfortably for the emigrants, was one of the essential ingredients in the esteem accorded to the American continent. It was also accompanied, however, by a palpable fall in the price of a passage that allowed the largest number of people to become expatriates. The *Sunday Times* showed this in 1852, while the liners were already cutting across the Atlantic and enabling their owners to profit from a first boom in emigration: 'During the coming season, great crossings of the Continent from Liverpool into New York are expected. They are caused by the low cost of passage in Liverpool.'[64]

Prices for steerage passengers, the immigrants, were already considerably lower. In 1825, a passage for America from Liverpool cost £20 sterling; in 1863, the steamships asked only £4.15s per emigrant, and sailing ships even less, £3 each. The £3 level had already been reached by the middle of the century.

Without cheap transport, itself facilitated by bitter competition between companies, the massive Irish and German emigration of the years 1847–1855 would not have developed as it did.

The crossing became inexpensive but it was also extremely frightening. Even at the end of the century, a director of Cunard might still tell an unhappy steerage passenger that the transatlantic voyage was a gruelling test to undergo. Nevertheless, conditions were considerably improved by then.

The embarkation ports

In the British Isles, the majority of the emigrants left from Liverpool, but also from Bristol, London and Glasgow, then Southampton on the south coast of England, a convenient port for foreign companies. The Irish ports of Londonderry, Belfast and Cork, used at the beginning of the nineteenth century, had been abandoned since the 1830s in favour of Liverpool, where Irish departures were concentrated, particularly for New York. In 1859, the Inman Line and Cunard opened the port of Queenstown where a certain number of Irish could take their places on ships coming from Liverpool.

The predominance of the latter port was increasingly clear: between 1860 and 1914, 4,750,000 passengers boarded there out of a total of 5,550,000 leaving Great Britain. British departures were concentrated in the Mersey port, as indeed were continental departures, since it received Germans and Scandinavians from Hull by train: thus, in 1887, out of a total number of 482,829 emigrants leaving Europe for the United States, Liverpool managed to send off 199,441 passengers, of which 68,819 were continental Europeans, 62,252 were British, and 68,370 were Irish, that is, almost 42 per cent of all departures. Liverpool, in that year, had boarded some 66 per cent of British emigrants, the total number of whom had risen to 93,375.

In France, Le Havre was the principal emigration port, eclipsing its rivals in Marseilles, Bordeaux and Nantes. It too profited from the concentration of passengers facilitated by railway traffic. From Basle and Strasbourg, Le Havre received southern Germans and Rheinlanders; from Modano they received Italians, although they were also received from Marseilles, arriving in this port by the Transatlantique's and the Fraissinet Company's liners, and then transported by train to Le Havre. This traffic in transalpine emigrants built up at the end of the nineteenth century, during the Mediterranean's migration boom: from 1894 to 1907 more than 3.5 million Italians left their peninsula for the New World, more than 2.5 million of whom left from 1900 to 1907.[65] The railways of the west, the east and the PLM agreed to significant price reductions, comparable to those taken by the transatlantic lines of Hamburg and Bremen for carrying emigrants to their ports. Le Havre's boarding capacity can partially be seen in the traffic of the

Compagnie Transatlantique in the port, but Cunard, the other British companies and the German lines also put in to this Norman port. In 1883 and 1884, years of declining traffic due to the economic crisis in the United States and the cholera epidemics rampant throughout France, the Compagnie Transatlantique made 33,000 and 46,000 places available for emigrants. In 1908, at the peak of the wave of emigration, the Transatlantique embarked some 60,000 emigrants in Le Havre, and equally as many in the following years until 1913, half of whom were Italians.[66]

Marseilles was France's second port for embarking emigrants, after Le Havre. Its uniqueness lay in being, more than any other port, tied up with Italian emigration: on departure from Marseilles, ships made calls in Genoa and Naples, or sometimes they waited in Marseilles for the arrival of ships hailing from those ports. In 1874, capacity was of the order of 10,000 emigrants a year, and a Marseilles emigration agency was founded in 1870 for undertaking the recruitment of passengers. Three companies were engaged in the traffic, favouring their links with South America – Brazil, Argentina and Uruguay. The Messageries Maritimes had gained the postal concession for South America in 1857, the Société Générale des Transports Maritimes and the Compagnie Fabre risked opening their first line to New York in 1881, after difficult beginnings, given the keen competition on this maritime route, and managed to maintain it by using cargo/passenger ships which, on their return, brought back cargoes of grain. It then added a second line to New Orleans. However, in 1900, at the beginning of the twentieth century, Fabre used the Italian port of Naples for a line to New York, with a service every three weeks. At the same time, it sent out a monthly ship via Genoa to Montevideo and Buenos Aires.[67]

In Bordeaux, which had been the major port for French departures for the Antilles in the eighteenth century, emigration also developed after the Second Empire. With more than 378,000 emigrants in the half-century from 1865 to 1920, Bordeaux ranked after Le Havre and Marseilles. The port dispatched passengers to South rather than North America: 46,000 departures to the United States, and 268,000 to South America, of which 200,000 went to Argentina alone.[68] This last country was in fact the favoured destination of Spanish (114,000) and Italian (46,560) emigrants, joined by 123,000 French emigrants. The strongest wave of emigration was attained in 1887–1890, with 75,634 departures, one-fifth of the total. In 1888, Argentina granted free passage and began the sale of prepaid tickets. The South of France railways also lowered their prices during these years. The companies, with the Messageries Maritimes in the first rank, having six ships to South America available to them in 1886, found a precious return cargo in the meats, leathers and cereals of the countries of La Plata. On board the ships there was the ethnic mix characteristic of the 'new immigration': Greeks in the 1880s, Turks and Syrians during the spectacular flood of the 1900s (5,247 in the three years from 1904 to 1906; 6,100 from 1908 to 1914).

Meanwhile, traffic slowed after the boom at the end of the 1880s, since Italian and German companies, departing from Genoa and putting in to Barcelona, became increasingly competitive in the transportation of Italians and Spaniards. After 1885, Genoa and Naples were the two ports for transalpine emigration, the Italians aiming to challenge the transport of their migrants by foreign companies. In Istria, Fiume took on great importance at the beginning of the twentieth century, when Austro-Hungarian departures began to increase; Cunard then endeavoured to take the majority share of this traffic, to the detriment of the continental companies. Around 1900, the Italian companies La Navigazione Generale Italiana, Italia, Veloce and Lloyd Italiana managed to handle slightly less than half of the emigrant departures. The former, which defeated its rivals, had 103 ships with a tonnage of 140,413 tonnes at its disposal in June 1908.[69]

The Italians successfully took part in the emigration boom of the 1890s and 1900s: 3,515,191 departures from their ports from 1894 to 1907, that is, more than 251,000 per year. The peak was reached in 1900 to 1907, with 2,575,776 departures.[70] Brazil alone received some 693,000 Italian immigrants from 1887 to 1902; Argentina was another frequent destination, but the United States also held a strong position when their eastern towns were crammed with strong Italian communities who could propagate the cult of American soil in their homeland, The practice of prepaid tickets to Brazil or Argentina, even of free passage and, in certain years, passage paid for by their governments, facilitated these departures. Companies were able to renew their fleets in the 1900s, ordering the construction of new liners in Italian or British shipyards. Two among them were, however, supported by German capital, the Veloce and the Italia. The latter was even directly dependent on the Hamburg Amerika Line. Their new ships, such as the *Italia*, the *Verona*, the *Taormina* and the *Ancona*, launched in 1908, were capable of transporting some 2,400 passengers in relatively comfortable conditions. For its lines to Santos and Buenos Aires, and even more for New York, Genoa was the principal boarding port, with companies using Marseilles and Barcelona as ports of call.

Since the middle of the century, Hamburg and Bremen had begun to challenge Liverpool's handling of Germans and even Scandinavians, but after the 1880s the most successful of these companies, the Hamburg Amerika Line, and Norddeutscher Lloyd, were certain to carry second-generation emigrants from their own national ports, and the Mediterranean ports in particular. Present in Genoa, Naples, Barcelona, La Coruña, Bilbao and Vigo as well as a French port like Le Havre, the German liners also had an excellent commercial network in the New World. Thus, for the United States alone, the Hamburg Amerika Line was able to set up a network of 3,200 agents, present in various states, qualified to sell

250

prepaid tickets bought in advance by an emigrant's fellow countrymen who were already settled there. They were also able to negotiate the best price agreements with German and French railways for carrying their passengers.

Together with Antwerp, from where the Red Star Lines' liners sailed, Hamburg and Bremen were the North Sea ports from which emigrants left. The two German companies competed with each other to offer their cabin passengers the greatest comfort, or even luxury, but were also able to improve considerably, better than Cunard had, the conditions of passage for the emigrants, who still brought in the highest receipts. German success sprang from the comparatively large number of the steerage passengers transported in 1891 across the North Atlantic to America by the Hamburg Amerika Line, the Norddeutscher Lloyd, the White Star Line and Cunard, as shown in Table 7.3.[71]

The massive influx of Slav and Austrian emigrants into German ports filled their ships in a way their rivals did not manage.

Table 7.3 Share of steerage passengers to America, 1891

Line	Passengers	% of total
Hamburg Amerika	75,835	17.9
Norddeutscher Lloyd	68,239	15.3
White Star	35,502	7.9
Cunard	27,341	6.1

Suffering in the Atlantic

The regular voyages of the liners, from the packet sailing ships of 1820 to 1840 right up to the first steamers in the middle of the century, due to their punctuality and their relative speed, were able to ensure emigrants acceptable conditions of passage, quite different from those experienced on board the 'occasionals' on the longest and most uncertain crossing. In fact, it would take until the end of the century to see even the larger companies, who nevertheless made their clearest profits from the steerage passengers, the emigrants, concern themselves with noticeably improving their lot. As competition became stronger, prices fell, and voyages were made, if not in comfort, then at least with the necessary security and a certain well-being. Meanwhile, Cunard remained famous over many years for the austerity and the discomfort of its berths and the frugality of the fare, whereas Collins, then Inman and Guyon had quite quickly been able to provide some degree of comfort.

Of course, the worst experiences were had when emigration had just begun. Adverts in the press certainly tried to reassure: in May 1818, the *Liverpool Mercury* announced in the most glowing terms the departure of the *Timoleon* for New Bedford, 'well suited for steerage passengers, being tall, with a large capacity between its decks, its cabin lodgings are excellent'.[72] In reality, the available space was amongst the smallest, and stayed that way for a long time on most ships. In the ships, most often with two decks, the emigrants were housed between the upper and lower decks, the hold beneath the upper deck was usually reserved for heavy freight, although sometimes exploiting this space would also serve to house the emigrants. There was generally less than 1.82 metres between the decks, although a tall man could stand upright. Around 1880, one of the directors of the Société Générale de Transports Maritimes in Marseilles finally grasped the reality and became concerned that emigrants were being crammed in, in order to ensure large freights for the company. He was not afraid to ask the authorities for permission to install three rows of berths in the 'false decks' on his ships, instead of the regulation two, for his third-class passengers. 'The false decks, measuring 2.4 m in height, would give every emigrant sufficient space, better even than is necessary, and we could increase the number of emigrants per ship by half.'[73] This was also a concern for the Compagnie Fabre – also from Marseilles – ships had to be filled to their maximum capacity:

> regarding the eight supplementary berths, it is easier to move the floating bulkheads slightly, and build them....It is also quite easy to suspend hammocks...a simple wooden bar wedged between the beams would suffice to hold the head of a hammock and another would hold the feet.

Although the ruling obsession amongst the shipowners was to make their ships as profitable as possible by cramming the steerage passengers in, this did not however prevent a preoccupation with maintaining moral standards in the course of the journey. The Marseilles Chamber of Commerce recognized that segregating the sexes on the emigrant ships dampened sexual desire, and was therefore of the mind that 'the complete separation of women and girls travelling alone is to be made obligatory'. Morals certainly did not always concern the companies: in Bordeaux in 1888, the port's commissioner was obliged to proceed with arrests on the steamships of the Messageries Maritimes, on the grounds of engaging in the white slave trade. Unscrupulous minds understood how to exploit the situation of a mass of people setting off alone on a distant and decisive voyage.[74]

The discomfort arose not only from the narrowness of the space offered the emigrant for resting, but also the sense of confinement created by weak light. Light only came in through a few hatchways and only a few hanging lamps gave a dull light, since there were rarely any portholes, certainly on the ships that predated the companies' liners, where efforts were made to make the steerage lighter. Melville has shown how, on his first voyage by sailing ship, in 1837 (an occasional), the conditions created by the crush of luggage and people turned the steerage into a kind of overpopulated prison. The crew of the *Highlander* had completely cleared the steerage, the cargo being stowed in the holds, in order to receive the 500 passengers whose luggage cluttered the decks. However, for a crossing that might last as long as five, or indeed six, weeks, water reserves had to be taken on:

> a greater tonnage on deck, rows of large tiercerons were stowed in the middle of the ship, in the steerage, running its entire length and dividing it into two long galleries, themselves cut into four compartments by lines of tiercerons crammed into the vessel's sides, three times one on top of the other. These compartments were soon closed with the help of rough planks, and more than anything else they resembled kennels; so much so that they were dark and stifling, since the only light that entered came from hatchways fore and aft.[75]

During storms, the steerage hatchways had to be closed and the passengers remained locked up, finding themselves in a fetid lair in which fevers and epidemics developed. Lines of rough berths, cutting into each other, left barely enough room to move between them.

It was not until after the first boom in Irish and German emigration that measures were taken in England and the United States, in 1854 and 1855, to reduce the number of migrants admitted on board a ship. The English law especially set a minimum quantity of provisions that each emigrant boarding in Liverpool had to bring. The packet boats transported a real farmyard for the well-nourished cabin passengers, waited on by obsequious black stewards: fowl, pigs, and a cow, milked daily. The often scrawny emigrants in the steerage, however, had of course no right to any of this. Their passage ticket enabled them only to obtain bread, salt meat and, in the best conditions, a sea biscuit, an imperishable foodstuff that could be kept from one year until the end of another, and that required no cooking. The emigrants' 'kitchen' was, in fact, often reduced to a single flame, hidden in one of the hatchways in the centre of the deck, which was far too narrow for such numbers. Passengers had to establish a rota for lighting their fire, despite the ship's pitching. Each disputed his turn, so that there were difficulties in cooking the basic food of the Irish emigrants, a broth of barley flour in water. In bad weather, the fire-places were too risky to be used, and since they were not allowed to light fires on deck, they had to eat an uncooked diet or suffer from hunger.

When contrary westerly winds delayed the vessel beyond the habitual five to six weeks, personal provisions became exhausted. Water could also be a problem: the ration for each adult's drinking, washing and other uses was four litres a day.

Before the law of 1855 was passed, a parliamentary White Paper in London revealed these conditions. Its author had made the crossing incognito in the steerage of the *Washington*, one of the liners that ran to New York. The 900 steerage passengers were assembled on the first day to receive their water ration, being insulted by sailors and some even being dealt blows, and only 30 got their water; provisions were not distributed for two days. Famished, the passengers sent a letter to the captain, but its bearer was beaten at the foot of the main mast. Finally, the following day, half of the expected provisions were distributed.[76]

As well as experiencing hunger, the passengers often had to face worse: shipwreck. In winter and spring, on approaching the Irish coasts and the waters off New York on the coasts of Long Island or New Jersey, the Newfoundland fogs prevented the helmsmen from seeing icebergs in time. In the midst of the Atlantic, when the sea's fury was unleashed, without a ship within reach to lend help, even sailing ships at full sail could not avoid sinking. Finally, on one occasion the fourth watch on the prow at night, half asleep, did not see a nearby ship approaching at full speed, and there was a collision that stove in the ship's side and sent it straight to the bottom.

When a boatload of emigrants sank, the crew were sometimes sufficiently humane to bring help to the unfortunate people in the grip of panic. Equally often, however, the brutality of men and the sea came out. Thus, the ship the *William Brown*, carrying emigrants for Philadelphia, five weeks out from Liverpool, struck an iceberg one night and began to sink.[77] Thirty-two sailors and passengers got away in a rowing boat with a boatswain, but the latter thought the little boat was too heavily laden and decided he had to throw several emigrants overboard like cheap merchandise. The federal tribunal that tried him for this crime in Philadelphia heard an Irishman, a certain Frank Carr, testify to a tragic death:

> I was not going to leave that little boat, I had worked bravely the whole time, until morning, I will work and do what is necessary to get the water out of the boat. Here are the five sovereigns in exchange for my life until dawn. When it comes, if the Lord does not help us, we will hold on to the end, and if my turn comes, I will go as a man...don't push me overboard until I have said a few words to Mrs Edgar....Mrs Edgar, can't you do anything for me?

The Irishman continued his deposition: 'She made no response that I could hear, and then they threw her into the sea.'

It is not until the famous wreck of the *Titanic*, on the night of 14–15 April 1912, also after striking an iceberg, that scenes of panic would be seen, showing contradictory evidence of generous help and hard-heartedness. In order to be able to extinguish a blaze that had broken out in the ship's holds by reaching New

York as early as possible, the packet boat increased its speed and the officer of the fourth watch was unable to avoid the iceberg in time. Only 703 people managed to take refuge in the lifeboats and more than 1,500 victims were dragged down with the ship over the 3,000 metres to the sea-bed. The steerage passengers were the majority of the victims, and it does indeed seem that some were refused help, and bars were even placed over the hatchways opening onto the steerage in order to enable the evacuation of the cabin passengers first.

It is certain that the emigrants paid the heaviest price, because, crammed in as they were, the panic that broke out was almost always fatal. This was the case in 1854 on the Inman Line's *City of Glasgow* which lost 460 people when wrecked, principally emigrants. Again, the *Powhatan*, in the same year, coming from Le Havre, was driven against the Jersey shoreline, so close that the screams of the passengers, some 200 German emigrants, could be heard as they were thrown into the sea. On the other hand, safety measures were sometimes adequate. Thus, the Black Ball Line's *Montezuma*, which was also driven aground on Long Island with its 500 emigrants, managed to save the passengers, thanks to the help that rushed from New York.

America welcomes the immigrants

Could the battalions of immigrants discovering New York once their ship had got past the Narrows and sailed along the shores of Staten Island hope to find there the warm welcome promised them by the agencies that had recruited them, as well as the means for settling quickly into the New World?

Above the coast of Staten Island flew the yellow flag of quarantine: as well as the poverty of the majority of the immigrants, the fear of epidemics reigned amongst New Yorkers and had inspired the construction of lazarets where the passengers stayed before being given permission to enter the port. The immigrants' agents sometimes managed to find ways of avoiding quarantine by letting them off in New Jersey. Perhaps a certain number of captains also did this, as Melville's captain did when, on coming in to port, he threw all the mattresses, blankets, pillows and straw mattresses overboard, and fumigated his ship, and having thus ended up with a healthy looking ship after this enormous cleaning operation, the passengers could avoid several weeks' detention in quarantine. Nevertheless, the *Highlander* had to throw 25 of its passengers overboard since they died of contagious diseases, with an epidemic being declared on board.

The boom given to immigration by the Irish famine required the establishment of more cumbersome quarantine services: the maritime hospital on Staten Island was exclusively reserved for contagious diseases, while the infirm, or non-contagious patients who needed care, were sent to Hellgate on Ward's Island.

However, once the barrier of quarantine had been cleared, the immigrants

255

found themselves confronted with the scourge of their disembarkation port on one of the wharves on the East River or the Hudson, where numerous 'runners', agents for guest houses who attempted to take advantage of them, stolen luggage, excessive travel costs and accumulated debts often found the immigrant totally stripped. Philanthropic associations such as the Hibernian Providence Society for the Irish, sought to secure a means for the new arrivals to leave New York as quickly as possible to look for work inland in the Union. After 1855, on the Battery, Castle Garden Fort was devoted to receiving immigrants, and a depot was erected there where they could be kept apart from the runners and their plundering. Here they were offered normal travel prices, and their luggage was guarded. In 1892, the reception was transferred to Ellis Island.

Conditions were changing during this period, however, and the total disarray of the Irish and indeed the German immigrant in the 1840s made way for something else. In fact, the ethnic communities of New York and the other large American towns were growing increasingly stronger, and were able to coordinate the welcome of the new arrivals. Kinsfolk and friends bought prepaid tickets for Sardinians, Piedmonters, Lithuanians, Bosnians, Magyars, Syrians and Slovaks. The immigrant's disorientation in the new world he was crossing, where he did not understand the language, remained real, but the more striking reality was a migration for which kinship or friendship bonds had prepared the way. At the end of the nineteenth century, more than 70 per cent of new arrivals on Ellis Island were to rejoin their kinsfolk or friends. We can employ the concept of a 'migration chain' for this.[78]

For voyages, the sailing companies had sold tickets covering the entire journey: from Finland, for example, immigrants would go to England, from England to an American port, and from there to their final destination. The Finnish who chose to go over to Minnesota, a favoured region among the immigrants from this country, could count on well-ordered time and space.

The voyage had also been prepared by letters from immigrants who had already settled and who made the migration chain effective through the detailed and generally optimistic information they provided. The classic example of a letter would contain information about America in general, about the American diet and the high salaries, while at the same time managing to complain of low employment and the hardships of life in the pioneer camps:

> Dear Brother, allow me to invite you to come to live and die here. Dear Brother, leave the country of our fathers and come here....I promise to help you to build your farm....Buy a railroad ticket for a town called Minneapolis, and I will come to meet you.[79]

The immigrant already settled in Minnesota was anxious to give every guarantee for the success of the voyage, about which another immigrant, from Ohio, is much more precise: 'If you are coming, send me a letter. And when you are in New York, telegraph me from there. I will come and meet you at the depot although you won't get lost.'

There was an enormous trust in the bonds of kinship or friendship amongst the immigrants who settled next to those who had paid for their voyage with prepaid tickets, and this must have contributed to making a success of the largest wave of immigration at the end of the nineteenth century and the beginning of the twentieth. The success of their elders served as an example to the young and gave them the necessary hope at a time of inevitable uprooting on departing their native land.

With this exceptional migration movement from the Old Continent to the New World, the Atlantic gave Europe and America the best grounds for believing in a better future. In fact, the disruptions imposed by the war and the crises prior to it were to change the life of the ocean profoundly.

Chapter 8

The Atlantic in the twentieth century

In the nineteenth century, under the maritime and commercial hegemony of Great Britain, the Atlantic was still dominated by European expansion as it had been in previous centuries. There was a strict complementarity between the New and the Old Worlds, the latter initially providing the manufactured goods, capital and men necessary to equipping it, while receiving the raw materials indispensable to its own development. On the eve of the First World War, this system of exchange saw the United States buying less than she sold. This was partially due to the protectionist tradition that was observed from early on, and reinforced by the McKinley tariffs in 1897, but it was also because of the Americans finding that they had to use their export surplus to pay the interest on the capital that Europe, their silent partner, invested in their country.[1] The development of intercontinental trade, with shipments of cereals, meats, minerals, and even petrol to Europe, created a global market in which Latin America too played a role in providing Europe and North America. In the majority of cases, the axes of exchange followed the parallels from the West to the East Atlantic.

The First World War swept this situation aside. In the face of a Europe whose populations and economies were badly affected and began to decline, a youthful America became all powerful. The conflict also began to question the basis of the Pax Britannica: its enhanced naval forces enabled America to challenge England for naval supremacy at the Washington Conference in 1921. It directly controlled the Caribbean where Saint Thomas, occupied in 1917, had become the Gibraltar of the Antilles, and its control of the Panama Canal allowed it to operate a double strategy, Atlantic and Pacific.

For almost a quarter of a century, Europe had nevertheless managed to maintain a certain predominance in the Atlantic, at least on its southern shores, in Latin America and Africa, from which it continued to draw raw materials, profit from the revenues of its colonies, and to send men there. The North Atlantic trades, however, that had until then been the most prosperous, were under serious threat from the new imbalance that the United States had brought with it.

Having profited from its neutrality, and even improved its economy during the war, it did not become a heavy importer from Europe although it expanded its trade with Asia, Africa and Latin America in order to find sources of energy or raw materials. On the other hand, exports flourished after 1918 as Europe was being reconstructed, and the United States gradually became the largest of Europe's creditors, although Europe was for a long time was incapable of paying it back.

The American economy reached maturity and settled into a strong position. The Union no longer felt the need to turn to its old home country and the other European countries to obtain capital, goods and men. The Americans gave in to the temptation of isolationism, and had to close off the ocean to the floods of migrants who, according to the character it had taken on over 30 years, seemed to threaten American identity. Withdrawing into itself, and thus exposing the real roots of the American soul, the inhabitants of the United States had to be protected from the excesses of alcoholism and drugs. This resulted in the infamous Prohibition of the 1920s and the beginning of the next decade. The Atlantic was to separate and no longer unite. Transatlantic companies saw a sharp fall in the numbers of passengers they carried, of which emigrants had until then formed the better part. They could only keep going by reorienting their traffic towards tourism and cruises that opened up the Caribbean Atlantic or the northern latitudes for both Americans and Europeans. Even migration to Latin America was affected around 1930.

To this must also be added the effects of the global crisis of 1929 that seriously lowered the movement of currency. It was, therefore, an Atlantic in crisis that faced a Second World War, and some slight restoration of traffic after 1933–1934 could not repair the losses it endured. Europe was to be torn to pieces and lose any hope of dominating the Atlantic for a long time to come. The British were obliged to give up their naval ambitions and a Pax Americana was to reign over an ocean that, moreover, had seen its strategic role affected by an interest in the Indian Ocean and the Pacific. Exchange had to be redirected again in accordance with the meridians as the United States sought to find its largest source of energy in Latin America and Africa.

However, after the 1960s, a new Atlantic appeared, at least as concerns the great flood of trade, controlled by a resurgent Old Europe. 'Spirals' of traffic crossed the ocean, once again connecting Africa, South and Central America to the North Atlantic to return either to Europe or the United States. At the same time, the actors changed: in place of the old tramps that were still fairly numerous before the Second World War and in the years following it, specialized container ships for the express purpose of transporting manufactured goods in the North Atlantic traffic between America and Europe, ore or petrol tankers, now sailed the Atlantic. Giving a better financial yield, flags of convenience considerably increased their share to the detriment of national flags. Specialized ports for the container ship and petrol tanker traffic – Antifer in Le Havre for France, Le Verdon for Bordeaux, and Rotterdam in Holland – maintained or even increased their trade while others found themselves in difficulties, as in the case of Liverpool in Great Britain.

The passenger traffic was finally killed off by the jets of the 1970s. All that remained for the liners was to embark tourists, dizzy and disoriented, at cruise sites. Meanwhile, tourism in the twentieth century opened new horizons in the Atlantic: the vast beaches of the Caribbean or Atlantic Europe, where a new-found familiarity binds men to the ocean.

Transformations in the Atlantic from 1914 to 1939

Threats to the Pax Britannica on the eve of the First World War

The Pax Britannica rested on Great Britain's naval hegemony over the Atlantic, a hegemony that was yet to be contested at the end of the nineteenth century. In fact, this power possessed an impressive network of naval bases ready to serve the movements of a war fleet of a tonnage of 2,714,000 tonnes in 1914, remaining significantly higher than the combined tonnages of the two most important fleets of the day: Germany's 1,305,000 tonnes and the United States' 985,000 tonnes The 14 Atlantic bases, from Halifax in Canada to the Falkland Islands in the South Atlantic, gave England the means to control the most useful commercial routes from the North Atlantic, the Caribbean, Latin America and Africa. In the Caribbean alone, the British possessed the bases at Trinidad, Santa Lucia, Antigua and Jamaica. South of the Equator, in the mid-Atlantic, the islands of Ascension and Saint Helena were also crucial bases; the first was traversed by the principal undersea telegraphic cables that came from Europe and were owned by the English, leading to South Africa and South America. On the west coast of Africa, the base of Lagos was added in 1898 to those in Gambia and Sierra Leone. One thousand kilometres from the Atlantic coast of the United States, the naval base in the Bermudas lay almost midway between the base in Halifax, further to the north, and the bases in the Caribbean. Ready for immediate intervention, some 39 ships were said to be in commission, stationed at these Atlantic bases. In its 10 naval bases in the Pacific, there were 43 ships in commission; with the same number of bases, the Indian Ocean had, on the other hand, only a dozen ships stationed there.[2] It was in the Pacific that an effort to create new naval bases appeared to come to fruition more than in the Atlantic: two bases in Australia, in Albany and Cape York, Weihaiwai in Northern China, and the Fiji Islands in the Pacific archipelagos.

Onto this network of naval bases an extremely dense network of coal-mining stations was superposed, providing steamships with the necessary supplies. There were a dozen of these on the Atlantic coast of South America, and an equal number on the African Atlantic coast.

These impressive resources were, in fact, inherited, since from the eighteenth century onwards Great Britain had been able to provide itself with the best naval logistics. It was this that enabled it to give its navy the necessary quality, just as much as its strengths. However, as Paul Kennedy puts it, Great Britain had retained supremacy by 'foregoing' an adversary to replace the one they lost by defeating France. Yet this was no longer the case in 1900, and still less in 1914. In fact, the rush for naval armaments had gripped all the powers, Germany in particular, and their battle fleet underwent a sudden boom: in 1880, it had only 88,000 tonnes, but in 1900, due to the numerous ships under construction, it could count on a tonnage already approaching 300,000 tonnes, and, at the beginning of the First World War, it exceeded 1.3 million tonnes[3] Wilhelm II's fleet had more than quadrupled its tonnage since 1900. Only the United States and Japan were able to provide their fleets with a rate of development that came close to this, each tripling their tonnage since 1900.[4] By contrast, France, which had 499,000 tonnes in 1900, not exceeding 900,000 tonnes in 1914, was then only in fourth place.

Above all however, in the maritime areas that until then were placed under direct British control, the powers began to give notice of new ambitions. The most remarkable case in the Atlantic was that of the Caribbean, continuing into South America. In the Caribbean, the United States aspired to inaugurate the reign of a Pax Americana, ensuring the necessary security for their commercial activities. American policies in the Caribbean, however, had been marked by prudence for a long time: the annexationist aims promoted by some in the southern states of the United States, in particular as regards Cuba, Puerto Rico and the Dominican Republic, were contained, and these expansionist projects were directed more to Hawaii, in the Pacific. It is true that the principal reason, to ensure the security of navigation in the Gulf of Mexico, was obscured to the extent that the old traffic from the Caribbean to the United States, from New Orleans to New York, had declined to the benefit of internal links by train and canal.

To transform the Gulf of Mexico into an American lake was, however, one of the permanent ambitions that was reinforced with the renewal of interest among American statesmen in the area of the Panama isthmus, which played a crucial role in linking the Atlantic and the Pacific for their battle fleet.[5] Two powers could oppose the United States' projects: England, present in Honduras, extremely close to Panama, was anxious to keep some control over the isthmus, and Spain, whose colonies in Cuba and Puerto Rico controlled the entrance to the Gulf of Mexico.

The American victory over Spain in the extremely short war of 1898, was the first step to building an American Caribbean. The famous doctrine of Admiral Mahan that sea power was indispensable to any great power, was strikingly confirmed by this. Theodore Roosevelt, a partisan of robust action made possible by the naval progress the Union had made, managed to take advantage of an incident – the explosion in Havana's harbour of the American battleship the *Maine*, on 15 February 1898 – to challenge Madrid in the Atlantic and the Pacific, in Cuba and the Philippines. With the Spanish squadron destroyed off Santiago in Cuba, and Puerto Rico attacked, Spain quickly sued for peace in 1898. The United States gained Puerto Rico, the position of which, controlling access to the Caribbean from the Atlantic, provided the crucial annexation. Cuba was freed from the Spanish regime and in 1901, was placed under *de facto* American protection: a right of intervention was granted to the United States to preserve order and maintain the island's independence.

Two years later, Roosevelt's 'cowboy diplomacy' also gave his country control over the Panama isthmus where they wanted to dig a canal from the Atlantic to the Pacific. England had already suffered one set-back in 1896, when its dispute with Venezuela over the border between that country and British Guyana was overseen by American arbitration (President Cleveland dared to advise London that the United States were, in effect, the continent's sovereigns).[6] In the midst of the Boer War in 1901, Britain had to give up its rights with regard to the future canal to be dug through the isthmus and permitted the United States to complete and own the canal. In 1903, Roosevelt managed to force Colombia to hand over an area of 16 kilometres for the canal to be dug. This acquisition constituted the pivot of American naval power in this sector, vital for its Atlantic–Pacific communications.

South of the Caribbean, in Venezuela, the American determination not to let the Europeans intervene in the New World had meanwhile been brought to a halt when Germany undertook to increase its influence there in 1900–1901. Highly influenced by Mahan's theory of sea power, the Kaiser introduced the concept of risk into his country's naval strategy. Roosevelt called Wilhelm II a maniac and a trickster, but nevertheless had to renounce his use of the 'big stick', the policy of standing fast employed against Spain and Colombia. Germany wanted to be reimbursed for Venezuela's debts and proposed the arbitration of the Court of The Hague, which President Castro in Caracas refused. Germany and England organized a naval blockade of Venezuela's ports in December 1902. Despite these threats, Roosevelt left the Germans to it. He showed himself to be the more firm and returned to his conception of the United States' right of intervention in the Dominican Republic, where Germany again demanded that its debts be settled. Declaring that he had the moral mandate to intervene, Roosevelt imposed American customs control on the country.

These various incidents reveal a rising tension that was taking place in the Atlantic at the beginning of the twentieth century. On the African Atlantic seaboard, Germany and France were at odds in Morocco over the Agadir incident in 1911. Confronting German ambitions, England was joined by France and Japan, and abandoned its policy of splendid isolation. The United States, tempted to respond to German challenges under the presidencies of Theodore Roosevelt and Taft, while maintaining a defence of the Monroe doctrine on their own continent, returned to neutrality regarding Europe with Wilson's presidency in 1913, on the eve of the First World War. On 4 August 1914, Wilson proclaimed that the European conflict was a war with which 'we have nothing to do'.[7]

The First World War and the Battle of the Atlantic

For more than a century, Europe had not experienced a single important maritime war. Since the beginning of the twentieth century, the naval arms race had given chiefs of staff the illusion of being able to use a powerful instrument that would ensure their victory. Battleships, accompanied by cruisers and torpedo boats on the high seas, with considerably increased speed and firepower, could be used in one supreme engagement that would deliver mastery of the seas by destroying the enemy's forces. It was only then that operations were mounted on enemy coasts or against enemy trade.

In fact, the maritime war was going to sweep these plans away, since the ships of the central empires were to remain in the shelter of their ports, with the exception of a few raids on the English coast, followed by limited engagements such as Dogger Bank in 1915. The only battle of the conflict, at Jutland on 31 May 1916, pitted the English home fleet against the German high sea fleet; the qualities of the latter were demonstrated, but the battle was not decisive. The British Admiralty, thanks to its fleet's superior tonnage, was able to maintain the blockade, which ran all the way from Scapa Flow to Harwich. In the absence of the necessary overseas coal bases, the German Admiralty could not contemplate prolonged actions on the part of its ships over the entire area of the Atlantic routes.

The Battle of the Atlantic was going to take place nevertheless, but it was to pit German submarines against allied trade. The United States, the principal trading partner for supplying the Europeans, intended to make sure that its neutrality, proclaimed by President Wilson in 1914, was respected. Both camps of combatants made their intentions against this neutrality known. In November 1914 Great Britain proclaimed the entire North Sea a war zone in order to place Germany in an effective state of blockade. Numerous German ships were seized by the navy. The central empires' trade with the United States was soon paralyzed: in 1914, it stood at $169 million, in 1916, it was reduced to little more than $1 million.[8] Germany's neighbouring neutral countries – Denmark, Holland, Norway and Sweden – increased their trade with the United States, which rose from $187 million to $279 million from 1914 to 1916. It could only partially compensate, however, for the collapse of German–American trade.

The decision that was to lead to the Battle of the Atlantic was one taken by Germany on 4 February 1915 to establish a war zone all the way around the British Isles. British and allied ships that turned up in this zone could be sunk by German submarines. President Wilson protested sharply: according to him, each submarine had to stop the allied ship it wanted to attack, look for contraband goods and make sure that the passengers and crew were safe. If the still extremely vulnerable submarines of 1914 did not want to be sunk by the guns that eventually armed merchant shipping, they had to sink them immediately, without warning.

On 25 March 1915, a single incident called the American experience into question: the English packet boat *Fallaba* was sunk, with a United States' citizen amongst the victims. However, off the south coast of Ireland, on 7 May 1915, the *Lusitania* was attacked and sunk with 128 Americans out of a total of 1,198 victims. This tragic event, in which women, children and innocent victims perished as the ship sank within minutes, unleashed anger on the other side of the Atlantic: 'the torpedo that sank the *Lusitania* also sank Germany in the opinion of humanity', a New York journalist wrote.[9] America threatened to break off diplomatic relations with Germany and the latter gave in to Wilson's demand by putting an end to unrestricted submarine war.

After the German defeats at Verdun and the indecisive Battle of Jutland, however, in January 1917, submarines re-entered an all-out war. With his 57 U-boats on the high seas, Ludendorf set himself to force England, through losses, to demand peace within six months. When this period was up, this decision brought with it the American entry into the war on 4 April 1917, after four of their ships were sunk. The daring U-boats forced their way through the barricade preventing passage through the Pas de Calais or took a long detour around the British Isles. The most effective response was then to organize protected convoys, since allied losses were increasingly heavy in the spring and the beginning of the summer of 1917: in May, England had no more than three weeks' provisions in stock, since between 540,000 and 880,000 tonnes were sunk every month.

Despite the success of the German submarine offensive, the English Admiralty immediately withdrew its cruisers from the home fleet for use as escorts. Prime Minister Lloyd George ordered the necessary escorts to act in concert with the Americans. The latter had demanded a report from the inventor Edison, which highlighted deficiencies in the allied side. From 1914 to 1917, British navigation had followed the same maritime routes as they had in peacetime; Edison advised that the routes be modified and recommended that ships be fitted with wireless radios, already installed before the conflict in some liners, so that when the *Titanic* was in distress, it was quickly able to get help. Wireless radios also made it possible to pin-point submarines quickly.

In May 1917, the first American destroyers left Halifax to escort convoys to Ireland, where, in Queenstown, the navy took over the escort.

It was in organizing the convoys necessary to transporting the arms and men of the American Expeditionary Corps that the Allies gained maximum effectiveness. Some 104 German merchant ships and liners had been interned in American ports at the beginning of the war. The liners served to transport troops. The first convoy of 14,000 men left Hampton Roads in Virginia on 14 June 1917. Divided into four groups according to their speed, the ships arrived safe and sound in Saint Nazaire between 26 June and 1 July. One officer declared 'we have lost nothing but a horse, and that was a mule'.[10] Every month until the end of 1917 and the beginning of 1918, 15,000 men crossed the Atlantic and as many as 10,000 a day were counted in July 1918. The convoys left from Virginia (Hampton Roads), New York, Halifax and Sydney in Nova Scotia. They comprised from 20 to 25 ships, protected by one or two destroyers and mine-sweepers as escorts. Four zones were organized: North Atlantic, Antilles and Gulf, South Atlantic and Mediterranean. Meanwhile, a large part of the traffic was still continued outside of the convoys.

Of course, the U-boats replied by trying to operate in the Western Atlantic: during the summer of 1918, six submarines sank 100,000 tonnes of shipping there, but they found themselves very far from their bases, and lacked the fuel to get down to the Gulf of Mexico, and could not hope to operate south of Cape Hatteras. Moreover, the English naval base in the Bermudas remained a difficult obstacle to surmount. In January 1918, the fleet of U-boats rose to 144: despite losses, their number had increased since January 1917, when there were 133; 63 were sunk, 12 lost. In total, throughout the entire war, the Germans built 373 submarines and lost at least 178 of them. The cordons of mines set up by the Allies in the North Sea between Scotland and Norway to prevent the U-boats leaving for the North Atlantic were of doubtful effectiveness, destroying only four submarines. The U-boats operated chiefly in the war zone around the British Isles and in the Atlantic waters east of the Azores.

Although the war had affected Allied sea-borne commerce, it had not, for all that, induce a weakening of the traffic; on the contrary, thanks to the supply contracts agreed between the shipowners and the state, it was an opportunity for undreamed-of profits. An enormous imbalance was created between supply and demand: in 1917–1918, freights were from 10 to 12 times higher than their level in 1913. In three voyages, a collier recouped the value of its purchase price.[11] For certain ports, this was an opportunity for a remarkable improvement in trade.

Thus, in France, whereas Le Havre was too exposed, Bordeaux experienced intense activity.[12] Here trade visibly improved; having collapsed in autumn 1914, it began to pick up again in 1915 and rose spectacularly after 1916, the year in which 8 million tonnes of shipping was reached, while in 1913 Bordeaux had made no more than 6 million tonnes. The port still received the traditional goods it was accustomed to importing – rum, sugar, wool, copper and oil-producing plants. However, new cargoes were unloaded during the war: petrol, refrigerated meats, horses from Argentina and Canada, machines and various materials. Bordeaux supplied neutral countries like Switzerland, hampered by the blockade.

Moreover, in July 1917, the Americans decided to set up their second French base, after Saint Nazaire, at Bassens in the Bordeaux suburbs. Less than a year later, New Bassens, remarkably fitted out with harbour trains and railway tracks, was in service. With Saint Nazaire, this port contributed to enabling the Americans to land more than two million men in 17 months.

The mastery of the sea held by the Allies was to prove a decisive asset for ensuring the blockade of the central empires, allowing the arrival at the front of a large British army at the time of Verdun, and the intervention of the United States reinforced the maritime blockade while also providing the new *matériel* leading to victory. The Atlantic collaboration was apparently without rifts. In reality, post-war crises were to show profound changes in the trade and the mind-set of the Atlantic.

The Atlantic in crisis: between the wars

Up until 1914, the Atlantic had connected Western Europe and the United States on the economic level, by exchange networks; on the human level, by opening American land to the enormous European migration; and on the political level, since the United States, tempted to give an ever higher priority to its interests in the New World, respected the leadership of Great Britain and indirectly of Europe as a whole.

Isolationism and the new American power

To understand why the United States, after having brought their Western Allies precious aid under the generous impulse of President Wilson, immediately after the armistice adopted a more than cautious attitude with regard to the negotiations of the Peace Treaty – only finally not to sign it, we should recall the very well-established orientation of American politics, as given by Washington himself at the end of his second term in office:

Europe possesses a system of interest that is essential for it, but that we do not understand, or at least, with which we are only distantly concerned. Discussions and frequent quarrels ensue, the causes of which are foreign to us. Why compromise our peace and our prosperity by allowing ourselves to get involved in the intrigues of the Old Continent, in its rivalries, its ambitions, its struggles between interests, its factions and its whims?[13]

The Atlantic separated two different worlds. Meanwhile, in the years that followed the First World War, the United States could no longer maintain a policy of total non-intervention. Its policies were prevented from becoming global since, for the first time in history, essential decisions concerning the stability of the world tended to be taken on the other side of the Atlantic. Old Europe had lost its capacity to insist on its own aspirations amidst the ruins, both human (almost 8 million killed, around 15 million wounded) and material, that accumulated throughout the war.

On the occasion of chairing the Washington Naval Conference in 1921, where the old balance resting on British hegemony was destroyed, a journalist from the London newspaper *The Times* perceived the real bearing of the new American power:

Almost without transition, they [the United States] have risen from the position of a simple commercial force to the dominant position of a power in financial control of the world. And now they realise to what extent this change must be reflected in their relations with the whole globe.[14]

The journalist goes on to specify that the United States has to have the resources for this new mastery in business, powerful battle fleets and trade, bases and means of communication.

The positions adopted by Charles Evans Hughes, President Harding's Secretary of State, at the Washington Conference favoured a generalized disarmament that would prevent a repeat of the naval arms race, but at the same time, they favoured the Americans. The fleets of the United States and Great Britain were placed on equal footing, which was something inconceivable in 1914. The American and British fleets had to be reduced and the construction of new battleships and cruisers would be halted for 10 years. They were to 'scrape away' at the strength of the three principal naval powers – America, Japan and England – by destroying almost two million tonnes of ships already constructed or under construction. One British observer declared, 'In five minutes, Mr Secretary Hughes has sunk more vessels than all the world's admirals have sunk in several centuries!'[15] In fact, the

United States and great Britain both reduced their fleets to 525,000 tonnes, Japan to 315,000 tonnes, France and Italy to 175,000 tonnes It is true that submarines and light surface ships were not included in this act.

The British Admiralty vehemently protested because it was in principle an attack on the country's naval superiority. In *Mein Kampf*, Adolf Hitler wrote that the Conference had from then on replaced the slogan *Britainnia rules the waves* with another, *On the seas of the Union*.[16] We should emphasize that Canada and South Africa had put pressure on the Conference to reduce the differences between the English and American navies, since imperial solidarity had not worked. It is true that Great Britain had hardly any choice, since its economic situation had become critical, with two million unemployed, and the boom of the immediate post-war period was over: any dream of returning to its prior hegemonic status was shattered. To do otherwise would have led to the financial ruin of the country whereas the Americans were pressing the Europeans to repay the loans they had taken from the United States to conduct the war. Great Britain therefore gave in to the demands of the Washington Conference and also had to abandon the Japanese alliance, the effects of which on the Pacific were feared by the Americans, since it was towards the Pacific that their preoccupations were increasingly directed in the domain of foreign policy. The reduction of British naval construction was drastic: in 1924, they built only 25 warships, while 111 were launched in 1914.[17] This sudden decline was going to weigh on the condition of the navy for a long time, and made rearmament on the eve of the Second World War all the more difficult.

When, a few years later, in 1932–1933, a project to return to the Pax Britannica was sketched out, with the Admiralty creating squadrons for the Antilles, North America, South America, the Cape, the Indian Ocean and China, its realization very quickly proved to be extremely difficult. They withdrew the squadron from South America and reduced the strength of the others. They had to be content to 'fly the flag'.[18] After 1933, while the menace of Hitler required a rearmament effort, but while financial conditions were still very difficult, the British naval budget rose from £53 million sterling in 1933 to more than £100 million in 1937.

The end of the Great Atlantic migration to the United States

Its new international power left the United States at liberty to practise a policy of closing itself off from Europe. It was an economic closure, by raising their customs duties with the goal of protecting their agriculture and their chemical and heavy industries under threat from Japanese and German competition. A corollary of this economic nationalism, however, was a human one. The barriers they erected on their borders against their competitors, to safeguard their country's production, also had to be raised against the threat represented by foreign emigrants, who were proving increasingly difficult to assimilate. In a difficult social situation – there were some 250,000 unemployed in New York, all foreigners, 150,000 in the textile mills of New England, 75,000 in Detroit[19] – the unions were claiming that immigrants were taking American jobs and sustaining a low-wage policy. The bosses, after having benefitted from their arrival for a long time, feared that they might be bringing revolutionary ideas with them from Europe.

The pressure in each case was sufficient for Congress to pass initial legislation, in summer 1921, restricting the volume of immigration to three per cent of the number of each nationality inhabiting the Union in 1910. They created the first quota, and three years later, in 1924, an even more restrictive quota was adopted in the National Origins Act: from then on, only two per cent of the representatives of each nationality residing in the Union in 1890 could gain entry to the United States. On this date, the southern and eastern Europeans were still low in number, while those from the north-west of Europe – the British, the Germans and Scandinavians – largely prevailed. The effect of the quotas was immediate: in 1921 the total number of immigrants had already fallen to less than 357,000 as against an annual average in excess of 860,000 before 1914, while in 1913, the flood of entrants had risen to more than 1.2 million. Calculating immigration in 1924 on the basis of an 1890 census, along with a threshold lowered from three to two per cent, induced an even more abrupt fall: the number of immigrants was reduced to 163,000. Only Northern Europe, Great Britain and the Scandinavian countries, and Germany in central Europe, were partially spared. In the legislative year ending on 30 June 1921, the date on which the first quota was imposed, the number of immigrants was still high, at 800,000; it then fell by more than two-thirds in 1921–1922 and by nearly four-fifths in 1924–1925.

At this heavily reduced level, immigration benefited the countries of north-western Europe, which were the only ones to maintain a relatively significant flow, although without being able to climb above the level imposed by the quota of 1924: on 1 July 1929, almost 150,000 immigrants a year were counted, and the global crisis was also affecting entrants, who were reduced to fewer than 70,000 in 1930–1931.

Having completely stopped Asiatic immigration and drastically reduced the Europeans', it was from their own continent, especially Mexico, that the Americans took the workforce they required during the years of renewal, in 1925–1929.

The massive secular flood of Atlantic migration from northern Europe to America over more than a century was finally plugged. On the other hand, European emigration towards Central or South America was maintained at quite a high level until as late as 1930, although arrivals were falling. Thus in Argentina in

1929, the arrival of some 192,000 immigrants was recorded, while in 1913 there were more than 300,000; Brazil kept its arrivals at a reasonable level, something in the order of 100,000 until the 1934 quota law. Canada absorbed quite a high proportion of British migrants, unless, however, it is compared with the situation prior to the First World War: in 1929, it received 140,000 immigrants, whereas it had welcomed 300,000 in 1913.[20]

In the Atlantic migration from Europe to America, above all in the North Atlantic, the American policy entailed a readjustment of traffic, which for some companies proved difficult.

Cunard, which had entertained great hopes in 1919 as emigration picked up again, and removed its port of embarkation from Liverpool to Southampton, so as to be able to use the largest tonnages, was badly affected. The number of its third-class passengers – the emigrants – fell from 49,305 in 1921 to 34,763 in 1922, but it could still count on British migrants, who were less affected by the quotas. It could not, however, transport Italians, since the Rome government, in order to strengthen its merchant navy, reserved the transport of its nationals for that purpose. The 1921 quota allowed no more than 42,000 Italians to enter, whereas, before the war, the transalpine immigrants were 10 times more numerous. Moreover, the Italians applied themselves to getting the principal of transporting emigrant nationals under the national flag onto the agenda of the Geneva Conference of December 1923. They reserved the monopoly on emigration to America for their own fleet. The Compagnie Française Transatlantique, which had made the 'French Line' famous over half a century before, was also seriously hit, the fall in emigration compromising its financial stability. In 1921–1922, its liners carried no more than 20,000 immigrants as against 55,000 the previous year. The German ports of Bremen and Hamburg, whose companies were weakened by the seizure of several of their liners under the rubric of reparations, also experienced a fall in the number of departures: the latter had risen in 1913 to almost 433,000, but there were no more than 74,000 in 1922.[21] They did not pass this number in 1924 although the new quota favoured Germany.

To stay within the limit of these sacrosanct quotas, the liners arrived in New York at midnight on the first of every month, and the first arrival exhausted the low contingents of Mediterranean people and Slavs at a stroke. They left Europe so as to arrive at the appropriate date and time. The ships anchored at the edge of American territorial waters and came closer as soon as the first of the month turned. To avoid their passengers' despair at being turned down, the companies tried to organize their departures. Registration offices were set up by the Atlantic Conference that gathered together the larger companies from Yugoslavia, Czechoslovakia, Poland and Romania, the countries where the quotas had the most disastrous consequences. Informed by cable from New York of the number remaining to be registered, the offices only then issued tickets. To avoid exclusions on arrival, American consuls in the various countries issued visas to these immigrants. Companies transporting foreigners without visas incurred penalties.

In this situation, companies all found themselves with a surplus of third-class berths and they had to restructure their transport by extending the tourist class. The possibilities open to them in this area were quite considerable, since from the United States and the Americas in general, a clientele of middle-class passengers came to Europe for business and pleasure. In consequence, unoccupied third-class cabins were converted for them and then liners were fitted out for one class only. Moreover, foreigners settled in the United States could briefly leave the Union without being counted among the quotas of new entrants on their return. The companies began to have great hopes for their carriage. In 1928, the President of the Norddeutscher Lloyd from Bremen wrote:

> Farmer Smith would like to see how his brothers are who stayed in the motherland, and Mr Meier, a geography teacher, would like to go to the United States so as to give his students the benefit of his own experience.[22]

The tourist class could take these foreign passengers at very acceptable price levels, with the passage from New York to Europe costing from $105 to $125. Thus, in this new political setting, the French Line was able to use the liner *Ile de France*, launched in 1927, for passengers, who much appreciated the comfort. With this new ship, the number of passengers the French company carried to New York rose from 75,000 in 1928 to reach the figure of 80,000 passengers in 1930. In that year, the Transatlantique put its new, single-class liner, the *Champlain* into service.

The American clientele came to sample fine fare and, especially during the 'dry' era, the abundantly available alcoholic drinks such as beers, and in particular, fine wines and champagnes. With its new policy of prohibition, virtuous America in fact found a new reason for closing its borders, the response to which was going to be a vast upsurge in smuggling.

Prohibition and the smugglers' Atlantic

In the 1920s and the beginning of the 1930s, Prohibition reinforced America's isolationist tendencies. Under the already considerable influence of the temperance societies before the War, particularly in the west and the centre of the Union, 'dry' America was going to be made a rule. In 1912, seven American states had already adopted prohibition measures against alcohol in their territory.[23] Two years later, an amendment to the Constitution was proposed to prohibit alcohol throughout the Union, but did not receive the requisite two-thirds majority in Congress. In fact, even at the onset of war, 36 states had either prohibited or limited the consumption of alcohol. During the war, the troops sent to Europe were used to show the dangers of alcohol. In 1917, a Bordeaux trader, anxious to defend his interests, induced his city's Chamber of Commerce to take a proposal to the French government for transporting their wines by the barrel, in a preferential price range, to the billets of English troops. 'Tommy' had discovered Bordeaux's wine in the course of the war, and, as the Bordeaux saying has it, wine consumption was the best means of fighting alcoholism![24] The American soldiers, like their British brothers-in-arms, doubtless had a notion to ask for 'a glass of wine'.

Morale had to be rebuilt: in January 1919, the Eighteenth Amendment was adopted, and on 17 January it was ratified by 46 of the 48 states of the Union, and the Volstead Act was entered into the statute books. It forbade the sale and consumption of alcohol in all its forms. The only drinks that were tolerated were those whose alcohol content was less than 0.5 per cent.

A trade in contraband and clandestine production sprang up, and 'bootleggers' could be seen popping up everywhere. These were traffickers whose name recalled the traffic already created by the whites for selling contraband bottles, hidden in the tops of their boots, to the Indians.[25] The mass of the contraband came across land borders from Mexico and Canada, but large quantities of rum, brandy and wine were also landed in secret on the coasts of America. The Atlantic has always had its illicit trades in which, in the eighteenth century, the North Americans found the source of much of their wealth in the Caribbean, on the islands and the coast of the Spanish Main, to the detriment of the French and Iberian crowns. This time, however, the Eldorado held out to the traders was due to the violation of American law.

To satisfy the United States' thirst for alcohol, the greatest ingenuity prevailed. All kinds of boats took part in smuggling, everything from the most modest craft, making only a single journey and fleeing with its cargo to a deserted creek, to as fast a launch as possible. Just like today's drug traffic, very high speed launches, capable of more than 30 knots, were the traffickers' major advantage, while the coastguards' vessels are limited to 14 or 15 knots. They used various smuggling techniques, and thought nothing of even the most gruesome: thus, there were an astonishing number of corpses repatriated in lead caskets that customs officers morally could not open up out of respect for the dead. This method meant that rum from Martinique, received in Puerto Rico, could be sent to the United States.

The major supply bases were found at Saint-Pierre and Miquelon, in the Bahamas, Bermuda and Cuba. From Bordeaux they sent cognac via Antwerp to Saint-Pierre, where intermediaries placed the goods with large Canadian clients such as the firm of Bronfman. In Saint-Pierre, one of the most important intermediaries who placed their cases with the bootleggers was the firm Chartier, who in 1930 managed to sell 6,000 cases of rum and 3,300 cases of liqueurs. Smuggling turned out to be the source of sudden wealth for the French colony.

The English colony of the Bahamas, whose economy was stagnant at the beginning of the twentieth century, attained a certain prosperity through prohibition. Nassau was an excellent port, close to the Florida coast, one of the great smuggling centres of the United States. Starting in 1920, England and Scotland flooded the bootleggers with barrels of whisky, which the bootleggers, who had just set up shop, could then trade. They set up 'legal' businesses and loaded ships in principle for Saint-Pierre and Miquelon, but in fact destined for the American coast. Nassau was transformed into a bustling town where people danced and played a great deal of poker. Hotels sprang up and Pan-Am opened an airline between Miami and Nassau in 1929, whose passengers were looking only to drink and have fun. The Bahamas' economy turned towards tourism, which has subsequently remained its largest resource.

Cuba was the last great beneficiary of Prohibition. There too, Florida's proximity made it an ideal base for the smugglers. Rich alcohol lovers came to settle in Florida, one of the Union's best-supplied states. Among others, Hemingway arrived at Key West in 1928, frequenting the bars, where he drank Cuban rum. More so than in Nassau, Havana was the place for gambling, and was associated with prostitution and alcohol. Pan-Am also opened an airline from New York to Havana, allowing Americans to go and sample Cuban rum. On the other hand, in Puerto Rico and on the Virgin Islands that the United States purchased from Denmark in 1917, Prohibition was rigorously enforced and people could only drink in secret.

Neapolitan Camorra and Sicilian Mafia, already very powerful in Italy in the second half of the nineteenth century, took advantage of the scale of the wave of Italian immigration to the United States in order to set up on the other side of the Atlantic before the First World War. Sicily's 'families' soon prospered on the American continent. Already well strengthened by their empire of crimes and rackets, they were able to find new wealth in the American policy against alcohol.

The Mafia built its trade on Prohibition which developed into widespread criminality since many gangsters enthusiastically set about manufacturing and distributing alcohol. In Chicago, Al Capone built an underground empire based first on beer and then on fruit machines, and could hope to make up to almost $60 million in annual revenues. He had 700 to 1,000 men at his disposal, and from 1920 to 1927 more than 250 men disappeared in Chicago's gang wars. In 1932, on the eve of the lifting of Prohibition, one assessment attributed the death of 5,000 policemen and customs officers and 2,000 civilians, the majority of whom were gangsters, to Prohibition.

However, although the Methodists and the Baptists made Prohibition the object of their faith and concern, especially in the rural areas in the south and west of the Union, the eastern towns were extremely hostile, especially the Catholics. The struggle proved to be hopeless since an insufficient budget meant that only around 1,000, poorly trained agents could be employed. Supervising almost 18,000 miles of coastline, controlling private residences where 'gin and bathwater' were drunk, turned out to be an impossible task, and disillusionment set in. In 1930, California permitted drinks with an alcohol content of 3.2 per cent. Resistance from the anti-alcohol leagues notwithstanding, the suspension of the Eighteenth Amendment took place in 1933. Only three states – Kansas, Mississippi and Oklahoma – remained dry in 1939.

The effects of Prohibition on the transatlantic liners made themselves felt when they put into port in New York, especially on the ships of the French Line, whose crews always aimed to drink their daily ration of wine. The necessary alcoholic drinks were kept under lock and key during the time in American territorial waters, and every morning customs officers helped to open the storeroom and take out the sailors' daily ration. Le Havre, however, was a hotbed of smuggling, cases of bottles were hidden in lifeboats, holds, and the bulkheads in gangways. American customs made strong-arm raids in New York's port, and fines could be imposed on the commander if alcohol was discovered, since he was held responsible. They took the view that the Compagnie Générale Transatlantique loading only drinks for the outward voyage, leaving the return 'dry', would have caused a notable reduction in business and so abandoned the idea.

The transatlantic lines on the eve of the world crisis

At the end of the 1920s a clear recovery had taken place for the liner companies, even in the North Atlantic, since transporting tourist-class passengers had turned out to be a source of considerable gains for them. They were also able to put their imaginations to the test by creating new lines. In this regard, an interesting example is that of Transatlantique, which was able to create a line from Bordeaux to Vigo to Halifax to New York, first by using passenger/cargo vessels and then by liners of average tonnage of around 15,000 tonnes. Mention could also be made of the Chargeurs Réunis, who through their South Atlantic subsidiary company revived the line from Bordeaux to Rio and La Plata, and, more importantly, created the 'imperial' line that was destined to bring great success to Bordeaux by way of its African route, serving the Senegal coast and the Gulf of Guinea as far as the mouth of the Congo.[26] Again, the Messageries Maritimes, which was still in business in Bordeaux, was a stopover for their line to Tahiti and New Caledonia via the Panama Canal. In 1924, Bordeaux managed to send off about 40,000 passengers, 10,000 of whom were heading for South America, the same number for the west coast of Africa, and more than 23,000 for Morocco. In Le Havre, Transatlantique also obtained favourable results on the routes to Central America and the Antilles, and had created passenger steam lines serving the American

Pacific coast via the Panama Canal. The new activity the canal created cannot be exaggerated: some 80 European lines went through it.

Receipts for the routes to the Antilles, to Africa and the Pacific compensated for the fall in those to New York, which were reduced by immigration restrictions. In the North Atlantic, however, one could count on the presence of an increasing amount of first-class passenger traffic. On Transatlantique's liners, therefore, bankers or great industrialists like the Vanderbildts or the Rockefellers could be seen arriving; in increasing numbers, however, one could also see representatives of the world of the theatre, cinema, fashion and sport. Reputation and notoriety spread across the Atlantic, and Maurice Chevalier, Charlie Chaplin and Marlene Dietrich were also guests on the prestige liner of the French Line, the *Ile de France*. Senators from the Union did not spurn appearing among the passengers, so that in 1929, Secretary of State Kellog made the crossing from New York to Le Havre on the *Ile de France*. These distinguished passengers were able to appreciate the large red-lacquered salon, picked out in gold, and the terraced café; splendour greeted the Compagnie's guests, who greatly appreciated the fine foods such as foie gras, pheasant, truffles and other national specialities which graced its rich menus, enhanced with the most prestigious wine lists.

Competition between the big companies remained ferocious. Francis Hyde gives us the market shares won by each one between 1924 and 1929.[27] Cunard then seemed to have the greatest advantage, since the quotas favourable to Anglo-Saxons favoured it: Cunard won 20 per cent of the North Atlantic traffic; the White Star Line, its only English rival, which it bought out in 1931, reached 7 per cent, as much as the French Line; the German Hamburg Amerika line and Norddeutscher Lloyd began to get back on their feet, putting the liners *Bremen* and *Europa* into service in 1928, which enabled them to resume a very respectable position, with some 11 per cent of the traffic.

The Cunard company made an enormous effort to retain its position in first-class passenger transport, carrying more than 30,000 a year from 1921 to 1929, but it also took action to develop tourist-class transport, and in 1930 it transported almost 42,000 passengers in this class.

The example of the liner *Ile de France* shows that the French Line was making the same effort. Put into service in 1927, the luxury liner made it possible to increase the number of first-class passengers transported on this route from 19,000 in 1926 to 24,000 in 1927 and 30,000 in 1928.

Trade crises and a difficult recovery, 1930–1939

In 1925–1928, during Coolidge's second term of office, America reached the peak of its prosperity, which could be seen as enabling relations between Europe and the United States to take on a new form. While the austerity of Prohibition was ravaging the Union, Europe had become familiar with a new face of America, one that was not dominated by the undivided authority of the temperance societies. In fact, the easy money of the 1920s, a good portion of which went on contraband and the bootleggers' traffic, allowed new ways of life to bloom that were going to cross the Atlantic. The urban societies were liberated from taboos of dress and sex. Coming into fashion among the young, who defied Prohibition by drinking beers and cocktails, jazz and the Charleston gave America the image of a country gripped by the joy of living. The new national heroes were actors such as Rudolph Valentino or Douglas Fairbanks, but also men of great courage such as the aviator Charles Lindberg who dared to complete the first non-stop flight across the Atlantic. Lindberg linked New York and Paris together on 27 May 1927 in 33 and a half hours on board his plane, the *Spirit of Saint Louis*. The year's most hailed man, he was given a hero's welcome in Europe and a dance, 'the Lindy', was created in his honour.

A little more than two years after Charles Lindberg's achievement, it was 'Black Thursday' on New York's Wall Street, on 24 October 1929. The market was suddenly inundated with orders to sell, and share prices fell catastrophically. For an Atlantic traffic that, despite the marked decline after the First World War, had also benefitted from its business booming, it was an extremely heavy blow. For almost half a century the delicate mechanisms of the forward markets for all the big products, such as cotton, coffee and wood, presupposed an advanced yet unwieldy financial organization with enormous movements of currency. Receipts were hit heavily by the cutting in half of the prices of raw material in 1930 and the simultaneous fall in freight charges.

Facing competition from the tramps that challenged them over freight, so that in the Gulf of Mexico freights fell from 61 to 31 cents per 100 pounds of cotton in a few months in 1930, and with a new passenger transport crisis in the North Atlantic, the fates of large companies were at stake. Cunard's accounts show losses of £533,000 in 1931, and £927,000 in 1932. The situation for the French Transatlantique company was even more difficult, with a deficit of 30 million francs in 1930 and 236 million in 1931. Only the state's intervention in June 1931 saved the company from liquidation. Receipts had fallen from 1 billion francs in 1930 to only 383 million in 1931. The company had to lay up 52 out of its 98 ships.

In 1933, the global level of freight had fallen to less than two-thirds that of 1913, despite there being more than 14 million tonnes of shipping lying unused throughout the world. The North Atlantic was still the worst affected, and the total number of passengers transported by all the companies, which in 1930 was still in excess of a million from America to Europe, was only 460,000 at the height of the crisis in 1934, having fallen by more than half. Trade was stifled by increasingly stringent protectionist barriers: in the United States, the cargo lines uniting Dunkirk, Le Havre and Bordeaux with New York, Philadelphia and Boston, showed a heavy deficit on each voyage. The American ships that took the largest proportion of this freight from French ports posed an unequal challenge. Moreover, the heavy goods trade – coal, cereals, raw textiles – like European exports, was stagnant. Only petrol began to initiate something of a recovery in trade around 1936–1937, its transport routes converging on western Europe. For this reason, the volume of trade in 1937 (490 million tonnes) was higher than it was in 1929 (470 million tonnes).[28]

Furthermore, the decline was not completely widespread. The merchant navies of the United States, Great Britain and France were affected in different ways. On the other hand, the German, Japanese and Norwegian fleets had increased from 1929 to 1939. Some favourable elements were the Scandinavians' anxiety about profits, and imports by Germany and Japan of strategic raw materials. By contrast, the French fleet was stagnating, having diminished from 3.5 million tonnes in 1929 to less than 3 million tonnes: insufficient return freights for the French ports, extremely heavy social costs and an oversized fleet were a few among many unfavourable factors, in the struggle against which public moneys had to be invested.

Meanwhile, in the North Atlantic, the decline was to a certain extent disguised by the efforts of the Transatlantique company, which brought new ships into service. First there was the *Champlain*, a single-class liner capable of transporting more than 1,000 passengers with a crew of 551 men at a speed that was already remarkable for this type of ship, 20 knots. The liner, aside from the summer route to New York, was used in winter for cruises from New York, the Antilles and the Mediterranean, which were very much in demand. However, in the face of competition, which was always very stiff – especially with the Germans' *Europa* and *Bremen*, the Italians' *Rex* and *Conte di Savola* – the French Line had wanted, since the beginning of the 1930s, at the height of the crisis, to meet these foreign challenges by beginning construction, in Saint-Nazaire, of a large liner capable of the highest speeds. On 29 May 1935 the *Normandie* made its maiden voyage. With a length of 313.75 metres and a breadth of 36.4 metres, it was at the time by far and away the world's largest liner. In tests, it came within a hair's breadth of 31 knots. Stringent precautions were taken to ensure the safety of her 2,000 passengers and 1,350 officers and crew: insulated, watertight compartments and electromagnetic iceberg detection. Her fittings boasted of luxury and splendour: the luxurious salons and dining room in first class spread over some 180 metres, a 400-seat theatre, an indoor pool, gaming rooms and sports halls, and a 'grill-room' with an illuminated dance floor, were to make the crossing a genuine delight.

Upon its arrival in New York, over Transatlantique's flag the liner hoisted a sky blue pennant, as many metres in length as the new speed record reached in knots. In fact, the *Normandie* had beaten the record of the Italian *Rex* by completing its crossing at a speed of 29.94 knots, in four days, three hours and 14 minutes. The Blue Ribbon went back with the French company. New York's welcome was marked by wild enthusiasm:

> hardly had we passed the Statue of Liberty than an immense chorus burst out as, ceaselessly, all the ships began to hiss, whistle and splutter cries, roars, and cheers of every note. Tirelessly, the huge voice of the *Normandie* answered and bellowed. This tumult was organized into a prodigious symphony whose leitmotiv was provided by the *Marseillaise* played from a loudspeaker on a plane....Manhattan's towers rushed to greet us. At each stage, thousands of hands and heads waved and screamed; the only part of New York visible from the port, Battery Place, was nothing but a swarming, dark human mass.[29]

In the *Revue de Paris*, Philippe Soupault conveyed this enthusiasm remarkably well as it gripped the New Yorkers, who, from the height of their skyscrapers, were celebrating the event.

Meanwhile, Cunard was not going to be slow to respond, it, too, having put in a construction order five years previously to its largest liner, the *Normandie*'s rival, the *Queen Mary*. This ship made its maiden voyage to New York in May 1936. On their ship, the British had wanted to create a degree of luxury, albeit not as striking as its French rival, to combine this with great comfort, and to give the *Queen Mary* superior power. Thus, the English snatched the Blue Ribbon from Transatlantique for the first time since the French liner took it back in 1937, reaching 31.20 knots, but lost it again the following year, when the *Queen Mary* completed her crossing at an average of 31.69 knots.

These two liners massively increased their companies' share of the transport of tourist-class passengers, which rose from 19,000 to 31,000 for Transatlantique from 1935 to 1937, and from 48,000 to 62,000 for Cunard in the same period. The English company's superiority was quite clear, but it should be noted that it had merged with the White Star fleet in 1931.

With the *Europa* and the *Bremen*, the Germans also increased their tourist traffic, albeit to a lesser extent, rising from 40,000 to 47,000. The respective shares of the traffic in this class were 28.9 per cent for Cunard, 14.4 per cent for Transatlantique and 22 per cent for the German lines. From May to the end of October 1935, the *Normandie* alone had completed nine voyages (18 crossings) and transported 17,872 passengers. Its success attracted a clientele to the French Line's other liners, the *Ile de France*, the *Paris* and the *Champlain*. In 1936, the *Normandie* transported 27,252 passengers in 15 voyages and, in 1937, it took as many as the company's other three liners, boarding 37,500 passengers, 14,400 of whom were in first class. With this liner, Transatlantique took on 21 per cent of the first-class traffic in the North Atlantic. The Universal Exhibition of 1937 in Paris contributed to reviving this traffic, and in the same year the French company, with more than 87,000 passengers, took almost 13 per cent of the total number of passengers in the North Atlantic.

The indisputable success gained by the fastest and most luxurious liners allowed them, on the eve of the Second World War, to absorb the most important share of the passenger traffic on the New York route, a quarter of which was carried by only four ships: the *Normandie*, the *Queen Mary*, the *Europa* and the *Bremen*.

Although the liners yielded satisfactory operating profits, they could not cover the very high financial charges generated by heavy loans taken out for their construction. The example of the *Normandie* alone is, in this regard, highly revealing: the total of these charges rose during the first year in operation to almost 96 million francs. The state had to agree to take responsibility for these charges, while the company kept operating profits for itself. Similar solutions were adopted in other countries. This was accompanied by an effort on the part of the companies to reduce their expenses by selling unused ships and cutting loss-making voyages.

The situation on the eve of the Second World War was still difficult, therefore. A slowing down in trade due to the crisis and its consequences burdened the Atlantic economy, and only certain protected sectors escaped: cruises and the New York route for the liners, petrol transportation, and the Antilles banana lines. The Atlantic world also retained the inheritance of the previous century that divided up the 'metropolises of the sea': New York, London, Le Havre, Antwerp, Rotterdam and Hamburg. Thanks to the presence of these great ports, Western Europe and the east coast of the United States remained, in 1938, the two major poles in the life of the ocean, their influence extending beyond the frame of the Atlantic alone, due to Suez and Panama. It would take the Second World War, which had an even greater effect than the First on Old Europe's health, to see some modifications in these structures appear, less in the ports than in the traffic. This was to be put into effect under the influence of a far more powerful America and, at the same time, of a new Europe arising out of the post-war reconstruction.

The Second World War and the new age of the Atlantic

The Atlantic and the Second World War

The naval disarmament decided upon by the Washington Conference was brushed aside on the eve of the Second World War. In 1938, Admiral Raeder had persuaded Hitler to develop his cruiser, destroyer and battleship fleets with a view to making them comparable with the English fleet within 10 years. It is true that in 1939 Admiral Doenitz had only 57 submarines available to him, while Raeder's Z-Plan predicted 250 by 1948.

On the British side, imperial defences were weakened by the unwillingness of the Canadians, South Africans and even the Irish to support it. The navy saw its share of the defence fund reduced to benefit the RAF: in 1938, only £127.2 million was allocated to it, against £133.8 to the RAF, whereas five years earlier the sailors received three times more than the aviators (£53.5 million against £16.7 million).[30] With the invasion of Manchuria in 1931, the threat of Japanese imperialism had shown the necessity of an effort in the Far East, where the base at Singapore received more funding. Meanwhile, on the eve of 1939, London was led more or less to abandon the Far East front in order to confront fascist Italy's ambitions in the Mediterranean. In fact, in August 1939, at the moment of Great Britain's and France's declaration of war on Germany, the Allies' Atlantic plans resembled those of 1914. They had to blockade German ports to prevent the surface fleet leaving, organize the defence of convoys in the North Atlantic, which was indispensable to the Allies supply lines. If the first objective, due to a net superiority in surface vessels, seemed realistic with the support of a young yet high-quality French fleet, the second was far less so, since the British lacked the resources for the escorts necessary to effectively protect the convoys, and did not have superiority in the skies. On this latter point, the 3,400 or so aircraft on the Allied side were theoretically capable of matching the 3,600 German aircraft, but a large number were outclassed by the enemy in arms and speed.

Due to the daring of the German 'raiders', the pocket battleships that managed to leave from the ports of the North Sea, and later from Brest, the blockade itself was quite ineffective. This was especially true when the Germans had occupied the ports of Denmark and Norway after the failure of the Allied campaign in the latter country at the end of spring 1940. The North Sea was no longer the 'net', tightly controlled by the home fleet, that it had been in 1914–1918, and Doenitz's submarines were able to take advantage of the extension of their bases from Oslo to the French ports in the Gulf of Gascony to launch into the Atlantic to attack the convoys.

After the French defeat of 1940, Great Britain's dependency on American resources increasingly became their Achilles heel, so that everything was at stake in the Battle of the Atlantic, which was therefore joined in thoroughly unfavourable conditions. This was all the more true since at the beginning of the conflict the United States was far from making a firm commitment, even to support the Allies' needs.

In 1935–1937, Congress in America had passed laws of neutrality that stipulated that the Union would not provide war *matériel* to possible combatants. The United States had managed to improve their relations with Latin America:

Roosevelt's 'good neighbour' policy made him give up the right of intervention claimed by the Americans at the beginning of the century, and thus had ended up having positive results. At the 1936 Inter-American Conference in Buenos Aires, Roosevelt had been very warmly welcomed, and the United States' president managed to gain recognition in principle for a policy directed against all European aggression, a principle extended to Canada in 1938. Reassured on their relations with the other states in the New World, the Americans were less so regarding the development of the situation in the Far East, where Japan's naval armament and the Chinese crisis was coming close to threatening their interests directly. In consequence, they were prompted not to interfere in the Atlantic or in Europe, just as their isolationist tradition, which still had its fervent supporters, had urged them.

At the very beginning of the conflict, President Roosevelt appeared to remain loyal to this policy, and decided that a neutral zone should be created for the western hemisphere across the Atlantic and the Gulf of Mexico, which the combatants' ships should not enter. In fact, the president gave an interpretation of his decision that was favourable to the British, since the 'neutrality patrol', a squadron of the United States' battle fleet charged with ensuring that its neutrality was respected, ought to help the Royal Navy to pin-point German traffic in the West Atlantic in order that the English could attack them. Besides, the Germans proved to be the aggressors: their pocket battleships, the *Graf Spee* and the *Deutschland,* left for the South Atlantic in August 1939, and the *Graf Spee* sank an English cargo vessel off Bahia at the beginning of September. Forced thereafter to take refuge in Montevideo, where the *Graf Spee* was scuttled, the second battleship nevertheless managed to return to Germany.

At the end of summer 1940, after Germany's clear victory over France, the danger seemed greater. In fact, in September the Axis powers, joining a tripartite pact between Germany, Italy and Japan, were able to extend their operations. In the Battle of the Atlantic that had been raging for more than a year, a considerable number of English ships were sunk every day, and the British were increasingly afraid that the vital link to the United States, which supplied their *matériel* and their army, could not be maintained. At the same time, Roosevelt had his chiefs of staff assess the condition of the Union's military, which was found sorely wanting: the Air Force was only 200 aircraft strong, there were not enough weapons, there were fewer than 60,000 ground troops, and the only significant force was the navy. Neutrality was imperative, but they still had to decide whether to grant Great Britain's pressing need for aid.

Doubtless turning indecisive during an electoral period, Roosevelt was completely informed of England's enormous needs by a British mission, and at the end of October was awaiting public support, which he received on being re-elected in November, in order to set in motion the aid process for the British.

A very authoritative yet deliberately candid letter from Churchill, on 8 December 1940, set before the president's eyes the needs of his country and the resources necessary to meet them.[31] The Americans were prepared to frustrate German plans for an all-out submarine war. For the prime minister, the only means of winning the Battle of the Atlantic was to have American merchant shipping transporting *matériel* to England, escorted by American warships. Hitler dared not attack ships thus escorted by the United States' navy. Churchill asked for 7,000 fighter planes and 3 million tonnes of shipping for spring 1942. He left the worry of finding a solution for payment in line with America's interests and the concern for England's survival, to Roosevelt. To cover the necessary investments, $2.7 billion was estimated to be the minimum required. Practically without available assets in the United States, the English could not pay cash.

A committee of the 'America First Movement', bringing together individuals who remained loyal to isolationism and hostile to aiding the English, rejected any concessions in matters of payment. Charles Lindburgh, the famous aviator, took part in this committee, and wrote in the *New York Times* of 24 April that the United States was not prepared to win wars in Europe, that they should spare their own lives and civilization by remaining loyal to America's independent destiny.[32] Of course, the same committee was opposed to any thoughts of an alliance.

In his 'fireside' speech on the radio, on 29 November 1940, Roosevelt was going to impose a solution: he had to defend the world's democracies, and the United States was 'the arsenal of democracy'. This was being done while preparing weapons, ships and cannons. An aggressive speech by Hitler on 30 January 1941, declaring that his navy would torpedo any ship transporting *matériel* to England, whatever its nationality, sent a wave of indignation across the other side of the Atlantic. Public support granted, the Lend-Lease project was passed by the Senate on 8 March 1941. It meant going back on all the legislation that forbade lending to combatants, which bore in mind the unpaid debts from the First World War. However, doing away with the dollar sign, the United States loaned goods rather than money. By the Lend-Lease Act, the president authorized expenses of $7 billion, as much as all the loans from 1914–1918 put together. Like any other, Lend-Lease shipping had to cross the Atlantic, and the Americans were duty bound to try anything so that the maritime route was kept safe from U-boat attacks. In spring 1941, U-boats were destroying almost half a million tonnes of shipping a month. However, Roosevelt would not risk having the convoys escorted all the way to England since the isolationists were still powerful in Congress. He made do with extending the neutral zone far into the Eastern Atlantic, almost as far as Iceland.

For controlling this zone, American naval resources were reinforced: ships from the Pacific fleet were transferred to the Atlantic, where, however, they had no bases. At one point, the Americans planned to set one up on the Azores, but

Portugal intended to defend them against attack, and the plan was dropped. Following Operation Catapult in Mers-el-Kebir, conducted with appalling brutality by the English against the French Algerian squadron – we can compare this takeover by force with the one led by Nelson in Copenhagen against the Danish fleet in 1801 – the British expedition against Dakar was born of the fear that this port must not be used by the Germans. These operations, in July and September 1940, did not add to the number of bases at the Allies' disposal in the Eastern Atlantic. The Americans elected to set up a base on Iceland on 9 April 1941, with the agreement of the Danish government which had removed to London. Thus the neutral zone could be extended into the Atlantic as far as the Azores, Iceland and Greenland. It became indispensable for improving the protection of the convoys. In February 1941, on the eve of voting on the Lend-Lease Act, the heavy cruiser *Hipper* had sunk seven ships from a convoy east of the Azores before returning to Brest. Some time later, on the Grand Bank, 500 miles from Newfoundland, it was to destroy 16 ships and disrupt several convoys.

In Iceland, aircraft were installed for locating U-boats and surface raiders. Despite this, the great German submarine offensive began in April 1941. Stationed in southern Greenland in order to attack the convoys, their attacks managed to block the maritime routes leading to Europe. British losses escalated and it was not until after the capture of Doenitz's code on U-boat 110, captured by an English destroyer, that a revival began to appear: from 1 June to 1 September, from Halifax to Liverpool, for the first time in the war, an unbroken defence of the convoys was developed, and not a single vessel was lost on this route. The American Atlantic fleet would engage more directly in escorting merchant shipping in the autumn, on 16 September, after an incident between a submarine and an American destroyer.

Despite Hitler's reluctance, being preoccupied with the Russian front, Doenitz decided on 14 September to plan an offensive against trade in Canadian and American waters. Losses were again heavy, and the submarines had no hesitation in attacking the American destroyers that escorted the ships (an American base had been established in Newfoundland in July). In the autumn of 1941, the German advance on the Baltic states blockaded Russia's Baltic ports. The only route open to the Allied convoys by way of the North Atlantic came to an end on the island of Kola in the port of Murmansk, which had already been used in 1916. Leningrad had been blockaded on 10 September 1941 and German efforts were redoubled to prevent the Russians from receiving any aid. The example of an attack carried out by the U-boat 'packs' on 15 October 1931 against a North Atlantic convoy makes clear the serious danger represented by submarine warfare. At 8.10 in the evening, in the dark, a Norwegian vessel at the centre of the convoy was suddenly struck by a torpedo from U-boat 558, exploded and sank. One hour later, the same submarine slipped silently into the heart of the convoy, began to surface, and torpedoed two more merchant ships. Half a dozen U-boats launched against the convoy and, at midnight, a Norwegian tanker was torpedoed, its explosion illuminating the whole convoy and showing the positions of all the ships. An escorting American destroyer was directly hit.[33]

This was the first United States warship to be hit during an engagement in the Battle of the Atlantic. On 31 October, another American destroyer was also hit, and 116 were killed. Despite this, the neutrality party remained strong and Roosevelt could still not put his war plan into action in the Atlantic, nor his defence plans in the Pacific, to attack Japan. On 7 December 1941, the destruction of a part of the American Pacific Fleet by a Japanese surprise attack on Pearl Harbor was to put the whole issue back on the table.

Despite the Americans' direct engagement in the war against the Axis, Allied losses in the Atlantic remained very heavy in 1942, with almost 8 million tonnes of shipping sunk. The U-boats were still dealing heavy blows to enemy forces in 1943, always using the tactic of surprise attacks by packs of between 10 and 40 submarines. Until as late as the summer of 1943, airborne protection, with aircraft coming from Newfoundland, Iceland and Northern Ireland, could not cover the entire crossing, and there was still a gap of 600 miles – a gap the submarines exploited. A few months later, the airborne escort was unbroken, and the radar carried by the escorting craft would get the better of the U-boats. In February–March 1943, four successive convoys thus lost 38 of the 191 merchant ships they comprised, and only three submarines were sunk.

The Allied landings in North Africa and then in Italy, crushing airborne superiority and the utilization of Dakar and Freetown on the African coast as stopovers, however, had restored the situation in the Allies' favour, and the Battle of the Atlantic gave the Germans no further opportunities. The 11,000 or so aircraft, 350 warships and 4,100 merchant ships deployed in the Allied landing in Normandy, consecrated the victory won in the Atlantic.

The cost of winning was, however, extremely heavy. Thus the British alone saw more than 11 million tonnes of their merchant shipping disappear, 60 per cent of their fleet in 1939, and Allied losses in general exceeded 21 million tonnes.[34] The war led to the disappearance of one out of every two ships afloat on the eve of the conflict. It had taken every effort by America's powerful industry to compensate for them: during the war, the United States launched more than 38 million tonnes, 5,171 ships, of which the famous 2,500 Liberty Ships formed the backbone of the Allied fleets. In the Battle of the Atlantic, England had won a Pyrrhic victory and, in reality, finally lost any chance of keeping a sea power that the First World War had already left extremely weakened.

The reconstruction of the Atlantic

The dependency on the United States in which Great Britain increasingly found itself during the war applied to the whole of western Europe in the period following the conflict, all the more so because of political constraints and economic requirements. In the face of Stalinist Russia's growing ambitions, the threat drove western Europe to turn towards its ally across the Atlantic. During 1949, the North Atlantic Treaty Organization was founded, in the context of the Cold War, by the signatories of the 1948 Brussels Treaty.[35] Through this, Canada and the United States came to support 10 European states, France and Great Britain among them.

American support proved indispensable for reconstructing Europe, and once again the Atlantic played the role of the vital link between the Old Continent and the New World. For importing the raw materials and manufactured goods they lacked, the countries of Europe, whose merchant fleets had been largely destroyed, received the necessary ships from America. Thus France found herself allocated some 75 Liberty Ships, that is, 760,000 tonnes fully laden, by the Blum–Byrnes Franco–American accord of 26 May 1946. The Compagnie Générale Transatlantique alone received 21 of them, and was already using 11 by charter. The Liberty's full load of 10,000 tonnes was enough to make crossings profitable; despite its low speed of 10 knots and the accidents, due to negligence and a rather hasty construction, this ship proved the best means for supplying Europe with coal, cereals, wool and cotton.

Meanwhile, the European companies devoted themselves to reconstituting their fleets, despite the difficulties caused by the rapid inflation common to all countries, where construction costs had increased.

Cunard and Transatlantique: two exemplary companies in the renewal of traffic

Due to purchasing four cargo liners and chartering, in 1948 the British company, Cunard, managed to achieve carriage of 2.7 million tonnes of goods, rediscovering a level of traffic comparable to the pre-war period. At the same time, Cunard were pursuing a construction programme for three fast cargo ships with refrigerated holds, ships which entered service in 1950.[36] At the beginning of the 1960s, receipts for this cargo traffic rose to £6.8 million (1961), and rose in 1965 to more than £12 million.[37] At that time, these receipts represented more than half the assured revenues from passenger traffic.

In 1948, thanks to the Liberty Ships, Transatlantique reconstituted its tonnage of 1939 and proceeded to launch new ships, five of which were on the Mexico and Antilles routes. This enabled them to have a tonnage of merchant shipping in 1950 that was half again as great as it was before the war.[38]

The two companies, however, aspired above all to bring their efforts to bear on the liner routes, in particular the North Atlantic that had made their flags famous. In this domain, the situation was extremely difficult: in 1938, 88 liners belonging to 11 nations were circulating in the North Atlantic; in 1946, no more than 13 were in use.

During the war, Cunard had contributed greatly to transporting Allied troops to theatres of operations. In the North Atlantic alone, the *Queen Mary* and the *Queen Elizabeth* had thus carried more than a million soldiers for Europe. In 1939, the company had 18 liners at their disposal carrying 434,689 tonnes; in May 1945, it had 9, carrying 345,921 tonnes[39] To restore the *Queen Mary*, the *Queen Elizabeth*, the *Mauritania* and the *Britannic*, its most prestigious ships, the company had to invest more than £7.6 million. In 1948, it put the *Caronia* into service, carrying 34,000 tonnes, but, lacking the amenities demanded by an American clientele, particularly air conditioning, it proved to be difficult to exploit. During the 1950s, Cunard adopted a new strategy, that is, to put the maximum number of ships into service on the New York route in high season – spring and summer – and to transfer a certain number of their ships to cruises during the winter.

After 1960, however, the North Atlantic route, even in high season, suffered increasingly from competition from the aeroplane. In 1957, passenger traffic was still equally split between air and sea: 1,041,000 passengers by plane, and 1,037,000 by boat. Ten years later, sea-going traffic amounted to no more than 7.5 per cent of the total, with only 504,000 passengers, as against 6,177,000 passengers by air routes.[40] The Cunard company was conscious of the importance of this competition from the plane and in 1959–1962 invested in airborne transport. At the first stage, Cunard, still believing in the complementarity of maritime and airborne transport, bought the company Eagle Airways in October 1959, which had put a route from London to Nassau, in the Bahamas, into service. The company then conducted more daring negotiations with BOAC and other transatlantic air carriers to operate over the North Atlantic route.[41] Using the new Boeing 707 and the De Havilland Comet IV, Cunard hoped to gain a service to New York for Eagle Airways. When, however, on 21 June 1961, Eagle Airways obtained a licence for this line, BOAC had it revoked. Negotiations with BOAC had broken down over this obstacle, but they were still highly original, since they foresaw that maritime and airborne services should be complementary: passengers would take an outward bound journey by sea and return by air, with great cost advantages.

The service on the London to Nassau route was extended in Miami, with a Nassau to New York journey, and achieved some success. In 1962, Cunard succeeded in taking out shares in BOAC and the results of this association remained considerable until as late as 1966. At this point, in the face of the heavy investments required by the introduction of jet planes, Cunard decided to with-draw totally from the airlines to dedicate all its capital to developing its traditional role of maritime transport, and in fact, the following year, the company launched the *Queen Elizabeth II*, which was to renovate its fleet and was able to compete with its rival, Transatlantique's *France II*.

The Compagnie Générale Transatlantique was also able to rebuild its fleet of liners in the years following the war, while competition was picking up over the North Atlantic. On the line from Le Havre to New York, the liners *de Grasse*, *Ile de France* and the *Liberté* (ex *Europa*) were put into service one after the other from 1947 to 1949. In spring 1950, with the *Ile de France* and the *Liberté*, the company ensured a weekly service to New York. In 1951, it had two liners going to the Antilles, and in the same year, the *Maroc* linked Bordeaux to Casablanca. Passenger movement was clearly increasing: in 1947, out of the 63,500 passengers registered in Le Havre, Transatlantique transported only 10,300 passengers on the *de Grasse* when three of Cunard's and four American vessels put into port there. In 1951, it had regained a more than respectable position, managing second place with a traffic of 79,200 passengers.

Transatlantique could not, like its rival, participate in airborne traffic. However, before the war, in July 1937, it had been the first company to complete a commercial crossing by the seaplane *Latécoère* from the Lac de Biscarosse in the Landes to New York. A company called Air France Transatlantique had then been founded but in June 1945 Air France was created, a nationalized firm, in which Transatlantique could only play a diminished role. This ruined all its hopes for launching itself into the airline business.

The lights go down on the transatlantics

With the new super liners *France II* and *Queen Elizabeth II* in the 1960s, Transatlantique and Cunard seemed to want to increase their Atlantic traffic even further. In reality, competition with the airlines already made this a vain attempt.

Transatlantique was the first to complete construction on a new liner. Under construction since 1957 in Penhoët, *France II* was launched in 1960 and entered service two years later. Its dimensions similar to the *Normandie* – 315 metres in length with a displacement of 65,000 tonnes – *France II* could, with the higher speed of 35 knots and a fuel consumption lower than 40 per cent, transport 2,033 passengers, divided into only two classes, 500 of which were in first. Anti-roll stabilizers, air conditioning, cabin telephones: everything was arranged for the comfort of the passengers. Luxury, although more discreet than on the *Normandie*, was present with decorations signed by Picasso, Dufy, Segonzac and Carzou, but the atmosphere was softer, and culture and sport were combined, with a 700-seat theatre and three swimming pools.

Five years later, on 20 September 1967, Cunard launched the *Queen Elizabeth II*. Planned since 1964, its smaller dimensions – 293 metres in length – allowed it to pass through the locks on the Panama Canal and to adapt to the requirements of cruises. Air conditioned, with a shopping hall, four swimming pools, a sauna and a Turkish bath, no expense had been spared to assure passengers of comfort in the manner of the British. Cunard then based great hopes on the combined liner-cruise. Its liners were to go in search of the sun and to serve the tourist industry. A summer service in great demand on the North Atlantic would be complemented by winter cruises to Nassau in the Bahamas, or to the Mediterranean.

After this success, problems were to pile up for the two companies. In 1967 and 1968 the *Queen Mary* and the *Queen Elizabeth* were retired from the North Atlantic line, the first sold to the town of Long Beach in California, and the second transformed into a floating university in Hong Kong. In 1969, Cunard had no more than three liners, including the *Queen Elizabeth II*.

The North Atlantic passenger traffic that had brought New York to the gates of Europe really disappeared in the face of increasing competition from the airlines. The jet killed the liners. In 1973, air traffic transported more than 14 million passengers, sea traffic fewer than 100,000, amounting to no more than 1 per cent of the traffic.

In the South Atlantic, where competition from the airlines was also making itself felt, a certain number of cargo/passenger ships remained for passengers and goods, the latter chiefly being refrigerated products in particular and specialized bulk, such as cereals, wools and leather goods. The English Blue Star Line, the Italia, with its two liners from Genoa to Buenos Aires still in service at the beginning of the 1970s, and American companies on the routes from the United States to South America, still managed to generate some traffic.

The situation was far worse on the North Atlantic, where decommissioning had been accelerating for every company since the beginning of the 1970s. The *United States* on the line from Southampton to New York was decommissioned in 1972, and the American flag disappeared from North Atlantic passenger traffic. At this time there was as yet only one Greek flag on this line (linking Piraeus and New York), one Norwegian flag (Oslo to New York), and one Swedish flag (Copenhagen to New York). In the autumn of 1974, *France II* was decommissioned. Despite heavy financial losses with the *Queen Elizabeth II*, Cunard made up its mind to maintain a presence, still completing 23 journeys between Southampton and New York in 1980. The cruise alone, however, had become profitable for the 'sacred monsters' that were the liners for almost a century.

The changes in the Atlantic then far exceed the transportation of passengers, since with the appearance of the container ships and other new modes of transport, the Atlantic, like the other oceans, experienced a revolution.

Changes in the Atlantic at the end of the twentieth century

Whereas the North Atlantic saw its passenger traffic all but collapse with the sudden expansion of air traffic, its merchant traffic responded to the global boom in large-scale maritime commerce in the 1960s, before the oil crisis of 1973 and, once this was over, continued to expand to reach its peak after the end of the 1970s.

A few months after Nasser's nationalization of the Suez Canal on 26 July 1956 there was a military occupation of the northern part of the canal by England and France, which was halted by an American intervention. The canal, obstructed during these operations, remained off-limits to international traffic for six months. In 1967, the Six Days' War showed the new fragility of the Suez route and large numbers of petrol tankers began to free themselves from the constraints of the route (the canal being closed from 1967 to 1975). The reopening of the Canal on 5 June 1975, after the great crisis of 1973, and after Egypt's attack on Israel on 5 October 1973, did not facilitate a revival of the situation to its previous state. The state of political insecurity was not removed, the very high costs of insurance rates, the price of tolls, and the insufficient depth of the canal all came together to direct traffic onto other routes. The entry onto the scene of the super tankers, which became familiar after the Suez crisis and the closing of the canal to petrol tankers of average tonnage, saw the Atlantic benefit from a stream of traffic opening to giants carrying 200,000 tonnes and even more. Due to their high tonnage, they could easily bear the cost of a detour round the Cape to reach western Europe and the United States. In fact, the trade in heavy tonnages had begun before the Suez crisis, since the Japanese had been working with these giants since the 1960s, being no longer dependent on the constraints of the Suez Canal, and the distances between the Middle East and Japan being great enough to justify larger sizes.

After the Six Days' War in 1967, the first European orders for super tankers were placed, and in 1972 the Atlantic shipyards of Saint-Nazaire received an order for two giant super tankers.

Vast reductions in costs are made possible by transporting hydrocarbons in these giants, fitted out by the great international petrol companies or independent shipowners such as Onassis and Niarchos, the Greeks whose vessels sail under a Liberian flag – and these reductions are increasing. Terminals like Antifer in Le Havre, adapted to the exceptional draughts of these giants – up to 29 metres – had to be constructed.

Petrol currently lies at the root of the most massive maritime traffic – almost 1,400 million tonnes of crude. The Atlantic is crossed by three great flows of traffic: the first comes from the Persian Gulf out of the Cape and then steers towards Europe (176 million tonnes) and the east coast of the United States (76 million tonnes);[42] the second links central and west Africa with Europe (41 million tonnes) and the east coast of the United States (44 million tonnes); the third is the one that leaves from Venezuela and Mexico in the Caribbean, the former country sending 101 million tonnes to the United States and 30 million tonnes towards Europe, and the latter, 12 million tonnes to Europe and 12 million tonnes to Brazil.

After petrol, bulk carrier goods have also done well from very high tonnage ships. In this field, it is the ore tankers that have taken a position in the Atlantic comparable to the petrol tankers in terms of the volumes of goods they transport and the size of the ships. Iron and bauxite demonstrate the importance of the traffic flows involved in transporting them. Three large areas of production, bordering the Atlantic, lie at the base of iron traffic. Brazil, exporting 115 million tonnes drives the first movement, from its Vitoria terminal where ore tankers of 120,000 tonnes can take on up to 8,000 tonnes per hour and are loaded in less than 15 hours. Brazil runs one-third of the world's exports. Africa, with several producer countries – Angola, Gabon, Guinea, Liberia and Mauritania – is taking an increasing share of this traffic. Loading here is subject to certain constraints due to the nature of the coastline. A system of convergent sea walls extends up to the sandbar, which has for a long time been an obstacle to African coastal navigation because of the enormous waves breaking over it. A quay with two mooring posts can be set up; a platform bears the loading machines and serves as a storage depot, and a railway line connects the port to the deposits. The ore-mining companies, themselves dependent on large steel-makers, finance these installations. The third great producer area consists of Labrador and Newfoundland in North America. The major traffic movements cross the Atlantic towards Europe and the United States.

Bauxite and aluminium show the intricate interdependence of the producers in the Caribbean, in Africa and Australia. In the Caribbean, Jamaica and Guyana are by far the dominant producers, with 40 per cent of the world's exports, followed in Africa by Guinea and Ghana, with 25 per cent. Australia, which exports more aluminium than bauxite, is the point of origin of the longest movement of ore transportation in the Atlantic, ascending to the Cape after crossing the Indian Ocean, as far as Western Europe. Africa exports particularly to Europe, and Jamaica, like Guyana, to the United States and Canada.

Bulk transport of ores, but also other products, such as wood and cereals, show an expansion in the traffic accompanied by a similar expansion in the tonnage of the ships. But the traffic in manufactured goods has seen a real revolution come about that has given the Atlantic, its ships and its ports a new face for the twentieth century.

With container ships, there was a total transformation in goods transport. The container ship solves one of the trickiest problems of maritime transport, that of loading and unloading various goods, avoiding the expenses of handling and immobilizing ships in port. The container ship allows a flexible, door to door service, and speed of port-side operations is astonishing: unloading a container carrier takes six times less than unloading an ordinary cargo vessel.

The container's breakthrough began in the United States at the beginning of the 1950s, for routes from New York to the Gulf of Mexico. In 1960–1962, the shipping outfit Sealand instigated a massive traffic on the routes between New York and the Caribbean (Puerto Rico). It was at the beginning of the 1960s that the container ships made their debut in the North Atlantic and the cargo ship began to be put back onto secondary lines. A battle between American and European outfitters was started in the Atlantic to ensure control of this new traffic. Three large American companies then found themselves in competition with the Europeans, who had joined forces to enable a more effective resistance. In 1967, Atlantic Container combined Cunard, Transatlantique, the Holland Amerika Line and the Svenska America Line; in 1968, Belgians, British and Germans found themselves in the Dart Container Line, and the Danish joined the British Blue Star Line in the Scantar consortium. In 1972, a pool brought together the Atlantic consortiums and the Europeans managed to gain a significant share of the traffic.

Containerization reached the peak of its development in the trade between countries with a high standard of living, having regular and plentiful movement of various products. This penalizes the developing countries which have only a limited share of various consumer goods, and in which transport is more seasonal. Meanwhile, an effort has been made by certain American and European shipowners to integrate these countries into their circuits. One can cite the case of the firm Africatainer, which brought the Chargeurs Réunis and the firm Fabre together to serve nine ports from Guinea to Matadi with cargoes reassembled or split up in Abidjan. Africatainer relies on local ports where traditional cargoes are used to exchange for lower tonnages, the container traffic arriving and leaving from Abidjan.

The features of this traffic have brought about a concentration of the majority of the movements of containers in the northern zone of the Atlantic in order to bind the east coast of North America – the United States and Canada – to western Europe. New York possesses the largest container terminal, with a storage area extending to some 317 hectares in 1975. As in other container terminals, giant gantry cranes can be seen lifting containers of 40 to 50 tonnes. In western Europe, Göteborg in Sweden, Bremerhaven and Hamburg in Germany, Rotterdam and Antwerp in particular in the Low Countries and Belgium, and finally Le Havre, with its Atlantic quay, all possess massive terminals. A port such as Bordeaux in the Gulf of Gascony found an opportunity in this container traffic to revive its trade, which was veering towards stagnation, with a terminal at the entrance to the Gironde estuary at Verdon. In England, London lacks sufficient storage areas and the terminal serving its port was set up in Suffolk.

Fast container carriers, the most recent running at 30 knots, with capacity for between 2,000 and 2,500 containers have created the greatest activity that North Atlantic traffic has known. On the rest of the Atlantic, the frequency and the capacity of the container carriers linking the United States to South America and South Africa, Europe to West Africa and South America, are clearly lower.

We must not ignore the serious problems that the introduction of container traffic has given rise to in ports. Although the highly specialized petrol and ore tanker traffic that serves industrial zones has often not given a boost to employment in these ports, they have not disrupted it. On the other hand, containerization threatens the traditional employment of the dockers. Its objective is in fact to limit the onerous recourse to the single process of quayside labour in favour of *several* compartmentalized tasks. In consequence, very early on there were fears of reductions in the workforce, and there has indeed been such a reduction: on the east coast of the United States, jobs fell from 51,000 in 1952 to 15,000 in 1972; in England, from 70,000 to 32,000 between 1961 and 1973; in France, from 15,000 in 1968 to 13,000 in 1973.[43]

This traffic, with ships for which production and maintenance costs require strict rules of productivity, has brought with it a transformation in the lives of sailors. One might think that the automation of tasks has clearly improved their lives when compared to their predecessors' experience in the steam age of the nineteenth century, where the men of the machine, the coal-trimmers, had an extremely hard life, or in the time of sailing ships, where conditions for topmen, who in all weathers had to work the rigging, were far from enviable. However, the search for acceleration in the rotation of ships puts a limit on the maximum time spent in port and has done away with stopovers, which crews often took very badly, since their shifts on board ship are long. In order to free themselves from social constraints and take advantage of beneficial taxation, shipowners use flags of convenience and take on crews from developing countries.

The size of the petrol, ore and container traffic, centred on Europe and America, could give rise to a belief in the existence of a 'bi-polar' Atlantic, perpetuating the tradition inherited from the nineteenth century. In fact, it is nothing of the kind, for two reasons.

On the one hand, the major poles of global development are not reducible to the two great zones of Europe and America. In addition, of course, there is also Japan and South-East Asia. Meanwhile, America is looking more towards the Pacific than the Atlantic. For a long time its privileged partner has been the Old Continent, but already, from 1980–1982, American trans-Pacific trade comes close to the level that the North Atlantic used to bear: before these dates, imports from Asia had exceeded those coming from western Europe, which, however, remained the market that absorbed the majority of the New World's produce. In 1983, the global volume of the United States' commercial relations with Asia exceeded that of her traditional European partners.

On the other hand, America, like Europe, has been led to develop 'spirals' of traffic, the majority oriented in accordance with the meridian, with others crossing it. Thus the United States has developed its relations with the Caribbean and Brazil so as to draw on them for strategic products such as petrol, iron and bauxite and to sell them various goods. Europe, inheriting the imperial routes, has developed its relations with West and Central Africa, and here again they have found the petrol and the minerals vital to their industries. Cutting across these routes, North America has also turned towards Angola and West Africa, as Europe has to Brazil. We may thus speak of a 'multi-polar' Atlantic, still, however, driven by the finance and trade decisions taken by America and Europe.

On the axes traced by traffic movements, ships gather in shipping lanes up to 50 miles long – they are not sent out arbitrarily over the ocean's surface. The 'track' – the route from New York to western Europe – is by far the most important of these axes, running from the entrance to the English Channel to the east coast of the United States, passing southern Newfoundland. In the 1960s, this 'track' held 61 per cent of the world's maritime traffic,[44] and kept 61 per cent of the fleets of every country within this oceanic horizon. Since then, it has undergone a reduction, and currently holds 40 per cent of the world's traffic.

Its pre-eminence can be explained by the relations it sustains between two of the world's three most powerful economic regions: the Northern Range in the east, the northern European seaboard between the Elbe and the Seine, whose hinterlands give it enormous economic potential; and the Megapolis in the west, from Boston to Hampton Roads in Virginia, passing New York in between.

The changes brought to bear on the movement of commercial exchanges could also be found in the exploitation of the Atlantic's wealth of fish. In fact, fishing had been in decline in certain areas: the available fish stocks had diminished, as was the case for Newfoundland at the end of the 1970s. Over the course of the preceding years, the fish stocks had been overexploited by the industrial trawler fleets from eastern states such as Russia and Poland, as well as French and Spanish deep-freeze trawlers. Canada reacted by evicting foreign fishing fleets to a distance of 200 miles from the area (including the 12 miles of territorial waters and the 104 miles of the economic exclusion zone). The last of these expulsions took place in 1988, the French having stayed there up until then by virtue of their historic rights. The north-east Atlantic was also overexploited in Greenland and Spitsbergen by Norwegian, Icelandic, German and French industrial fisheries. Also imposing a 200-mile exclusion zone, the European Community strove to maintain the necessary reserves. From Esbjerg, the Danish practised fishing in order to manufacture flour from fish, for which they were heavily criticized by other countries. The last area of the Atlantic to be affected by rules aiming to control stocks, was from Patagonia to the Islas Malvinas (the Falkland Islands) in the South Atlantic. On this archipelago, the English sold fishing licences to the

Spanish and the Argentinians, and created a restricted area of 200 miles around the islands. In Patagonia, the Argentinians imitated them, and without hesitation turned to gunfire to evict Russian trawlers at the end of 1980. Therefore, there was a real decline in fishing in certain areas and a withdrawal of Russian ships, but on the whole, no measures taken to maintain the world's fish stocks at an optimum level for the future can yield completely positive results in the absence of any real consensus between states.

Just as spectacular for the life of the Atlantic was the overthrow of naval strategy created by the debut of nuclear submarines with missile launching capabilities. In 1958, the United States began the Polaris submarine project: nuclear propulsion enabled it to spend a long time in the deep, and there was the transpolar navigation of the USN *Nautilus* in July 1958. By the beginning of the 1960s, the Soviet navy had its first nuclear submarines, the capacities of which were enormously increased in the 1970s, and until the end of the 1980s the Soviets maintained the underwater patrols *Delta* and *Typhoon* in the Arctic Ocean, submarines carrying long-range missiles, which seemingly, however, had only a slim chance of survival against American attack submarines.

While not taking into account the other nuclear submarine forces – France and Great Britain – we must note how impressive the size of the forces in place in the United States and Russia is, although geopolitical upheavals in the latter country over the last few years have certainly contributed to reducing its real capacity for action. In 1990, Russia had 116 submarines in the North Atlantic alone, against 39 in the Baltic, 21 in the North Sea and 105 in the Pacific.[45] On the same date, the United States possessed a total fleet of 132 submarines. Confronting this situation, attempts were made to restrict the use of naval forces in the ocean: thus a zone where nuclear arms cannot be deployed was considered in the South Atlantic, South Pacific and the Antarctic, but the weapons carried by these nuclear submarines appear to have made this a futile policy.

No picture of the most recent transformations experienced by the Atlantic could be painted without recalling how, while offering transport operations axes of trade that are still the most powerful on the planet, the ocean becomes a resource for the leisure industries whose exploitation is rapidly growing.

After 1965, when the decline in the regular passenger transport lines was making itself felt, companies already foresaw a double service – crossings and cruises. During the 1970s, British, Scandinavian and Italian shipowners ordered specialized cruise ships or converted old liners. The best known case is that of a Norwegian, Kloster, who transformed the *France* into the *Norway* so that he could put Caribbean cruises from Miami into operation. In winter, in fact, the Antilles attracts sun-seeking tourists, while in spring and autumn the cruisers head more for the Mediterranean and the Atlantic archipelagos of the Azores, Madeira and the Canaries. Summer brings Spitsbergen in Norway a clientele eager to discover a northern change of scenery under the midnight sun.

The cruise industry has made Miami its capital, with a third of the world's liner fleets based in its port, loading more than a million passengers (1978). New York comes next with 300,000 passengers.

The number of cruise-loving tourists we can expect at the end of the century is far higher, some 10 million in the United States, and more than a million in Europe. The names of the floating palaces announce the era of a new mythology of the sea and the Atlantic – *Sovereign of the Seas*, *Splendour of the Seas* – which is filtering into this new form of maritime hotel.

Is there any familiarity with the sea amongst the holiday-makers thus boarded for a few dream-like days? It would be rash to assert this. The secret creeks of the Virgin Islands are threatened with an eruption of noise from thousands of tourists, gregarious urbanites taking over the beaches from their discoverers, and who, moreover, often prefer crowds of shoppers and casinos in the cities of the free zones to the solitude of a shoreline. On these distant beaches, we find the same mass tourism as on the Atlantic coasts of Europe and America.

Pleasure sailing can nevertheless discover the secrets of the sea. With these very light craft, from the simple canoe to the sailing dinghy, genuinely inhabitable sailboats allow a cruise to be taken where real navigators learn how to come to terms with the sea. Although the Mediterranean holds a large number of them, the Atlantic offers these pleasure-seekers subtropical cruises from the Bahamas to Trinidad, as well as in the Mediterranean Atlantic of the Phoenicians, to the Canaries or Madeira. Trophies for monohulls and catamarans, in the English Transat or in the rum and coffee races, have given these daring navigators the opportunity to smash record crossing times. At the cost of long nights awake, combining the science of navigation with the art of anticipation to prevent accidents at sea, these solitary skippers have managed to link Le Havre to Cartagena or Plymouth to Newport in record times: it took 14 days, 16 hours, 1 minute and 30 seconds for Yves Parlier in the English Transat of June 1992 to complete the race with a crossing of 2,800 miles in a monohull of less than 19 metres.

At the end of the twentieth century, therefore, the Atlantic retains the attraction of the wide open sea for the pleasures of sport or holiday-making. Still a Mecca for the most intense human efforts to reconnect the continents, is it so much better known today than it used to be? While in the various countries of Europe and America the push to the sea is a response to the increasingly pronounced taste for fleeing the tedium of everyday life during the summer months, it seems by no means certain that 'going to the seaside' might lead Europeans or Americans to understand an ocean that was one of humanity's great questions, contributing to the history of the continents bordering it a large part of their character.

Chapter 9

Conclusion

Clouds cover the abyss, and the spirit of God floats on the waters.

(Genesis I.1)

Antiquity's pervasive consciousness of the infinite ocean holding nothing but the threat of destruction was replaced, under medieval Christianity – which appropriated elements of the Arab imaginary, by a belief in the presence at the heart of the abyss of the Fortunate Isles, the lands of refuge. In the clouds over the Land of the Dead that was the ocean, the Isles of the Blessed represented the necessary halt before acceding to Paradise itself. Ancient memories resurface in this imaginary in its attachment to the *mirabilia*, to the prodigies that these islands offered to whosoever dared to cross the Sea of Perpetual Gloom to lead a life of ease there, with neither pain nor labour.

If the time of discoveries, followed by centuries of Atlantic prosperity for Europe and then the New World, saw reality emerge from legend and create a completely different consciousness along the ocean's shorelines of the riches given up by the sea, then the ancient myths have survived and new ones have been created. They too form part of the history of the Atlantic.

Spanish dreams of a New Jerusalem in the lands of the New World where Spaniard and Indian would live in Christian brotherhood – certainly a utopia presaging the dreams of Don Quixote – were cruelly shattered at the beginning of the conquest.[1] We must also emphasize the slowness with which Columbus's legacy was integrated into the mentality of the West, so that pioneering Spanish works such as Sahagun's *General History of New Spain* were only published later. The European mind had turned inwards for good, although a good number of her citizens always turn with interest to the utopias that remain forever dreams, such as the one the Iberians were unable to bring into being.

Inherited from pagan and Christian legend, the myth of the islands was one of the most enduring, one that sustained generations. In *The Tempest*, Shakespeare

296

situates an island close to the Bermudas. On this island, nature provides everything in abundance to feed an innocent people in a New World proud to shelter
such extraordinary creatures. Was he inspired by the New Lands described in
Montaigne's *Essays*? They harbour 'the true, most useful, and natural virtues....
These nations...are still very close to their original simplicity.'[2] Beyond the
dream of this island, it was the predominance of virtue that attracted the
humanist. To a troubled Europe, torn apart by religious divisions during the
Reformation, he brought a vision of original innocence. The land of refuge across
the Atlantic welcomed the Founding Fathers of the English colonies in 1620, the
Pilgrim Fathers coming to establish the City of Christ, as well as to found a
community where virtue would be preserved to inspire just and equal laws. Half
a century later, the Quakers dared to set up a radically different society within
their colony, certainly managing far better than the Puritans of New England.
While the colonies of Massachusetts were massacring Indians, who were no more
than miserable savages to them, barely endowed with a soul, the Friends refused
to have recourse to weapons, placing their trust in honesty and tolerance.

In the eighteenth century virtue was still admired in the New World, but it
gave rise to a will to freedom. 'Freedom will never again lack a sanctuary', wrote
La Fayette, the hero of two worlds, on 1 January 1783, in the aftermath of the
American War of Independence.[3] The states managed to join together to defy
European intrigues and henceforth held fiercely to the land, virtue and liberty.
Jefferson wanted his country to remain an Arcadia that might be saved from a
Europe in permanent crisis.

It is true that things changed in the nineteenth century, when the Atlantic separated and united more than ever. Europe sent its migrants to a United States in a
sudden expansion, and the burdens of the industrial world became increasingly
heavy on the other side of the Atlantic. At this time, Old Europe seemed to most
Americans to be a land of real freedom. In contrast to La Fayette, from a France
in crisis sailing to receive homage from Congress on 18 June 1784, and also to
recognize the virtues of the Founding Fathers, is the image of the American
writers crossing the Atlantic in the other direction, to ask Europe to return their
roots. Thus Henry James came to London in 1876: 'He was not waving the star-
spangled banner in a provocative manner, convinced that his country is the best in
the world and that Americans could put the whole of Europe in their pockets'.[4]

And in *Tropic of Capricorn*, Henry Miller condemns an American civilization
that has become exclusive and no longer tolerant of differences: 'If you dream
something different you are not in America, of America American, but a
Hottentot in Africa, or a Kalmuck, or a chimpanzee. The moment you have a
"different" thought you cease to be an American.'[5]

In *Babbit*, Sinclair Lewis describes the tranquil despair of an American *petit
bourgeois* who sacrificed his life for the collective lie. Of course, this is clearly

overstated, and when *Babbit* was published in 1922 Europe warmly embraced American customs, exemplified by jazz or the Charleston. After the Second World War, the American model penetrated even further into the daily lives of Europeans, and the Atlantic looked as if it was uniting more than ever. Of course, it is no longer as dominant as it was in the past, since at the end of the twentieth century America (and Europe) are looking increasingly towards Asia, where the power of the younger economies – the 'tiger economies' of south-east Asia – increasingly astonishes the West. However, the legacy of the Atlantic rests not so much on the qualities of any one culture as on wealth alone.

In the era of the greatest wealth, at the end of the twentieth century, fascinating dreams are again being dreamt in the hope that the men of the Atlantic will manage to revive their souls:

> The people have sampled the salt of the sea
> and the strength of the winds
> labouring at the ends of the earth.
> The people have taken the earth
> like a resting place and a cradle of hope.
>   (Carl Sandburg, *The People Will Live On*, 1936)

Notes

Introduction

1 Homer, *The Odyssey* Bk V, p. 410.
2 Christian Buchet, 'Des routes maritimes Europe–Antilles et de leurs incidences sur la rivalité franco-britannique', *Histoire, Economie, Société* 4, 1994, p. 576.
3 Herman Melville, *Moby Dick*, London: Dent, 1961, p. 9.

1 Atlantic legends and Atlantic reality before the Iberian discoveries

1 Seneca, *Medea* I, pp. 374–379.
2 Homer, *The Odyssey* Bk I, p. 51.
3 Alexandre Bessmertny, *L'Atlantide, exposé des hypothèses relative à l'énigme de l'Atlantide*, Paris: Payot, 1949, p. 235.
4 Ibid., p. 249.
5 The Breton legends are cited in Wolfgang Geiger, 'De la navigation des moines de l'abbaye de Saint-Mathieu au voyage de Cristoph Columb; le recherche du paradis terrestre à l'ouest' in *Dans le Sillage de Columb: l'Europe du Ponant et la découverte du Nouveau Monde, 1450–1630*, Rennes: Presses Universitaires de Rennes, 1995, pp. 297–314. The reference to the Celestial Jerusalem can be found in the Book of Revelations, Ch. 21, vv. 11 and 21.
6 Michel Mollat, *L'Europe et la mer*, Paris: Seuil, 1993, p. 64.
7 *Encyclopaedia Britannica* II, p. 698.
8 Virgil, *The Aeneid* Bk XI, pp. 623–628.
9 Alexandre Bessmertny, op. cit., p. 256.
10 Jean Favier, *Les grands découvertes d'Alexandre à Magellan*, Paris: Fayard, 1991, p. 53.
11 Cristophe Picard, *Récits merveilleux et réalités d'une navigation en océan Atlantique chez les auteurs musulmans*, p. 3.
12 Pierre Rouillard, *Les Grecs et la péninsule ibérique du VIIIe au IVe siècle avant JC*, Paris: De Boccard, 1991.
13 Ezekiel 27.12.
14 Pliny the Elder, *Natural History* vi, p. 36, cited by André Jodin, *Les établissements du roi Juba II aux Iles Purouraires*, Mogador, 1967.
15 Jérôme Carcopino identifies Cerné with an island situated much further south than

Mogador, in the bay of Rio de Oro, past Cape Juby. André Jodin gives an impression of wavering: Mogador could by turns bear the name of the Purple Islands or of Cerné; Carcopino's interpretation gives greater scope to those who derive certainty from Hanno.

16 André Jodin, *Mogador, Comptoir phénicien du Maroc atlantique*, Tangiers, 1963.

17 Jérôme Carcopino, *Le Maroc Antique*, Paris: Gallimard, 1943, p. 33.

18 Jérôme Carcopino, op. cit., p. 154.

19 Herodotus, *The Histories* IV, 196f. Quoted in Jérôme Carcopino, op. cit., p. 108.

20 Jérôme Carcopino, op. cit., p. 161.

21 Raoul Lonis, 'Les conditions de la navigation sur la côte atlantique de l'Afrique dans l'Antiquité, le problème du retour' in *Afrique noire et mode méditerranéen dans l'Antiquité*, Dakar: Nouvelles Editions Africaines, 1978, p. 147.

22 Lucretius, *On the Nature of the Universe* Bk IV, 946ff. Seneca, *Medea*, 318–320. Virgil, *The Aeneid* Bk V, pp. 830–832.

23 Monies have been found since the eighteenth century. The author would like to thank Mme Geneviève Bouchon for having kindly brought this to his attention.

24 Pierre Rouillard, op. cit., p. 237.

25 Pindar, *Nemean Odes* iv, 69; iii, 21; Aristophanes, *The Frogs*, p. 475.

26 Jean Favier, op. cit., p. 67.

27 Pierre Rouillard, op. cit., pp. 68–69.

28 Charles R. Whitehaker, *Les frontières de l'empire romain*, Paris: Les Belles Lettres, 1989, pp. 54–57.

29 Roland Delamaire, 'La région Manche-Mer du Nord dans l'espace politique et économique romain', in *Revue du Nord*, 1, 1986, pp. 153–161.

30 Pliny the Elder, *Natural History* ix, p. 60.

31 Pierre Chaunu, *L'expansion européenne du XIIIe au XVe siècle*, Paris: PUF, 1969, p. 111.

32 Cristophe Picard, 'L'éventualité de relations maritimes musulmans dans l'océan atlantique, IXe–XIIIe siècles', *115e Congrès national des sociétés savantes*, Avignon 1990, pp. 409–416.

33 Ibid, p. 409.

34 Ibid, p. 413.

35 Ibid, p. 416.

36 G. J. Marcus, *The Conquest of the North Atlantic*, Suffolk: Boydell Press 1980, pp. 9–10.

37 Ibid, p. 25.

38 Saint Columba (540–610), who was born in Ireland and was a monk in Bangor, went to Gaul in 590 to found the monastery at Luxeuil.

39 G. J. Marcus, op. cit., p. 26.

40 Ibid, p. 27.

41 Gokstad is, with Oseberg, the site where Viking ships were found, on the western shore of a fjord near Oslo.

42 Paul Adam, 'Problèmes de navigation dans l'Atlantique Nord' in Regis Boyer (ed.) *L'Age Viking, les Vikings et leur civilisation, problèmes actuels* , Paris: Payot 1978, pp. 49–60.

43 Johannes Brondsted, *The Vikings*, London: Penguin, 1965, p. 139.

44 Régis Boyer, *Les sagas islandaises*, Paris: Payot 1978, p. 20.

45 G. J. Marcus, op. cit., p. 64.

46 Ibid, p. 60.

47 Cited by G. J. Marcus, op. cit., p. 75.

48 G. J. Marcus, op. cit., p. 76.

49 Paul Adam, op. cit., pp. 55–57.

50 Ibid, op. cit., p. 54.

51 G. J. Marcus, op. cit., pp. 106, 116.

52 Ibid, p. 89.

53 Ibid, p. 92.

54 Ibid, p. 80.

55 Ibid, p. 90.

2 A new Atlantic: from the fifteenth to the begining of the sixteenth centuries

1 Michel Mollat, *L'Europe et la mer*, Paris: Seuil, 1993, p. 90.

2 An anonymous eighteenth-century versifier, quoted in Michel Mollat, op. cit., p. 117.

3 In his *Colomb ou la logique de l'imprévisible* (Paris: François Bourin, 1993), Pierre Chaunu provides a perfect form in which to describe the coasters and fishermen, both Breton and Basque, as '*bricoleurs* of the ocean's blue-green bordering seas and the abundant fish of the continental rim'. [A *bricoleur* is someone who 'makes do' with materials around him or her to patch up a problem. The term has acquired great theoretical currency since it was used by the anthropologist Claude-Lévi Strauss to describe the structuralist methodology he advanced. – trans.]

4 Michel Mollat, op. cit., p. 93.

5 Charles Higounet, *Histoire de Bordeaux*, Toulouse: Privat, 1980, p. 139.

6 Michel Mollat, op. cit., p. 97.

7 Jean Favier, *Les grandes découvertes d'Alexandre à Magellan*, Paris: Fayard, 1991, p. 441.

8 Pierre Chaunu, op. cit., p. 24.

9 Jean Favier, op. cit., p. 321.

10 See Chapter1.

11 Jean Favier, op. cit., pp. 446–447.

12 Ibid, p. 453.

13 Alain Huetz de Lemps, *Le vin de Madère*, Grenoble: Glénat, 1989, p. 25.

14 Jean Meyer, *Histoire du sucre*, Paris: Desjonquères, 1989, p. 69.

15 Charles Verlinden, 'Les débuts de la production et de l'eportation du sucre à Madère, quele rôle jouèrent les Italiens?', in *Studi in memoria di Luigi dal Pane*, Bologna, 1982, p. 305. Verlinden estimates the 'arroba' at 14.06 kg, so that 400 cantars is equal to 23,200 kg or 1,650 arroba.

16 Ibid, p. 303.

17 Ibid, p. 302.

18 Ibid, p. 310.

19 Cited by Jean Meyer, op. cit., p.53.

20 Jean Favier, op. cit., p. 483.

21 Michel Mollat, op. cit., p. 120.

22 Fernand Braudel, *Civilisation matérielle et capitalisme*, Paris: Colin, 1967, p. 310. Trans. Miriam Kochan, *Capitalism and Material Life, 1400–1800*, New York: Harper and Row, 1973.

23 Michel Mollat, op. cit., p. 81.

24 Ibid, p. 130.

25 Randles, *De la terre plate au globe terrestre, une mutation épistémologique rapide, 1480–1520*, Paris: Colin, 1980, p. 25.

26 Ibid., p. 44.

27 Pierre D'Ailly, *Image du Monde*, cited by Jean Favier, op. cit., p. 279.

28 Pierre Chaunu, op. cit., pp. 24 and 130.

29 *The Great Atlas of Explorations*, London: Universalis, 1991, p. 60.

30 Jean Favier, op. cit., p. 454.

31 *Great Atlas* , op. cit., p. 79.

32 Michel Verge-Francheschi, *Henri le navigateur, un découvreur au XVe siècle*, Paris: Editions du Félin, 1994, p. 247.

33 Ibid., p. 249.

34 Ibid., p. 304.

35 Ibid., p. 314.

36 *Great Atlas*, op. cit., p. 79.

37 Philip D. Curtin, *The Rise and Fall of the Plantation Complex: Essays in Atlantic History*, Cambridge: Cambridge University Press, 1990, pp. 37 and 43.

38 The 'monsoon' wind of the African west, blowing from the south-west in the Gulf of Guinea during the summer, represented a significant obstacle to the return journeys of ships out of São Tomé and the ports of the Gold Coast.

39 Carmen Bernand and Serge Gruzinscki, *Histoire du nouveau monde II: Les Méttissages*, Paris: Fayard, 1993, p. 14.

40 *Great Atlas*, op. cit., p. 80

41 Ibid., p. 65.

42 Jean Favier, op. cit., p. 495.

43 *Great Atlas*, op. cit., p. 63.

44 Michel Mollat, op. cit., p. 152. See also Charles Verlinden, 'L'engagement maritime et la participation économique des Flamands dans l'exploration et la colonisation ibériques pendant la seconde moitié du XVe siècle' in Jean-Pierre Sanchez, (ed.), *Dans le Sillage de Colomb, l'Europe du Ponant et la découverte du Nouveau Monde, 1450–1650*, Rennes: Presses Universitaires de Rennes, 1995, pp. 228–229. For Verlinden, there were voyages before Van Olmen's, giving rise to the question of knowing whether the Seven Cities were one large island, an archipelago, or a continent.

45 Bartolomé Bennassar, *1492, un monde nouveau?*, Paris: Perrin, 1991, p. 211.

46 Pierre Chaunu, op. cit., p. 128.

47 Jean Favier, op. cit., pp. 490–491.

48 Cited by Bartolomé Bennassar, op. cit., p. 213.

49 *Great Atlas*, op. cit., p. 67.

50 Jean Favier, op. cit., pp. 482–483.

51 Bartolomé Bennassar, op. cit., p. 197.

52 Klaus A. Vogel, *Les découvertes maritimes et les humanistes allemands*.

53 The texts from Brant and Munzer are cited in Klaus A. Vogel, op. cit.

54 Bartolomé Bennassar, op. cit., p. 235.

55 Cited by Bartolomé Bennassar, op. cit., p. 237.

56 Jean Favier, op. cit., p. 506.

57 Bartolomé Bennassar, op. cit., p. 194.

58 Ibid., p. 202.

59 *Great Atlas*, op. cit., p. 83.

60 Frédéric Mauro, *Le Brésil du XVe à la fin du XVIIIe siècle*, Paris: Sedes, 1977, pp. 31–32.

61 Frédéric Mauro, op. cit., p.1 9.

62 *Great Atlas*, op. cit., p. 85.

63 Jean Favier, op. cit., pp. 573–574.
64 D. B. Quinn, *England and the Discovery of America, 1481–1620*, London: George Allen and Unwin, 1974, p. 53.
65 Ibid., p. 53.
66 Ibid., p. 86.
67 Ibid., p. 6.
68 Charles Verlinden, op. cit., p. 227.
69 *Great Atlas*, op. cit., p. 95.
70 Ibid., p. 92.

3 The Atlantic and the Iberians: sixteenth to seventeenth centuries

1 Bartholomé Bennassar, *1492, un monde noveau?*, Paris: Perrin, 1981, pp. 221–222.
2 John H. Elliott, 'The seizure of overseas territories by the European powers' in Hans Pöhl (ed.) *The European Discovery of the World and its Economic Effects on Preindustrial Society, 1500–1800*, Stuttgart: Franz Steiner Verlag, 1990, pp. 47–48.
3 Francisco Lopez de Gomara, *Histoire générale des Indes*, cited by Elliot, op. cit., p. 48.
4 Pierre Chaunu, *Séville et l'Amérique, XVI–XVIIe siècles*, Paris, Flammarion, 1977, p. 149.
5 Ibid., p. 205.
6 Ibid., p. 92.
7 Antonio Garcia Baquero Gonzales, *Cadix y el Atlantice, 1717–1778. El comercio colonial bajo el monopolio gaditano*, Seville, 1976.
8 Alain Huetz de Lemps, *Le climat des Canaries*, Paris: Sedes, 1969, p. 20.
9 Ibid., p. 89.
10 Pierre Chaunu, op. cit., p. 176.
11 Ibid., pp. 166–167.
12 Ibid., p. 172.
13 Ibid., p. 173.
14 Ibid., p. 183.
15 Ibid., p. 99.
16 Ibid., pp. 342–345.
17 Samuel Champlain *Voyages to the Antilles and Mexico in 1599–1602*, in A. Wilmere (ed.), London: Hakylut Society, 1869.
18 Thomas Gage, *Nouvelle Relation contenant les voyages de Thomas Gage dans la Nouvelle Espagne*, Paris and Geneva: Ressources, 1979.
19 Pierre Chaunu, op. cit., p. 333.
20 Ibid.
21 Bernard Lavalle, 'Séville et le siècle d'or du commerce américain (1503–1610)' in B. Lavalle (ed.) *Séville, vingt siècles d'histoire*, Bordeaux: Maison des Pays Ibériques, 1992, p. 95.
22 Bernard Lavalle, op. cit., p. 97.
23 Pierre Chaunu, *L'Amérique et les Amériques de la Préhistoire à nos jours*, Paris: Armand Colin, 1964, pp. 90–91.
24 Michel Morineau, *Histoire économique et sociale du monde t.2: les hésitations de la croissance, 1580–1730*, Paris: Armand Colin, 1978, p. 84.
25 Pierre Jeannin, *Les marchands au XVIe siècle*, Paris: Seuil, p. 28.
26 The *peso* was a piece of beaten silver weighing 27.5g.

27 Renalt Pieper, 'The volume of African and American export of precious metals and its effects in Europe, 1500–1800' in Hans Pöhl, op. cit., pp. 97–117.

28 François Crouzet, *La Grande Inflation, La monnaie en France de Louis XVI à Napoléon*, Paris: Fayard, 1993, p. 23.

29 Cited by Pierre Jeannin, op. cit., p. 28.

30 Fernand Braudel, *Civilisation matérielle et capitalisme*, Paris: Armand Colin, 1967, p. 353. Trans. Miriam Kochan, *Capitalism and Material Life, 1400–1800*, New York: Harper and Row 1973, p. 310.

31 Jean-Pierre Moreau, *Les Petites Antilles de Christoph Colomb à Richelieu*, Paris: Karthala, 1992, p. 44.

32 Kenneth R. Andrews, *Trade, Plunder and Settlement: Maritime Enterprise and the Genesis of the British Empire, 1480–1630*, Cambridge: Cambridge University Press, 1984, pp. 61–62.

33 Kenneth R. Andrews, op. cit., pp. 116–117.

34 Jacques Bottin, 'La rédistribution des produits américains par les réseaux marchands rouennais, 1550–1620' in *Dans le Sillage de Colomb, l'Europe du Ponant et la découverte du Nouveau Monde, 1450–1650*, Rennes: Presses Universitaires de Rennes, 1995, p. 28.

35 Paul Butel, *Les Caraïbes au temps des flibustiers, XVIe–XVIIe siècles*, Paris: Aubier, 1982, p. 43.

36 Paul Butel, op. cit., p. 53.

37 Kenneth R. Andrews, op. cit., p. 133.

38 Jonathan I. Israel, *Dutch Primacy in World Trade, 1585–1740*, Oxford: Clarendon, 1989, p. 31.

39 Ibid., pp. 56–57.

40 Ibid., p. 60.

41 Ibid., p. 62.

4 The Atlantic and the growth of the naval powers: the seventeenth century

1 Jonathan Israel, *Dutch Primacy in World Trade*, op. cit., p. 24.

2 Israel has doubtless put his argument in too rigid a manner through his criticisms of Fernand Braudel's Mediterranean perspective, which locates the origins of Amsterdam's fortune in the massive transportation of seeds to the north.

3 Jonathan Israel, op. cit., p. 55. Venice took more than 1,250,000 ducats in remittances; France, 800,000 ducats; England, 300,000 ducats and the United Provinces, 150,000 ducats.

4 Ibid., p. 93, table 4.6.

5 Ibid., p. 91, cites this memoir from the 1620s concerning Dutch trade and navigation.

6 Pierre Jeannin, 'Les comptes du Sund comme source pour la construction d'indices généraux de l'activité économique en Europe (XVIe–XVIIIe siècle)' in *Revue Historique*, 1964, p. 72.

7 Murdo J. MacLeod, *Spanish Central America, a Socioeconomic History 1520–1720*, Berkeley: California University Press, 1973, p. 83. Each year from 1606 to 1620, Seville imported 240,000 lbs of indigo.

8 P. C. Emmer, 'The Dutch and the making of the second Atlantic system' in Barbara Solow (ed.) *Slavery and the Rise of the Atlantic System*, Cambridge: Cambridge University Press, 1991, p. 82.

9 Pierre Chaunu, *Séville et l'Atlantique*, Paris: 1955–1956, VIII. 2, pp. 1519–1521.

10 Michel Morineau, *Incroyables gazettes et fabuleux métaux, les retours des trésors américains d'après les gazettes hollandaises, XVIe–XVIIIe siècles*, Paris, 1985.

11 Jonathan Israel, op. cit., p. 125.

12 Jaap R. Bruijn, *The Dutch Navy of the Seventeenth and Eighteenth Centuries*, Augusta SC: University of South Carolina Press, 1993, p. 26.

13 Jaap R. Bruijn, op. cit., p. 28.

14 Jonathan Israel, op. cit., p. 162.

15 Ibid., p. 169.

16 Frédéric Mauro, *Le Portugal et l'Atlantique au XVIIe siècle*, Paris: Sevpen, 1960, pp. 237–238.

17 Jonathan Israel, *European Jewry in the Age of Mercantilism, 1550–1750*, Oxford: Oxford University Press, 1989, p. 51.

18 P. C. Emmer, op cit., p. 78.

19 Ralph Davis, *The Rise of the English Shipping Industry in the 17th and 18th Centuries*, Newton Abbott: David & Charles, 1962, p. 12. Davis gives the total of captures by the Navy and the corsairs: during the first Anglo–Dutch war of 1652–1654, 1,000 to 1,700 captures; during the Anglo–Spanish war of 1658–1660, 400; in the second Anglo–Dutch war of 1664–1667, 522; in the third, of 1672–1674, 500; and, during the Anglo–French war of 1689–1697, they took 1,279 ships (ibid., p. 51).

20 Ralph Davis, op. cit., p.15.

21 Ralph Davis, op. cit., pp. 18 and 298–299; the number of ships leaving London for the mainland colonies rose from 43 to 114.

22 Paul Butel, *Les Caraïbes au temps des Filbustiers, XVIe–XVIIe siècle*, Paris: Aubier, 1982, p. 75.

23 Richard Sheridan, *Sugar and Slavery, an Economic History of the British West Indies, 1623–1775*, Aylesbury: Ginn & Co., 1974, p. 272.

24 Ibid., p. 44.

25 Ibid., p. 47.

26 Ibid., p. 50.

27 Ibid., p. 97.

28 Ibid., pp. 397–398.

29 Henry Rosavaere, *Markets and Merchants of the Late Seventeenth Century, the Marescoe-David Letters, 1668–1680*, Oxford: Oxford University Press, 1987.

30 Henry Rosavaere, op. cit., p. 51.

31 K. G. Davis, *The North Atlantic World in the Seventeenth Century*, Minneapolis: University of Minnesota Press, 1977, p. 32.

32 Ralph Davis, op. cit., p. 280. London's position can also be measured against traffic going in other directions (op. cit., p. 210):

No. of Ships	Arrivals	Departures
Mediterranean	118	79
North America	110	114
Iberian Peninsula	247	182
(of which the Canaries	24	—
Northern Europe	412	165
Western Europe	820	496
(of which Ireland	41	68)
Total	1,973	1,285

33 Ralph Davis, op. cit., p. 298. The total number of ships arriving in England from the Antilles in 1686 was 275, while 219 ships left England for the Antilles.

34 Paul Butel, op. cit., p. 206.

35 In Jamaica, the pinnacle of the sugar trade (more than 5,000 tonnes of sugar in 1680) enabled the English Antilles to become the primary producer by the end of the century, yielding 24,000 tonnes in 1700 against 18,000 in 1683, when the French Antilles were producing more than 9,400 tonnes and Brazil almost 21,000 tonnes.

36 Jacques Bernard, in Charles Higounet (ed.) *Histoire de Bordeaux t.IV*, Bordeaux, 1966, p. 135.

37 Josette Pontet, 'Bayonne et l'Océan au XVIe siècle' in P. Masson and M. Verge-Francheschi (eds) *La France et la Mer au Siècle des Grandes Découvertes*, Paris: Tallandier, 1993, p. 133.

38 Laurier Turgeon and Evelyne Picot-Bermond, 'Echange d'objets et conquête de l'autre en Nouvelle France au XVIe siècle' in *Découvertes et explorateurs*, Paris: L'Harmattant, 1994, p. 269.

39 Laurier Turgeon, 'Vers une chronologie des occupations basques du Saint Laurent du XVIe à XVIIIe siècle' in *Recherches amérindiennes au Québec*, XXIV, 1994, p. 3.

40 Evelyne Picot-Bermond, 'Mirage ou réalité économique, les armements pour les Indes à Bordeaux dans la deuxième moitié du XVIe siècle' in *Bulletin du Centre d'histoire des Espaces Atlantiques*, 5, 1990, p. 128.

41 Jean-Pierre Moreau, *Les Petites Antilles de Christoph Colomb à Richelieu*, Paris: Karthala, 1992, p. 95.

42 Paul Butel, 'Richelieu fonde les bases d'une politique maritime nationale', *Mer*, September–October 8, 1983, p. 15.

43 Jean-Pierre Moreau, op. cit., p. 193.

44 Michel Verge Franceschi, *Abraham Dusquene, Huguenot et Marin du Roi Soleil*, Paris: France-Empire, 1992, p. 83.

45 Guy Saupin, 'Les marchands nantais et l'ouverture de la route antillaise, 1639–1650' in Jean Pierre Sanchez (ed.) *Dans le sillage de Colomb*, Rennes: Presses Universitaires de Rennes, 1995, pp.173–175.

46 Jean Meyer, 'Nantes au XVIe siècle' in *La France et la Mer au Siècle des Grandes Découvertes*, Paris: Tallandier, 1993, p. 112.

47 Sold at 10 livres per pound in 1629, Saint Christopher tobacco raised no more than 1 livre 5 sous in Dieppe in 1635, where, moreover, at the end of 1639, it was sold for only 4 sous.

48 Paul Butel, *Histoire des Antilles*, Toulouse: Privat, 1980, p. 89.

49 Jean Meyer, 'Fouquet, Colbert et l'état de la Marine en 1661' in *La France et la Mer*, op. cit. p. 22.

50 Paul Butel, *Histoire des Antilles*, op. cit., p. 95.

51 Paul Butel, op. cit., p. 199.

52 Ibid., p. 202.

53 Ibid., p. 197.

54 Jean Meyer, *Histoire du sucre*, Paris: Desjonquères, 1989, p. 112.

55 Numbers given by Jean Meyer, op. cit., pp. 125–126.

56 Henry Rosevaere, op. cit., p. 69.

57 Ibid., p. 539.

58 Ibid., p. 69.

5 The golden age of the colonial Atlantic: the eighteenth century

1 Jacob M. Price, 'What did the Merchants Do? Reflections on British Overseas Trade, 1660–1790', *The Journal of Economic History* XLIX, 2,1989, p. 270.

2 Jean-Pierre Poussou, 'Inerties et Révolutions, 1730–1840' in Pierre Léon (ed.) *Histoire économique et sociale du Monde*, vol. 3, Paris: Colin, 1978, p. 147.

3 Jordan Goodman, '*Excitantia*, or how Enlightenment Europe took to soft drugs' in Jordan Goodman, Paul E. Lovejoy and Andrew Sherralt (eds) *Consuming Habits: Drugs in History and Anthropology*, London: Routledge, 1995, p. 126.

4 Paul Butel, *Histoire du Thé*, Paris: Desjonquères, 1989, p. 46.

5 Ibid., p. 50.

6 Ibid., p. 58.

7 Jean Meyer, *Histoire du Sucre*, Paris: Desjonquères, 1989, p. 188. In fact, Italian cuisine inherited the uses of these ingredients from the Ottoman empire.

8 Goodman, op. cit., p. 136.

9 Paul Butel, op. cit., p. 77.

10 Ibid, p. 56.

11 Richard B. Sheridan, *Sugar and Slavery: an Economic History of the British West Indies, 1623–1775*, Aylesbury: Ginn, 1974, p. 35.

12 Seymour Drescher, *Econocide: British Slavery in the Era of Abolition*, Pittsburgh: University of Pittsburgh Press, 1977, p. 127.

13 Richard B. Sheridan, op. cit., p. 28.

14 Ibid., p. 31.

15 Louis M. Cullen, *An Economic History of Ireland since 1660*, London: Batsford, 1972, p. 92.

16 Jordan Goodman, *Tobacco in History: the Cultures of Dependence*, London: Routledge, 1993, p. 59.

17 Jordan Goodman, 'Excitantia', op. cit., p.129.

18 Jordan Goodman, *Tobacco in History*, op. cit., p. 62.

19 Jacob M. Price, 'Tobacco use and tobacco taxation: a battle of interests in Early Modern Europe' in *Consuming Habits*, op. cit., p. 166.

20 Jordan Goodman, op. cit., p. 74.

21 François Crouzet, *De la supériorité de l'Angleterre sur la France*, Paris: Perrin, 1985, p. 142.

22 Jacob M. Price, *Capital and Credit in British Overseas Trade. The View from the Chesapeake, 1700–1776*, Cambridge, MA: Harvard University Press, 1980, pp. 112–113.

23 Jacob M. Price, op. cit., p.172.

24 Ibid., p. 173.

25 For a general explanation of this question, see Jacob M. Price, *France and the Chesapeake: A History of the French Tobacco Monopoly, 1674–1791, and its Relationship to the British and American Tobacco Trades*, 2 vols, Ann Arbor, MI: University of Michigan Press, 1973.

26 Paul Butel, 'Le grand commerce maritime' in Pierre Léon (ed.) *Histoire économique*, op. cit., pp. 68–69.

27 Jacob M. Price, 'What did the merchants do?', op. cit., p. 274.

28 John J. McCusker, *Rum and the American Revolution: the Rum Trade and the Balance of Payments of the Thirteen Continental Colonies*, New York and London: Garland, 1989, vol. 1, p. 149.

29 Ibid., p. 158.

30 Kenneth Morgan, *Bristol and the Atlantic Trade in the Eighteenth Century*, Cambridge: Cambridge University Press, 1993, p. 209.

31 Seymour Drescher, op. cit., p. 44.

32 Jacob M. Price, op. cit., p. 274.

33 Ibid., p. 275.

34 John J. McCusker and Russell R. Menard, *The Economy of British America, 1607–1789*, Chapell Hill, NC and London: North Carolina University Press, 1985, p. 286.

35 John J. McCusker, op. cit., p. 319.

36 Ibid., p. 428.

37 Ibid., p. 476.

38 Ibid., p. 496.

39 Ibid.

40 Paul Butel, 'Le grand commerce maritime', op. cit., p. 86.

41 Cited by François Crouzet, op. cit., p. 106.

42 Cited in ibid., p. 107.

43 Paul Butel, *La grande commerce maritime*, op. cit., p. 70.

44 Pierre Deyon, 'La concurrence internationale des manufactures lainières' in *Annales ESC*, 1972, p. 29.

45 Charles Frostin, 'Les Pontchartrain et la pénétration commerciale en Amérique espagnole (1690–1715)', *Revue Historique*, April–June 1971, p. 326.

46 François Crouzet, 'Angleterre et France au XVIIIe siècle, essai d'analyse comparée de leurs croissances économique', *Annales ESC*, March–April 1966, p. 261.

47 Ibid., p. 263. The expression is François Crouzet's.

48 Blanche Maurel and Etienne Taillemite (eds) 'Moreau de Saint Méry', *Description de la partie française de Saint Domingue*, Paris, 1951, p. 321.

49 Paul Butel, 'Le modèle urbain à Saint Domingue au XVIIIe siècle: l'investissement immobilier dans les villes de Saint Domingue' in Paul Butel and Louis M. Cullen (eds) *Cities and Merchants: French and Irish Perspectives on Urban Development, 1500–1900*, Dublin, 1986, p. 161. A worker in a Bordeaux port then earned from 200 to 250 livres per year, that is, from 4,000 to 5,000 francs.

50 Paul Butel, 'Traditions and changes in the French Atlantic trade between 1780 and 1830 in the Age of European maritime expansion', *Renaissance and Modern Studies* XXX, 1986, p. 132.

51 Seymour Drescher, op. cit., pp. 49–50.

52 Page, *Traité d'économie politique et du commerce*, Paris: Year IX, cited in Paul Butel, 'Traditions et change', op. cit., p. 125.

53 Observations of the manager of the Fleuriau plantation, in a letter of 14 August 1787, cited in Jacques de Cauna, *Au temps des Isles à sucre. Histoire d'une plantation de Saint Domingue au XVIIIe siècle*, Paris: Karthala, 1987, p. 130.

54 For Barbados, see Hilary Beckles, *A History of Barbados: from Amerindian Settlement to Nation State*, Cambridge: Cambridge University Press, 1990, pp. 72–73; for Guadeloupe, see Paul Butel, *Les négociants bordelais, l'Europe et les Iles au XVIIIe siècle*, Paris: Aubier, 1974, p. 222.

55 Justin Girod de Chantrans, *Voyage d'un Suisse dans différentes colonies d'Amérique*, Paris: Tallandier, 1980, p. 209.

56 Justin Girod de Chantrans, op. cit., p. 194.

57 Seymour Drescher, op. cit., p. 44.

58 Jacques de Cauna, op. cit., p. 196.
59 Gabriel Debien and Pierre Pluchon, 'L'habitation Fevret de Saint Mesmin (1774–1790)', *Bulletin du Centre d'histoire des Espaces Atlantiques* 3, p. 185.
60 A letter from the Marseilles firm of Roux dated 26 January 1785. See Charles Carrière, *Négociants marseillais au XVIIIe siècle t.1*, Aix-Marseille, 1973, p. 334, n. 112.
61 Louis Dermigny's analysis from his *Cargaisons Indiennes* is cited by Charles Carrière, op. cit., p. 334.
62 Paul Butel, *Les négociants bordelais*, op. cit., p. 255.
63 Ibid., p. 274. For the eight Nantes traders, see Jacob M. Price, 'Credit in the slave plantation economies' in Barbara A. Solow (ed.) *Slavery and the Rise of the Atlantic System*, Cambridge: Cambridge University Press, 1991, p. 335.
64 See Jacob M. Price, 'Credit in the slave plantation economies', op. cit., pp. 334–335, for the complete analysis of these settlements.
65 David Richardson, 'Slavery, trade and economic growth in eighteenth century New England', in Barbara A. Solow (ed.) *Slavery*, op. cit., p. 261, n. 73.
66 Charles Frostin, *Les révoltes blanches à Saint-Domingue au XVIIIe siècle*, Paris: L'École, 1970, pp. 374–375.
67 Letter of 5 January 1786, in ibid., p. 407.
68 Paul Butel, 'Traditions and changes', op. cit., p. 126.
69 John J. Coatsworth, 'American trade with European colonies in the Caribbean and South America, 1790–1812', *William and Mary Quarterly* 2, 1967, p. 246.
70 Paul Butel, 'Traditions and changes', op. cit., p. 129.
71 Paul Butel, *Les négociants bordelais*, op. cit., p. 276.
72 Ibid., p. 275.

6 Men and powers in the Atlantic: seventeenth and eighteenth centuries

1 Christopher J. French, 'Crowded with traders and a great commerce: London's domination of English overseas trade, 1700–1775', *London Journal* 17.1, 1992, p. 27.
2 Anon., *An Essay on the Increase and Decline of Trade in London and the Outports*, London, 1749, cited by Christopher French, op. cit.
3 John J. McCusker and C. Gravesteijn, *The Beginnings of Commercial and Financial Journalism*, Amsterdam: Rodopi, 1991, pp. 292–326.
4 Marc de Bombelles, *Journal de voyage en Grande-Bretagne et en Irlande, 1784*, London: The Voltaire Foundation at the Taylor Institute, 1989. In 1790, the traffic in London exceeded 12,000 ships per year.
5 Memorandum from the director, Pierre Desclaux Sr, cited in Paul Butel, *Histoire de la Chambre de Commerce et d'industrie de Bordeaux*, Bordeaux: Chambre de Commerce, 1988, p. 130.
6 Bernard Lavalle, *L'Amérique espagnole de Colomb à Bolivar*, Paris: Belin, 1993, p. 142.
7 J. N. Biraben, 'Le peuplement du Canada français', *Annales de Démographie Historique*, 1966, p. 112.
8 John J. McCusker and Russell Menard, *The Economy of British America, 1607–1789*, Chapel Hill, NC: University of North Carolina Press, 1988, p. 212.
9 J. N. Biraben, op. cit., p. 116.
10 Jean Berenger, Yves Durand and Jean Meyer, *Pionniers et Colons en Amérique du Nord*, Paris: Colin, 1975, p. 232. From 1751 to 1760, the birth rate was 61 out of 1,000,

and 40 per 1,000 in Europe; however, there was still a high infant mortality rate of 33 per thousand.

11 John J. McCusker and Russell Menard, op. cit., pp. 223–224.

12 Paul Butel, *Histoire des Antilles* (ed.) Pierre Pluchon, Toulouse: Privat, 1982, p. 73.

13 Jean Meyer, *Les Européens et les Autres*, Paris: Colin, 1975, pp. 137 and 152.

14 François Crouzet, in Charles Higounet (ed.) *Histoire de Bordeaux*, Bordeaux: Fédération Historique du Sud-Ouest, 1968, vol. 5, p. 218.

15 R. J. Dickson, *Ulster Emigration to Colonial America*, London: Routledge, 1966, pp. 66–67.

16 Cited in McCusker and Menard, op. cit., p. 212.

17 Cited by Jean Meyer, op. cit., p. 155.

18 R. J. Dickson, op. cit., pp. 108–109.

19 Ibid., p. 109, 'report to the Justices of the Peace'.

20 Ibid., p. 119.

21 Ibid., pp. 123–124.

22 Peter H. Wood, *Black Majority: Negroes in Colonial South Carolina from 1670 through the Stono Rebellion*, New York: Norton, 1976.

23 Ibid., p. 150.

24 Paul Butel, 'L'essor de l'économie de la plantation à Saint Domingue dans la deuxième moitié du XVIIIe siècle' in Martine Acerra, Jean-Pierre Poussou and Michel Verge-Francheschi (eds) *Etat, Marine et Société, Mélanges Meyer*, Paris: Sorbonne, 1996, p. 96.

25 Pierre Pluchon, *Histoire de la Colonisation Française*, Paris: Fayard, 1991, vol. 1, p. 402.

26 Jacques Cauna, *Au temps des Isles à sucre, Histoire d'une plantation de Saint Domingue*, Paris: Karthala, 1987, p. 194.

27 Pierre Pluchon, op. cit., p. 422. To appreciate these costs, it is well known that it represents around 10 times the annual total pay of a worker in the Bordeaux port in 1788.

28 Richard B. Sheridan, *Sugar and Slavery: An Economic History of the British West Indies, 1623–1775*, Aylesbury, Ginn, 1974, p. 256.

29 Pierre Pluchon, op. cit., p. 422.

30 Frédéric Mauro, *Le Brésil du XVe à la fin du XVIIIe siècle*, Paris: SEDES, 1977, p. 176.

31 Joseph C. Miller, 'Legal Portuguese Slaving from Angola', in *Revue française d'histoire d'outre-mer*, 1975, p. 135.

32 For Cuba, see Herbert S. Klein, 'The Cuban Slave Trade in a period of transition, 1790–1843', in *Revue française d'histoire d'outre-mer*, 1975, p. 61. For Cartagena, see Dominique Morales, *L'esclavage en Colombie*, Masters' Dissertation, University of Bordeaux 3, 1980.

33 Kenneth Morgan, *Bristol and the Atlantic Trade in the Eighteenth Century*, Cambridge: Cambridge University Press, 1993, p. 133.

34 Daniel P. Mannix, *Black Cargoes: A History of the Atlantic Slave Trade*, Harmondsworth: Penguin, 1976, pp. 70–71.

35 Eric Saugera, *Bordeaux port négrier, XVIIe–XIXe siècles*, Paris: Karthala, 1995, p. 201.

36 Kenneth Morgan, op. cit., p. 135.

37 Ibid.

38 Ibid., pp. 137–138.

39 Daniel P. Mannix, op. cit., p. 72.

40 Kenneth Morgan, op. cit., p. 149. The slave-traders of Liverpool reduced their costs by settling their bills of exchange.

41 Roger Anstey, 'The volume of the North American slave carrying trade from Africa, 1761–1810', *Revue française d'histoire d'Outre-Mer*, 1975, p. 49.

42 Ibid., p. 51.

43 Paul Kennedy, *The Rise and Fall of British Naval Mastery*, New York: Charles Scribner's Sons, 1965, p. 4.

44 François Crouzet, *De la supériorité de l'Angleterre sur la France*, Paris: Perrin, 1985, p. 11.

45 Cited by Jean Meyer, op. cit., p. 221.

46 N. A. M. Rodger, 'La mobilisation navale au XVIIIe siècle' in Martine Acerra, Jean-Pierre Poussou and Michel Verge-Francherchi (eds) op. cit., pp. 365–374.

47 N. A. M. Rodger, op. cit., p. 369.

48 Ibid. Rodger is citing the memoirs of Louis XVI's naval minister, La Luzerne.

49 Jean Meyer, 'Les problèmes de personnel de la marine de guerre française aux XVII et XVIIIe siècles. Les Hommes et la mer dans l'Europe du Nord-Ouest, de l'antiquité à nos jours', *Revue du Nord*, 1986, p. 111.

50 Ibid., p. 123.

51 Christian Buchet, 'La Royal Navy et les levées d'hommes aux Antilles (1689–1763)', *Histoire, Economie et Société* 4, 1990, pp. 521–543.

52 Paul Butel, *L'économie française au XVIIIe siècle*, Paris: SEDES, 1993, p. 245.

53 Jaap R. Bruijn, *The Dutch Navy of the Seventeenth and Eighteenth Centuries*, Greenville: University of South Carolina Press, 1993, p. 148.

54 Jean Meyer, *Marines et Révolution*, Rennes: Ouest France, 1988, p. 59.

55 Christian Buchet, 'Essai de comparaison du système de ravitaillement français et anglais dans l'espace caraibe au XVIIIe siècle', *Actes du colloque de Bordeaux: La Guerre dans la Caraibe, XVIIIe–XIXe siècles*, 1996.

56 Christian Buchet, 'La logistique française en *matériel* naval dans l'espace Caraibe (1672–1763)', *Service Historique de la Marine*, 1993, p. 67.

57 Paul Kennedy, op. cit., pp. 81–82.

58 Etienne Taillemite, 'Guerre et commerce maritime au XVIIIe siècle', *Bulletin du Centre d'histoire des Espaces Atlantiques* 7, 1995, p. 199.

59 Paul Butel, 'Le transport maritime à Bordeaux au XVIIIe siècle', *Cahiers d'histoire* XXXIX, 1989, p. 259.

60 Ibid., p. 260.

61 Etienne Taillemite, op. cit., pp. 200–201.

62 Ibid., p. 201.

63 Paul Kennedy, op. cit., p. 108.

64 Philippe Loupes, 'L'état défensif des colonies espagnoles vers 1761–1762', *Actes de colloque de Bordeaux*, op. cit.

65 Jean Meyer, *Marines et Révolution*, op. cit., p. 57.

66 Paul Kennedy, op. cit., pp. 144–145.

67 Jean Meyer, op. cit., p. 259.

68 After Trafalgar, Great Britain had 128 armed vessels and 88 either unarmed or under construction; France, at the time, had 20 armed vessels. British superiority therefore became overwhelming. In 1792, at the beginning of the French Wars, it was far lower: almost 160 vessels were theoretically available in England, but many were not capable of entering service; at the time, France had 80 vessels at its disposal.

7 The Atlantic in the nineteenth century: tradition and change

1 François Crouzet, 'Remarques sur la formation d'une économie mondiale', *Histoire, Economie et Société*, 4, 1986, p. 615.

2 Paul Butel, *Les négociants bordelais, l'Europe et les Iles au XVIIIe siècle*, Paris: Aubier, 1973, p. 219.

3 Herman Melville, *Redburn, or, Her First Cruise*, Paris: Gallimard, 1980, pp. 460–462.

4 François Crouzet, *De la supériorité de l'Angleterre sur la France*, Paris: Perrin, 1985, p. 301.

5 Stanley Chapman, *Merchant Enterprise in Britain from the Industrial Revolution to World War I*, Cambridge: Cambridge University Press, 1992, p. 84.

6 François Crouzet, op. cit., p. 300.

7 François Crouzet, *L'Economie britannique et le blocus continental*, Paris: Economica, 1987, pp. xii–xiii.

8 François Crouzet, op. cit., pp. xv and 885. British exports of manufactured goods in 1806 rose to a total of £25 million sterling, while those to the United States amounted to £6,860,000; exports in 1807 rose to a total of £27.4 million, with £7,743,000 pounds' worth going to the United States.

9 John J. Coatsworth, 'American trade with European colonies in the Caribbean and South America', *William and Mary Quarterly* vol. 24 no. 2, 1967, p. 243.

10 See Chapter 5, 'The American invasion'.

11 François Crouzet, op. cit., p. 303.

12 John J. Coatsworth, op. cit., p. 250.

13 François Crouzet, op. cit., p. 58. These figures represent the annual average from 1803–1805.

14 Ibid., p. 885.

15 François Crouzet, 'Angleterre–Brésil, 1697–1850, un siècle et demi des échanges commerciaux', *Histoire, Economie et Société*, 1990, pp. 300–301.

16 François Crouzet, op. cit., p. 302.

17 Stanley Chapman, op. cit., p. 83.

18 Elie Halévy, *Histoire du peuple anglaise au XIXe siècle*, Paris: Hachette, 1913, p. 167.

19 Robert W. Love, *A History of the US Navy, 1775–1841*, Harrisburg, PA: University of Pennsylvania Press, 1982, pp. 21 and 37.

20 Ibid., p. 139.

21 François Crouzet, op. cit., p. 305.

22 Ibid., p. 307.

23 Ibid., p. 308.

24 D. C. M. Platt, *Latin America and British Trade, 1806–1914*, London: Adam and Charles Black, 1972, p. 56.

25 *Universal British Directory 1791*, cited in Stanley Chapman, *Merchant Enterprise*, op. cit., p. 82.

26 Ibid., p. 83.

27 Ibid., p. 84.

28 André Siegfried, *Tableau des Etats-Unis*, Paris: Colin, 1958, p. 25.

29 Robert Greenhalgh Albion, *The Rise of New York Port, 1815–1860*, Newton Abbot: David & Charles, 1972, pp. 95–121.

30 Ibid., p. 119.

31 Ibid., p. 112.

32 Ibid., p. 117.
33 See Francis E. Hyde, *Liverpool and the Mersey*, Newton Abbot: David & Charles, 1971; and Robert Albion, op. cit.
34 Robert Albion, op. cit., p. 220.
35 Ibid., p. 222.
36 Francis E. Hyde, op. cit., p. 91.
37 Ibid., p. 48.
38 Stanley Chapman, op. cit., p. 89.
39 Robert Albion, op. cit., p. 52.
40 Ibid., p. 319, quoting from a New York newspaper.
41 Francis E. Hyde, *Cunard and the North Atlantic, 1840–1973*, Newton Abott: David & Charles, 1976, p. 38.
42 The *Titanic* displaced 60,000 tonnes and was 271 metres in length.
43 Francis E. Hyde, op. cit., p. 52.
44 Daniel Hillion, *L'Atlantique à toute vapeur*, Rennes: Ouest France, 1993, p. 44.
45 Daniel Hillion, op. cit., p. 52.
46 Ibid., p. 56.
47 Marthe Barbance, *Histoire de la Compagnie Générale Transatlantique*, Paris: Compagnie Générale Transatlantique, 1955, pp. 85–86.
48 Ibid., p. 128.
49 Francis E. Hyde, op. cit., p. 110. These prices come close to those charged over 40 years earlier, in 1863: on their steamships, Cunard asked for £4. 15s, and only £2.17s on their sailing ships.
50 Francis E. Hyde, op. cit., p. 114.
51 François Caron, in Pierre Léon, *Histoire économique et sociale du monde* vol. 4, Paris: Colin, 1972, p. 171.
52 All the above data are taken from Thomas Brinley, *Migration and Economic Growth: a Study of Great Britain and the Atlantic Economy*, Cambridge: Cambridge University Press, 1954.
53 A. N. Porter (ed.), *Atlas of British Overseas Expansion*, London: Routledge, 1991, p. 85.
54 Gilbert Garrier, in Pierre Léon, *Histoire*, op. cit., p. 27.
55 Thomas Brinley, op. cit., p. 308, table 117.
56 André Siegfried, *Tableau*, op. cit., p. 40.
57 Jean Heffer, in Pierre Léon, *Histoire*, op. cit., p. 225.
58 Robert Albion, op. cit., p. 349.
59 Ibid., p. 254.
60 Following annual data from Thomas Brinley, op. cit., pp. 25–26.
61 Ibid., p. 166.
62 Ibid., p. 170.
63 On these seasonal displacements, see Rudolph Vicoli (ed.), *A Century of European Migration*, Chicago: University of Illinois Press, 1991, pp. 25–26.
64 Thomas Brinley, op. cit., p. 96.
65 Ludovico de Courten, *La Marina Mercantile Italiana nella Politica di Espansione, 1860–1914*, Bulzoni, 1987, p. 173.
66 Marthe Barbance, op. cit., p. 160.
67 Paul Bois, *Armements marseillais, compagnies de navigation et navires à vapeur, 1831–1988. Histoire du commerce et de l'industrie de Marseilles, XIXe–XXe siècles*, Marseilles, 1988, pp. 219–220.

68 Philippe Roudie, 'Bordeaux port d'émigration lointaine (1865–1918)', *Revue historique de Bordeaux* XXX, 1984, pp. 137–188.

69 Ludovico de Courten, op. cit., p. 186.

70 Ibid., p. 173.

71 Francis E. Hyde, op. cit., p. 100.

72 Robert Albion, op. cit., p. 339.

73 Paul Bois, op. cit., p. 73.

74 Philippe Roudie, op. cit., p. 164.

75 Herman Melville, op. cit., p. 360.

76 Robert Albion, op. cit., p. 343.

77 Ibid., p. 345.

78 Dirck Hoerder, 'International labour market and community building by migrant workers' in Rudolph Vicoli (ed.) *A Century of European Migration*, op. cit., p. 97.

79 Reino Vero, 'Migration traditions from Finland to North America' in Rudolph Vicoli (ed.) *A Century of European Migration*, op. cit., p. 128.

8 The Atlantic in the twentieth century

1 European investments in United States' industries and services rose to almost $7 million in 1914. See Paul Kennedy, *The Rise and Fall of the Great Powers*, New York: Vintage, 1989, p. 245.

2 See *Atlas of British Overseas Expansion*, A. N. Porter (ed.), London: Routledge, 1991, p. 123 for the data from 1898.

3 Paul Kennedy, op. cit., p. 203.

4 Japan: 187,000 tonnes in 1900, and 700,000 tonnes in 1914. United States: 383,000 tonnes in 1900, 985,000 tonnes in 1914.

5 During the Spanish–American War of 1898, the cruiser *Oregon* had to make a detour that lasted three months via Cape Horn in order to reach the Atlantic.

6 Robert W. Love, *A History of the US Navy, 1775–1941*, Harrisburg, 1992, pp. 380–381.

7 Ibid., p. 468.

8 J. B. Duroselle, *La politique extérieur des Etats-Unis I*, Paris: CDU, 1955, p. 55.

9 Ibid.

10 Robert W. Love, op. cit., p. 499.

11 Philippe Masson, *Marins et Océans*, Paris: Imprimerie Nationale, 1982, p. 209.

12 Georges Dupeux, in Paul Butel (ed.), *Histoire de la Chambre de Commerce de Bordeaux*, Bordeaux: Chambre de Commerce, 1988, pp. 228–231.

13 Cited by André Siegfried, *Tableau des Etats-Unis*, Paris: Colin, 1958, p. 324.

14 Ibid., p. 327.

15 Richard N. Current, Harry William and Frank Freidel, *American History: a Survey*, New York: Alfred A. Knopf, 1975, vol. 2, p. 644.

16 Paul Kennedy, *The Rise and Fall of British Naval Mastery*, New York: Charles Scribners' Sons, p. 275.

17 Ibid., p. 287.

18 Ibid., p. 279.

19 Marthe Barbance, *Histoire de la Compagnie Générale Transatlantique*, Paris: Compagnie Générale Transatlantique, 1955, p. 235.

20 Philippe Masson, op. cit., p. 213.

21 Ibid.

22 Ibid., p. 217.
23 My colleague and friend, Professor Alain Huetz de Lemps, wanted me to read the still unpublished manuscript of his *History of Rum*, forthcoming from Desjonquères, for which I extend my warmest gratitude to him. I have drawn on this manuscript a great deal in my presentation of Prohibition.
24 Georges Dupeux, in Paul Bartel (ed.) *Histoire* op. cit., p. 229.
25 The word 'bootleg' designates the upper part of a high boot.
26 Georges Dupeux, in Paul Bartel (ed.) *Histoire* op. cit., p. 236.
27 Francis E. Hyde, *Cunard and the North Atlantic, 1840–1973*, London: Macmillan, 1975, pp. 234–235.
28 Philippe Masson, op. cit., p. 221.
29 Quoted by Philippe Masson, op. cit., p. 205.
30 Paul Kennedy, op. cit., p. 286.
31 J. B. Duroselle, op. cit., pp. 118–125.
32 Richard Current, Harry William and Frank Freidel, op. cit., p. 702.
33 Robert W. Love, op. cit., p. 651.
34 For British losses, see Paul Kennedy, op. cit., p. 317; for general Allied losses, see Philippe Masson, op. cit., p. 257.
35 Yves Lacoste (ed.), *Dictionnaire de Géopolitique*, Paris: Flammarion, 1993, p. 117.
36 Francis E. Hyde, op. cit., p. 284.
37 Ibid., p. 311.
38 Marthe Barbance, op. cit., p. 314.
39 Francis E. Hyde, op. cit., p. 267.
40 Philippe Masson, op. cit., p. 281.
41 Francis E. Hyde, op. cit., p. 297.
42 Statistics from 1988, from André Vigarie, *Echanges et transports internationaux*, Paris: Sirey, 1991, p. 74.
43 André Vigarie, *Ports de commerce et vie littorale*, Paris: Hachette, 1979, p. 455.
44 André Vigarie, *Echanges*, op. cit., p. 210.
45 Captain Richard Sharpe, RN (ed.), *Jane's Fighting Ships 1990–1991*, Coulsdon, 1990, p. 579.

9 Conclusion

1 G. V. Scammell, *Ships, Oceans and Empires*, London: Varorium, 1995, p. 411.
2 Michel de Montaigne, *Essays* I.31, Harmondsworth: Penguin, 1985, p.109.
3 Etienne Taillemite, *La Fayette*, Paris: Fayard, 1989, p. 103.
4 Léon Edel, *Henry James, une vie*, Paris: Seuil, 1990, p. 253.
5 Henry Miller, *Tropic of Capricorn*, London: Panther, 1966, p. 52.

Bibliography

Adam, Paul (1976) 'Problèmes de navigation dans l'Atlantique nord', in Régis Boyer (ed.), *L'Age Viking, les Vikings et leur civilisation, problèmes actuels*, Paris, Mouton.

Albion, Robert G. (1972) *The Rise of New York Port 1815–1860*, Newton Abbott, David & Charles Ltd.

Andrews, Kenneth (1984) *Trade, Plunder and Settlement: Maritime Enterprises and the Genesis of the British Empire 1480–1630*, Cambridge, Cambridge University Press.

Barbance, Marthe (1955) *Histoire de la Compagnie Générale Transatlantique*, Paris, Compagnie Générale Transatlantique.

Bennassar, Bartolomé (1991) *1492, un monde nouveau?*, Paris, Perrin.

Bernard, Antoinette (ed.) (1991) *Le Grand Atlas des Explorations*, Encyclopaedia Universalis, London, HarperCollins.

Bessmertny, Alexandre (1949) *L'Atlantide, exposé des hypothèses relative à l'origine de l'Atlantide*, Paris, Payot.

Brinley, Thomas (1954) *Migration and Economic Growth: a Study of Great Britain and the Atlantic Economy*, Cambridge, Cambridge University Press.

Bruijn, Jaap R. (1993) *The Dutch Navy of the Seventeenth and Eighteenth Centuries*, Columbia, SC, University of South Carolina Press.

—— (1982) *Les Caraibes au temps des filibustiers, XVIe–XVIIe siècle*, Paris, Aubier-Montaigne.

Buchet, Christian (1994) 'Des routes maritimes Europe–Antilles et de leur incidence sur la rivalité franco–britannique', *Histoire, Economie, Société*, 4.

Butel, Paul (1974) *Les négociants bordelais, l'Europe et les Iles au XVIIIe siècle*, Paris, Aubier-Montaigne.

Carcopino, Jérôme (1943) *Le Maroc antique*, Paris, Gallimard.

Carrière, Charles (1973) *Négociants marseillais au XVIIIe siècle*, Marseilles, Institut Historique de Provence.

Cauna, Jacques de (1987) *Au temps des Isles à sucre, histoire d'une plantation de Saint-Domingue au XVIIIe siècle*, Paris, Karthala.

Chapman, Stanley (1992) *Merchant Enterprise in Britain from the Industrial Revolution to World War I*, Cambridge, Cambridge University Press.

Chaunu, Pierre (1977) *Séville et l'Amérique, XVIe–XVIIe siècle*, Paris, Flammarion.

—— (1993) *Colomb ou la logique de l'imprévisible*, Paris, François Bourin.

Coatsworth, John J. (1967) 'American Trade with European Colonies in the Caribbean and South America 1790–1812', *William and Mary Quarterly*, 2.

Courten, Ludovico de (1987), *La Marina mercantile italiana nelle Politica di Espansione*, Milan, Bulzoni.

Crouzet, François (1966) 'Angleterre et France au XVIIIe siècle, essai d'analyse comparée de deux croissances économiques', *Annales ESC*, March–April.

—— (1985) *De la supériorité de l'Angleterre sur la France, l'économie et l'imaginaire, XVIIe–XXe siècle*, Paris, Perrin.

—— (1986) 'Remarques sur la formation d'une économie mondiale', *Histoire, Economie et Société*, 4.

—— (1987) *L'économie britannique et le blocus continental*, Paris, Economica.

—— (1990) 'Angleterre–Brésil, 1670–1850, un siècle et demi d'échanges commerciaux', *Histoire, Economie, Société*.

Cullen, Louis M. (1972) *An Economic History of Ireland since 1660*, London, Batsford.

Curtin, Philip D. (1990) *The Rise and Fall of the Plantation Complex: Essays in Atlantic History*, Baltimore, Johns Hopkins.

Davies, K. G. (1977) *The North-Atlantic World in the Seventeenth Century*, Minneapolis, Minnesota University Press.

Davis, Ralph (1962) *The Rise of the English Shipping Industry in the 17th and 18th Centuries*, Newton Abbott, David & Charles Ltd.

—— (1973) *The Rise of the Atlantic Economies*, London, Weidenfeld & Nicolson.

Dickson, R. (1966) *Ulster Emigration to Colonial America*, London, Routledge.

Drescher, Seymour (1977) *Econocide: British Slavery in the Era of Abolition*, Pittsburgh, University of Pittsburgh Press.

Favier, Jean (1991) *Les grandes découvertes d'Alexandre à Magellan*, Paris, Fayard.

French, Christopher (1992) 'Crowded with traders and a great commerce, London's domination of English overseas trade 1700–1775', *London Journal*, 17.1.

Goodman, Jordan (1993) *Tobacco in History, the Culture of Dependence*, London, Routledge.

Halévy, Elie (1913) *Histoire du peuple anglais au XIXe siècle*, Paris, Hachette.

Hillion, Daniel (1993) *L'Atlantique à toute vapeur*, Rennes, Ouest-France.

Hyde, Francis E. (1971) *Liverpool and the Mersey*, Newton Abbott, David & Charles Ltd.

—— (1976) *Cunard and the North Atlantic, 1840–1973*, Newton Abbott, David & Charles Ltd.

Israel, Jonathan (1989) *Dutch Primacy in World Trade 1585–1740*, Oxford, Clarendon.

Kennedy, Paul (1965) *The Rise and Fall of British Naval Mastery*, New York, Charles Scribners' Sons.

—— (1989) *The Rise and Fall of the Great Powers*, New York, Vintage.

Léon, Pierre (ed.) (1968–1972) *Histoire économique et sociale du monde*, 4 vols, Paris, Colin.

Love, Robert W. (1992) *A History of the US Navy 1775–1841*, Harrisburg, University of Ohio Press.

McCusker, John (1989) *Rum and the American Revolution, the Rum Trade and the Balance of Payments of the Thirteen Continental Colonies*, New York and London, Garland Publishers.

McCusker, John and Russell Menard (1985) *The Economy of British America 1607–1789*, Chappel Hill, NC, University of North Carolina Press.

MacLeod, Murdo (1973) *Spanish Central America, a Socio-Economic History, 1520–1720*, Berkeley, CA, California University Press.

Marcus, G. J. (1980) *The Conquest of the North Atlantic*, Woodbridge, Suffolk, Boydell & Brewer.

Masson, Philippe (1982) *Marins et Océans*, Paris, Imprimerie Nationale.

Mauro, Frédéric (1977) *Le Brésil du XVe à la fin du XVIIIe siècle*, Paris, Sedes.

Meyer, Jean (1975) *Les Européens et les autres*, Paris, Colin.

—— (1989) *Histoire du sucre*, Paris, Desjonquères.

Mollat, Michel (1993) *L'Europe et la mer*, Paris, Seuil.

Morgan, Kenneth (1993) *Bristol and the Atlantic Trade in the Eighteenth Century*, Cambridge, Cambridge University Press.

Platt, D. C. M. (1972) *Latin America and British Trade 1806–1914*, London, Adam and Charles Black.

Pluchon, Pierre (1991) *Histoire de la colonisation française*, Paris, Fayard.

Price, Jacob M. (1980) *Capital and Credit in British Overseas Trade. The View from the Chesapeake, 1700–1776*, Cambridge, MA, Harvard University Press.

—— (1989) 'What did the merchants do? Reflections on British overseas trade 1700–1776', *The Journal of Economic History*, June.

Saugera, Eric (1995) *Bordeaux, port négrier, XVIIe–XIXe siècle*, Paris, Karthala.

Sheridan, Richard (1974) *Sugar and Slavery, an Economic History of the British West Indies 1623–1775*, Aylesbury, Ginn.

Solow, Barbara (1991) *Slavery and the Rise of the Atlantic System*, Cambridge, Cambridge University Press.

Verge-Francheschi, Michel (1994) *Henri le navigateur, un découvreur au XVe siècle*, Paris, Editions du Félin.

Vigarie, André (1979) *Ports de commerce et vie littorale*, Paris, Hachette.

—— (1991) *Echanges et transports internationaux*, Paris, Sirey.

Index